Remembering
The Sabbatical
Years of 2016

The Calderon Family

336 253 6140
(USA)

Cover; The Vineyard Project. We at Sightedmoon.com and those who donated to this project have come to an agreement with Boaz and Rinah Dreyer of Be'er Milkah Isreal, to see the results and blessings of keeping the Sabbatical year. Together we began to build and to plant this vineyard in October of 2012.

We have agreed to supply the new grape vines, trellises, electric fences, water lines and all that is needed to plant and water and grow them. In exchange we have been given 10% of the grapes vines. This 10% will rest in the Sabbatical year of 2016 to 2017; Aviv to Aviv as we are about to prove to you in this book. The other 90% will keep the Jewish Sabbatical year in 2014, 5775 according to the Hillel calendar, from Tishri to Tishri.

Our Portion of the vineyard will keep each Sabbatical cycle up to the Jubilee year of 2045 (2016, 2023, 2030, 2037, 2044). At this time the entire vineyard will be returned to Boaz and Rinah.

We will then watch and let Yehovah show us which year is right by the blessing He bestowes on each section of the vineyard. Although we may not agree on doctrinal issues we are united in our love for Yehovah the God of Abraham, Isaac and Jacob, the people of Israel and the Land of Israel.

We have in faith, invested in our belief and are waiting on HASHEM (The Name), Yehovah, to show us, which Sabbatical year is right according to the results in the vineyard.

Remembering The Sabbatical Years of 2016

2023 2030 2037 2044

Breaking The Curses By Obedience

Isaiah 49:16 I have engraved you on the palms of my hands. Your walls are always in my presence

By
Joseph F. Dumond

To order additional copies of this book, contact:
Xlibris Corporation
1-888-795-4274
www.Xlibris.com
Orders@Xlibris.com
125561

Table of Contents

Foreword

5 "See, I am sending you Ěliyahu (Elijah) the Prophet before the coming of the great and awesome day of יהוה. **6** And he shall turn the hearts of the fathers to the children, and the hearts of the children to their fathers, lest I come and smite the earth with utter destruction." (**Malachi 4:5-6**)

16 "And he shall turn many of the children of Yisra'ĕl to יהוה their Elohim. **17** And he shall go before Him in the spirit and power of Ěliyahu (Elijah), to turn the hearts of the fathers to the children, and the disobedient to the insight of the righteous, to make ready a people prepared for יהוה." (**Luke 1:16-17**)

3 The voice of one crying in the wilderness, "Prepare the way of יהוה; make straight in the desert a highway for our Elohim. **4** Let every valley be raised, and every mountain and hill made low. And the steep ground shall become level, and the rough places smooth. **5** And the esteem of יהוה shall be revealed, and all flesh together shall see it. For the mouth of יהוה has spoken." (**Isaiah 40:3-5**)

19 "Repent therefore and turn back, for the blotting out of your sins, in order that times of refreshing might come from the presence of the Master, **20** and that He sends יהושע Messiah, pre-appointed for you, **21** whom heaven needs to receive until the times of restoration of all *matters*, of which Elohim spoke through the mouth of all His set-apart prophets since of old. **22** For Mosheh (Moses) truly said to the fathers, יהוה your Elohim shall raise up for you a Prophet like me from your brothers. Him you shall hear according to all *matters*, whatever He says to you. **23** 'And it shall be that every being who does not hear that Prophet shall be utterly destroyed from among the people.' **24** And likewise, all the prophets who have spoken, from Shemu'ĕl (Samuel) and those following, have also announced these days." (**Acts 3:19-24**)

25 "... and it speaks words against the Most High, and it wears out the set-apart ones of the Most High, and it intends to change appointed times¹ and law², and they are given into its hand for a time and times and half a time. (**Daniel 7:25** | **Footnotes:** ¹This is another word for festivals. ²Changing the law amounts to lawlessness.)

Many today look to see the Sunday law enforced as fulfillment of this prophecy. What they do not realize is that it has *already* taken place. The Feasts and Festivals (or Appointed Times) have *already* been changed and the laws to uphold them already promote and beget lawlessness. What you're about to read is going to shock you.

Satan has *already* changed the Laws of Yehovah and most continue to have no idea and remain clueless. This book is a witness and attestation to the actual return to the original Torah for those who have ears to hear and eyes to see. This includes:

- The Restoration of *all* things.
- The Restoration of the Sabbath.
- The Restoration of the Sabbatical & Jubilee Years.
- The Restoration of the Holy Days as outlined in Leviticus 23.

This phenomenon has not happened through one man, but through many over the years, of whom it can be said Yehovah's Spirit of Elijah has rested upon and spoken through. It is my desire that all I am about to put forth in this book will powerfully and conclusively illustrate the errors of our fathers (including our forefathers) and how they came to be. It is also my hope to be thorough in demonstrating what the Torah *actually* stipulates on *how* these errors are to be undone and what kind of understanding we need to come into. It is my intent to not only lay a solid foundation for you when it comes to a firm grasp of the heart of Torah, but a sure foundation you can build upon with regard to growing in your understanding of what being Torah observant is supposed to look like and what keeping Torah is really all about.

Speaking on my own behalf, just as I once believed the name of the Creator God was pronounced Yahweh, I now believe His name to be pronounced Yehovah. Yet, I also know of many others who operate under the conviction His name is spelled in a wide variety of other ways and have since discovered our brother Judah chooses not to mention His sacred name at all, but instead uses Ha Shem or The Name.

Originally I had set out to only use the Hebrew spelling of His name or "יהוה" so as to not offend anyone, but after I read Nehemia Gordon's book, *Shattering the*

Conspiracy of Silence[1], I realized I would still be guilty of hiding His name given the level of understanding He has brought me into with regard to His name. Once we have been shown something, we must be true to that which we have been shown. To not be true to or to conceal that which we've been shown is sin.

Moreover, I was extremely moved by Gordon's book and no longer want to be a "co-conspirator" with regard to hiding the Creator's mighty name. You are most welcome to use whatever version of His name you have come to understand as being His true name. But as for me, I am going to use Yehovah throughout the course of this book—except for those places where I quote from a given Bible translation (e.g., The Scriptures 1998)[2] or from someone else using another version of His name. Other than that, I will not depart from it.

We are told in Psalms that if we forget the name of Yehovah and use some other name instead, then He will search our heart to know just who it is, exactly, we are trying to talk to:

> **20** If we have forgotten the Name of our Elohim, or stretched out our hands to a foreign mighty one, **21** would Elohim not search this out? For He knows the secrets of the heart. (**Psalm 44:20-21**)

In I Corinthians we are told:

> **10** For the Spirit searches *all* matters, even the depths of Elohim. (**I Corinthians 2:10**)

I do not want His special and set-apart name to be argued over, but I have recently made a decision to not keep what I believe His glorious name to be a secret any longer. We are commanded to call upon His name. If we do not know it, then we can't call upon it. I also have purposed throughout this book only to set forth and prove the truths Yehovah has revealed to me and it is not my intent to speak disrespectfully against any one ministry, teacher, or group of people who have come to believe the very things I am about to debunk as being false. But once Yehovah makes the truths known, which I am about to put forth and they bear witness with your spirit, to go back to the lies you once believed would be nothing short of wrong. Test and prove my words then, and after having done so, *obey*. May the Creator Yehovah Himself guide you as you study out these truths and as my website clearly states: Prove All Things[3] and…[4].

---

1 http://www.nehemiaswall.com/shattering-the-conspiracy-of-silence
2 http://isr-messianic.org/downloads/free-scriptures-downloads.html
3 http://www.sightedmoon.com/index.php
4 http://www.sightedmoonnl.com/index.php

Acknowledgments

I would like to thank Lora Skeahan, Judith Dennis, Vicki Brady, Irene Varner and Joli Darling[5] —all of the United States; and Annamarie Marrier D'unienville, of South Africa; and Schalk and Elsa Klee of Holland; for their individual and collective contributions to the development, formation, organization, layout, readability and clarity of this book.

Lora has taken on a great deal of extra research on my behalf and continuously says she does not wish for her name to be mentioned. She has also been helping me write the weekly newsletters I post on my website each week, in order to give me more time to concentrate on the writing of this book. Whenever I have asked, Lora has researched subjects from a perspective other than my own and also, from a woman's point of view. I owe her a huge debt of gratitude.

Judith Dennis, Vicki Brady, Irene Varner and Annamarie Marrier D'unienville were the people I used to objectively read this book and let me know, once having read it from cover to cover, if they understood it. Each one of them is at different levels of understanding in their walk and in their knowledge of the Bible and this is exactly why I asked this of them. They have written back to me expressing how appreciative they were to finally be able to understand certain things that had bothered them for some time and were not readily explained by others they turned to for answers. They all came away from the experience with a much clearer understanding of history and feeling like they now know *why* they believe what they believe.

Here are some examples of feedback-based comments I received from my sneak preview readers:

---

5 http://www.wordforwordlineuponline.com/

I enjoyed so much your testimony in the beginning of the book and it sounds so very similar to my own, and probably will to others as well.

Again Joseph, you have hit the proverbial nail on the head. Yah is not the author of confusion and all these calendars and their changes are mind boggling, especial for those of us who are seeking to do His will alone.

Chapter 6: Love this chapter! It is finally all coming together! And I see the one ditch for sure!

I have read up to chapter 7 and it is really well done. You explained everything very nicely and I am in agreement with everything thus far.

I have been through chapters 11-17 now of your book, and I love them. Cannot say I would change anything. Great job!!!

Man, I'm really loving this book more and more. And I actually understand most of it. A year ago this time, Joseph, it would have mostly been Greek to me, except for the weekly Sabbath. I love it. It's a hit.

I also would like to conclude this section with a letter from one of my sneak preview readers of this book:

Shalom Joseph,

Just wanted you to know I'm almost finished with the book. Man, I really, *really* love it. It is so wonderful. And most things you've explained so wonderfully. I'm sure it will be a huge success.

It is a very good presentation, well put together, you are going to blow these people away with all the information.

Shabbat Shalom

To each of these ladies I thank you all so very much. In *The Prophecies of Abraham*, I was explaining a subject that was very deep for a lot of people—especially given the fact that most of them had never considered the Sabbatical Years at all. In this book, I try to better explain those things I put forth in my last book, on a more entry-level basis that everyone might more readily and easily understand. Based on the previous comments and feedback, I think I have achieved this, so again, *thank you*.

To Schalk and Elsa Klee who have also proofread this book, a special thanks goes out to them personally, who are independently researching the Sabbatical Years topic with regard to each of its many facets and have made every effort to explain the ins and outs of it in their own words to their own growing readership of Set Apart People[6]. They have done such an exceptional job at this that I decided to include two of their articles to more succinctly explain certain aspects of the Sabbatical Years I had difficulty explaining in my own words. So I tip my hat to them for this.

I have also used, with his permission, two articles written by Nehemia Gordon,[7] whom I consider a friend. His insights and understandings have been a *great help* to me over the years on many subjects. So I acknowledge and thank him for all his work over the years.

Last, but not least, those who know me and read my articles know for a fact I cannot spell and my sentence structure is atrocious. You all should know I graduated from high school with a 51% average in English in each grade and I only got that because they did not want me back the following year.

Therefore, I have asked Joli Darling, once again, to do the editing. She is brilliant with regard to this subject and also did the editing on my last book, The Prophecies of Abraham[8]. This is why I did not utilize the other ladies in this capacity with regard to this book. Joli also knows her Bible and has helped in certain areas she felt were deficient. Her contribution to this book makes much of what I say sound intelligent. I cannot thank her enough. If you need to have your work(s) edited, I highly recommend Joli who does this for a living.

I must also acknowledge and thank Yehovah, YHVH the Creator of all things who has reached down from His Throne and revealed these truths to me. It has now been 7 years since He first began to show me these things from the pages of His Torah and from history. Over these 7 years, since 2005, I have had to answer and prove each and every question that has come along about the Sabbatical Years and the plan of Yehovah and He has revealed them to me slowly over this time. This book Remembering the Sabbatical Year[9] 2016 is

---

6 http://www.setapartpeople.com/

7 http://www.karaite-korner.org/

8 http://www.authorhouse.co.uk/Bookstore/BookDetail.aspx?Book=286642 By Joseph F. Dumond Published: February 2010 ISBN: 9781449047528

9 The sabbath year (shmita Hebrew: הטימש‎, literally "release") also called the sabbatical year or sheviit (Hebrew: תיעיבש‎, literally "seventh") is the seventh year of the seven-year agricultural cycle mandated by the Torah for the Land of Israel and still observed in contemporary Judaism. (Lev. 25:2-7; comp. Ex. 23:10, 11, 12; Lev. 26:34, 35). Whatever grew of itself during that year was not for the owner of the land, but for the poor and the stranger and the beasts of the field.

my way of sharing the answers to all of the hard questions and putting them down on paper so that everyone can study them out for themselves.

May Yehovah Bless you, and shine His face upon you, and reveal these truths to you as well, as you search them out and strive to understand His Torah.

Introduction

I, Joseph F. Dumond, was born in 1958 and raised a Catholic. In 1978, after graduating from Orangeville High School in Ontario, Canada; I married my high school sweetheart, Barbara. We had our daughter in 1981, our son in 1982 and then later, our third child—another son, in 1990.

In 1982, I first heard Herbert Armstrong teaching about the Sabbath on my car radio late one night on my way to work in Eastern Ontario. A few days later, I heard him again as I left from work. I wrote in to request some material and found myself compelled to prove what he said about the Sabbath wrong. I worked seven days a week as a foreman supervising natural gas pipeline workers. There was *no way* I could possibly take a day off to attend church on Saturday. But finally, after six months of solid day and night study, I could no longer discount just how clear Yehovah has always been on this matter and that we all should be keeping the Sabbath. I was forced to conclude the seventh day Saturday Sabbath had never changed and that it was the Catholic Church[10] that was to blame for changing the Saturday Sabbath to a Sunday—a counterfeit Sabbath which all Christian churches have continued to observe once the Catholic mold was cast and the heretical dye set.

When Yehovah opened a door, I began to attend the Worldwide Church of God and not long after my first visit, I was told about the Holy Days. It was through those Holy Days—all of which are found in Leviticus 23—that I was able to learn of Yehovah's divinely inspired plan for mankind and how it was all to come together. For quite some time thereafter, I operated under the mistaken conviction I knew of His plan *in full* in this regard until I came to understand the Sabbatical Years—both past and future. The last Sabbatical

---

10 http://www.newadvent.org/cathen/13287b.htm

Year was from Aviv (March-April) 2009–Aviv 2010. This was also the first one I had ever kept.

I began to study in earnest each week, while attending church regularly, from that moment forward (from 1982 until 1994). I then had to leave the Worldwide Church of God because, somewhere along the way, they were starting to bear a striking resemblance to the Catholic Church I had already walked away from in 1982. It was also at this time that I was told all I had learned in the World Wide Church of God, was "wrong."

So, for the next two years I no longer attended any church and went back to working seven days a week. Then, in 1996, as the Holy Days were fast approaching, I felt a deep desire to start keeping the Sabbath and the Holy Days once again. Not having the remotest clue this time where to go or who to turn to, I began to keep the Holy Days myself by venturing out in my car, parking at the end of a dead end road and praying and crying out to Yehovah with all my heart.

During this time, I also had to rethink everything I understood to be true up until that point. I had to do this without using any church literature from any group and without listening to any pre-canned sermons or scholarly lectures. I had to prove the Sabbath by the Bible itself and other credible reference materials—including applicable encyclopedia volumes. It was while I was engaged in this period of intense study that I learned of Noah's Ark, the Red Sea Crossing, Jabal Al Lawz in Saudi Arabia, the *real* Mount Sinai, and many other things that created in me an insatiable, spiritual desire to prove everything the Bible claimed to be true.

A few years later, in September 2001, came the attack on the World Trade Center and I feared we were going to war, but I had no clue as to what our response as individuals or as a nation should or would be. So I broke down and called some friends who told me they were attending the United Church of God—one of the many Church of God splinter groups to have sprung up from the disintegration of the Worldwide Church of God. There are now over 800 Church of God groups around the world—each of them, of course, claiming to be the one "true" church.

Once I began attending United, however, my quest for truth, by no means ended there. I diligently kept searching and tirelessly researching. With the help of the Internet, which was finally coming of age, it became increasingly easier with each passing year to unearth the information my soul so desperately longed for. It was during this time I began to write short articles for United's *Good News* magazine,[11] which had already attained a global readership consisting primarily of United Church of God brethren. That was when I realized the "power of the pen" and began writing more articles for United on a regular basis. It was also during this time they began grooming me to become a church deacon.

In 2004 however, I came to the stark realization I had stopped growing; I had started to stagnate spiritually and was, in fact, regarding sin in my heart, while justifying and excusing my sin. In December of 2004, I listed all my sins in an article and then read the article, in its entirety, to my pastor at the time. I was determined to never again return to my old ways. I was doing as Daniel had done when he confessed the sins of Israel; only I was confessing my own sins.

Immediately thereafter, I heard about the Sighted Moon versus the Conjunction Moon as an alternative and altogether biblical way by which to determine the start of any given month. This was a critical turning point for me, especially when I realized the gravity of how choosing wisely or choosing poorly in this regard could change the days as to when the Holy Days are to be observed. For me, it was no different than keeping the Sabbath on a Sunday. If you kept the Holy Days on any of the wrong days you were *still* missing the mark and therefore, sinning.

But I had not yet acquired biblical proof.

Even after subjecting myself to a great deal of heavy reading and intense study, I still could not prove which way was right. So I retreated into my prayer closet and prayed about it. Within just a few days' time, the biblical passages nearly leaped off the page at me and proved to be a direct answer to this question. That answer which I had sought was in Isaiah 7 and Revelation 12. But in the finding of it, I was immediately given a test to pass. With the Holy Spirit's help, I had proven to myself, beyond all reasonable doubt, the Sighted Moon was to be *THE* moon by which to determine *when* the Holy Days were to be observed. However, the 2005 Passover was just around the corner and there arose a conflict. There was a thirty day difference between the Sighted Moon Calendar and the Hebrew Calendar which most groups were at this time still using. This was very upsetting to me, as I had hoped to be able to keep the Sighted Moon Calendar and, in so doing, have it slip by *unnoticed*

---

11 http://www.ucg.org/doctrinal-beliefs/how-will-you-be-remembered/; http://www.ucg.org/marriage-and-family/mates-not-church-three-true-stories/; http://www.ucg.org/search/gss?query=Living%20with%20an%20unconverted%20mate

by the brethren of the United Church of God who would have been keeping the Hebrew or Conjunction Moon Calendar.

Still not yet 100% sure, I kept *both* calendars that year just to see. The Conjunction Moon observance (Hebrew Calendar observance) was scheduled to take place thirty days *after* the Sighted Moon Calendar observance. So, Passover and the Days (Feast) of Unleavened Bread, according to the barley being ripe and the Sighted Moon, would occur one month *earlier* than the Hebrew-based or Conjunction Moon or calculated calendar.

As soon as I kept the Passover according to the Sighted Moon Calendar, however, the Holy Spirit gave me revelation regarding the Sabbatical and Jubilee Years and their relationship with the curses of Leviticus 26. I could not believe it and yet, I could not dismiss or disprove it either.

I instinctively then began to write out my notes in keeping with what I was learning. This was no coincidence, for these notes would later become an integral part of my website newsletters. As I did this, I began to see irrefutable evidence of the curses of Leviticus 26 happening all around me and thought I was imagining it all. After all, I was not a learned theologian, scholar or eschatologist. Nor was I a pastor, priest or rabbi. I was nothing more than a blue collar, working class ditch digger. How could I *possibly* understand what no one else seemed able to grasp or have any knowledge of?

> **13** And seeing the boldness of Kepha (Peter) and Yohanan (John), and perceiving that they were unlearned and ordinary men, they marveled. (**Acts 4:13**)

> **27** But Elohim has chosen the foolish matters of the world to put to shame the wise, and Elohim has chosen the weak of the world to put to shame the strong. (**1Co 1:27**)

At the Feast of Tabernacles according to the Sighted Moon calendar that year (2005), I asked the host if I could talk to him about this newfound understanding I had acquired of the Sabbatical Years. He wrote me back and told me I *had to* teach what I had been shown to an entire group of individuals who would be attending Sukkot (Feast of Tabernacles, Feast of Booths) in New Hampshire that year. I had never spoken at one of Yehovah's Feasts before and had no desire to do so. I even told the host as much, but the host insisted I share this teaching with those who would be presiding that year.

As a result, I felt the need, once again, to retreat into my prayer closet. It was at that time in prayer I threw a fleece before Yehovah as if to say, "Here am I, send me" if it really *was* true—that there was no one else teaching this. I was, at that point, more open and willing to share the things I had come to understand, including the very scary prophecies they revealed and their relationship to the end of the age. In the end, my final answer was "Yes" if Yehovah again, *truly* had no one else who was willing, able or in a place of understanding to do it and *even if* it meant I would run the risk of being called a fool; if this was, indeed, what He really wanted me to do.

In all honesty, however, it has only been recently that I actually read all of what Yehovah told Isaiah in the part where Isaiah said to Yehovah, "Here am I. Send me."

> **8** And I heard the voice of יהוה saying, "Whom do I send, and who would go for Us?" And I said, "Here am I! Send me." **9** And He said, "Go, and you shall say to this people, 'Hearing, you hear, but do not understand; and seeing, you see, but do not know.' **10** Make the heart of this people fat, and their ears heavy, and shut their eyes; lest they see with their eyes, and hear with their ears, and understand with their heart, and shall turn and be healed." **11** Then I said, "יהוה, until when?" And He answered, "Until the cities are laid waste and without inhabitant, and the houses are without a man, and the land is laid waste, a ruin, **12** and יהוה has removed men far away, and the forsaken places be many in the midst of the land. **13** But still, there is a tenth part in it, and it shall again be for a burning, like a terebinth tree and like an oak, whose stump remains when it is cut down. The set-apart seed is its stump!" (**Isaiah 6:8-13**)

Yehovah is going to send a message the people will hear, but will not understand or know. They will grow fat with knowledge learning many things and yet they will not understand, repent or be healed. In other words, they will be just like a people who are:

> **7** "... always learning and never able to come to the knowledge of the truth." (**II Timothy 3:7**)

This is actually quite remarkable what Yehovah is saying here. We would all do well to sit up and take note and have Yehovah put us on notice!

The following Scriptures in Timothy also jump off the page at me:

> **1** But know this, that in the last days hard times shall come. **2** For men shall be lovers of self, lovers of money, boasters, proud, blasphemers, disobedient to parents, thankless, wrong-doers, **3** unloving, unforgiving, slanderers, without self-control, fierce, haters of good, **4** betrayers, reckless, puffed up, lovers of pleasure rather than lovers of Elohim, **5**

having a form of reverence but denying its power. And turn away from these! **6** For among them are those who creep into households and captivate silly women loaded down with sins, led away by various lusts. (**II Timothy 3:1-6**)

12 And indeed, all those wishing to live reverently in Messiah יהושע, shall be persecuted. **13** But evil men and impostors shall go on to the worse, leading astray and being led astray. (**II Timothy 3:12-13**)

5 For the earth has been defiled under its inhabitants, because they have transgressed the Torot[1], changed[2] the law, (and) broken the everlasting covenant[3]. (**Isaiah 24:5 | Footnotes:** [1]Torot—plural of Torah, teaching. [2]**Jeremiah 23:36**. [3]This is the only reason, according to all Scriptures, why the earth shall be burned in the Day of Judgment | **See also: Isaiah 13:9, 13:11, 26:21, 66:24; Micah 5:15; Zephaniah 1:2-18**)

6 Therefore a curse shall consume the earth, and those who dwell in it be punished. Therefore, the inhabitants of the earth shall be burned, and few men shall be left. (**Isaiah 24:6**)

That year, I taught the Sabbatical Years—also known as 'Shmita'—at the New Hampshire feast and again in Israel, thirty days later, due to the fact I was keeping both the Holy Days of the Sighted Moon Calendar and the Hebrew Calendar. These two feasts constituted the first time I had ever met and talked with those who identified themselves as a part of a growing movement—the Hebraic Roots Movement—which was just beginning to take shape and was still, for all intents and purposes, in its inception at the time.

In 2006, I spoke again about the Sabbatical Years in Windsor, Ontario and then in Toronto. The groups in Toronto were comprised of former members of the splinter churches of the Worldwide Church of God and it was with them I had met with my first real resistance. They did not want to hear any talk of the Sabbatical Years.

Each time I was asked questions I did not have the answers to, I would go and find the answers so I would have a ready defense the next time for what the Spirit would have me say to the churches or those present. And if I could not find the answers in the many hours I spent reading, I would pray about it and within days the answer would surface in a study of some sort or even through a Christian radio station I was listening to.

In July of 2006, the United Church of God wanted me to either stop talking about the things I was speaking of or leave, so my feet left and the rest of my body followed. That same week, I created my website:

http://www.sightedmoon.com I then began writing educational, informative, and provocative articles about the Sighted Moon versus the Conjunction Moon Calendars, and about the Sabbatical and Jubilee Year Cycles as well.

Before I was asked to leave once and for all, my pastor had asked me many times if I considered myself to be Elijah. I assured him I was *not* each and every time he asked. Yet, as it stands at present, I do believe I have been granted the privilege by Yehovah to be numbered amongst those in the last days, along with an untold number of others, Hebraically speaking, to help usher in the restoration of all things—including the Sabbath and Holy Days in accordance to the Sighted Moon and Sabbatical Years.

At Passover in 2007, I began writing a weekly newsletter that was to go only for seven weeks until Shavuot (Pentecost) and yet, it has not stopped since that time except for when I am away at The Feasts (Appointed Times) each year. I have continued to write this newsletter faithfully each week explaining the Sabbatical and Jubilee Years and the prophecies they have revealed and continue to reveal to us. Each week I learn more and more about the Sabbatical Years—and those things, which are directly interrelated—so as to share them with those who sincerely want to learn.

My website readership exceeded 11,000 readers in 2009 and is now nearing the 2,000,000 hit mark in 2012.

It was in March of 2008 that Yehovah made it possible for me to visit ten cities in the USA over the course of a twelve day period speaking about the Sabbatical and Jubilee Years for *The Prophecy Club*[12]. At the end of this tour, they made a DVD, called The Chronological Order of Prophecies in the Jubilees.[13] It became one of their bestsellers and the message therein has yet to be proven false or to be in need of modification. It is still available on my website to those who wish to learn about the Sabbatical Years and the curses that come upon a person for not keeping them.

Many of the things I spoke of on this DVD have *already* happened. How did I know these things? I took great pains to ensure I did not take Scripture out of context and made sure I quoted Scripture accurately. I also made a point to only let Scripture interpret Scripture versus relying on my own biblical interpretations that stem from my own finite understanding of

---

12 http://www.prophecyclub.com/
13 http://www.prophecyclubresources.com/CHRONOLOGICAL-ORDER-OF-PROPHECIES-IN-JUBILEES/productinfo/D-COO01/

Scripture. For we ALL only see *in part*, and even then, through a mirror dimly (I Corinthians 13:12).

In 2009, I was told by some of my readers to take the things I had written in my newsletters and encapsulate them in a book. Having never written a book before, I was not at all sure I could pull it off. My readership insisted I pursue this, however, as they felt the information I was sharing was crucial to the times in which we live. I quickly discovered that the most powerful way to convey the truths contained in Yehovah's Word, were with the charts I had already developed about the Sabbatical and Jubilee Cycles.

So I worked on the book for the greater part of 2009 and in February 2010, *The Prophecies of Abraham* was published. This same book, *The Prophecies of Abraham*, was then nominated for the 2011 Nobel Prize in literature that very same year, because of the many things I had shared about the curses outlined in Leviticus 26, and the coming wars.

Although my book did not win the Nobel Prize, I consider it an honor that it was nominated at all and wish to once again, thank Professor Liebenberg for the noble effort he put into trying to persuade others to consider my book for the Nobel Prize in Literature. On the following page I have enclosed his letter of nomination for my book, *The Prophecies of Abraham*. Please see Appendix "A" at the back of the book for additional information and to see all of what went into the effort Professor Liebenberg put forth on my behalf in this regard.

To The Norwegian Nobel Committee: Date: July 9th, 2010

RE: Nomination of Joseph F. Dumond for a Nobel Humanitarian Prize

Dear Sir or Ms:

Since 1901, the Nobel Prize has been awarded to men and women from all corners of the globe for outstanding achievements in physics, chemistry, physiology or medicine, literature, and for their efforts in bringing about greater world peace. The Norwegian Nobel Committee defines humanitarian efforts as an essential part of promoting "fraternity among nations."

To my understanding, The Committee focuses on a basic aspect of the word "humanitarian": Helping to improve the lives of mankind and reduce suffering. Repeatedly, it has chosen human symbols; people who, through their good deeds, serve as examples for present day and future generations. According to The Committee, these "champions of brotherly love" or "self-sacrificing" men and women served the cause of peace by holding out a helping hand to victims of armed conflicts, etc. The existence of men and women who wish to heal the wounds of war or help to prevent or minimize a future catastrophic event, is, in and of itself an important factor in their deliberations.

The Committee strongly stressed how we all have a global responsibility and that the proud tradition of humanitarianism must also be put on the agenda of world politics. Therefore, I would like to nominate Mr. Joseph F. Dumond from Canada as a Laureate for the humanitarian prize, who, in my mind, has put forth a tremendous effort to lay out before us a gravely imminent, cataclysmic event of epic proportions through his book, *The Prophecies of Abraham.*

He has, in a way that is above and beyond, successfully proven when the Sabbatical and Jubilee Years were throughout history and has, in the most painstaking and accurate of manners, connected them to past and near future events that are going to affect every person on this planet. His exegesis of history as it relates to the Sabbatical Cycles will cause many historians to rethink chronologically when certain events took place. Current world news stories, without question, also more than confirm and corroborate the Sabbatical Years by the devastating events that are taking place around the globe even as we speak.

As a professor and teacher of Biblical History and Theology, *The Prophecies of Abraham* is a truly brilliant explanation of why certain things happen at certain times, whether those things be past, present or future.

Yours Sincerely,

Professor W.A. Liebenberg

Calvary University
HRTI | POB 36035
Annlin, Pretoria, South Africa
Tel: +27 (0) 83 273 1144 (Cell) | Fax: +27 (0) 86 528 3461
E-mail: admin@hrti.co.za **http://www.hrti.co.za**

I also feel impressed to share with you some of the inexplicable things that have happened over the years from 2005 to present. I will do that in Appendix "B" (also at the back of the book).

This year, I began a speaking tour that clearly indicated to me just *how much* those who are being called out (whether they have only just begun, or are farther along or are somewhere in the middle) hunger and thirst to know so much more about the very things Yehovah has already revealed. What struck me the most profoundly with regard to this speaking tour was how so many appeared to have been provided with little to no information pertaining to the Sabbatical and Jubilee Years and how unequipped they still were with respect to how best to put it to the test and prove the information to be true. This is *precisely why* I wrote this current book. For it is written:

6 My people perish for a lack of knowledge. (**Hosea 4:6**)

As I mentioned earlier, I first learned in 2005 of the Sabbatical Years and the respective curses for not keeping them. It has been a spiritually sobering and awe inspiring journey from that moment on as I continue to learn more and more about this Great Commandment and look back on all that has happened since then.

And now, as we enter 2013, I would like to present to you what Yehovah has been showing me since 2005. I am doing this with the sincere hope you too will begin to see the wisdom in and the necessity of keeping this blessed and Great Commandment and, in so doing, break the curses that have come upon you and your family, your friends and co-workers, and our entire society and nation at large for not respecting and obeying our Creator Yehovah and keeping His Sabbaths, Holy Days and Sabbatical Years.

With this book in hand, you too can then teach those in your family, your circle of friends, your church, assembly, fellowship or synagogue—as well as all Yehovah puts in your path—the truth about the Sabbatical Years and how it applies to their life in the here and now and, even more so, in the dark days still to come.

Now is the time to break the curses and keep the Sabbatical Year in 2016! Break the curses of Leviticus 26 and begin to, at long last, reap the blessings of obedience.

May Yehovah now bless *each and every one of you* who choose, in earnest, to repent of your former ways and to do whatever it takes to effectually work toward keeping the next Sabbatical Year from Aviv 2016–Aviv 2017, followed by Aviv 2023–Aviv 2024 and, after that, Aviv 2030–Aviv 2031.

Chapter 1 | Going From One Ditch Into Another

When I first began to learn about the Sabbath, I figured the best place to learn more was at a local synagogue. But the nearest one to me was over an hour's drive away and when I finally was able to check it out, I was not exactly welcomed with open arms.

I believed in the Messiah and at that time I believed His name was Jesus. It wasn't until many years later that I came to know Jesus was the Greek name ascribed to our Messiah who was not a Greek, but very much a Jew—the exciting part being, His true name has been in Hebrew all along and it actually *means* something. The word "Jesus," according to Brad Scott, is a man inspired or man manufactured name.[14] The name Jesus does not mean anything, but the Hebrew Jewish Messiah called Yeh Shua *does mean* something very important:

In English this means, "YHWH's salvation" or "YHWH saves." If you have a different understanding of how to pronounce the name of our Messiah and our Elohim, the Creator then I am happy we both know they have real names, which we can call upon. But I am not going to get into any disputes over the "proper" pronunciation or spelling of their respective names. In this book, unless it is a direct quote, I will use Yehshua for the Son and Yehovah for the Father. Period. This is clearly a case where I cannot please everyone. As I stated earlier, I must stay true to what Yehovah has revealed to me and write this book as unto Him and not unto man.

Today some believe the Messiah was the late Rabbi Menachem Mendel Schneerson, even though Schneerson himself scoffed at such claims.

---

14 http://walkingintheancientpaths.blogspot.com/2011/03/jesus-or-yeshua-whats-in-name.html

Throughout the ages, Jews have also believed those I have listed below to be the Messiah.

In Judaism, "messiah" originally meant a divinely appointed king, such as David, Cyrus the Great or Alexander the Great. Later, especially after the failure of the Hasmonean Dynasty (37 B.C.) and the Jewish–Roman wars (A.D. 66–A.D. 135), the figure of the Jewish Messiah was one who would deliver the Jews from oppression and usher in an Olam Haba ("world to come") or Messianic Age.[15]

- ❖ **Jesus of Nazareth** (ca. 3 B.C.E.–31 C.E.), leader of a small Jewish sect who was crucified; Jews who believed him to be the Messiah were the first Christians, also known as Jewish Christians.

- ❖ **Simon of Peraea** (ca. 4 B.C.E.), a former slave of Herod the Great who rebelled and was killed by the Romans. https://acrobat.com/clients/677768/app.html - cite_note-2

- ❖ **Athronges** (ca. 3 C.E.), a shepherd turned rebel leader.

- ❖ **Vespasian**, (A.D. 69–A.D. 79), according to Josephus https://acrobat.com/clients/677768/app.html - cite_note-4

- ❖ **Menahem ben Judah** (aka, as Menahem ben Hezekiah) (133 C.E.–135 C.E.), allegedly son of false messiah, Judas of Galilee, partook in a revolt against Agrippa II before being slain by a rival zealot leader.

- ❖ **Simon bar Kochba** (ca. 132–135 C.E.), founded a short-lived Jewish state before being defeated in the Second Jewish-Roman War.

- ❖ **Moses of Crete** (circa 440–470 C.E), who convinced the Jews of Crete to attempt to walk into the sea to return to Israel; he disappeared after that disaster.

- ❖ **Ishak ben Ya'kub**https://acrobat.com/wiki/Abu_Isa (aka, Isa al-Isfahani, Abu 'Isa) (A.D. 684–A.D. 705), who led a revolt in Persia against the Umayyad Caliph 'Abd al-Malik ibn Marwan.

  - • **Yudghan** (8th-century), a disciple of Abu 'Isa who continued the faith after 'Isa was slain.

- ❖ **Serene** (circa 720 C.E.), who claimed to be the Messiah and advocated expulsion of Muslims and relaxing various rabbinic laws before being arrested; he then recanted.

---

15 http://en.wikipedia.org/wiki/Messiah_claimants

❖ **David Alroy** (circa 1160 C.E.), born in Kurdistan, who agitated against the caliph before being assassinated.

❖ **Nissim ben Abraham** (circa 1295 C.E.)

❖ **Moses Botarel** of Cisneros (1413 C.E.), who claimed to be a sorcerer able to combine the names of God.

❖ **Asher Lämmlein** (1502 C.E.), a German near Venice who proclaimed himself a forerunner of the Messiah.

❖ **David Reubeni** (1490 C.E.–1541 C.E.) and **Solomon Molcho** (1500 C.E.–1532 C.E.), adventurers who traveled in Portugal, Italy, and Turkey; Molcho was eventually burned at the stake by the Pope.

❖ A mostly unknown Czechoslovakian Jew from around 1650 C.E. A page from the Jewish Museum of Prague about Solomon Molcho mentions this nameless Czech Jew.

❖ **Sabbatai Zevi** (1626 C.E.–1676 C.E. & 1687 C.E.), an Ottoman Jew who claimed to be the Messiah, but then converted to Islam; still has followers today in the Donmeh.

  · **Barukhia Russo** (**Osman Baba**), (1695 C.E.–1740 C.E.) successor of **Sabbatai Zevi**.
  · **Jacob Querido** (1690 C.E.), claimed to be the new incarnation of Sabbatai; later converted to Islam and led the Donmeh.
  · **Miguel Cardoso** (1630 C.E.–1706 C.E.), another successor of Sabbatai who claimed to be the "Messiah ben Ephraim."
  · **Mordecai Mokia** (1650 C.E.–1729 C.E. or, 1678–1683 C.E.), "the Rebuker," another person who proclaimed himself Messiah after Sabbatai's death.
  · **Löbele Prossnitz** (1750 C.E.), attained some following amongst former followers of Sabbatai, calling himself the "**Messiah ben Joseph**."

❖ **Jacob Joseph Frank** (1726 C.E.–1791 C.E.), who claimed to be the reincarnation of King David and preached a synthesis of Christianity and Judaism.

❖ **Menachem Mendel Schneerson** (1902 C.E.–1994 C.E.), the seventh Chabad Rabbi who tried to "prepare the way" for the Messiah. An unidentifiable number of his followers believed him to be the Messiah, (although he himself never said this and actually scoffed at such claims which were made during his lifetime). https://acrobat.com/clients/677768/app.html - cite_note-6

I bring this up because Judah now openly becomes upset with those who are keeping Torah—or, all The Commandments in the first five books of the Bible—especially with those who are not Jewish and yet believe in Yehshua as the Messiah.

Yet, the truth of the matter remains. Many of us, who once called ourselves "Christian," are now waking up to the truth of Torah and coming to understand like never before just *how much* we have been lied to in the *very* denominations we are being called out of, no matter which ones. This phenomenon has left in its wake an earnest desire in many of us to want to become Torah obedient and come under the True Covenant of Yehovah, the Creator.

In our newfound zeal, however, we mistakenly assume Judaism has all the right answers. And it is with this misplaced, newfound zeal that many of us climb our way out from the religious ditch of Christianity, only to haplessly fall right back into another religious ditch of Orthodox Judaism. Yet neither one, as a rule, is following Yehovah. Yes, you read that right—*neither one* is following the Torah that Moses wrote which was given to him directly from Yehovah at Mount Sinai. And if either one is, they are only doing it in part, at best, and not in full. But you either do Torah all the way or not at all. For if you break one commandment, you break them all (James 2:10).

Q: What is the one test Commandment that Yehovah gave to test *all* mankind as to whether or not they would obey and follow Him?

A: The Fourth Commandment.

> **4** And יהוה said to Mosheh (Moses), "See, I am raining bread from the heavens for you. And the people shall go out and gather a day's portion every day, in order to try them, whether they walk in My Torah or not. **5** And it shall be on the sixth day that they shall prepare what they bring in, and it shall be twice as much as they gather daily." (**Exodus 16:4-5**)

The weekly seventh day Saturday Sabbath is a weekly test to see *if* we will obey Yehovah *or not*. "But Judah keeps the Fourth Commandment," you say. We shall examine this more closely and see if, in truth, they actually do or if they have perverted Scripture. But Judah is, by no means, alone in this. It is even more obvious that those who are still caught up in Christendom do *not* keep the Fourth Commandment. And because of this, Christians will be told by Yehshua:

> **13** "Enter in through the narrow gate! Because the gate is wide–and the way is broad–that leads to destruction, and there are many who enter in through it. **14** Because the gate is narrow and the way is hard pressed which leads to life, and there are few who find it. **15** But beware of the

false prophets, who come to you in sheep's clothing, but inwardly they are savage wolves. **16** By their fruits you shall know them. Are grapes gathered from thornbushes or figs from thistles? **17** So every good tree yields good fruit, but a rotten tree yields wicked fruit. **18** A good tree is unable to yield wicked fruit, and a rotten tree to yield good fruit. **19** Every tree that does not bear good fruit is cut down and thrown into the fire. **20** So then, by their fruits you shall know them." (**Matthew 7:13-20**)

21 "Not everyone who says to Me, 'Master, Master,' shall enter into the reign of the heavens, but he who is doing the desire of My Father in the heavens. **22** Many shall say to Me in that day, 'Master, Master, have we not prophesied in Your Name, and cast out demons in Your Name, and done many mighty works in Your Name?' **23** And then I shall declare to them, 'I never knew you, depart from Me, you who work lawlessness!' **24** Therefore everyone who hears these words of Mine, and does them, shall be like a wise man who built his house on the rock, **25** and the rain came down, and the floods came, and the winds blew and beat on that house, and it did not fall, for it was founded on the rock. **26** And everyone who hears these words of Mine, and does not do them, shall be like a foolish man who built his house on the sand, **27** and the rain came down, and the floods came, and the winds blew, and they beat on that house, and it fell, and great was its fall." (**Matthew 7:21-27**)

23 "I never knew you, depart from Me, you who work lawlessness!" (**Matthew 7:23**)

4 Everyone doing sin also does lawlessness, and sin is lawlessness. (**I John 3:4**)

It all comes down to the keeping of The Commandments—all ten. You keep Torah (The Law) when you obey The Commandments, and when you do not keep them, you are said to be lawless.

Will Judah be told the same thing?

Let me show you what Torah has to say in response and then you can decide who does or does not keep The Law. Then you will know whether or not you should blindly go and subscribe to another religion.

We are *commanded* to go and tell our brother when we see him sinning in the Torah and the Brit Chadasha (New Covenant or New Testament).

17 Do not hate your brother in your heart. Reprove your neighbor, for certain, and bear no sin because of him. (**Leviticus 19:17**)

12 "What do you think? If a man has a hundred sheep, and one of them goes astray, would he not leave the ninety-nine on the mountains, going to seek the one that is straying? **13** And if he should find it, truly, I say to you, he rejoices more over that sheep than over the ninety-nine that did not go astray. **14** Thus it is not the desire of your Father who is in the heavens that one of these little ones should be lost. **15** And if your brother sins against you, go and reprove him, between you and him alone. If he hears you, you have gained your brother. **16** But if he does not hear, take with you one or two more, that 'by the mouth of two or three witnesses every word might be established.' **17** And if he refuses to hear them, say it to the assembly. And if he refuses even to hear the assembly, let him be to you like a gentile and a tax collector." (**Matthew 18:12-17**)

Let us now read in *Clarke's Commentary* what these two verses *actually* mean.

Clarke's Commentary On the Bible[16]

Thou shalt not hate thy brother—Thou shalt not only *not* do him any kind of evil, but thou shalt harbor *no* hatred in thy heart towards him. On the contrary, thou shalt love him as thyself, Leviticus 19:18. Many persons suppose, from misunderstanding our Lord's words, John 13:34, A new commandment give I unto you, that ye love one another, etc., that loving our neighbor as ourselves was first instituted under The Gospel. This verse shows the opinion to be unfounded: but to love one another as Christ has loved us (i.e., to lay down our lives for each other), is certainly a new commandment; we have it simply on the authority of Jesus Christ alone.

> And not suffer sin upon him—if thou see him sin, or know him to be addicted to anything by which the safety of his soul is endangered, thou shalt mildly and affectionately reprove him, and by no means permit him to go on without counsel and advice in a way that is leading him to perdition. In a multitude of cases, timely reproof has been the means of saving the soul. Speak to him privately if possible; if not, write to him in such a way that himself alone shall see it.

In Scripture we read:

> **3** "If your brother sins against you, rebuke him, and if he repents, forgive him." (**Luke 17:3**)

> **9** But the one who says he is in the light, and hates his brother, is in the darkness until now. (**I John 2:9**)

---

16 http://bible.cc/leviticus/19-17.htm

11 But whoever hates his brother is in the darkness and walks in the darkness, and does not know where he is going, because the darkness has blinded his eyes. (**I John 2:11**)

15 Everyone hating his brother is a murderer, and you know that no murderer has everlasting life staying in Him. (**I John 3:15**)

If we do not tell our brother of his sins as we become aware of them, it is the same as hating our brother and walking in darkness—or, the same as if we had murdered him.

Contained within the 613 Mitzvot is the command to warn your brother and it, along with insightful commentary, is as follows:

(**30**) Do not cherish hatred in your heart.[17]

17 You shall not hate your brother in your heart. (**Leviticus 19:17**)

Could it be that the rabbis actually got one right? This is apparently a no-brainer, the converse of Mitzvah (#26), "You shall love your neighbor as you do yourself." But look at what follows, (for) it almost sounds like a contradiction: "You shall surely rebuke your neighbor, and not bear sin because of him." In light of this close contextual connection, we shouldn't automatically assume Moses has moved on to a different subject. Actually, I believe the second phrase defines what it is to "hate your brother." And the truth that emerges if we make this connection has stunning relevance for us today: we are *not* to be tolerant of false teaching, but are rather to "rebuke" those in error—to neglect this correction is to hate our brother. Remember the rabbinical Mitzvah (#27) that said, "Do not stand by idly when a human life is in danger?" This is the practical outworking of the principal: if your brother is in spiritual error, if he espouses doctrines that Yahweh's Word says will kill him in the end, then to withhold rebuke and admonition is to hate him. By tolerating his heresy, you are sending him to hell, (very much like offering an alcoholic a drink or) like indulging a diabetic's sweet tooth.

There is a way that seems right to a man, but its end is the way of death. (**Proverbs 14:12, 16:25**)

What does it mean to "bear" sin? The Hebrew word is 'nasa,' meaning to 'lift,' or 'carry.' It is "used in reference to the bearing of guilt or punishment for sin" leading to the "representative or substitutionary bearing of one person's guilt by another."

---

17 http://theownersmanual.net/The_Owners_Manual_02_The_Law_of_Love.Torah

In the Amplified Bible we read:

> **2 Bear (endure, carry) one another's burdens *and* troublesome moral faults, and in this way fulfill *and* observe perfectly the law of Christ (the Messiah) *and* complete what is lacking (in your obedience to it). 3** For if any person thinks himself to be somebody (too important to condescend to shoulder another's load) when he is nobody (of superiority except in his own estimation), he deceives *and* deludes *and* cheats himself. **4** But let every person carefully scrutinize *and* examine *and* test his own conduct *and* his own work. (**Galatians 6:2-4**)

Yahweh did not want false teaching tolerated in Israel because the guilt incurred—and thus the punishment—would eventually be borne by the entire nation. He would have spared them that pain. He would spare us that pain.

This ought to then shed new light on Yahshua's confirmation of the principle that loving Yahweh and our fellow man is the path which leads to life.

> **25** And see, a certain one learned in the Torah stood up, trying Him, and saying, "Teacher, what shall I do to inherit everlasting life?" **26** And He said to him, "What has been written in the Torah? How do you read it?" **27** And he answering, said, "You shall love your Elohim with all your heart, and with all your being, and with all your strength, and with all your mind, and your neighbor as yourself." **28** And He said to him, "You have answered rightly. Do this and you shall live." (**Luke 10:25-28**)

Friends don't let friends fall prey to false teaching.

Knowing this now and taking on the name of our Father, with respect to us, His children, brings a whole new understanding of the following commandment found in Exodus:

> **7** "You do not bring the Name of יהוה your Elohim to *naught*, for יהוה does not leave the one unpunished who brings His Name to *naught*." (**Exodus 20:7**)

The word 'naught' is Strong's # **H7723 אושׁ ושׁ**° shâv' shav *shawv, shav*

Significantly similar to **H7722** in the sense of *desolating; evil* (as *destructive*), literally (*ruin*) or morally (especially *guile*); figuratively *idolatry* (as false, subjectively), *uselessness* (as deceptive, objectively; also adverbially in *vain*): false (-ly), lie, lying, vain, vanity.

H7722 אוש האוש האוש shô' shô'âh shô'âh *sho, sho-aw' sho-aw'*

From an unused root meaning to *rush* over; a *tempest*; by implication *devastation:* desolate (-ion), destroy, destruction, storm, wasteness.

We are not to be called the Children of Yehovah only to have the professing of His name come to represent allowing sin to prevail or remain unaddressed on our part. And it is this very sin of the breaking of the Fourth Commandment that will be addressed in this book.

It has been said, "The only thing necessary for evil to triumph is for (good) men to stand idly by and do nothing." We let evil triumph when we are unwilling to be as Ezekiel watchmen who warn our brother or sister if they are sinning or missing the mark. Their blood is on our hands if we don't love them enough to tell them the truth.

> **17** "Son of man, I have made you a watchman for the house of Yisra'el. And you shall hear a word from My mouth, and shall warn them from Me. **18** When I say to the wrong 'You shall certainly die,' and you have not warned him, nor spoken to warn the wrong from his wrong way, to save his life, that same wrong man shall die in his crookedness, and his blood I require at your hand. **19** But if you have warned the wrong and he does not turn from his wrong, nor from his wrong way, he shall die in his crookedness, and you have delivered your being. **20** And when a righteous one turns from his righteousness and shall do unrighteousness, when I have put a stumbling-block before him, he shall die. Because you did not warn him, he shall die in his sin, and his righteousness which he has done is not remembered, and his blood I require at your hand. **21** But if you have warned the righteous one that the righteous should not sin, and he did not sin, he shall certainly live, because he has been warned; and you have delivered your being." (**Ezekiel 3:17-21**)

But in so doing, we must also take care to do it in the right spirit:

> **1** Brothers, if a man is overtaken in some trespass, you the spiritual ones, set such a one straight in a spirit of meekness, looking at yourself lest you be tried too. (**Galatians 6:1**)

For even greater clarity, the Amplified Bible translation reads:

> **1** Brethren, if any person is overtaken in misconduct *or* sin of any sort, you who are spiritual (who are responsive to and controlled by the Spirit) should set him right *and* restore *and* reinstate him, without any sense of

> superiority *and* with all gentleness, keeping an attentive eye on yourself,
> lest you should be tempted also. **(Galatians 6:1)**

It has always deeply troubled me to know just *how* persecuted Judah has been throughout history. Yet, if the keeping of Torah was to bring blessings (and still is), then *why* have those who claim to have been keeping the Torah all along (and still claim to be the only ones who do so) been so persecuted in every generation? Why are they so hated by most of the world? And why has the rest of the world not seen the blessings the Jews are supposed to have been given and have continuously bestowed upon them for keeping Torah? I would think the world, once they saw the benefits of keeping Torah, would then *also* be found wanting to obey Torah.

But, as it stands, we have *not* seen the blessings in any kind of significant or sit up and take note kind of way down through the ages and therefore, do *not* see anything to cause us to also want to keep Torah. And yet, a light is to be seen from far off. It is not heard at all, just seen. We should be able to *see* the benefits of keeping Torah in a way that we can't ignore, explain away, or dismiss and should not have to be *told* why we should.

> **13** "You are the salt of the earth, but if the salt becomes tasteless, how shall it be seasoned? For it is no longer of any use but to be thrown out and to be trodden down by men. **14** You are the light of the world. It is impossible for a city to be hidden on a mountain. **15** Nor do they light a lamp and put it under a basket, but on a lampstand, and it shines to all those in the house. **16** Let your light so shine before men, so that they see your good works and praise your Father who is in the heavens."
> **(Matthew 5:13-16)**

So let's once again look at *what* we are commanded to do and see if Judah does this. If they do not, then we should not just go and follow them blindly thinking this is the way to go. And too, we already know Christianity is overladen with lies and falls short of the truth. Now let's see just what that truth looks like and how close you are to it or how far you are from it.

Below is another verse, also from Mitzvot 613, which states we must follow the majority *even when they are wrong.* This Mitzvah is as follows:

> **(248)** Give the decision according to the majority when there is a difference of opinion among the members of the Sanhedrin as to matters of law.[18]

---

18 http://theownersmanual.net/The_Owners_Manual_07_The_Rule_of_Law.Torah

1"You shall not circulate a false report. Do not put your hand with the wicked to be an unrighteous witness. 2 You shall not follow a crowd to do evil; nor shall you testify in a dispute so as to turn aside after many to pervert justice." (**Exodus 23:1-2**)

This is one of those instances (thankfully rare—they usually just *miss* the point) where the rabbi's Mitzvah is *diametrically opposed* to the (very) Scripture they've cited to support it. (In essence), they're saying, "The majority opinion among us, the ruling elite of Israel, will become law." It's the (very) same system America uses, subject to the (very) same abuses. And by the way, it's the (very) same system the Sanhedrin used to condemn Yahweh's Anointed One to death—proving that it's anathema to Yahweh. (Yet), Yahweh (Himself) is saying something *completely* different: Don't follow the crowd, and don't lead them into falsehood, either.

1 Blessed is the man who shall not walk in the counsel of the wrong, and shall not stand in the path of sinners, and shall not sit in the seat of scoffers. 2 But his delight is in the Torah of יהוה. (**Psalm 1:1-2**)

Seek truth, mercy, and justice, even if you're (nothing more than) "... a lone voice crying in the wilderness." Yahweh could *care less* about the majority opinion. In fact, He flatly stated that the majority is lost:

13 "Enter by the narrow gate; for wide is the gate and broad is the way that leads to destruction, and there are many who go in by it. 14 Because narrow is the gate and difficult is the way which leads to life, and there are few who find it." (**Matthew 7:13-14**)

8 He has declared to you, O man, what is good. And what does יהוה require of you but to do right (justly), and to love kindness (mercy), and to walk humbly with your Elohim? (**Micah 6:8**)

Continuing on in Mitzvot 613, the gross distortion of Scripture the rabbis make in (248) also finds its way into (249) below:

(**249**) In capital cases, do not decide according to the view of the majority when those who are for condemnation exceed those who are for acquittal by only one.[19]

Yet again, what is said in Exodus should make it clear that no high court or high tribunal of *any* kind is to be a law unto themselves:

---

19 http://theownersmanual.net/The_Owners_Manual_07_The_Rule_of_Law.Torah

1 You shall not circulate a false report. Do not put your hand with the wicked to be an unrighteous witness. **2** You shall not follow a crowd to do evil; nor shall you testify in a dispute so as to turn aside after many to pervert justice. (**Exodus 23:1-2**)

They're saying a simple majority isn't enough to condemn a man to death—you need at least two tie-breakers. Sorry, folks. Wrong again. This is merely man's flawed wisdom. In the case of the most significant trial in history, we know of only two dissenting (or was it abstaining?) voices out of the seventy—Nicodemus and Joseph of Arimathea. Clearly, the idea of majority rule has some holes in it. How many in that assembly were swayed by the vituperative attitude of Annas and Caiaphas? How many were nudged over the line by the false witnesses who were brought in to testify against Yahshua? How many were cowed into silence by the weight of peer pressure?

Next, we will take a closer look at where Judah has changed the Torah and now adheres to and follows what has been voted on by the "moral" majority.

Chapter 2 | Sabbath Sunset To Sunset, Not Three Stars

We are told in the passage below we *are* to keep the Sabbath. It is the very first Feast day in that it precedes all of the Feast Days—a day in which Yehovah wants us to earnestly remember all of His holy, set-apart (appointed) times. In doing so, we become much better equipped to keep our divine appointments with Him by weekly setting aside this day to meet with Him, to spend time with Him and learn more about Him.

> 1 Andיהוה spoke to Mosheh (Moses), saying, 2 "Speak to the children of Yisra'ĕl, and say to them, 'The appointed times of יהוה, which you are to proclaim as set-apart gatherings, My appointed times, are these: 3 Six days work is done, but the seventh day is a Sabbath of rest, a set-apart gathering. You do no work, it is a Sabbath to יהוה in all your dwellings.'" (**Leviticus 23:1-3**)

We are told in the first chapter of Genesis that the evening comes first and then the day. Shabbat, therefore, begins at sunset. We know this because in chapter one of the story of creation in Genesis it says, "And there was evening, and there was morning, one day." From this, we infer that a day begins with an evening, that is, sunset. We are also told in Leviticus 23, regarding the Day of Atonement, how this High Holy Day is from 'evening to evening.' In other words, the Sabbath goes from 'sunset to sunset.' From the moment the sun sets in the western horizon at the end of the sixth day on any given Friday, the Sabbath begins.

In Judaism 101[20], after stating that the Shabbat begins at sunset because of the Genesis 1 account it then goes on to say:

---

20 http://www.jewfaq.org/shabbat.htm

Shabbat ends at nightfall, when three stars are visible, approximately forty minutes after sunset.

There is *nothing* in Scripture that tells us to begin when we see three stars. This is an invention of the rabbis and is found in the Talmud.[21] It is a fence they have put on the Sabbath to help keep you from breaking the Sabbath.

Yet *nowhere* in Torah or the Bible do we have the Sabbath beginning or ending by the sighting of three stars. Yet we *do* find in Genesis the following statements:

> **5** And Elohim called the light 'day' and the darkness He called 'night.' And there came to be evening and there came to be morning, the first day. (**Genesis 1:5**)

> **8** And Elohim called the expanse 'heavens.' And there came to be evening and there came to be morning, the second day. (**Genesis 1:8**)

> **13** And there came to be evening and there came to be morning, the third day. (**Genesis 1:13**)

> **19** And there came to be evening and there came to be morning, the fourth day. (**Genesis 1:19**)

> **23** And there came to be evening and there came to be morning, the fifth day. (**Genesis 1:23**)

> **31** And Elohim saw all that He had made, and see, it was very good. And there came to be evening and there came to be morning, the sixth day. (**Genesis 1:31**)

With this pattern of evening and morning now set before us, Yehovah then tells us about the seventh day of rest.

> **1** Thus the heavens and the earth were completed, and all their array. **2** And on the seventh day Elohim completed His work which He had done, and He rested on the seventh day from all His work which He had made. **3** And Elohim blessed the seventh day and set it apart, because

---

21 Nightfall is determined by the appearance of three medium-sized stars in the evening sky (Bi'ur Halakha 261 s.v. She-hu and Bi'ur Halakha 293 s.v. Gimmel kokhavim ketanim). [For further research, see Shabbat 35b (compare with Megilla 20b, Pesachim 2a, and Berakhot 2a-b). See also Nechemia 4:15, Rambam Shabbat 5:4 (compare with Rambam Terumot 7:2 and Shulchan Arukh OC 235:1)].

on it He rested from all His work which Elohim in creating had made. (**Genesis 2:1-3**)

And to again show us the importance of when the day begins, Yehovah tells us point blank in Leviticus 23 when the most solemn day was to start and end just to make sure we all would understand.

> **27** "On the tenth day of this seventh month is the Day of Atonement. It shall be a set-apart gathering for you. And you shall afflict your beings, and shall bring an offering made by fire to יהוה. **28** And you do no work on that same day, for it is the Day of Atonement, to make atonement for you before יהוה your Elohim. **29** For any being who is not afflicted on that same day, he shall be cut off from his people. **30** And any being who does any work on that same day, that being I shall destroy from the midst of his people. **31** You do no work—a law forever throughout your generations in all your dwellings. **32** It is a Sabbath of rest to you, and you shall afflict your beings. On the ninth day of the month at evening, from evening to evening, you observe your Sabbath." (**Leviticus 23:27-32**)

There are, among us, in these last days, a couple of rogue groups who adamantly claim the Sabbath is during the day *only* (the daylight or sunlight hours exclusively of any given twenty-four-hour period) or that the Sabbath begins 'seven days' *after* the New Moon. And yet, neither one of these groups have authoritative or exhaustive enough proof historically or biblically to support either school of thought. Nevertheless, the two groups are comprised of a surprising and alarming number of former Christians who, more recently, have converted from Christianity to these errant forms of observing and keeping the Sabbath. Yet not *one* group or governing body of Jews throughout history operated in accordance with either one of these misguided groups.

The Lunar Sabbath Theory (and I *stress* theory) has only been in existence since 1998:

> Jonathan David Brown was the first known Sabbath keeper to begin the practice of counting the Sabbath from the New Moon day rather than using the modern seven day week. He published the book *Keeping Yahweh's Appointments* in 1998, which explained the practice. The Lunar Sabbath movement has grown among the Messianic Judaism, Armstrong/Worldwide Church of God and Christian Identity movements.[22]

---

22 http://en.wikipedia.org/wiki/Jonathan_David_Brown#cite_note-2

But thankfully, there *are* ample proofs from *well documented* sources—proofs of which, line upon line and precept upon precept, show *both* of these approaches to be fraught with error. And that's not discounting just plain, good old common sense, for Yehovah makes it so obvious in Scripture how we are to go about keeping the Sabbath according to His dictates. I am not, however, going to elaborate on these wrong teachings for they will only confuse those of you who are earnestly seeking the truth of Torah and how it relates to *all* of Scripture. But, at the very least, I had to make you aware of the doctrinally unsound teachings and warn you of their deceptive nature, which lead you down a slippery slope—away from truth, Yehovah, His Sabbath and all of His other set-apart days as well.

Let me give you one proof for you to use although there are many. Yehshua was killed on the 14th day of the first month. This is the preparation day for the Passover meal. This day was a Wednesday. He had to be in the grave before sunset as it was the High Holy Day of the 1st Day of Unleavened Bread. Thursday was this 1st day of Unleavened Bread and it was the 15th day of the first month. Friday was the Preparation day for the weekly Sabbath and was the day that the women were preparing the spices for Yehshua and they planned to give Yehshua a proper burial after the weekly Sabbath. Friday was the 16th day of the first month.

Friday evening was the 3rd night Yehshua was in the grave. Saturday was the 3rd day He was in the grave, thus fulfilling the prophecy that the only sign He would give of His Messiah ship was that He would be in the grave for 3 days and 3 nights just as Jonah was 3 days and 3 nights in the belly of the fish.

Saturday was the 17th day of the first month. And when the Sabbath was over on the first day of the week we are told that the women came to the grave and Yehshua was gone. It was still dark, and was the first day of the week. That Sunday was the 18th day of the month. This shows you that this day, which was still dark on the first day of the week, includes the night part and the day part together, thus disproving the day only groups.

The Lunar Sabbath people claim the Sabbath to be on the 7th or the 8th day of the month every month. So if we just do the math, the second week according to them, the second Sabbath would be the 14th or the 15th depending on which group you are following. And the third Sabbath would be the 21st or 22; again depending upon which group you follow.

But your bible clearly says that the women came on the 1st day of the week a Sunday and you can calculate that this day was the 18th day. The weekly Sabbath that they observed was on the 17th day of the month that year. Clearly the Lunar Sabbath people have a gaping hole in their theory. Do not get caught up in this false teaching.

If you feel led to want to explore this subject more, here are two sources you can use. *The Lunar Sabbath Lie*[23] at **sightedmoon.com** and *The Lunar Shabbat Calendar Issues* by Yochanan Zaqantov.[24]

23 http://www.sightedmoon.com/?page_id=194
24 http://www.karaitejudaism.org/talks/The_Lunar_Shabbat_Calendar_Issues.htm

Chapter 3 | The New Moon

We must now look at the New Moon. We do this because it is *by the moon* that we determine the beginning of the month.

Today, as I stated earlier, there are two commonly known biblical calendars in use to show when each of the Holy Days are. One is the Sighted Moon Calendar and the other is, the more popular Hillel II Calendar (aka, the Hebrew Calendar or the rabbinical calendar).

Before 70 C.E. and before the Temple was destroyed, the Jewish calendar was determined during the proceedings of a special Sanhedrin committee meeting at the Temple. The declaration of the New Moon did not take place until two witnesses came forward and described the Sighted New Moon to the committee. The entire Jewish community outside the Land of Israel waited to hear official word on the calendar sanctioned by the Sanhedrin, being it was deemed essential for the unified observance of the Jewish Holy Days. But, as religious persecution set in, beginning with the destruction of the Temple in 70 C.E. and continuing up to the time of Hillel II while he held the office of Nasi (or, Chief Rabbi) from 330 C.E.–365 C.E., it became impossible to receive reports of moon sightings or barley status from the Land of Israel.

Nevertheless, during the Diaspora, Hillel II devised an authorized calendar everyone could use; not only for those who still remained in Israel, but even more importantly, for those who had been exiled and cut off from Israel. However, in so doing, he severed the ties that united the Jews of the Diaspora to the Land of Israel and to the Sanhedrin. Yet, during the Diaspora this calendar was considered vital so that those outside of Israel could keep the Holy Days in unison with those in Israel.

> The Hebrew calendar has evolved over time … the months were set by observation of a New Crescent Moon, with an additional month added

every two or three years to keep Passover in the spring, again based on observation of natural events, namely the ripening of the barley crop, the age of the kids lambs and doves, the ripeness of the fruit trees, and the relation to the Tekufah (seasons). Through the Amoraic period and into the Geonic period, this system was displaced by mathematical rules. The principles and rules appear to have been settled by the time Maimonides compiled the (Mishneh) Torah in the 12th-century.[25]

You can learn about the Hillel II Hebrew calendar[26] by researching it online. While doing so, be sure to take note of the year this calendar came into effect. It was 358 C.E. when Hillel II shared the methods used by the Sanhedrin to calculate the months and the Holy Days. It was further modified throughout history into the 11th-century C.E. until it became what it is today, as referenced in the quote above in accordance with Maimonides' fourteen-volume Mishneh Torah.[27] But again, this is a *man-made*, calculated calendar. It is *not* at all the one instituted by Yehovah.

As I am about to show you, the original, biblical, non-rabbinical, Sighted Moon Calendar has always been:

"... based directly on celestial observation and inspections of the young barley crop in Israel. These observations were meticulously catalogued and corroborated. Armed with a tabulation of this data spanning centuries, ancient astronomers could model celestial phenomena with mathematical equations, enabling them to predict lunar cycles and other celestial events far in advance. This allowed a new month to be accurately reckoned even when the weather prevented direct observations. However, *the observations drove the math, and not vice versa*."

(After the Diaspora), the Beit Din's (aka, Sanhedrin's) Provisional Calendar (came to rely) entirely on the math model to the *exclusion* of celestial observation. Neither was there any explicit provision (put in place) for recalibrating this purely mathematical calendar with the heavens.

By 10th-century C.E., it (became) clear to some that "Hillel's Calendar" needed refining. In 921 C.E., Aaron ben Meir, while presiding over the Judean Sanhedrin, announced a calendar reform that, naturally, would place the holidays on *different days* than those prescribed by Hillel's Calendar. Thousands adopted this reform. However, the Jewish academic

25 http://en.wikipedia.org/wiki/Hebrew_calendar
26 http://www.jewfaq.org/calendr2.htm
27 http://en.wikipedia.org/wiki/Maimonides & http://en.wikipedia.org/wiki/Mishneh_Torah

communities of Babylon, in part represented by Saadia ben Yosef (Saadia Gaon), strongly opposed Meir's proposition. Both authorities had considerable influence and the issue threatened their cohesion (solidarity). In the end, Babylon won out, and Judaism has been loath to court the fragmentation that could well result from serious calendar reform discussion, preferring to defer the matter to Messiah.[28]

Evidence From *The Talmud*[29]

The Talmud is *not* Scripture, and *The Talmud* is *not* inspired. However, *The Talmud* does give us a good historical record of the thoughts of the Jewish rabbis in ancient times. This can be very good information to have.

The Talmud tells us that the rabbinical calendar was not in use in Yeshua's day, in that the New Moon was still being declared by observation (rather than prediction). For example, *The Talmud Mishna Tractate Rosh Hashanah* ("Head of the Year") account discusses how to properly interrogate witnesses (of) the Hodesh ("New Moon").

The Talmud Tractate Rosh Hashanah (excerpt below) details a dispute between the rabbis as to whether a certain pair of witnesses who had observed the New Moon formed a reliable basis for officially declaring the New Moon that month. The passage reads:

> 7 Rabbi Jose (aka, Rabbi Yose) said: "It happened once with Tobiyah (Tobias) the physician, that he saw the New Moon in Jerusalem, along with his son and his emancipated slave; and the priests accepted his evidence and that of his son (but disqualified his slave); but (then) when they appeared before the (Rabbinic) Beit Din they accepted his evidence, and that of his slave, but disqualified his son." (**Talmud Tractate Rosh Hashanah 1:7**)

Clearly this passage refers to physical sightings of the New Moon, telling us that the New Moon was being observed in Yeshua's time, because if the New Moon was already being calculated (or predicted) there would be no need to sight it.

Next, *The Talmud Mishna Tractate Rosh Hashanah* tells us:

> 7 "Whether it was seen in its time or not seen in its time (i.e. on or before the 30th day of the preceding month), it is sanctified

28 http://yahoshuafoundation.org/calendararticle.pdf
29 http://www.sightedmoon.com/?page_id=126 as quoted from *About Calendars* by www.nazareneisrael.org

(i.e. the New Moon day is declared by default). Rabbi Eleazar ben (aka, bar) Tsadoq says, 'If it is not seen in its time (i.e. on the 30th) we (the court) do not (even bother to) sanctify it; for it has already been sanctified by heaven." (**Talmud Mishna Tractate Rosh Hashanah 2:7**)

Further, *The Babylonian Talmud Tractate Rosh Hashanah* tells us:

The Halachah (Traditional Law) is according to R. Eleazar ben (aka, bar) R. Tsadoq. (**Babylonian Talmud Tractate Rosh Hashanah 24a**)

As (you have) just read, R. Eleazar ben (aka, bar) Tsadoq said that the New Moons (New Months) were to be declared based upon observation (and not pre-calculation). Then (you were) told that the Halachah (the legal practice) is in agreement with R. Eleazar's ruling.

Since the rabbinical calendar does depend on pre-calculation, the rabbinical calendar could not have been the calendar in use during Yeshua's time.

Still not convinced? Keep reading.

No Calculations

(You) should further note that (the) Babylonian Talmud Tractate Rosh Hashanah 24a (as cited above) makes no reference to: calculation, lunar conjunction (or any other consideration). Rather, it makes reference only to the direct observation of the New Moon Crescent. This tells us that the established practice of Second Temple Times (i.e., Yeshua's time), was (based on the fact) that the Hodesh (New Moon) was declared when the First Crescent Sliver of the New Moon was physically seen (and then reported) by at least two reliable witnesses. This logically demolishes the argument of the so-called "Obscuration Method" of establishing the Hodesh, since it is not possible to require witnesses to physically sight something that cannot physically be seen. *Again they didn't have the technology*

Moreover, (you) should note that Yeshua was a Second Temple Period (Post-Babylonian-Exilic) Jew, whose "modus operandi" was to adhere to the Second Temple Period Halachah, except in those cases where the Second Temple Period Halachah conflicted with His Father's Torah.

In this case, the New Moon day was determined by direct observation (and not any form of prediction at all). If (you) think about this, (you) should be able to see that the reason Yeshua never said anything against (this) method of declaring the New Moon or, Head of the Year (was

NO MAN at the time

22

because) this (was) one of the (few) things the rabbis were still doing correctly in His time. As (you) will see below, the (heretical) calculated calendar only came into use after Yeshua's death.

Ask (yourself) one question: "If Yeshua did not have a problem with the Torah-based calendar that was in use at the time of the Second Temple Period, then why would (you) want to (use) anything else?"

'Messengers' In *The Talmud*

For yet more witnesses, *The Talmud Mishna Tractate Rosh Hashanah* 1:4 tell us that messengers were sent out to those still in Exile, to relate when the New Moon was sighted. As (you) will see later, this appears to have continued to be the case during the entire time the Second Temple still stood.

In other words, the rabbis considered it ... important for those of the Exile to keep the Festival times in-sync with the Land of Israel (as determined by the Abib barley and the New Moons, in the Land of Israel). In fact, the rabbis felt it was so important those in the outlying areas (knew what) the "correct" calendar was, that these emissaries were even required to violate the Shabbat in the first and seventh months, so those in the far distant areas of Northern Syria would receive the news in time to keep the festivals (during) those months!

Given the seriousness (in) which the rabbis have always taken the Sabbath, it (would appear) the rabbis considered it vitally important for those (of) the Exile to know the "correct" calendar, so they could (remain in step) with it—and, this also makes sense.

However, this also begs the rhetorical question: If the rabbis had known the date of the Hodesh (New Moon) long in advance (because they were using a pre-calculated calendar, rather than relying on observation), then why would it be necessary to require the messengers to violate the Sabbath? If the rabbis had the benefit of a pre-calculated calendar (such as the modern rabbinical calendar), then why was the date not simply calculated months (or even years) in advance, as the rabbis do (it) now?

The answer is simply that the rabbis in Yeshua's day did not use a pre-calculated calendar to determine the start of the New Month, or the (Head) of the New Year. Rather, the rabbis in Yeshua's day still relied on physical observation, as outlined in the Torah.

However, if the rabbis were still keeping the calendar properly during the time of Yeshua's ministry, then when (and why) did they stop? The

Not a respected source.

answer is simply that it was time for the next phase of YHWH's divine plan for the Two Houses.

I will explain later in this book, why these changes took place when I discuss with you the events of the Simon Bar Kochba Rebellion.

In the event you still remain a skeptic, I would now like to provide you with a final piece of evidence (as far as this chapter is concerned) as to which new moon method should be employed as your authoritative guide by sharing with you what the Israeli New Moon Society has to say on the matter. They are connected with the Temple Mount Movement in Israel today and are currently engaging in the practice of sighting the Moon each month in preparation for, and in keeping with, when the Sanhedrin once again will sit and rule from the Temple Mount.

> The Commandment (Mitzvah)[30] of sanctifying the month is the first one which the Children of Israel were commanded upon leaving Egypt. This commandment is of great importance because the dates of the festivals, including over sixty (additional) commandments, depend on it. In addition to sanctifying months according to the appearance of the New Moon, the Hebrew Calendar depends on leap years (extended by an extra month) that depend on the position of the Sun, ripeness of grains, *etc.*
>
> For over a thousand years, the Hebrew Calendar has been fixed by calculation. Today, the Hebrew Calendar does not match that (which is) fixed by observing the Moon. Even though the gap between the two calendars continues to increase, we do not have the authority to alter the calendar until a new Sanhedrin (Religious High Court) is re-established and is widely recognized. While sanctification of the month according to observation is not practiced today, it is (still very) important to carry out calculations and practice observing the New Moon in order to be ready for when the Sanhedrin is re-established. Likewise, there is increasing involvement in the Temple, red heifer, *etc.* Of course, we are *not* intending to change the current calendar (this is a task for an authorized Sanhedrin), but just to increase involvement in and embellish the Torah.

In summary, you have now just read how the members of the ruling Jewish body openly admit the current Hebrew Calendar does *not* match its fixed counterpart of observing the Moon and, as a result, now hopefully, you agree and can see that the Holy Days, which are determined by the First

---

30 https://sites.google.com/site/moonsoc/

Visible Crescent of the Moon, will be off by as much as three days on any given month, as I have already pointed out. You also have been shown how the calculated Hillel II Calendar does not concern itself with the maturity of the barley—as I we are about to explained in chapter 5, *Abib (Barley) Biblical Leap Years* to begin the year—but instead, uses a set number of Leap Years in a nineteen-year cycle. I will explain this aspect in much greater detail in chapter 6, *The 360 Days Calendar; Was There Ever Such A Thing?* So, in addition to the three day discrepancy, there can also be an entire month's difference between the two systems of keeping the Holy Days throughout the course of any given year.

That being said, read on to discover how the Karaite Jews observe the beginning of the month.

Chapter 4 | The New Moon In the Hebrew Bible[31]

The Biblical month begins with the Crescent New Moon, also called First Visible Sliver. The Hebrew word for month (Hodesh) literally means New Moon and only by extension the period between one New Moon and the next.

The Rabbanite Midrash relates that when God said to Moses "This month (HODESH) shall be for you the beginning of months" (Exodus 12:2), the Almighty pointed up into the heavens at the Crescent New Moon and said "When you see like this, sanctify! [declare (the) New Moon day]." This Rabbinic fairy-tale highlights an important point, namely that the Bible never comes (right) out and says we should determine the beginning of months based on the New Moon. The reason for this is that the term for "month" (Hodesh) itself inherently implies that the month begins with the Crescent New Moon. As will be seen, this would have been self-evident to any ancient Israelite present when Moses recited the prophecies of YHWH to the Children of Israel and therefore, there was no need to elucidate this concept any more than such terms as "light" or "dark." However, due to the long Exile, we have lost the use of Biblical Hebrew in day-to-day speech. Therefore, we will have to reconstruct the meaning of Hodesh from the usage of the word in the biblical text using sound linguistic principles.

He Created the Moon for Holidays

There can be no doubt that the Biblical Holidays are dependent upon the Moon. The strongest proof of this is the passage in the Psalms which declares:

---

31 By Nehemia Gordon, http://www.karaite-korner.org & http://www.karaite-korner.org/new_moon.shtml; used by permission.

19 He created the moon for Mo'adim [appointed times]. (**Psalm 104:19**)

The Hebrew term Mo'adim [Appointed Times] is the same word used to describe the Biblical Holidays. Leviticus 23, which contains a catalogue of the Biblical Holidays, opens with the statement: "These are the Mo'adim [Appointed Times] of YHWH, Holy Convocations which you shall proclaim in their Appointed Times [Mo'adim]." So when the Psalmist tells us that God created the Moon for Mo'adim [Appointed Times], He means that the Moon was created to determine the time of the Mo'adim of YHWH, that is, the Biblical Holidays.

"Hodesh" Is Related To the Moon

The above verse clearly teaches us that the holidays are related to the Moon. But when the Torah was given, Psalm 104 had not yet been written by the Levitical prophets, and the question still remains of how the ancient Israelites could (possibly) have known this. The answer is that the Hebrew word for month (Hodesh) itself indicates a connection to the Moon. We can see this connection in a number of instances in which Hodesh (month) is used interchangeably with the word "Yerah," the common Biblical Hebrew word for Moon, which by extension also means "month." For example:

Hodesh

1 "... in the month (Yerah) of Ziv, which is the second month (Hodesh) ..." (**I Kings 6:1**)

2 "... in the month (Yerah) of Eythanim... which is the seventh month (Hodesh) ..." (**I Kings 8:2**)

Another proof that Hodesh is related to the Moon (Yerah) is the phrase, "A Hodesh (month) of days" (Genesis 29:14; Numbers 11:20-21) [meaning a period of 29-30 days], which is equivalent to the phrase, "A Yerah (month/moon) of days" (Deuteronomy 21:13; II Kings 15:13). Clearly then Hodesh is related to "Yerah," which itself literally means "moon."

"Hodesh" Means New Moon (Day)

The primary meaning of Hodesh (month) is actually "New Moon" or "New Moon Day" and it is only by extension that it came to mean "month," that is, the period between one New Moon and the next. This primary meaning is preserved in a number of passages such as: I Samuel 20:5, in which Jonathan says to David, "Tomorrow is the New Moon (Hodesh)." Clearly, in this verse Hodesh is used to refer to the specific day on which the month begins and not the entire month. Another passage which uses Hodesh in its primary sense is Ezekiel 46:1, which talks about, "The Day (Yom) of the New Moon (Ha-Hodesh)." Clearly in this verse Hodesh (New Moon) is a specific event and the beginning of the month is the day on which this event (New Moon) occurs.

The Biblical New Moon Is the "First Crescent"

"Hodesh" (New Moon), is derived from the root H.D.SH. (or, .ש.ד.ה) meaning "new" or "to make new/renew." The Crescent New Moon is called Hodesh because it is the first time the Moon is seen *anew* after being concealed for several days at the end of the lunar cycle. At the end of the lunar month, the Moon is close to the Sun[32] and eventually reaches the point of "conjunction" when it passes between the Sun and the Earth.[33] As a result, around the time of conjunction very little of the Moon's illuminated surface faces the earth and it is not visible through the infinitely brighter glare of the Sun. After the Moon moves past the Sun, it continues (in its trajectory) toward the opposite side of the Earth. As it gets farther away from the Sun, the percentage of its illuminated surface facing the Earth increases and one evening, shortly after sunset, the Moon is seen anew after being invisible for 1 ½–3 ½ days. Because the Moon is seen anew after a period of invisibility, the ancients called it a "New Moon" or "Hodesh" (from Hadash meaning "new").

Crescent New Moon vs. Astronomical New Moon

Many people have been led astray by the inaccurate use in modern languages of the term "New Moon." Modern astronomers adopted this otherwise unused term, which had always referred to the First Visible Sliver, and used it to refer to *conjunction* (when the Moon passes between the Earth and the Sun, at which time it is not visible). The astronomers soon realized that the inaccurate use of "New Moon" to refer to conjunction would lead to confusion, so to be more accurate, scientists now distinguish between "Astronomical New Moon" and "Crescent New Moon." "Astronomical New Moon" means New Moon as the term is used by astronomers, (i.e. conjunction). In contrast, (the term) "Crescent New Moon" (retains its) original meaning (or, First Visible Sliver). A good English dictionary should

---

32 From the perspective of an observer on Earth.
33 (i.e., it is on the same plane as the Sun & the Earth)

reflect both meanings. For example, the Random House Dictionary of the English Language, Unabridged Edition defines New Moon as:

> The Moon, either when in conjunction with the Sun or soon after being either invisible [Astronomical New Moon] or visible [Crescent New Moon] only as a slender crescent. (Brackets added by Nehemia Gordon)

The Supposed Evidence For (the) "Concealed Moon"

Having been confused by the use of the term New Moon in modern astronomy, some people have sought biblical support for this incorrect meaning of the term. Psalms 81:3 [Heb 81:4] is usually cited in this context:

> **3** Blow on a horn for the Hodesh (New Moon), on the Keseh (Full Moon) for the Day of our Hag (Feast). **(Psalms 81:3)**

According to the "Concealed Moon Theory," the term "Keseh" is derived from the root K.S.Y. meaning "to cover" and thus means "Covered Moon" or "Concealed Moon." According to this interpretation, when the verse says to blow on a horn on the day of Keseh, it actually means "[blow on a horn] on the day of the Concealed Moon." However, the language does not sufficiently support this argument, for the second half of the verse also refers to the day of Keseh as "the Day of our Feast (Hag)." In the Bible, Feast (Hag) is a technical term which **always** refers to the three annual pilgrimage-feasts (Matzot, Shavuot, Sukkot; see Exodus 23, 34:18, 34:22-23).[34] New Moon Day (Hodesh) is **never** classified as a "Pilgrimage-Feast" so Keseh/Hag cannot possibly be synonymous with New Moon Day (Hodesh). It has further been suggested that Keseh refers to the Biblical holiday of Yom Teruah (Day of Shouting), which always falls out on New Moon Day. However, the Bible describes Yom Teruah as a *Moed* (Appointed Time) and never as a *Hag* (Pilgrimage-Feast) so Keseh/Hag cannot refer to Yom Teruah either.

---

34 (See BDB pp.290b-291a.) Even in the few instances where Hag does not refer to the three biblical Pilgrimage-Feasts, it refers to non-biblical pilgrimage-feasts. For example, in Judges 21:19, Hag refers to the annual Pilgrimage-Feast held around the shrine of Shiloh. Also, in Exodus 10:9, Moses tells Pharaoh that the Israelites must leave Egypt to celebrate a Hag to YHWH in the desert, which clearly is a Pilgrimage-Feast. It is worth noting that Moses says they have a Hag, meaning they must make a pilgrimage—in this case, to Mt. Sinai, and thus, they *must* leave Egypt in order to observe the Hag properly.

What Does Keseh *Really* Mean?

It is likely that "Keseh" is related to the Aramaic word "Kista" and the Assyrian word "Kuseu," (both of) which mean "full moon" (see Brown-Driver-Briggs, p.490b). [Hebrew, Aramaic, and Assyrian are all Semitic languages and often share common roots.] This fits in perfectly with the description of Keseh as the Day of the Hag since two of the three Pilgrimage-Feasts (Hag HaMatzot and Hag HaSukkot) are on the fifteenth of the month, which is about the time of the Full Moon!

More On (the) "Concealed Moon"

Another point to consider is that there is no actual "day" of (the) Concealed Moon. In fact, the moon stays concealed anywhere from 1 ½–3 ½ days in the Middle East. It has been proposed that the "day" of (the) Concealed Moon is actually the Day of Conjunction (when the Moon passes between the Earth and Sun). However, it was only 1,000 years after Moses that the Babylonian astronomers discovered how to calculate the Moment of Conjunction. Therefore, the ancient Israelites would have had *no way* of knowing when the Moment of Conjunction (took) place and would not have known on which day to observe (the) "Concealed Moon Day."

It has been suggested that the ancient Israelites could have looked at the "Old Moon" and determined the Day of Conjunction by when the Old Moon was no longer visible in the morning sky. However, such a method would not work in the Middle East where the so-called "Concealed Moon" can remain concealed for as many as 3 ½ days! It is, in fact common, for the Moon to stay concealed for 2 ½ days and in such instances *how* would the ancient Israelites have known *which day* was the Day of Conjunction?

In contrast, the ancient Israelites would have been well aware of the Crescent New Moon. In ancient societies people worked from dawn to dusk and they would have noticed the Old Moon getting smaller and smaller in the morning sky. When the morning Moon had disappeared, the ancient Israelites would have anxiously awaited its reappearance 1 ½–3 ½ days later in the evening sky. Having disappeared for several days and then appearing anew in the early evening sky, they would have called it the "New Moon" or "Hodesh" (from Hadash meaning "New").

Chapter 5 | Abib (Barley) Biblical Leap Years

One of the other factors the Hebrew Calendar fails to take into account is whether or not the barley is Abib. It is not even considered at all. Yet, the barley *must be* Abib (or almost ready to harvest) in order for it to qualify, along with the sighting of the First Visible Sliver of the Moon, as part of the primary basis by which we determine the beginning or Head of the Year.

Rosh Hashanah is *not* the beginning of the year, contrary to popular belief. It is the seventh month and *not* the first. You need the barley in order to fulfill one of The Commandments in Leviticus 23. So now, let me share again with you from the Karaite Jews about the barley.

Abib (Barley)[35] Biblical Leap Years

The Biblical Year begins with the first New Moon after the barley in Israel reaches the stage in its ripeness called Abib. The period between one year and the next is either twelve or thirteen lunar months. Because of this, it is important to check the state of the barley crops at the end of the twelfth month. If the barley is Abib at this time, then the following New Moon is Hodesh Ha-Aviv ("New Moon of the Abib"). If the barley is still immature, we must wait another month and then check the barley again at the end of the thirteenth month.

By convention, a twelve-month year is referred to as a "Regular Year" while a thirteen-month year is referred to as a Leap Year. This should not be confused with Leap Years in the Gregorian (Christian) Calendar, which involve the "intercalation" (addition) of a single day (February 29th). In contrast, the Biblical Leap Year involves the intercalation of an entire lunar month ("Thirteenth Month," also called "Adar Bet"). In

---

35 by Nehemia Gordon, http://www.karaite-korner.org, used by permission. http://www.karaite-korner.org/abib.shtml

general, it can only be determined whether a year is a Leap Year a few days before the end of the twelfth month.

Where Is Abib Mentioned In the Hebrew Bible?

The story of the Exodus (indicates):

> **4** "This day you are going out in the month of the Abib." **(Exodus 13:4)**

To commemorate that we left Egypt in the month of the Abib, we are instructed to bring the Passover sacrifice and celebrate the Feast of Unleavened Bread (Hag Ha Matzot) at this time of year. In Deuteronomy we are commanded:

> **1** "Keep the month of the Abib and make the Passover (sacrifice) to YHWH your God at night, because in the month of the Abib YHWH your God took you out of Egypt by night." **(Deuteronomy 16:1)**

Similarly, we are commanded in Exodus:

> **15** "You will keep the Feast of Unleavened Bread; seven days you will eat unleavened bread, as I have commanded you, at the time of the month of the Abib, because in it you went out of Egypt." **(Exodus 23:15)**

> **18** "You will keep the Feast of Unleavened Bread; seven days you will eat unleavened bread, as have I commanded you, at the time of the month of the Abib, because in the month of the Abib you went out of Egypt." **(Exodus 34:18)**

What Is Abib?

Abib indicates a stage in the development of the barley crops. This is (made) clear from (the following account in) Exodus which describes the devastation caused by the plague of hail:

> **31** And the flax and the barley were smitten, because the barley was Abib and the flax was budding (Giv'ol). **32** And the wheat and the spelt were not smitten because they were dark (Afilot). **(Exodus 9:31-32)**

The above passage (indicates) that the (flax and) barley crops were destroyed by the hail while the wheat and spelt were not damaged. To understand the reason for this, we must look at how grain develops. When grains are (still in the) early (stage of) their development, they are flexible and have a dark green color. As they become ripe, they take on a light yellowish hue and become more brittle. The reason the barley was destroyed and the wheat was not (was because) the barley had reached the stage in its development called Abib and, as a result, had become brittle enough to be damaged by the hail. In contrast, the wheat and spelt were still early enough in their development, at a stage (where) they were flexible and not susceptible to being damaged by hail. The description of the wheat and spelt as "dark" (Afilot) indicates that they were still in the stage when they were a deep green and had not yet begun to lighten into the light yellowish hue which characterizes ripe grains. In contrast, the barley had reached the stage of Abib at which time it was no longer "dark" and at this point, it probably had begun to develop golden streaks.

Parched Abib

We know from several passages that barley, which is in the state of Abib, has not completely ripened, but has ripened enough so that its seeds can be eaten parched in fire. Parched barley was a commonly eaten food in ancient Israel and is mentioned in numerous passages in the Hebrew Bible as either "Abib parched (Kalui) in fire" (Leviticus 2:14) or in the abbreviated form "parched Kalui/ Kali" (Leviticus 23:14; Joshua 5:11; I Samuel 17:17, 25:18; II Samuel 17:28; Ruth 2:14).

While still early in its development, barley has not yet produced large enough and firm enough seeds to produce food through parching. This early in its development, when the "head" has just come out of the shaft, the seeds are not substantial enough to produce any food. At a later stage, the seeds have grown in size and have filled with liquid. At this point, the seeds will shrivel up when parched and will only produce empty skins. Over time, the liquid is replaced with dry material and, when enough dry material has amassed, the seeds will be able to yield "barley parched in fire."

Abib & the Harvest

The month of the Abib is the month which commences after the barley has reached the stage of Abib. Two-three weeks after the beginning of the month, the barley has moved beyond the stage of Abib and is ready to be brought as the "Wave-Sheaf Offering" (Hanafat HaOmer). The "Wave-Sheaf Offering" is a sacrifice brought from the first stalks cut in the harvest and is brought on the Sunday which falls out during Passover (Hag HaMatzot). This is described (below) in Leviticus:

> **10** "When you come to the land which I give you, and harvest its harvest, you will bring the sheaf of the beginning of your harvest to the priest. **11** And he will wave the sheaf before YHWH so

you will be accepted. On the morrow after the Sabbath the priest will wave it." **(Leviticus 23:10-11)**

From this it is clear that the barley, which was Abib at the beginning of the month, has become harvest-ready fifteen–twenty-one days later (i.e by the Sunday during Passover). Therefore, the month of the Abib cannot begin unless the barley has reached a stage where it will be harvest-ready two–three weeks later.

That the barley must be harvest-ready two–three weeks into the month of the Abib is also (made) clear (in) Deuteronomy which states:

> **9** "From when the sickle commences on the standing grain, you will begin to count seven weeks." **(Deuteronomy 16:9)**

From (the passage in) Leviticus (below) we know that the seven weeks between Passover (Hag Hamatzot) and Pentecost (Shavuot) begin on the day when the Wave-Sheaf Offering is brought (i.e. the Sunday which falls out during Passover):

> **15** "And you shall count from the morrow after the Sabbath, from the day you bring the sheaf of waving; they will be seven complete Sabbaths." **(Leviticus 23:15)**

Therefore, the "sickle commences on the standing grain" on the Sunday during Passover, (i.e. two–three weeks after the beginning of the month of the Abib). If the barley is not developed enough so that it will be ready for the sickle two–three weeks later, then the month of the Abib cannot begin and we must wait (until) the following month.

It should be noted that not all the barley ripens in the Land of Israel at the same time. The Wave-Sheaf Offering is a national sacrifice brought from the first fields to become harvest-ready. However, the first-fruit offerings brought by individual farmers can vary in ripeness anywhere from "Abib parched in fire" to fully ripe grain which may be brought "crushed" or "coarsely ground." This is what is meant in Leviticus (where we read):

> **14** "And when you bring a first-fruit offering to YHWH; you shall bring your first-fruit offering as Abib parched in fire or crushed Carmel." **(Leviticus 2:14)**

Carmel is grain which has hardened beyond Abib to the point where it can be "crushed" or "coarsely ground."

All of the above passages have been translated directly from the Hebrew and it is worth noting that the King James translators seem to have only understood the various Hebrew agricultural terms very poorly (at best). In Leviticus 2:14 they translated Carmel as "full ears" and "Abib" as "green ears," whereas in Leviticus 23:14 they translated Carmel as "green ears!"

In summation, barley which is in the state of Abib, has three characteristics:

1. It is brittle enough to be destroyed by hail & has begun to lighten in color (it is not "dark").
2. The seeds have produced enough dry material so it can be eaten parched.
3. It has developed enough so that it will be harvest-ready two–three weeks later.

We have the Omer ceremony that is recorded in the Mishna, but it has been corrupted by the rabbis. This record even records the dispute between the Pharisees and the Sadducees about when the ceremony was to take place. The Sadducees had it right.

The Omer was to be marked by the priest the night of the fourteenth of Aviv (Nisan). After the weekly Sabbath came to a close during the days of the Feast of Unleavened Bread, then the Omer (grain or corn) was to be cut and brought into the Temple courts to be prepared for the Wave Offering on the morrow after the weekly Sabbath. This was to take place on the Sunday morning in the night time (or wee morning hours) between sunset Saturday and sunrise Sunday morning. This was a huge celebration that has now been lost to history, but the meaning of this great day is explained when you understand what it stood for and how Yehshua fulfilled it by way of His Sunday morning ascension.

To learn more about this awesome event you can read *Pentecost's Hidden Meaning.*[36]

---

36 http://www.sightedmoon.com/?page_id=21

Chapter 6	The 360 Day Calendar; Was There Ever Such A Thing?

In preparing this book, a number of people have asked me about the 360 Day Calendar.[37] In order to properly explain this, I must first provide you with some historical background so you might better understand the "who, what, when, where, how and why" of certain changes that took place.

We are currently on a 365 Day Gregorian Calendar, and the Hebrew Calendar is 354 days with an additional or thirteenth month added in at the tail end of select years of a nineteen-year time cycle.

The current Hebrew Calendar that is being used today was originally created by Hillel II because of the growing Roman persecution against anything that was Jewish during the 4th Century. Hillel II wanted to make sure Jews the world over would know when each of the Holy Days occurred during the first and seventh months of the year.

With persecution on the rise, being in any kind of position to sight the Moon in Jerusalem became a luxury at best. To send out messengers to the various Jewish enclaves during the Diaspora (Exile) was not exactly the easiest of undertakings either. However, with Hillel II's calculations published somewhere between 358 C.E.–359 C.E., the New Moons of Nisan 1 and Tishri 1 could be determined far in advance, and would only need to be verified by direct observation. But over time, the practice of observation was either abandoned or forgotten altogether and only the calculated method was then used.

Take special note that the direct observation method was initially used by Hillel II to determine the beginning of the month *and* to confirm his calculations. This means a given month began with a Sighted Moon not a

---

37 http://en.wikipedia.org/wiki/360-day_calendar

39

"Moon in Conjunction"—that is, a moon that was directly in line with the Earth and the Sun that could not be seen—a dark moon, in other words. Back then, the months were always determined by the sighting of the First Visible Crescent of the New Moon after the Sun had set.

Included in Hillel II's calculations was the use of the Babylonian nineteen-year time cycle I mentioned earlier. Hillel II determined that a thirteenth month was to be added with regard to select years (3, 6, 8, 11, 14, 17, and 19) of this nineteen-year time cycle. This process would then be duplicated in the subsequent nineteen year time cycle and for all nineteen-year time cycles yet to come.

You might ask, "How does this apply to us now?" The answer is simple once the right foundation has been laid. In the years 2000, 2003, 2008, 2011, 2014, and 2016 an additional thirteenth month either already was or in the future will be added to the Hebrew Calendar. And this will continue to be the case until a new Sanhedrin comes into play (or Yehshua returns) irrespective of what I have already explained to you about the barley having to be Abib in order to begin the year. (See previous chapter: *Abib (Barley) Biblical Leap Years.*)

The addition of a thirteenth month during these years (3, 6, 8, 11, 14, 17, 19) of the nineteen-year time cycle, automatically made all the Holy Days, fall one month later in the Solar Year, keeping these days in harmony with the harvest seasons.

> The current 19-year cycle began in the Jewish year 5758 (the year that began October 2, 1997).[38]

To elaborate on the above quote, the Jewish Year begins in the seventh month of Tishri. At the time of this writing, the year 2012, the current Jewish Year is 5772. It became 5773 on Tishri 1, which was September 17th, 2012. On Tishri 1 in the year 2016, the nineteenth year of this current cycle will have come to a close.

But to give you a taste of how the Jewish community began to witness a gradual departure from Hillel II's Calendar, I have added The Second Rule of Four Rules with regard to: *Dehioth (Dechiyot): Rules of Postponements,* which I will touch upon in much greater depth in the following chapter: *The Jewish Holy Days Are Not "Kosher."*

I felt it important to make you aware of The Second Rule for starters so you might gain a better working knowledge of how the Hebrew Calendar

---

38 http://www.jewfaq.org/calendar.htm

works in its present form. But again, it was not always this way. Hillel II devised this calendar with the understanding it was supposed to continue to operate on the Sighting of the Moon to begin the month. This was not only stated as such in Hillel II's calculations, but even in *Dehioth (Dechiyot): Rules of Postponements* we find the following surprising statement: "So that the Moon is not sighted in another part of the world before it is sighted in Jerusalem." Although, one cannot know precisely when these *Rules of Postponements* were enacted and came into full force, the incorporation of the Four Rules into Hillel's II Calendar *as a whole* proved to be even more of a deviation from Yehovah's Calendar.

This is the current Hebrew Calendar as developed by Hillel II back in 358 C.E. with its modifications since then.

However some people believe that the one true calendar was the 360-Day Calendar. One individual, whose name continues to come up quite often in this context, is the late Immanuel Velikovsky—especially with regard to his highly controversial and yet ground breaking book, *Worlds In Collision*.

> *Worlds In Collision* is a book written by Immanuel Velikovsky and first published April 3rd, 1950. The book postulated that around the 15th-century B.C.E., Venus was ejected from Jupiter as a comet or comet-like object, and passed near Earth (an actual collision is not mentioned). The object changed Earth's orbit and axis, causing innumerable catastrophes that were mentioned in early mythologies and religions around the world. The book was met with a very hostile reception by the scientific community at the time of publication.[39]

Velikovsky made the following assertion in his book, *Worlds In Collision*, in the chapter entitled, *The Year of 360 Days*:

> Numerous evidences are preserved which prove that prior to the year of 365 ¼ days, the year was only 360 days long. Nor was that year of 360 days primordial; it was a transitional form between a year of still fewer days and the present year.

> In the period of time between the last of the series of catastrophes of the fifteenth century and the first in the series of catastrophes of the eighth century, the duration of a seasonal revolution appears to have been 360 days.[40]

---

39 http://en.wikipedia.org/wiki/Worlds_in_Collision
40 http://www.britam.org/megaliths/velikovskyworlds.html, *The Year of 360 Days*, p. 316, Part II, CHAPTER VIII

I once had very little regard for Velikovsky's works. This was based on what others had said about him, his observations, his findings and his publications. I had prematurely judged a matter never having looked into it in detail or researched it for myself. With your permission, I would like to now delve into a summary of Velikovsky's works: *Velikovsky's Ghost Returns: The Electric Universe*, written by Michael Goodspeed.

To fill the void, I'll briefly summarize the story—[6]

The Russian-born scholar was a friend and colleague of Albert Einstein, a student of Freud's first pupil Wilhelm Stekel, and Israel's first practicing psychoanalyst. Some of his writings appeared in Freud's *Imago*. In 1930, he published the first paper to suggest that epileptics would be characterized by abnormal encephalograms. He was the founder and editor of the scholarly publication, *Scripta Universitatis*, the physics and mathematics section being prepared by Einstein.

It was while researching a book on Freud and his heroes that Velikovsky first wondered about the catastrophes said to have accompanied the Hebrew Exodus, when fire and hailstones rained upon Egypt, earthquakes decimated the nation, and a pillar of fire and smoke moved in the sky. Biblical and other traditional Hebrew sources speak so vividly that Velikovsky began to wonder if some extraordinary natural event might have played a part in the Exodus.

To explore this possibility, Velikovsky sought out a corresponding account in ancient Egyptian records, finding a remarkable parallel in a papyrus kept at the University of Leyden Museum, called the *Papyrus Ipuwer*. The document contains the lamentations of an Egyptian sage in response to a great catastrophe overwhelming Egypt, when the rivers ran red, fire blazed in the sky, and pestilence ravaged the land.

Velikovsky also encountered surprising parallels in Babylonian and Assyrian clay tablets, Vedic poems, Chinese epics, and North American Indian, Mayan, Aztec, and Peruvian legends. From these remarkably similar accounts, he constructed a thesis of celestial catastrophe. He concluded that a very large body—apparently a "comet"—passed close enough to Earth to violently perturb its axis, as global earthquakes, wind and falling stone (and) decimated early civilizations.

Before Velikovsky could complete his reconstruction, he had to resolve an enigma. He had found that in the accounts of far-flung cultures, the "cometary" agent of disaster was identified as a planet. And the closer he looked, the more clear it became to him that this planet was Venus: The converging ancient images included the Babylonian "Torch-Star" and "Bearded Star" Venus, the Mexican "Smoking Star" Venus, the Peruvian "Long-Haired Star" Venus, the Egyptian "Great Star" Venus ("scattering its flame in fire") and the widespread imagery of Venus as a flaming serpent or dragon in the sky. In each instance, the cometary language is undeniable, for these were the very symbols of "the comet" in the ancient languages.

By following the evidence, Velikovsky discovered that Venus holds a special place among the world's first astronomers. In both the Old World and the New, ancient stargazers regarded Venus with awe and terror, carefully observing its risings and settings, and claiming the planet to be the cause of world-ending catastrophe. These astronomical traditions, Velikovsky reasoned, must have had roots in a traumatic human experience, though modern science has always assumed that the planets evolved in quiet and undisturbed isolation over billions of years.

Based on extensive cross-cultural comparison, Velikovsky concluded that the planet Venus, prior to the dawn of recorded history, was ejected violently from the gas giant Jupiter, displaying a spectacular comet-like tail. Its later catastrophic approach to the Earth (around 1500 B.C.) provided the historical backdrop to the Hebrew Exodus, Velikovsky claimed.

In *Worlds In Collision*, Velikovsky argued that the terrifying "gods" of the ancient world were planets—those inconspicuous specks of light we see moving with clock-like regularity, as if to deny their chaotic roles in the past. The book recounted two close encounters of the comet or protoplanet Venus with the Earth. Included in the same volume was a large section on the ancient war god, whom Velikovsky identified as the planet Mars. He claimed that centuries after the Venus catastrophes, Mars moved on an unstable orbit intersecting that of Earth, leading to a series of Earth-disturbing events in the seventh and eighth centuries B.C.

With the first reviews of the book, the publisher Macmillan came under fire from astronomers and scientists. But sales of *Worlds In Collision* skyrocketed, and it quickly soared to the top of the bestseller lists. Dr. Harlow Shapley, director (of) the Harvard Observatory, branded the book "nonsense and rubbish," but without (even) reading it. A letter from Shapley to Macmillan threatened a boycott of the company's textbook division. The astronomer Fred Whipple threatened to break his relations with the publisher. Under pressure from the scientific community, Macmillan was forced to transfer publishing rights to Doubleday, though *Worlds In Collision* was already the number one bestseller in the country. Macmillan editor James Putnam, who had been with the company for twenty-five years and had negotiated the contract for *Worlds In Collision*, was summarily dismissed.

In the wake of Macmillan's publication of *Worlds In Collision*, one scientific journal after another denounced Velikovsky's work. The eminent astronomer and textbook author Donald Menzel publicly ridiculed Velikovsky. Astronomer Cecilia-Payne Gaposchkin launched a campaign to discredit Velikovsky, (also) without reading *Worlds In Collision*. The *Bulletin of Atomic Scientists* produced a series of articles grossly misrepresenting Velikovsky. And Gordon Atwater, curator of the respected Hayden Planetarium, was fired after having proposed in *This Week* magazine that Velikovsky's work deserved open-minded discussion.

For many years after publication of *Worlds In Collision*, Velikovsky was persona non grata on college campuses. He was denied the opportunity to publish articles in scientific journals. When he attempted to respond to critical articles in such journals, they rejected these responses. The attitude of established science was typified by the reactions of astronomers. Michigan astronomer Dean McLaughlin exclaimed, "Lies—yes, lies." In response to a correspondent, astronomer Harold Urey, wrote: "My advice to you is to shut the book and never look at it again in your lifetime."

For Velikovsky, this was the beginning of a personal "dark age." But remarkably, his friendship with Albert Einstein was unaffected, and Einstein met with him often, maintaining an extended correspondence as well, encouraging Velikovksy to look past the misbehavior of the scientific elite. In discussion with Einstein, Velikovsky predicted that Jupiter would be found to emit radio noises, and he urged Einstein to use his influence to have Jupiter surveyed for radio emission, though Einstein himself disputed Velikovsky's reasoning. But in April 1955 radio noises were discovered from Jupiter, much to the surprise of scientists who had thought Jupiter was too cold and inactive to emit radio waves. That discovery led Einstein to agree to assist in developing other tests of Velikovsky's thesis. But the world's most prominent scientist died only a few weeks later.

Velikovsky expected other discoveries (would come about) through space exploration. He claimed that the planet Venus would be found to be extremely hot, since in his reconstruction, the planet was "candescent" in historical times. His thesis also implied the likelihood of a massive Venusian atmosphere, residue of its former "cometary" tail. And he claimed that the Earth would be found to have a magnetosphere reaching at least to the Moon, because he was convinced that in historical times the Earth exchanged electrical charge with other planetary bodies.

Arrival of The Space Age was a critical juncture for Velikovsky, as data returned from the Moon, from Mars, and from Venus began to recast (popularly held) views of these celestial bodies. In 1959, Dr. Van Allen discovered that the Earth has a magnetosphere. In the early sixties, scientists realized, much to their surprise, that the planet Venus has a surface temperature as high as 900°F, hot enough to melt lead. "The temperature is much higher than anyone would have predicted," wrote Cornell Mayer.

Things grew more promising for Velikovsky. In 1962, two scientists, Valentin Bargmann, professor of physics at Princeton, and Lloyd Motz, professor of astronomy at Columbia, urged that Velikovsky's conclusions "be objectively re-examined." In support of this reconsideration, they cited his prior predictions about radio noises from Jupiter, the terrestrial magnetosphere, and an unexpectedly high temperature of Venus.

In July 1969, on the eve of the first landing on the Moon, the *New York Times* invited Velikovsky to summarize what he expected the Apollo missions to find. Velikovsky responded by listing nine "advance claims," including "Remanent (residual, remaining) Magnetism," a steep thermal gradient, radioactive hot spots, and regular moonquakes. All told, it was a remarkably accurate summation of later findings. But still, the scientific community was silent.

Then, in 1972, at the invitation of the Society of Harvard Engineers and Scientists, Velikovsky returned to the (very) site from which the original boycott was launched. His presentation produced a standing ovation. "I survived, as you see," he said. "I have been waiting for this evening for twenty-two years. I came here to find the young, the spirited, the men who have a fascination for discovery."

Also in 1972, a small student journal in Portland, Oregon called *Pensée* began publishing a series of full issues devoted to Velikovsky, with contributions from the pioneer himself. The Pensée series *Immanuel Velikovsky Reconsidered* recounted the history of the Velikovsky affair, bringing international attention to the scientific misbehavior involved, and reviewing Space Age findings lending support to Velikovsky's revolutionary thesis of planetary catastrophe. Clearly, it was time for a reassessment of Velikovsky's work, and the *Pensée* series produced a groundswell of interest in the Velikovsky debate. The first issue became the number one bestseller on several college campuses and inspired stories in *Reader's Digest, Analog, Time, Newsweek, Physics Today*, (the) *National Observer*, and many other publications.

Now filled with optimism, Velikovsky began receiving numerous invitations from university campuses. The British Broadcasting

Corporation produced a special documentary on Velikovsky, (which aired) twice because of popular interest. The Canadian Broadcasting Corporation also (aired) a documentary on Velikovsky. And an international symposium was held in Toronto, Ontario. Velikovsky also gave a talk at the N.A.S.A. Ames Research Center, suggesting experiments and procedures to test his claims.

For about two years after the appearance of *Immanuel Velikovsky Reconsidered*, the scientific elite (still) remained eerily quiet. The resurrection of a "heretic," long presumed dead, seemed all too easy.

Then came a counterattack through the American Association for the Advancement of Science. America's largest scientific organization scheduled a symposium on *Worlds In Collision* for an "open discussion of Velikovsky." The proceedings of the 1974 San Francisco A.A.A.S. gathering would feature the popular astronomer Carl Sagan in a direct "debate" with Velikovsky.

The gathering had all the trappings of a media event, and like so many such events, it brought no clarity to the subject at all. Yet for years afterward it was dutifully remembered in mainstream journals as the "definitive refutation" of Velikovsky.

The A.A.A.S. meeting was the beginning of a relentless (smear) campaign against Velikovsky. In the years that followed, Sagan devoted a substantial section of each book he published to debunking Velikovsky. And science editors of newspapers across the country, no longer accustomed to looking up anything for themselves, simply reported what they were told by local astronomers. (Hence), the Velikovsky question (became) a dead issue.

Before he died in 1979, Velikovsky grew darkly pessimistic, telling those close to him that the battle was over, that the critics had won. Mainstream science, he said, would never permit an objective hearing on the subject of *Worlds In Collision*.

Whereas I am not inclined to agree with Velikovsky that the "gods" of ancient times were, in fact, the planets, I do believe however, that if indeed these great events took place as suggested by Velikovsky, that it was Yehovah who was bringing them about. But we have drifted away from the primary purpose of this chapter: to determine if the calendar in question is comprised of 354 days or 360 days in a given year. If nothing else, I wanted to give Velikovsky's theory and postulations a fair hearing, as some will mention him with regard to this subject matter.

Yair Davidiy[41] also takes a close look at Velikovsky's 360 day question as he compares it to each of the ancient civilizations at that time. I strongly urge you to read it when you get a chance, but I am about to present you with an answer most do not see or even begin to consider.

Many people are all too easily convinced there are 360 days in a given year based on the Bible passages below in Genesis and Daniel:

> **11** In the six hundredth year of Noah's life, in the second month, the seventeenth day of the month, on that day all the fountains of the great deep were broken up, and the windows of the heavens were opened. **12** And the rain was on the earth forty days and forty nights. (**Genesis 7:11-12**)

> **3** And the waters receded steadily from the earth, and at the end of the hundred and fifty days the waters diminished. **4** And in the seventh month, the seventeenth day of the month, the ark rested on the mountains of Ararat. **5** And the waters decreased steadily until the tenth month. In the tenth month, on the first day of the month, the tops of the mountains became visible. (**Genesis 8:3-5**)

It is in reading these passages in Scripture that many have concluded, with all certainty, that the five months between the second month of Genesis 7:11 and the seventh month of Genesis 8:4, coupled with the additional information presented in Genesis 8:3 on the 150 days, all prove that the time consisted of five months of thirty days in duration each.

Which begs the question, did the 150 days during the Great Flood consist of five, thirty-day months?

Each month, the Moon revolves around the Earth in exactly 29.53059 days (roughly 29½ days). It is my position that this has *always* been the case and has not changed since Yehovah created the Earth. Given how Velikovsky's theory is said to pertain to the time of Moses and the Exodus during the years 1386 B.C.–1380 B.C.,[42] it would also stand to reason the events prior to that time would not have changed.

The calendar used by Adam and passed down to Noah is the very same calendar that uses the Sighting of the Moon to begin the month with. As I state on the previous page, it takes the Moon exactly 29.53059 days to

---

41 http://www.britam.org/megaliths/velikovskyworlds.html
42 See Charts at: http://www.sightedmoon.com/files/jubilees_corrected.pdf The history of man from creation up to our day now based on the Sabbatical & Jubilee Years

complete one revolution around the earth. This is roughly 29½ days each month; and it is that ½ day part that is so pivotal to our point.

Because the potential always exists for the Moon to be sighted on the twenty-ninth day, a given month could easily be only twenty-nine days in length. Then, of course, on other months, the Moon could just as easily be sighted on the thirtieth day. It is this variable that is our proof.

Each month is made up of either twenty-nine or thirty days, depending on the Sighting of the Moon on any given month. The Modern Hebrew Calendar has a dynamic already in place to account for the months to fluctuate between twenty-nine to thirty days.[43] But as I will continue to demonstrate to you, the Hebrew Calendar is not without fault. This assignment of a particular number of days to each month is another point which cannot possibly be correct once you understand how the months were always sighted and, as a result, would always end up being either twenty-nine or thirty days, but you never knew which until you (or someone else) actually *saw* the First Visible Sliver or Crescent Moon. (The month was *never* thirty-one days—no, not ever. That only came about as a result of Julian reforms to the calendar in 46 B.C. by Julius Caesar.[44] We have him to thank for that.)

When I explain *The Thirty Days of Noah*,[45] I remind people that the Moon must be a Sighted Moon in the biblical sense in order to declare it "New Moon Day." Noah, of course, was shut up inside the ark for this amount of time. It was also raining and overcast the entire time. If we do not see the Moon on the twenty-ninth day, then it is automatically New Moon Day on the thirtieth day. As you now know, there is no such thing as thirty-one days in a month, in other words. Noah was not able to see the New Moon during his time spent inside the ark. It was not until he opened the window and was able to behold the sky at long last while releasing the raven—then and only then could Noah finally sight the New Moon. But inside the ark all he could do was keep counting to thirty each month.

> As explained by Mr. Dumond, whenever it is overcast on the 29th day of the month, thus obscuring the sighting of the New Moon that evening, by default we declare the next day to be "day 30."[46]

43 http://www.jewfaq.org/calendar.htm
44 http://www.crystalinks.com/romecalendar.html
45 http://www.sightedmoonnl.com/?page_id=486 COUNTING THE 30 DAYS OF EZEKIEL & THE 30 DAYS OF NOAH
46 http://www.sightedmoon.com/files/Ezekiels%2030%20days.pdf THIRTEENTH MONTH (Ezekiel's 30 days)

With the window of the ark being shut up before the rain set in, we do not read of Noah opening it again until verse six of Genesis which, consequently, was *after* the 150 days spoken of in verse three.

> **6** And it came to be, at the end of forty days, that Noaḥ opened the window of the ark which he had made, **7** and he sent out a raven, which kept going out and turning back until the waters had dried up from the earth. (**Genesis 8:6-7**)

While shut up inside the ark, it is a given Noah could not sight the Crescent Moon on any given month. He had no visual access to the night sky until he opened the window in verse six. Before he was given the "OK" to open the window again, which includes the period before the flooding stopped and the floodwaters began to recede, it had been, as we all know, raining torrentially and non-stop forty days and forty nights to the point of the Earth being flooded on a scale unprecedented before or since. This, in and of itself, tells you the sky would have been overcast with clouds that would have completely obscured Noah's ability to see much of anything, even if the window had been open the entire time.

Another Scripture people often fall back on, for the sake of argument, is the one in Daniel below. Let's now take a look at what is said here:

> **6** And one said to the man dressed in linen, who was above the waters of the river, "How long until the end of these wonders?" **7** And I heard the man dressed in linen, who was above the waters of the river, and he held up his right hand and his left hand to the heavens, and swore by Him who lives forever, that it would be for a time, times, and half a time. And when they have ended scattering the power of the set-apart people, then all these shall be completed. **8** And I heard, but I did not understand, so I said, "My master, what is the latter end of these *matters*?" **9** And he said, "Go, Dani'ēl, for the words are hidden and sealed (until) the time of the end."[1] (**Daniel 12:6-9** | Footnote: [1]See v. 4)

> **10** "Many shall be cleansed and made white, and refined. But the wrong shall do wrong—and none of the wrong shall understand, but those who have insight shall understand. **11** And from the time that which is continual is taken away, and the abomination that lays waste is set up, is one thousand two hundred and ninety days. **12** Blessed is he who is waiting earnestly, and comes to the one thousand three hundred and thirty-five days. **13** But you, go your way (until) the end. And rest, and arise to your lot at the end of the days." (**Daniel 12:10-13**)

It is my belief the two men involved in the discourse in Daniel above happen to be the two witnesses as spoken of in Revelation. I cannot prove it but that is my firm belief. One of them understands the Sabbatical and Jubilee chronology and is able to know when the end is to come. But this is just a side note.

We read again in verse seven:

> 7 "... time, times, and half a time." (**Daniel 12:7**)

All biblical narratives equate "time, times, and half a time" to 3 ½ years. We also read of this same description as we continue in Daniel:

> 24 "And the ten horns are ten sovereigns from this reign. They shall rise, and another shall rise after them, and it is different from the first ones, and it humbles three sovereigns, 25 and it speaks words against the Most High, and it wears out the set-apart ones of the Most High, and it intends to change appointed times and law, and they are given into its hand for a time and times and half a time." (**Daniel 7:24-25**)

In *both* cases it 3 ½ years.

But we *also* read in Revelation of forty-two months and 1,260 days:

> 2 "But cast out the court which is outside the Dwelling Place, and do not measure it, for it has been given to the gentiles, and they shall trample the set-apart city under foot for forty-two months. 3 And I shall give unto my two witnesses, and they shall prophesy one thousand two hundred and sixty days, clad in sackcloth." (**Revelation 11:2-3**)

> 6 And the woman fled into the wilderness, where she has a place prepared by Elohim, to be nourished there one thousand two hundred and sixty days. (**Revelation 12:6**)

> 14 And the woman was given two wings of a great eagle, to fly into the wilderness to her place, where she is nourished for a time and times and half a time, from the presence of the serpent. (**Revelation 12:14**)

> 5 And he was given a mouth speaking great *matters* and blasphemies, and he was given authority to do so forty-two months. (**Revelation 13:5**)

All the Bible verses I cited above are what some use to prove a given month always consisted of 30 days for any given month (30 x 42=1,260). Are they correct in their conclusions?

As you can see in the following three scriptures below, Yehovah does not change; therefore His calendar and His method of beginning the month will also never change.

> **6** "For I am יהוה, I shall not change, and you, O sons of Ya'qob, shall not come to an end. (**Malachi 3:6**)

> **8** יהושע Messiah is the same yesterday, and today, and forever. (**Hebrews 13:8**)

> **17** Every good gift and every perfect gift is from above, coming down from the Father of lights, with whom there is no change, nor shadow of turning. (**James 1:17**)

So what are we to make of all the Scriptures I have just provided, which on the surface seem to be saying that each and every month of the last 3 ½ years to all be thirty-day months? Are they actually saying this? Part of the answer lies in what Yehshua is explaining in the Gospel accounts to His disciples with regard to the Last Days:

> **1** And going out, יהושע went away from the Set-apart Place, and His taught ones came near to point out to Him the buildings of the Set-apart Place. **2** And יהושע said to them, "Do you not see all these? Truly, I say to you, not one stone shall be left here upon another, at all, which shall not be thrown down." **3** And as He sat on the Mount of Olives, the taught ones came to Him separately, saying, "Say to us, when shall this be, and what is the sign of Your coming, and of the end of the age?" (**Matthew 24:1-3**)

During this discourse Yehshua then tells them:

> **29** "And immediately after the distress of those days the sun shall be darkened, and the moon shall not give its light, and the stars shall fall from the heaven, and the powers of the heavens shall be shaken. **30** And then the sign of the Son of Adam shall appear in the heaven, and then all the tribes of the earth shall mourn, and they shall see the Son of Adam coming on the clouds of the heaven with power and much esteem." (**Matthew 24:29-30**)

The Gospel of Mark issues a similar warning:

> **23** "And you, take heed. See, I have forewarned you of it all. **24** But in those days, after that distress, the sun shall be darkened, and the moon shall not give its light, **25** and the stars of heaven shall fall, and the powers in the heavens shall be shaken." (**Mark 13:23-25**)

In the Old Testament we find that Joel also speaks of this same time period and adds some information we need to consider in the solving of this riddle. Notice that there will be columns of smoke and the Sun is turned into darkness.

> 29 "And also on the male servants and on the female servants I shall pour out My Spirit in those days. 30 And I shall give signs in the heavens and upon the earth: blood and fire and columns of smoke, 31 the sun is turned into darkness, and the moon into blood, before the coming of the great and awesome day of יהוה." (Joel 2:29-31)

Right now, as you read my book, all around the world many of the dormant volcanoes are becoming active again and columnar plumes of smoke are rising from them. When they erupt you then have the fire part. A great example of this in recent years is the **Eyjafjallajökull**[47] volcanic eruption of 2010.[48] **Eyjafjallajökull** means "island mountain glacier." I have shared a link if you wish to look at some pictures that graphically depict this event. Iceland is the only country I know of where you can be sitting in a hot spring, looking out upon a glacier. Hot springs alone have been known to be a sporadic hotbed of young volcanic activity—as in the case of Old Faithful[49] in America's Yellowstone National Park.

The Icelandic 2010 event is just one example of the evil still yet to come that will befall the physical world in which we live, but we can read more of this coming destruction in Isaiah:

> 7 I form the light and create darkness, I make peace (national well-being) and I create (physical) evil (calamity); I am the Lord, Who does all these things. (**Isaiah 45:7 | Amplified Bible**)

> 6 Howl, for the day of יהוה is near! It comes as a destruction from the Almighty. 7 Therefore all hands go limp, every man's heart melts, 8 and they shall be afraid. Pangs and sorrows take hold of them, they are in pain as a woman in labor; they are amazed at one another, their faces aflame! 9 See, the day of יהוה is coming, fierce, with wrath and heat of displeasure, to lay the earth waste, and destroy its sinners from it. 10 For the stars of the heavens and their constellations do not give off their light. The sun shall be dark at its rising, and the moon not send out

---

47 http://www.armageddononline.org/Volcanic-ash-relentless-as-tremors-rock-Iceland. html
48 http://en.wikipedia.org/wiki/2010_eruptions_of_Eyjafjallaj%C3%B6kull
49 http://en.wikipedia.org/wiki/Old_Faithful

its light. **11**"And I shall punish the world for its evil, and the wrong for their crookedness, and shall put an end to the arrogance of the proud, and lay low the pride of the ruthless. **12** I shall make mortal man *scarcer* than fine gold, and mankind *scarcer* than the gold of Ophir. **13** So I shall make the heavens tremble, and the earth shall shake from her place, in the wrath of יהוה of hosts and in the day of the heat of His displeasure." **(Isaiah 13:6-13)**

Again we read of the both the sun and the moon not giving their light in Joel.

14 Crowds, crowds in the Valley of Decision! For the day of יהוה is near in the Valley of Decision. **15** Sun and moon shall become dark, and stars shall withdraw their brightness. **16** And יהוה shall roar from Tsiyon (Zion), and give forth His voice from Yerushalayim (Jerusalem). And the heavens and earth shall shake, but יהוה shall be a refuge for His people, and a stronghold for the children of Yisra'ĕl. **(Joel 3:14-16)**

We also read of the Sun and the Moon not giving their light in Revelation right after the martyrdom of the saints.

9 And when He opened the fifth seal, I saw under the altar the beings of those having been slain for the Word of Elohim and for the witness which they held, **10** and they cried with a loud voice, saying, "How long, O Master, set-apart and true, until You judge and avenge our blood on those who dwell on the earth?" **11** And there was given to each one a white robe, and they were told that they should rest a little while longer, until both *the number of* their fellow servants and their brothers, who would be killed as they were, was completed. **12** And I looked when He opened the sixth seal and saw a great earthquake came to be. And the sun became black as sackcloth of hair, and the moon became as blood. **13** And the stars of the heaven fell to the earth, as a fig tree drops its unripe figs, being shaken by a strong wind. **14** And heaven departed like a scroll being rolled up, and every mountain and island was moved out of its place. **15** And the sovereigns of the earth, and the great ones, and the rich ones, and the commanders, and the mighty, and every slave and every free one, hid themselves in the caves and in the rocks of the mountains, **16** and said to the mountains and rocks, "Fall on us and hide us from the face of Him sitting on the throne and from the wrath of the Lamb, **17** because the great day of His wrath has come, and who is able to stand?" **(Revelation 6:9-17)**

And Isaiah again speaks of the heavens dissolving during this time of Great Tribulation.

2 For the displeasure of יהוה is against all the gentiles and His wrath against all their divisions. He shall put them under the ban, He shall give them over to the slaughter, **3** and their slain be thrown out, and their stench rise from their corpses. And mountains shall be melted with their blood. **4** And all the host of the heavens shall rot away. And the heavens shall be rolled up like a scroll, and all their host fade like a leaf fading on the vine, and like the fading one of a fig tree. **5** "For My sword shall be drenched in the heavens. Look, it comes down on Edom, and on the people of My curse, for judgment. **(Isaiah 34:2-5)**

We read above about the sun being turned into sackcloth. What does this mean? It is describing a solar eclipse.

It is evident that the sun darkening (as if putting on 'sackcloth of hair') and the moon not shining and turning into a blood moon refer to solar/lunar eclipses.[50]

Along with the above, Pastor Mark Blitz[51] has found that in 2014 and 2015, **FOUR** Total Lunar Eclipses (Four Blood Moons) appear in a row (known as a "Tetrad") accompanied by two Solar Eclipses and they all fall on Jewish Feasts.

It is extremely *rare* that four Blood Moons appear in a row and it is forecasted that this kind of event will never happen again in this century. Pastor Blitz noted that Tetrads did happen back in 1967-1968—the year Jerusalem was, miraculously, recaptured by Israel and back in 1949-1950—a year after Israel declared its independence. (But *do* make a note that the declaration took place on May 14th, 1948, and Arab-Israeli war broke out right next day lasting until January 7th, 1949.)

Not only that, (the) 1949-1950 Tetrad, likewise with the 2014-2015 Tetrad, fell *exactly* on either Passover or the Feast of Tabernacles. Only back in 1500's, Pastor Blitz further noted, (how) there were six Tetrads (meaning there were none between the 1600's–1900's), but none of them fell on Jewish Feasts.[52]

I have now quoted the passages in Scripture to you that describe the Sun becoming darkened and the Moon not giving her light and then followed it up with what your bible had to say about the Blood Moons, which are *always* harbingers of bad tidings. But now, add to that the passage in Isaiah I quoted

50 http://facingend.wordpress.com/2011/01/03/celestial/
51 http://www.elshaddaiministries.us/
52 http://facingend.wordpress.com/2011/01/03/celestial/

where he mentions plumes of smoke. You can anticipate more of the same in this regard, for in Revelation we are told of the smoke that rises up from the burning and destruction of Babylon:

> 8 "Because of this her plagues shall come in one day: death and mourning and scarcity of food. And she shall be burned up with fire, because יהוה Elohim who judges her is mighty. 9 And the sovereigns of the earth who committed whoring and lived riotously with her shall weep and mourn over her, when they see the smoke of her burning, 10 standing at a distance for fear of her torture, saying, 'Woe! Woe, the great city Babel, the mighty city, because your judgment has come in one hour!'" (**Revelation 18:8-10**)

Knowing that the Sun and the Moon will not give their light in the Last Days, Yehovah has told us to count the days of each month in Daniel. We do this by looking for the First Visible Sliver of the New Crescent Moon (aka, the Sighted Moon) to begin the month. And yet, the Moon will not be able to give her light because of the volcanic ash covering the skies and obscuring it. Many nations will also be destroyed at this time from wars. They will be set ablaze and burning. Babylon will be destroyed suddenly and will be burning also—maybe even more so, given the extent of her iniquity. The burning of Babylon and the destruction of other cities on a global scale—coupled with the volcanic activity taking place all over the world—will result in smoke thick enough to cause the Sun and the Moon to no longer be visible. Yet, we need not feel as though we've been left in the dark *entirely*, for we now know that when the Moon is not seen on the twenty-ninth day of the month due to smoke infused or overcast skies, the month automatically defaults to a thirty day month.

In the book of Daniel we are told there will be 3 ½ years or 42 months when we will not be able to see the Moon to begin the month with. And yet, irrespective of how difficult and trying these times will be for us and for all mankind, we will still be expected to know when to keep the Holy Days in the first and seventh months of each year. These are days when Yehovah is going to act in mighty ways and we must be ready for them.

Just like in the days of Noah and the Great Flood when the Moon was not visible to Noah (so that he might plainly see when the month was to begin), *so shall it be* for us in the Last Days. We will not have a way of determining with our naked eye or a telescope when a month is to begin either because the Moon will be totally obscured by the collective smoke from volcanic eruptions and cities burning all over the world on a cataclysmic, unprecedented scale unlike anything mankind has ever known before or since the days of Noah. And there's no telling how far reaching the combined effect of urban areas being ravaged by fire and volcanic activity giving way to fires will have on both urban and rural areas.

To presume then that all years should be 360-day years is nothing more than an erroneous assumption based on a faulty and incomplete understanding of things. We are told in Daniel of the 1,260 days, the 1,290 days and the 1,335 days for a very specific purpose and for good reason: To be ever mindful of the fact the Moon would not always be visible in each and every instance of a given month and the barley would not always be available to usher in the head of the year with as I have already explained in the previous chapter, *Abib (Barley) Biblical Leap Years.*

Chapter 7 | The Jewish Rabbinic Holy Days Are Not Kosher

With the background I've provided you with so far on how the calendar was to be used (and was then confused), I will now compare what the rabbis have done with what was originally in place and then you will be able to see *the difference* and know why the Jewish people continue to be persecuted. It is because they do *not* keep the Holy Days—at least not at the proper time Yehovah commanded them to (and commands us all to) in Torah. But nonetheless, they are keeping them as best they can. The rest of us have not even tried to keep them and be in compliance with Yehovah's laws. The punishments that come are there to cause us to repent and return to the true ways of Torah.

In Exodus we are told *when* the beginning of the year is.

> 2 "This month is the beginning of months for you, it is the first month of the year for you." (**Exodus 12:2**)

Yehovah was speaking to Moses about the month of Aviv—also known as Nisan. This is the month when Passover occurs. It is *not* the month of Tishri, which is what Judah now calls Rosh Hashanah. Keeping Rosh Hashanah on the first day of the seventh month of Tishri is just another rebellious act against the Creator.

Leviticus tells us to count out fourteen days to Passover in the context of the first day of Aviv (the first month) being the beginning or head of the year.

> 5 "In the first month, on the fourteenth day of the month, between the evenings, is the Passover to יהוה." (**Leviticus 23:5**)

But if you start your month according to the Conjunction Moon, which the Hebrew Calendar does, then you will be off by one to three days depending on when the Moon is sighted. So this is another in the list of errors we need to take a closer look at. This error is off due to using the calculated Conjunction Moon Method and not the scriptural Sighted Moon Method to determine the start of the month with.

> 6 "And on the fifteenth day of this month is the Festival of Unleavened Bread to יהוה—seven days you eat unleavened bread. 7 On the first day you have a set-apart gathering, you do no servile work." (**Leviticus 23:6-7**)

In the following verse, the errors become even more evident still:

> 10 "Speak to the children of Yisra'ĕl, and you shall say to them, 'When you come into the land which I give you, and shall reap its harvest, then you shall bring a sheaf of the first-fruits of your harvest to the priest. 11 And he shall wave the sheaf before יהוה, for your acceptance. On the morrow after the Sabbath the priest waves it.'" (**Leviticus 23:10-11**)

This is precisely why you *must have* ripe barley to usher in the head of the year with. If you do not, then you *cannot* keep this command.

The "morrow after the Sabbath" *is* the first day of the week. Judah insists it is the day after the first High Holy Day or the fifteenth day of Aviv as referenced in Leviticus 23:6 above. And they base this claim upon the following passage in Joshua:

> 10 "And the children of Yisra'el ... performed the Passover on the fourteenth day of the month at evening ..." (**Joshua 5:10**)

Yet, as many of you already know, Passover can fall on *any* day of the week. That particular year, as referenced in the Leviticus passage on the previous page, Passover fell on the weekly Sabbath. But in order to hold on to this view, that the wave sheaf is done on the 16 of Aviv and not the day after the weekly Sabbath, the rabbis must also ignore the additional passages in Leviticus below:

> 10 "Speak to the children of Yisra'ĕl, and you shall say to them, 'When you come into the land which I give you, and shall reap its harvest, then you shall bring a sheaf of the first-fruits of your harvest to the priest.'" (**Leviticus 23:10**)

> 15 "And from the morrow after the Sabbath, from the day that you

brought the sheaf of the wave offering, you shall count for yourselves: seven completed Sabbaths. **16** Until the morrow after the seventh Sabbath you count fifty days, then you shall bring a new grain offering to יהוה." (**Leviticus 23:15-16**)

The "morrow after the seventh Sabbath" can *only ever be* a Sunday or, the *first day* of any given week. Period. Pentecost is *always* going to fall on the first day of the week if we are careful to obey the passage in Leviticus above.

But Judah chooses not to obey this and would rather hold on to the Sivan 6 false teaching based on the misapplied view of Joshua 5:10 I mentioned previously. In counting forward from the fifteenth of Nisan (as they do), you will always arrive at the sixth day of Sivan, the third month which could be on any day of the week and not "the morrow after the seventh Sabbath you count fifty days."

The following passages in Leviticus then tell us what we need to know with regard to the fall Holy Days:

> **24** "Speak to the children of Yisra'ěl, saying, 'In the seventh month, on the first day of the month, you have a rest, a remembrance of blowing of trumpets, a set-apart gathering.'" (**Leviticus 23:24**)

Yehovah does not tell us anywhere in His Word that this is to be the beginning of the year. It is the seventh month, *not* the first month. Yet the rabbis claim Rosh Hashanah to be the head of the year all the same.

> **27** "On the tenth day of this seventh month is the Day of Atonement. It shall be a set-apart gathering for you. And you shall afflict your beings, and shall bring an offering made by fire to יהוה. **28** And you do no work on that same day, for it is the Day of Atonement, to make atonement for you before יהוה your Elohim. **29** For any being who is not afflicted on that same day, he shall be cut off from his people. **30** And any being who does any work on that same day, that being I shall destroy from the midst of his people. **31** You do no work—a law forever throughout your generations in all your dwellings. **32** It is a Sabbath of rest to you, and you shall afflict your beings. On the ninth day of the month at evening, from evening to evening, you observe your Sabbath." (**Leviticus 23:27-32**)

This has been lauded as the most sacred day of the year in Judah and is from sunset to sunset. This is deemed to be such a special day, to the extent the entire country shuts down. But as I am about to show you, they have again broken the commandment to keep the right day.

34 "Speak to the children of Yisra'ĕl, saying, 'On the fifteenth day of this seventh month is the Festival of Booths for seven days to יהוה. **35** On the first day is a set-apart gathering, you do no servile work. **36** For seven days you bring an offering made by fire to יהוה. On the eighth day there shall be a set-apart gathering for you, and you shall bring an offering made by fire to יהוה. It is a closing festival, you do no servile work.'" **(Leviticus 23:34-36)**

From the start, I have been explaining to you how it is *sin* in Yehovah's sight if you keep any of these Holy Days spoken of in Leviticus 23 at the *wrong* time. The Hebrew Calendar, by default, causes all who adhere to it to sin by keeping each Holy Day at the wrong time by as much as three days—due to the use of the conjunction moon to begin the month versus the sighted moon. Failure to keep the Holy Days (Appointed Times) on the specific day commanded by Yehovah in Leviticus 23 is the same as keeping the weekly Sabbath on any other day of the week, but not on Saturday. Yet, doing so on any other day is wrong and is sin for you are breaking the Fourth Commandment.

So, first of all, by using the wrong starting point of the Moon in Conjunction and not one that is Sighted, those who follow the Hebrew Calendar fall into sin by keeping the Holy Days each year on the wrong day by, again, as much as three days. But then, to make matters worse, the rabbis do something very special for the fall Holy Days and compound the error they are already making.

> In addition to the long-term drift of the popular Jewish calendar off the celestial clock, it has other features to which we take exception.
>
> Among these are what are called *dachiyot (dehioth)* or postponements. These artificially delay dates in order to accommodate the sensibilities of certain oral traditions. For example, Yom haKippurim (Yom Kippur) is prevented from occurring on a Friday or a Sunday in order to circumvent challenges in observance of the weekly Shabbat. The last day of Sukkot is prevented from occurring on a Shabbat. To accomplish this, Yom Teru'ah (commonly known as Rosh haShanah) is fixed to either a Sunday, a Wednesday or a Friday. Since Yom Teru'ah is the first day of Tishrei (aka, Tishri), the seventh month, this convention shifts the calendrical month off the natural lunar month. Such adjustments not prescribed in the Bible are unacceptable to us.[53]

As I stated before, each of the fall Holy Days are postponed or moved by as much as three days. These same postponement rules are not applied to the spring Holy Days.

---

53 http://yahoshuafoundation.org/calendararticle.pdf

I want you to now read the *Dehioth: The Rules of Postponement* and I want you to take special notice of the second rule because it is referring to the Crescent Moon.

Dehioth: The Rules of Postponement[54]

Let us begin with some background on the Postponements and why some of the Jewish leaders felt it was necessary to postpone God's Holy Days. The Holy Day arrangement for the year is determined by rules that are designed to prevent Yom Kippur (Atonement) from occurring either before or after the Sabbath. They changed God's Holy Days to suit their own needs, in the society existent (during) that time in history.

There are seven rules to the Postponements, but we (will just look at) the first four.

THE FIRST RULE

This rule explains that Trumpets (Rosh Hashanah), the first day of the (Jewish) New Year, may not occur on Sunday, Wednesday, or Friday. If Trumpets (Rosh Hashanah) were on Sunday, Hosha'na Rabbah (the seventh day of the Feast of Tabernacles) would be on Saturday, and this must be avoided because it would prevent the proper celebration of the Festival of Willows. If Trumpets (Rosh Hashanah) were on Wednesday, Atonement (Yom Kippur) would be on a Friday and this would cause undue hardship because, there would be two days in a row with severe restrictions. If Trumpets (Rosh Hashanah) were on a Friday, Atonement (Yom Kippur) would be on a Sunday and, again, we would have two days in a row with severe restrictions. Therefore, if the New Moon (Molad) is on either Sunday, Wednesday or Friday, the first day of Tishri (seventh month) is postponed to the following day.

THE SECOND RULE

If the New Moon (Molad) of Tishri (the seventh month) occurs at noon or later, New Moon (Rosh Hodesh) is declared to be the following day. Thus, if the Molad (New Moon) is Monday at noon or later, Tuesday is declared to be (the) Rosh Hodesh (New Moon). The reason is that if the Molad (New Moon) is before noon, it is certain that the New Crescent will be visible in some part of the world before sunset of the same day. If however, the New Moon (Molad) occurs after midday, the New Crescent will not be visible before sunset of the same day. If the following day is Sunday, Wednesday, or Friday on which the first day of

---

54 http://www.ironsharpeningiron.com/postponements2.htm

Tishri may not occur, it is further postponed to the next following day, so that the first of Tishri is the third day counting from, and including, the day of the Molad (New Moon).

THE THIRD RULE

If the Molad of Tishri in an ordinary year is on Tuesday at 3:204/1080am or later, the first of Tishri is postponed to Thursday. It cannot be on Tuesday because then the next year's New Moon (Molad) of Tishri would be on Saturday afternoon and (the) New Moon (Rosh Hodesh) would have to be postponed to Sunday. This would make the year in question 356 days long, which is more than the statutory limit of 355 days.

THE FOURTH RULE

This occurs if the New Moon (Molad) of Tishri, in a year succeeding (following) a Leap Year, is on a Monday after 9am (ie. the fifteenth hour from the beginning of the night before) and 589/1080 parts. If this year were to begin on Monday, Trumpets (Rosh Hashanah) of the preceding year would have fallen on Tuesday (at) noon, and would have been postponed to Wednesday. This would make the current year 382 days in length, which is lower than the statutory limit of 383 days.

If you want to do some more research into the calendar issues, then I urge you to read *Conjunction or Sighted Which?*[55] and *The Return of Yehshua*[56] for a more complete understanding.

Nowhere in the Torah do we have any suggestions or hints from Yehovah that we can postpone each of the fall Holy Days in order not to have a Holy Day next to the weekly Sabbath. In the spring we do not have postponement rules to keep us from having the high Holy Days of the Days of Unleavened Bread fall next to the weekly Sabbath. In fact we already know that Pentecost is always two Holy Days in a row. The weekly Sabbath followed by the Holy Day of Pentecost on Sunday. These Postponement rules are man made and are not from Yehovah. We are not to keep them and to change the actual Holy Day and make it or change it into another.

But because we do not keep the Holy Days at the right time; this is why we see Judah being punished over and over throughout history. It is to provoke them to return to the truth. To keep the Holy Days as we are told in Leviticus 23 and not to make exceptions or postpone them.

---

55 http://www.sightedmoon.com/?page_id=22
56 http://www.sightedmoon.com/?page_id=20

Chapter 8 | The Holy Days of Leviticus 23 Are Not Jewish

A schematic on how to build something, everyone would agree, is written for an engineer. A blueprint for a high rise is designed for an architect. Books on war strategies are written for military personnel. Anatomy books are written for medical students and aspiring doctors. Yet, how much trust would we place in a heart surgeon who decided to forgo the segment of his/her medical schooling that taught him/her about the atrial valve? How safe and operational would an airplane be if built by engineers who chose not to utilize their understanding of physics both on a conceptual level and in the actual designing of it? How well would Noah's Ark have held up against the Great Flood had Yehovah not given Noah specific instructions as to how to build an ark best suited for such a cataclysmic event? Finally, would a military commander who skipped the unit on how to clean a weapon really be effective in the heat of battle?

Yet we do this from cover to cover with our Father's Word and without even giving it a second thought. Which begs the following question, "Who are the Scriptures written for?" And also, "Why were they written?" All believers, no matter the denomination, would claim the Word of Yehovah was written for them. Why do so many professing believers make such a sweeping claim and yet, fail to act in a manner in keeping with the claim they have just made? All peoples throughout history and of the world have taken the Word of Yehovah, added to it, subtracted from it, taken Scriptural passages out of context, and taken single doctrines and built fences around them. People have dissected and vivisected the Bible to the point of it having been amended away, just like the U.S. Constitution. We, as Yehovah's bride selectively pick and choose only what we would have ourselves believe applies to us—very much like a spouse who distances his or herself by engaging in selective hearing, only hearing what he/she wants to hear. Yet Yehovah has something to say about this—His Instructions (His Word)—that has been from the beginning, before the foundation of the world and those of us He foreknew—His "called out" peculiar people. Yehshua addresses this grave reality very candidly in the passage below:

> **8** "This people draw near to Me with their mouth, and respect Me with their lips, but their heart is far from me. **9** But in vain do they worship Me, teaching as teachings the commands of men." (**Matthew 15:8-9**)

> And יהוה says, "Because this people has drawn near with its mouth, and with its lips they have esteemed Me, and it has kept its heart far from Me, and their fear of Me has become a command of men that is taught (**Isaiah 29:13**)

The Holy Days are not exclusively Jewish; they are for *all* men of *all* nations. The Holy Days were given to the Twelve Tribes of Israel at Mount Sinai, and they *all* agreed to them. Judah is only but one tribe. All Jews are Israelites but not all Israelites are Jews. It is the same in the U.S.A. Not all Americans are New Yorkers but all New Yorkers are Americans.

We are told a number of times that the Torah is for all mankind and not just for Israel. There is one Torah for the Israelite and the same Torah for the stranger amongst them.

> **22** "You are to have one right-ruling, for the stranger and for the native, for I am יהוה your Elohim." (**Leviticus 24:22**)

> **49** "There is one Torah for the native-born and for the stranger who sojourns among you." (**Exodus 12:49**)

> **29** "For him who does *whatever* by mistake there is one Torah, both for him who is native among the children of Yisra'ĕl and for the stranger who sojourns in their midst. **30** But the being who does *whatever* defiantly, whether he is native or a stranger, he reviles יהוה, and that being shall be cut off from among his people." (**Numbers 15:29-30**)

Today Jews claim that the Goyem (Gentiles) who want to keep Torah only have to keep the "Seven Noahide Laws", but do not have to keep all the laws. This is *not supported* in Scripture as we have already read what Scripture has to say on this matter. The Noahide Laws are part of the Oral Torah and have *nothing* to do with the truth of Torah itself.

The Seven Noahide Laws[57]

To the Jewish people, Yehovah gave the *entire* Torah (teaching) as their Law. They therefore have a special responsibility—with special commandments—to be the priesthood of the world, a "light unto the nations."

What about the *rest* of the world? What is God's will for them?

God gave Noah and all his descendants (*B'nei Noach* or "Children of Noah") Seven Commandments to obey. These seven universal laws (known as the "Seven Noahide Laws") were reaffirmed with Moses and the Jewish people at Mount Sinai in what is now known as the Oral Torah, establishing modern observance of these laws. These Seven Commandments (*Mitzvos*), (which) actually (include) seven categories of hundreds of specific laws, are God's will for *all* non-Jews.

Non-Jews who (1) reject all idolatrous ideas and accept the kingship of the one God, (2) accept the priesthood of the Jewish people as the guardians and teachers of Torah, and (3) commit to following the Seven Noahide Laws as revealed in the Oral Torah from Mount Sinai are "Hasidic Gentiles" or "Noahides." The term "Hasidic Gentile" is derived from a classic commentary by the Rambam, Rav Moshe ben Maimon (Maimonides), in The Laws of Kings:

11 Anyone who accepts upon himself the fulfillment of these Seven Mitzvos (Commandments) and is precise in their observance is considered one of the Hasidei Umos Ha'olam ("Hasidim of the nations of the world") and will merit a share in the World to Come. (**Kings 8:11**)

The Seven Noahide Laws are the minimal observance for non-Jews. The source of these laws and the basis of their understanding is the Oral Torah, which God gave to the Jewish people at Mount Sinai along with His Written Law. By learning from the Jews and performing the *Mitzvos*, non-Jews (play) a crucial role in God's creation.

The Seven Noahide Laws actually encompass numerous details and applications within hundreds of laws, each with specific applications. One should also keep in mind that these laws are only the *minimal* basis for a Hasidic Gentile's service to God, since there are many Jewish Mitzvos that non-Jews are encouraged to adopt to accomplish more. Through these laws, a Gentile refines himself and the creation as a whole, fulfilling his purpose for existence.

---

57 http://www.noahide.com/7laws.htm

But I must point out something else with regard to the Noahide Laws before we go any further. These laws claim the Jewish people are to be the teachers (See rule #2 above). Therefore, we are to *accept* the priesthood of the Jewish people as the guardians and teachers of Torah.

Yet we read in II Chronicles:

> 3 "... and said to the Lewites (Levites) who were teaching all Yisra'el, who were set-apart to יהוה ..." (**II Chronicles 35:3**)

With just a little bit of research we can easily discover it was *Levi* that was to instruct the people and *not* Judah.

1. The tribe of *Levi*[58] was elevated to perform holy service, in the Tabernacle of the desert and in the Temple. Hence, it is an affirmative command for all Levites to be available and prepared for Temple Service, as stated in the Torah, "The Levites shall be for Me" (**Numbers 18:14**), indicating that the special relationship with the tribe of *Levi* is permanent. The prophet Jeremiah relates God's promise that there will always be *Kohanim* and Levites fit to serve:

> 20 "As I will never renege on My covenant with day and night,
> 21 ... so is my covenant with ... the Levites, the *Kohanim*, My servants." (**Jeremiah 33:20-21**)

2. The choice of the tribe of *Levi* for the highest spiritual service was due to their ability to channel their strong character in the service of God. Levi, the son of Jacob, was chastised for his anger by his father:

> 7 "Cursed is their zealousness for it is brazen and their wrath for it is hard. I will separate them in Ya'akov (Jacob) and scatter them throughout Israel." (**Genesis 49:7**)

Also, in *The Scriptures* the same verse reads:

> 7 "Cursed be their displeasure for it is fierce, and their wrath for it is cruel! I divide them in Ya'aqob (Jacob) and scatter them in Yisra'el." (**Genesis 49:7**)

Four generations later, Moses blessed the same tribe of *Levi*: "Your righteous men ... keeper of Your Word and covenant; He shall teach Your judgment in Ya'akov (Jacob) and Your Torah in Israel ... Blessed of God is his valor and his actions are pleasing ..." (Deuteronomy 33:8-11). The Levites were able to apply their physical and spiritual strength

---

58 http://www.cohen-levi.org/the_levites/role_of_the_levites.htm

to the fulfillment of God's will and gain forever the role of God's trusted servants.

3. The name *Levi* is derived from the words, "he shall accompany." This name was given to the third son of Jacob and Leah to indicate that he was to bring a strengthening of relationship between his parents, for now with three children, Jacob would need to accompany his wife Leah.

It was a natural development, therefore, that the task of the Levite became to accompany the Divine Presence and serve in the Temple. His role as teacher and spiritual example is to lead and, thereby, accompany others back to their spiritual purpose. The *Midrash* relates that in the future, Levites will lead the people of Israel back to their Father in Heaven.

4. Levi ben Ya'akov, the father of the tribe of Levites, lived 137 years, the longest of all of the sons of Ya'akov (Jacob). He had a particularly strong influence on the spiritual development of his progeny, and lived to see his great-grandsons Moshe (Moses) and Aharon (Aaron).

The tribe of *Levi* developed separately from the other tribes of Israel. During the period of the Egyptian bondage, the Levites avoided the slavery suffered by the others, by maintaining their separateness in the land of Goshen immersed in the tents of learning, and maintaining the spiritual tradition of the Fathers.

5. The loyal nature of the Levites was most clearly demonstrated at the episode of the Golden Calf. The general populace was influenced by the evil promptings of the mixed multitude. The Levites, however, rallied to the side of Moshe to avenge Yehovah's honor. They were rewarded with the spiritual service lost at that time by the firstborn of the other tribes. The Levites were tested and proved themselves able, thereby earning their elevated spiritual status.

The Levites were constantly willing to risk their lives for God's service. They carried the sanctified vessels of the Tabernacle, which if mishandled, resulted in death.

Again, this claim that non-Jews only need to follow the Noahide Laws, cannot be found anywhere in Torah. It is, instead, found in the Talmudic writings, which are *not* Torah but are the opinions of Jewish sages over the centuries.

49 "There is one Torah for the native-born and for the stranger who sojourns among you." (**Exodus 12:49**)

11 "Therefore remember that you, once gentiles in the flesh, who are called 'the uncircumcision' by what is called 'the circumcision' made in the flesh by hands, 12 that at that time you were without Messiah, excluded from the citizenship of Yisra'el and strangers from the covenants of promise, having no expectation and without Elohim in the world. 13 But now in Messiah יהושע you who once were far off have been brought near by the blood of the Messiah. 14 For He is our peace, who has made both one, and having broken down the partition of the barrier, 15 having abolished in His flesh the enmity—the Torah of the commands in dogma—so as to create in Himself one renewed man from the two, thus making peace..." (**Ephesians 2:11-15**)

Dogma[59] is the established belief or doctrine held by a religion, or a particular group or organization. (**1**) It is authoritative and not to be disputed, doubted, or diverged from, by the practitioners or believers. Although it generally refers to religious beliefs that are accepted without reason or evidence, they can refer to acceptable opinions of philosophers or philosophical schools, public decrees, or issued decisions of political authorities. (**2**) The term derives from the Greek δόγμα "that which seems to one, opinion or belief" (**3**) and that from δοκέω (dokeo), "to think, to suppose, to imagine." (**4**) Dogma came to signify laws or ordinances adjudged and imposed upon others by the 1st century. The plural is either dogmas or dogmata, from Greek δόγματα. Today, it is sometimes used as a synonym for systematic theology.

Yehovah called out a nation of people unto Himself. Those who were not biological descendants of the twelve sons of Jacob (Yisra'el) were strangers or foreigners but were grafted in and assimilated into the Twelve Tribes. Joseph's sons were born in Egypt—as were all those called out by Yehovah from Egypt and we would now call them "Egyptians" by nationality. These two sons of Joseph were adopted into the sons of Jacob. All people, all nations, all men and women of the earth have this same opportunity and privilege—to be counted amongst those of Yehovah's "called out" nation. For again, the Word of Yehovah does not change:

49 "There is one Torah for the native-born and for the stranger who sojourns among you." (**Exodus 12:49**)

7 What then? Yisra'el has not obtained what it seeks, but the chosen did obtain it, and the rest were hardened. 8 As it has been written, "יהוה has given them a spirit of deep sleep, eyes not to see and ears not to hear, unto

---

59 http://en.wikipedia.org/wiki/Dogma

this day." **9** Dawiḏ (David) also says, "Let their table become for a snare, and for a trap, and for a stumbling-block and a recompense to them, **10** let their eyes be darkened, not to see, and bow down their back always." **11** I say then, "Have they stumbled that they should fall? Let it not be! But by their fall deliverance has come to the gentiles, to provoke them to jealousy. **12** And if their fall is riches for the world, and their failure, riches for the gentiles, how much more their completeness! **13** For I speak to you, the gentiles, inasmuch as I am an emissary to the gentiles, I esteem my service, **14** if somehow I might provoke to jealousy *those who are* my flesh and save some of them." (**Romans 11:7-14**)

15 For if their casting away is the restoration to favor of the world, what is their acceptance but life from the dead? **16** Now if the first-fruit is set-apart, the lump is also. And if the root is set-apart, so are the branches. **17** And if some of the branches were broken off, and you, being a wild olive tree, have been grafted in among them, and came to share the root and fatness of the olive tree, **18** do not boast against the branches. And if you boast, *remember*: you do not bear the root, but the root *bears* you! **19** You shall say then, "The branches were broken off that I might be grafted in." **20** Good! By unbelief they were broken off, and you stand by belief. Do not be arrogant, but fear. **21** For if Elohim did not spare the natural branches, He might not spare you either. (**Romans 11:15-21**)

22 See then the kindness and sharpness of Elohim: on those who fell sharpness, but toward you kindness, if you continue in *His* kindness, otherwise you also shall be cut off. **23** And they also, if they do not continue in unbelief, shall be grafted (back) in, for Elohim is able to graft them in again. **24** For if you were cut out of the olive tree which is wild by nature, and were grafted contrary to nature into a good olive tree, how much more shall these who are the natural *branches*, be grafted into their own olive tree? **25** For I do not wish you to be ignorant of this secret, brothers, lest you should be wise in your own estimation, that hardening in part has come over Yisra'ěl, until the completeness of the gentiles[1] has come in. (**Romans 11:22-25** | Footnote: [1]**Genesis 48:19**)

26 And so all Yisra'ěl shall be saved, as it has been written, "The Deliverer shall come out of Tsiyon (Zion), and He shall turn away wickedness from Ya'aqoḇ (Jacob), **27** and this is My covenant with them, when I take away their sins."[1] (**Romans 11:26-27** | Footnote: [1]**Isaiah 59:20-21**)

If the Torah was written for all men in every generation in every land around the world then the Holy Days spoken of in Lev 23 also apply to every man in each and every country around the world. They are not Jewish but are for all mankind and for the betterment of all of us. We all need to embrace them and not keep our distance from them.

Chapter 9 | Chesed—Love & Grace Are the Standard

Everyone believes they are inherently good. Even when her people and her own family were subject to Nazi occupation and persecution, Anne Marie Frank could be found penning in her diary:

> I still believe, in spite of everything, that people are truly good at heart.[60]

Good, but by *what* standard? An expression that has been all too commonly heard for some time now is, "I am a good person" or, "he/she is a good person." But what does this statement *mean* exactly? Automatically the person making such a claim sets a precedent. Yet is the person making such a claim *truly* being objective or is this person ascribing the quality of being good onto another strictly by using his or her own standards as the gauge by which to judge goodness by? What set of criteria is the foundation for people making such judgments? What worldviews and cultural filters are at work? I think we can all agree the answer to this would vary profoundly based on just who, exactly, is setting the standard. Disturbingly enough, the logistics of this can be likened to the dynamic the media relies so heavily upon—when we see or hear something (despite its particular slant or bias) printed in black and white or on the nightly news, we believe it *must* be true.

To make things even more complex, Yehshua Himself spoke of being *in* this world but not *of* this world when He said:

> 14 "I have given them Your Word, and the world hated them because they are not of the world, as I am not of the world. 15 I do not pray that

---

60 http://en.wikiquote.org/wiki/Anne_Frank

You should take them out of the world, but that You keep them from the wicked one." (**John 17:14-15**)

So *even when* we have been "raised up in the way we should go," we are still, to some extent (whether it be lesser or greater), the sum of the culture we were born into or have spent the greater portion of our life being a part of. This is an inescapable reality—one from which we could never escape even in part if it were not for Yehovah. We cannot be transformed into His likeness if we remain conformed to this world in other words.

How do you remain conformed to this world? We remain conformed to the world in accordance to the culture we are by-products of. This includes our home environment, government-sanctioned public education (school curriculums), the media, Hollywood (TV, movies), and so on. The more exposure we have to what makes our culture what it is, the more it becomes a part of who we are. The measuring rods then by which we gauge human goodness all stem from a humanistic ideology or worldview derived from the culture we are born into. Do these man-inspired systems change over time with regard to culture and religion? Do they change with respect to the distinction made between secular and sacred, as well as with respect to relativism and absolutes? Of course they do. How can any kind of hard and fast criteria be put in place then by which to accurately determine whether you are good or someone else is good when everything is in a constant state of flux culturally and the winds of change keep blowing?

Again by whose standard do we rightfully determine who and what is good and who and what is not? Do we go by man's standards and ideals, which are ever-changing and shifting? Or do we go by Yehovah's standards which are timeless, unchanging and in which there are no shifting shadows?

> **17** Every good thing given and every perfect gift is from above, coming down from the Father of lights, with whom there is no variation or shifting shadow. (**James 1:17 | NAS**)

Man has been in the business of making new laws (and constantly modifying old ones) for nearly 6,000 years now. Each day governments around the world are busy making new laws and modifying or doing away with old ones. Yehovah, on the other hand, gave us "Ten Laws" to obey and has not changed with regard to His attributes or deviated from His Laws since creation.

We read in Ezekiel:

4 The being that is sinning shall die. (**Ezekiel 18:4**)

Another translation of this verse reads:

4 The soul that sins, it shall die.. (**Ezekiel 18:4 NKJV**)

It does not say, "… go to hell or purgatory." The soul that sins dies; plain and simple. Period.

In case you missed it, a little later in the same chapter of Ezekiel, Yehovah underscores what he said earlier in the chapter:

20 The soul who sins shall die. (**Ezekiel 18:20**)

Many Christians will counter this reassertion by asserting they are New Testament believers. My response to this is what Paul wrote in Romans:

23 "…the wages of sin is death." (**Romans 6:23**)

Knowing that the wages of sin is death and that this means our very souls, too, can die, it behooves us to learn exactly *what* sin is. Your opinion (or mine) of what sin is does not count. Again, we must go by Yehovah's standards and *not* our own.

We find the answer to what sin is in I John:

4 Whoever commits sin also commits lawlessness, and sin is lawlessness. (**I John 3:4**)

To put it even more pointedly, in the New King James version of this same passage it says:

4 Everyone who practices sin also practices lawlessness, for sin is lawlessness. (**I John 3:4**)

We now know that in not keeping or in breaking The Law we commit sin. We are to keep The Commandments. It really is *that* simple and the King James translation could not have put it more plainly. Not only are we to keep them, but we are to guard them as well and it is by obeying and doing His Commandments that we become perfected in Him.

3 And by this we know that we know Him, if we guard His commands. (**I John 2:3**)

4 The one who says, "I know Him," and does not guard His commands, is a liar, and the truth is not in him. (**I John 2:4**)

5 But whoever guards His Word, truly the love of Elohim has been perfected in him. By this we know that we are in Him. (**I John 2:5**)

24 And the one guarding His commands stays in Him, and He in him. And by this we know that He stays in us, by the Spirit which He gave us.[1] (**I John 3:24** | Footnote: [1]**John 14:23-24, Acts 5:32, Romans 8:7-11, I John 2:5, I John 4:13**)

6 Everyone staying in Him does not sin. Everyone sinning has neither seen Him nor known Him. (**I John 3:6**)

1 And it came to be when Aḇram was ninety-nine years old, that יהוה appeared to Aḇram and said to him, "I am Ěl Shaddai—walk before Me and be perfect." (**Genesis 17:1**)

1 Blessed are the perfect in the way, who walk in the Torah of יהוה! (**Psalm 119:1**)

48 "Therefore, be perfect, as your Father in the heavens is perfect." (**Matthew 5:48**)

1 Therefore, having left the word of the beginning of the Messiah, let us go on to perfection, not laying again the foundation of repentance from dead works, and of belief toward Elohim. (**Hebrews 6:1**)

The more submitted we are to Yehovah, the more He empowers us to keep His Commandments. The more we keep His Commandments, the more we learn to and come to love Yehovah. It is in keeping His Commandments that we can increasingly walk before Yehovah perfectly, just like Abraham, and most profoundly and persuasively demonstrate to Yehovah we love Him.

6 "... but showing kindness to thousands, to those who love Me and guard My commands." (**Exodus 20:6**)

Hidden in plain sight, in the actual Ten Commandments, we are told about kindness and how to love Yehovah.

H2617 חסד chêsêd *kheh'-sed*

From **H2616**; *kindness*; by implication (towards יהוה) *piety*; rarely (by opprobrium: harsh criticism or censure) *reproof*, or (subjectively) *beauty*:

favor, good deed (-liness, -ness), kindly, (loving-) kindness, merciful (kindness), mercy, pity, reproach, wicked thing.

Khesed (Chesed) is the word for "grace." The Hebrew translation of "saved by grace" is "Nosha be-Khesed." Yehovah tells us in Exodus 20 we are saved by grace *if* we keep His Commandments.

> **10** "... but showing kindness to thousands, to those who love Me and guard My commands." (**Deuteronomy 5:10**)

Again, the word kindness is "chesed" or "grace." Here, with your own eyes, you can see that GRACE has always been the heart of our Father. It is not just a "New Testament" concept.

> **9** "And you shall know that יהוה your Elohim, He is Elohim, the trustworthy Ĕl guarding covenant and kindness for a thousand generations with those who love Him, and those who guard His commands." (**Deuteronomy 7:9**)

> **1** "And you shall love יהוה your Elohim and guard His Charge[1]: even His laws, and His right-rulings, and His commands, always." (**Deuteronomy 11:1** | Footnote: [1]See **Genesis 26:5**)

> **5** "Only, diligently guard to do the command and the Torah which Mosheh (Moses) the servant of יהוה commanded you, to love יהוה your Elohim, and to walk in all His ways, and to guard His commands, and to cling to Him, and to serve Him with all your heart and with all your being." (**Joshua 22:5**)

> **5** "... and I said, 'I pray, יהוה Elohim of the heavens, O great and awesome Ĕl, guarding the covenant and kindness with those who love You, and with those guarding Your commands.'" (**Nehemiah 1:5**)

> **47** That I might delight myself in Your commands, which I have loved; **48** that I might lift up my hands to Your commands, which I have loved; while I meditate on Your laws. (**Psalm 119:47-48**)

> **127** Therefore I have loved Your commands. More than gold, even fine gold! (**Psalm 119:127**)

> **4** And I prayed to יהוה my Elohim, and made confession, and said, "O יהוה, great and awesome Ĕl, guarding the covenant and the kindness to those who love Him, and to those who guard His commands." (**Daniel 9:4**)

15 "If you love Me, you shall guard My commands." (**John 14:15**)

21 "He who possesses My commands and guards them, it is he who loves Me. And he who loves Me shall be loved by My Father, and I shall love him and manifest Myself to him." (**John 14:21**)

10 "If you guard My commands, you shall stay in My love, even as I have guarded My Father's commands and stay in His love." (**John 15:10**)

2 By this we know that we love the children of Elohim, when we love Elohim and guard His commands. 3 For this is the love for Elohim, that we guard His commands, and His commands are not heavy. (**I John 5:2-3**)

Did you notice it? These last 4 verses mentioned are from the Apostle John and it is Yehshua that is saying to His followers the method how to show Him they love Him. It was then and it is still to this very day, by keeping the commandments and by guarding them. If you do this, then the Father will love you. Do we comprehend this? All we have to do is keep the commandments- all of them.

In keeping with His commands not being heavy, the following verse in Matthew further supports this idea:

30 "For My yoke is gentle and My burden is light." (**Matthew 11:30**)

6 And this is the love, that we walk according to His commands. This is the command, that as you have heard from the beginning, you should walk in it. (**II John 1:6**)

We show our love for Yehovah by keeping His Commandments and obeying them. He then, in turn, loves us and shows us grace or kindness if we keep His Commandments. This becomes so apparent when we just take and make the time to read His Word.

The *Old Testament Word Studies* facet of the Christian Leadership Center[61] website defines "Khesed" as:

"Loyal Love, Lovingkindness"

One of the most important words in the Bible, and certainly in the Book of Psalms, is the word *khesed*, most often translated as "lovingkindness."

---

61 http://www.christianleadershipcenter.org/otws8.htm

Not only is the word descriptive of a divine attribute, but it is also the key word for covenant relationships, whether between God and His people, or between people themselves. It is important to have a good grasp of this word because this word (is) found in so many passages of the Old Testament.

ETYMOLOGY

Dictionary Definitions

The dictionaries are in general agreement over the meaning of this word. The *Brown-Driver-Briggs Hebrew & English Lexicon* (aka, the BDB), written by Francis Brown, S.R. Driver and Charles A. Briggs, says it means "goodness, kindness." It then breaks this down to its meanings for people: "mercy, affection, lovely appearance," and then to its meanings for God: "lovingkindness, deeds of mercy, deeds of kindness" (the latter two being in the plural).

The *Hebrew & Aramaic Lexicon of the Old Testament*[62] (aka, the KBL) by Ludwig Kohler, L. Koehler and W. Baumgartner says the word means: "the mutual liability of those who are relatives, friends, master and servant, or belonging together in any other way, the solidarity, (and) joint liability." The dictionary then specifies that the word can describe single proofs of that solidarity.

Cognate Languages

The root is found only in Aramaic (including later Syriac) and Hebrew. It is used in <u>later Hebrew</u> (MH) where it clearly parallels the usage of Biblical Hebrew. Jastrow defines the word for this <u>later rabbinic use</u> as "grace, kindness, love, charity," and in the plural as "acts of kindness." Syriac exhibits meanings closely related to that of Biblical Hebrew as might be expected.

Khesed (Chesed) is the word for "grace." The Hebrew translation of "saved by grace" is "Nosha be-Khesed." Yehovah tells us in Exodus 20 we are saved by grace if we keep His Commandments.

You are saved by grace if you repent and keep the commandments. Yeshua died on the tree to pay the penalty for your sinning. This is the grace that is given for you. It does not mean you can go on and continue to sin, or continue to not keep the commandments; in particular the 4th one which is what we have been talking about this whole book.

---

62 http://www.amazon.com/The-Hebrew-Aramaic-Lexicon-Testament/dp/9004124454

Having been forgiven you are now expected to return, repent, and begin to keep all ten commandments, including the 4th one of keeping the 7th day weekly Sabbath, the Holy Days of Lev 23 and the Sabbatical years of Lev 25. If you do not then you have not repented and your sins are not forgiven.

> **10** "... but showing kindness (grace) to thousands, to those who love Me and guard My commands." (**Deuteronomy 5:10**)

This is something to seriously consider.

Chapter 10 | So What Is "The Law?"

I have now armed you with a foundational knowledge of what love is from a Torah-based perspective and have shown you that the only way we can appropriate our love for Yehovah is by keeping His Commandments. The beautiful part being, that when we do, He extends to us His loving-kindness or "Chesed" (expounded upon in Chapter 9) in return, which also means grace. That being said, we must now review The Commandments of His we are to guard and keep. Of course we are to keep all of His Commandments, for it is written:

> 10 For whoever shall guard the Torah, and yet stumble in one point, he is guilty of all. (**James 2:10**)

But it is my desire to first lay the right foundation by focusing on the greatest of The Commandments we are to keep. By now you know that sin is the transgression of His Commandments and that your very soul can die for not keeping them.

> 28 "And do not fear those who kill the body but cannot kill the soul. But rather fear Him who is able to destroy both soul and body in hell." (**Matthew 10:28**)

And that person, of course, is Yehovah.

- The soul who sins shall die.
- Sin is the transgression of The Law.
- The Law is The Commandments.

> 8 Owe no one any *matter* except to love one another, for he who loves another has filled the Torah. 9 For this, "You shall not commit adultery,"

"You shall not murder," "You shall not steal," "You shall not bear false witness," "You shall not covet," and if there is any other command, is summed up in this word, "You shall love your neighbor as yourself."**10** Love does no evil to a neighbor. Therefore, love is completion of the Torah. (**Romans 13:8-10**)

Again, Paul tells us that love is to keep Yehovah's Commandments. That being said, it should be your ongoing, all-consuming goal to:

1 "Make love your aim ..." (**I Corinthians 14:1**)

I will now share with you which commandments are considered to be the greatest by Yehshua Himself.

34 But the Pharisees, having heard that He had silenced the Sadducees, were gathered together, **35** and one of them, one learned in the Torah, did question, trying Him, and saying, **36** "Teacher, which is the great command in the Torah?" **37** And יהושע said to him, "'You shall love יהוה your Elohim with all your heart, and with all your being, and with all your mind.' **38** This is the first and great command. **39** And the second is like it, 'You shall love your neighbor as yourself.' **40** On these two commands hang all the Torah and the Prophets." (**Matthew 22:34-40**)

Yehshua has just told us in the passage above what the two greatest commandments are.

Both Yehshua and Paul can be found quoting the Ten Commandments, as first revealed to man by Yehovah, directly from Exodus 20. In so doing, both make it clear to us what the two greatest commandments are and the ways in which they singularly and jointly reveal to us how we are to love Yehovah—by keeping His Commandments, but also, by loving our fellow man as we love ourselves. And it is only in loving our fellow man that we are completed in our love for Yehovah. Keeping His Commandments is not enough if we do not do it in love, in other words. The First Great Commandment tells us how to love Yehovah and the Second Great Commandment, which is *just like* it, tells us how to love our fellow man. On these *two* hang *all* that the Torah teaches us and all the prophets who have come and gone have prophesied to us.

In the previous chapter, I demonstrated how The Commandments teach us how best to properly love Yehovah and that when we do; He loves us and is merciful to us in like manner. Insofar and inasmuch as we do it unto the least of our brothers or sisters, we do it unto Yehovah. We are known of Yehovah by what we do and do not do—by the things we have done and by the things we have neglected or left undone. That is how Yehovah separates us, His sheep (those who worship Him in Spirit and in truth, know His voice and do His will), from those who are goats and tares at best and ravenous wolves in sheep's clothing at worst. Moreover, we only love Yehovah as much as we love our neighbour the least. May we not condemn ourselves then in Yehovah's sight as Cain or the Pharisees did who quipped, "Am I my brother's keeper?" or "Who is my neighbour?" respectively.

Finally, whereas the second greatest commandment is *just like* the first and sums up the last six of the Ten Commandments which teach us specifically how to love our fellow man, the first greatest commandment sums up the first four of the Ten Commandments which teach us specifically how to love Yehovah.

The last six commandments pertaining to loving our neighbour (or fellow man) are as follows:

The **Fifth Commandment** is:

12 "Respect your father and your mother, so that your days are prolonged upon the soil which יהוה your Elohim is giving you." (**Exodus 20:12**)

The **Sixth Commandment** is:

13 "You do not murder." (**Exodus 20:13**)

The **Seventh Commandment** is:

14 "You do not commit adultery." (**Exodus 20:14**)

The **Eighth Commandment** is:

15 "You do not steal." (**Exodus 20:15**)

The **Ninth Commandment** is:

16 "You do not bear false witness against your neighbor." (**Exodus 20:16**)

The **Tenth Commandment** is:

17 "You do not covet your neighbor's house, you do not covet your

neighbor's wife, nor his male servant, nor his female servant, nor his ox, nor his donkey, or whatever belongs to your neighbor." (**Exodus 20:17**)

Again, what is the Greatest Commandment according to Yehshua?

37 "You shall love יהוה your Elohim with all your heart, and with all your being, and with all your mind. 38 This is the first and great command." (**Matthew 22:37-38**)

That being said, I will now review the first four commandments:

The **First Commandment** is:

1 And Elohim spoke all these Words, saying, 2 "I am יהוה your Elohim, who brought you out of the land of Mitsrayim (Egypt), out of the house of slavery. 3 You have no other mighty ones against My face." (**Exodus 20:1-3**)

The **Second Commandment** is:

4 "You do not make for yourself a carved image, or any likeness of that which is in the heavens above, or which is in the earth beneath, or which is in the waters under the earth, 5 you do not bow down to them nor serve them. For I, יהוה your Elohim am a jealous Ěl, visiting the crookedness of the fathers on the children to the third and fourth generations of those who hate Me, 6 but showing kindness to thousands, to those who love Me and guard My commands." (**Exodus 20:4-6**)

And here, once again, Yehovah is depicted as showing grace to those who love Him and guard His Commandments.

The **Third Commandment** is:

7 "You do not bring[1] the Name of יהוה your Elohim to naught, for יהוה does not leave the one unpunished who brings His Name to naught." (**Exodus 20:7** | Footnote:[1] Or *lift* up, or *take*)

The **Fourth Commandment** is:

8 "Remember the Sabbath day, to set it apart. 9 Six days you labor, and shall do all your work, 10 but the seventh day is a Sabbath[1] of יהוה your Elohim. You do not do any work—you, nor your son, nor your daughter,

nor your male servant, nor your female servant, nor your cattle, nor your stranger who is within your gates. (**Exodus 20:8-10** | Footnote: [1]There are other Sabbaths, but this is the weekly Sabbath)

11 "For in six days יהוה made the heavens and the earth, the sea, and all that is in them, and rested the seventh day. Therefore יהוה blessed the Sabbath day and set it apart." (**Exodus 20:11**)

But just as Rome was not built in a day, neither are we perfected overnight. We are commanded to "be perfect as the Father in heaven is perfect," yet perfection is never a state we fully attain to on earth in our fallen state. But it is a state that we are to continually make our aim. Yehovah knows we can't keep all His Commandments straight off the bat, however. So we would do well, like I mentioned earlier, to start with His first Great Commandment, which tells us how to love Him, yet not, forgetting His second Great Commandment, which tells us how to love our fellow man. Together, they sum up the Ten Commandments or The Law and The Prophets in the same manner in which Yehshua did in Matthew 22:36-40.

Again:

- The soul who sins shall die.
- Sin is the transgression of The Law.
- The Law is the Ten Commandments.

Some Christians are hopefully and prayerfully now becoming convicted and even a little uncomfortable.

1 At that time the taught ones came to יהושע, saying, "Who, then, is greatest in the reign of the heavens?" **2** And יהושע called a little child to Him, set him in their midst, **3** and said, "Truly, I say to you, unless you turn and become as little children, you shall by no means enter into the reign of the heavens. **4** "Whoever then humbles himself as this little child is the greatest in the reign of the heavens. **5** And whoever receives one little child like this in My Name receives Me. **6** But whoever causes one of these little ones who believe in Me to stumble, it is better for him that a millstone be hung around his neck, and that he be drowned in the depth of the sea. **7** Woe to the world because of stumbling-blocks! For it is necessary that stumbling-blocks come, but woe to that man by whom the stumbling-block comes!" (**Matthew 18:1-7**)

If you choose to deceive little ones by teaching them lies, you may as well tie a millstone to your neck and toss yourself into the sea.

In like manner:

> **30** "And if your right hand causes you to stumble, cut it off and throw it away from you. For it is better for you that one of your members perish, than for your entire body to be thrown into Gehenna (hell)." **(Matthew 5:30)**

Most Christians will proceed to quote the following passage:

> **11** In Him you were also circumcised with a circumcision not made with hands, in the putting off of the body of the sins of the flesh, by the circumcision of Messiah, **12** having been buried with Him in immersion, in which you also were raised with Him through the belief in the working of Elohim, who raised Him from the dead. **13** And you, being dead in your trespasses¹ and the uncircumcision of your flesh, He has made alive together with Him, having forgiven you all trespasses …" **(Colossians 2:11-13** | Footnote: ¹**Ephesians 2:1)**

Reading from *The Scriptures* in Colossians, we see that:

> **14** "…having blotted out the certificate of debt against us—by the dogmas—which stood against us. And He has taken it out of the way, having nailed it to the stake. **(Colossians 2:14)**

The Scriptures Bible translation of the passage I have just quoted above is correct, however. It is *the debt* we owe for our sins that was blotted out and *not* The Law that shows us our sin.

> **1** "And you were dead in trespasses and sins …" **(Ephesians 2:1** | and also see: **Ephesians 5:14, Matthew 8:22, Romans 8:6, Colossians 2:13, I Timothy 5:6, I John 3:14, Revelation 3:1)**
>
> **2** "… in which you once walked according to the course of this world, according to the ruler of the authority of the air, of the spirit that is now working in the sons of disobedience …" **(Ephesians 2:2** | Footnote: ¹**Ephesians 5:6, Colossians 3:6)**
>
> **3** "… among whom also we all once lived in the lusts of our flesh, doing the desires of the flesh and of the mind, and were by nature children of wrath, as also the rest. **4** But Elohim, who is rich in compassion, because of His great love with which He loved us, **5** even when we were dead in trespasses, made us alive together with Messiah—by favor you have been saved—**6** and raised us up together, and made us sit together in the heavenlies in Messiah יהושע, **7** in order to show in the coming

ages the exceeding riches of His favor in kindness toward us in Messiah **יהושע**. 8 For by favor you have been saved, through belief, and that not of yourselves, it is the gift of Elohim, 9 it is not by works, so that no one should boast." (**Ephesians 2:3-9**)

Yehovah has chosen you from amongst all the people on this earth and made the scales fall away from your eyes so you can see. You have not come to this understanding on your own. You have nothing to boast about. But if you do choose to boast, may it only be in the following context:

17 But "He who boasts, let him boast in **יהוה**." (**II Corinthians 10:17**)

Using the verses I cited recently (and others), Christian preachers and teachers now wrongly teach others that the Ten Commandments are done away with and they use the verses in Colossians (to give an example) as their basis.

Remember the words of Yehshua with regard to one being better off tying a millstone around his or her neck and taking the plunge versus misleading a little one? Take heed also of the warning issued in the following passage:

1 Not many of you should become teachers, my brothers, knowing that we shall receive the greater judgment. (**James 3:1**)

In other words, does this mean we are free to be lawless like Satan and have license to lie, steal, murder, worship idols, and commit adultery? Are we free, as Paul mentioned, to do evil so Yehovah may bring good from it? If so, should we even, on this basis, be allowed into Yehovah's Kingdom? And yet this is exactly what "good Christians" claim—that they do not have to keep The Law.

We would also do well to remember what Yehovah's view of an unprofitable servant is and how we provoke Him to jealousy when we take the words of Paul and misapply them (v. 23 especially):

21 You are not able to drink the cup of the Master and the cup of demons, you are not able to partake of the table of the Master and of the table of demons. 22 Do we provoke the Master to jealousy? Are we stronger than He? 23 All is permitted me (all is lawful), but not all do profit (but not all is profitable). All is permitted me (all is lawful), but not all build up. 24 Let no one seek his own, but each one that of the other. (**I Corinthians 10:21-24**)

Here are a few more unprofitable servant verses as food for thought: Matthew 18:25, 20:1-16, 14-30, Luke 17:7-10.

So, the answer is "no." We are still commanded to keep The Commandments. It was only *the debt* for breaking The Commandments that was nailed to the tree. The debts have been paid for; for those who repent. You must be doing the commandments at His return to receive your reward. But for those who do not repent:

> **11** "He acting unjustly, let him still act unjustly. And the filthy, let him be filthy still. And the righteous, let him be righteous still. And the holy, let him be holy still. **12** And behold, I am coming quickly, and My reward *is* with Me, to give to each according as his work is. **13** I am the Alpha and the Omega, the Beginning and the Ending, the First and the Last. **14** Blessed *are* they who do His commandments, that their authority will be over the Tree of Life, and they may enter in by the gates into the city. **15** But outside *are* the dogs, and the sorcerers, and the fornicators (i.e. violators of the 7th Commandment) and the murderers, (i.e. violators of the 6th Commandment) and the idolaters, (i.e. violators of the 1st & 2nd Commandments) and everyone who loves and makes a lie (i.e. violators of the 9th Commandment)." (**Revelation 22:11-15**)

You will notice that those who DO His Commandments will be over the Tree of Life and allowed entrance into the Holy City of His Kingdom. But outside are those who do not keep The Commandments.

Humans can only be saved by the grace of Yehovah, through the blood sacrifice of Yehshua. There is *nothing* that we can ever possibly do to save ourselves. We don't have the power to do it, and no amount of "law keeping," "righteous acts," "Levitical rituals," or "works" can possibly make Yehovah owe us anything or make it so He is in our debt. To the contrary! We will always forever be in His debt, come what may and no matter how great our achievements or how much we accomplish here on earth. We can't *earn* our salvation, in other words. Our salvation is made possible *only* by His grace, but *whether or not* we will be saved depends upon our repentance and obedience to Yehovah and His Commandments.

Yehovah isn't going to grant His gift of eternal life to those who refused on earth to obey Him (which would, in effect, create more rebellious, immortal, devilish individuals in His Kingdom who, like Satan, chose for themselves not to obey Yehovah, and who, worse yet, taught others not to obey Him). If that were allowed, the same people who made life a living hell on earth for the rest of us would be in the same business of making life in Yehovah's Kingdom a living hell for everyone there also. There would still be tears and all manner of evil if this ended up being the case. To prevent this outcome, the unrepentant lawless and the unrepentant teachers of lawlessness (who the lawless ones follow), are going to find themselves in the Lake of Fire, right along with the wicked and lawless Satan.

> **17** "Do not think that I have come to destroy the Law (Torah) or the Prophets. I have not come to destroy but to fulfill (complete). **18** For truly I say to you, until the heaven and the earth pass away, not one jot or one tittle shall in any way pass from the Law (Torah) until all is fulfilled.' **19** Therefore whoever shall relax one of these commandments, the least, and shall teach men so, he shall be called the least in the kingdom of Heaven. But whoever shall do and teach *them*, the same shall be called great in the kingdom of Heaven." (**Matthew 5:17-19**)

Chapter 11 | "But Why Do You Call Me 'Lord, Lord?'"

How true the words of Peter ring in the following passage:

> 15 "… and reckon the patience of our Master as deliverance, as also our beloved brother Sha'ul (Paul) wrote to you, according to the wisdom given to him, 16 as also in all *his* letters, speaking in them concerning these *matters*, in which some are hard to understand, which those who are untaught and unstable twist to their own destruction, as they do also the other Scriptures." (**II Peter 3:15-16**)

> 17 You, then, beloved ones, being forewarned, watch, lest you also fall from your own steadfastness, being led away with the delusion of the lawless, 18 but grow in the favor and knowledge of our Master and Savior יהושע Messiah. To Him be the esteem both now and to a day that abides. Amĕn. (**II Peter 3:17-18**)

We are warned not to be led down the slippery slope of lawlessness or led astray by those who teach us to do away with The Law.

I find it very ironic that Christians feel "commissioned" to convert the Jews to Christianity. They are, in fact, trying to get the Jew who may very well already be keeping The Law to follow *another* "messiah" who is said to have "done away" with The Law. If only those who profess to be "Christian" would come to realize what Yehshua the Messiah actually *did* say, they would be mortified over the grave ramifications of believing the delusion of lawlessness themselves and trying to win others over into believing this very same delusion. It is not the Jew who needs to convert to Christianity, but it is the Christian who needs to return to keeping Torah—just as the Messiah, who was without sin, kept Torah. Keeping Torah is what made Yeshua sinless. If He had broken it, in even the smallest of ways, He would not have been a perfect Sacrifice for us. So if that is what made Yeshua sinless, would it not be the same for us?

I have to say that again:

It is not the Jew who needs to convert to Christianity, but it is the Christian who needs to return to keeping Torah.

This could not be more clearly and poignantly illustrated than it is in the story of the Prodigal Son. The son who went away and squandered his inheritance is symbolic of those of us who have been scattered, (The Ten Lost Tribes) but also, even more so, those of us who profess to be Christian or "Christ followers" and yet openly embrace and condone lawlessness. Conversely, the son who remained at home with his father is representative of the Jews. The Jews may be still waiting for the Messiah's first coming, not having recognized Him when He was walking amongst them, true. In addition, they may not be 100% right in the way that they go about keeping the Law- that has already been pointed out in previous chapters. However, unlike so many who call themselves "Christians" at least the Jewish people are still acknowledging the fact that Yehovah has a standard that He designed for us to observe and guard. That standard is called Torah; that is the Law, the Ten Commandments and the Holy Days. The Christian "Prodigal Son" has done *everything "but"* keep The Law and some are only just now waking up to *how wrong* they have been.

> 11 And He said, "A certain man had two sons, 12 and the younger of them said to his father, 'Father, give me the portion of goods falling *to me.*' And he divided his livelihood between them. 13 And not many days after, the younger son, having gathered all together, went away to a distant country, and there wasted his goods with loose living. 14 And when he had spent all, there arose a severe scarcity of food throughout that land, and he began to be in need. 15 And he went and joined himself to one of the citizens of that country, and he sent him to his fields to feed pigs. 16 And he was longing to fill his stomach with the pods which the pigs were eating, and no one gave to him." (Luke 15:11-16)

> 17 "But having come to himself, he said, 'How many of my father's hired servants have bread enough and to spare, and I am perishing with hunger!' 18 Having risen, I shall go to my father and say to him, 'Father, I have sinned against the heaven, and before you, 19 and I am no longer worthy to be called your son. Make me like one of your hired servants.' 20 And having risen, he went to his father. And while he was still a long way off, his father saw him and was moved with compassion, and ran

and fell on his neck and kissed him. **21** And the son said to him, 'Father, I have sinned against the heaven, and before you, and I am no longer worthy to be called your son.' **22** But the father said to his servants, 'Bring out the best robe and put it on him, and put a ring on his hand and sandals on his feet. **23** And bring the fattened calf here and slaughter it, and let us eat and rejoice, **24** because this son of mine was dead and is alive again, and he was lost and is found.' And they began to rejoice." **(Luke 15:17-24)**

25 "And his older son was in the field, and when he came and approached the house, he heard music and dancing. **26** And having called one of the servants he asked what this meant. **27** And he said to him, 'Your brother has come, and your father has slaughtered the fattened calf because he received him back in health.' **28** And he was wroth and would not go in. So his father came out and pleaded with him. **29** And answering, he said to his father, 'See, these many years I have been serving you, and I have never transgressed a command of yours, but to me you have never given a young goat, so I could rejoice with my friends. **30** But when this son of yours came, who has devoured your livelihood with whores, you slaughtered the fattened calf for him.' **31** Then he said to him, 'Son, you are always with me, and all I have is yours. **32** And we had to rejoice and be glad, for your brother was dead and is alive, and was lost and is found.'" **(Luke 15:25-32)**

As I have already shown you, sin *is* the transgression of The Law.

In keeping with what this chapter is all about, you find Yehshua asking a question to end all questions in the passage from Luke below:

46 "But why do you call Me 'Master, Master,' and do not do what I say?"[1] **(Luke 6:46** | Footnote: [1]see vv. 47-49, **Matthew 7:24-28, Luke 8:21, John 3:36, James 2:17-24)**

Yehshua also goes on to say:

47 "Everyone who is coming to Me, and is hearing My words and is doing them, I shall show you whom he is like: **48** He is like a man building a house, who dug deep and laid a foundation on the rock. And when a flood came, the stream burst against that house, but was unable to shake it, for it was founded on the rock." **(Luke 6:47-48)**

20 And it was reported to Him, saying, "Your mother and Your brothers are standing outside, wishing to see You." **21** And He answering, said to them, "My mother and My brothers are those who are hearing the Word of Elohim and doing it." **(Luke 8:20-21)**

The passages referenced above are perfect examples of those who keep The Commandments that we spoke about in a chapter 10. In chapter 10 we discussed the two greatest commandments that both Yeshua and the Apostle Paul made notable mention of from Exodus chapter 20. The passage below, however, pertains to those who are hearers of Yehovah's Word but not doers. They do not keep His Commandments- and note the results: The foundation is not there (The Commandments) and thus, the house falls.

> **49** "But the one hearing and not doing, is like a man who built a house on the earth without a foundation, against which the stream burst, and immediately it fell. And the ruin of that house was great." (**Luke 6:49**)

Attending church once a week with a Bible in hand will not be what saves you. You must also obey what the Bible says—to where it becomes a permeating, pivotal and foundational part of your normal, everyday life; in other words, a lifestyle or your way of life.

> **36** "He who believes in the Son possesses everlasting life, but he who does not obey the Son shall not see life, but the wrath of Elohim remains on him." (**John 3:36**)

> **17** So also belief, if it does not have works, is in itself dead. **18** But someone might say, "You have belief, and I have works." Show me your belief without your works, and I shall show you my belief by my works. **19** You believe that Elohim is one. You do well. The demons also believe—and shudder! **20** But do you wish to know, O foolish man, that the belief without the works is dead? **21** Was not Aḇraham our father declared right by works when he offered Yitsḥaq (Isaac) his son on the altar? **22** Do you see that the belief was working with his works, and by the works the belief was perfected? **23** And the Scripture was filled which says, "Aḇraham believed Elohim, and it was reckoned to him for righteousness." And he was called, "Elohim's friend." **24** You see, then, that a man is declared right by works, and not by belief alone. **25** In the same way, was not Raḥaḇ the whore also declared right by works when she received the messengers and sent them out another way? **26** For as the body without the spirit is dead, so also the belief is dead without the works. (**James 2:17-26**)

Yehshua brings this chapter of my book into even sharper focus in the passage below. He gives us even more reason to sit up, take note and, like the demons, shudder.

15 "But beware of the false prophets, who come to you in sheep's clothing, but inwardly they are savage wolves. **16** By their fruits you shall know them. Are grapes gathered from thornbushes or figs from thistles? **17** So every good tree yields good fruit, but a rotten tree yields wicked fruit. **18** A good tree is unable to yield wicked fruit, and a rotten tree to yield good fruit. **19** Every tree that does not bear good fruit is cut down and thrown into the fire. **20** So then, by their fruits you shall know them." (**Matthew 7:15-20**)

21 "Not everyone who says to Me, 'Master, Master,' shall enter into the reign of the heavens, but he who is doing the desire of My Father in the heavens. **22** Many shall say to Me in that day, 'Master, Master, have we not prophesied in Your Name, and cast out demons in Your Name, and done many mighty works in Your Name?' **23** And then I shall declare to them, 'I never knew you, depart from Me, you who work lawlessness!' **24** Therefore everyone who hears these words of Mine, and does them, shall be like a wise man who built his house on the rock, **25** and the rain came down, and the floods came, and the winds blew and beat on that house, and it did not fall, for it was founded on the rock. **26** And everyone who hears these words of Mine, and does not do them, shall be like a foolish man who built his house on the sand, **27** and the rain came down, and the floods came, and the winds blew, and they beat on that house, and it fell, and great was its fall." **28** And it came to be, when יהושע had ended these words, that the people were astonished at His teaching, **29** for He was teaching them as one possessing authority, and not as the scribes. (**Matthew 7:21-29**)

There will be people in the Last Days who will make these kinds of unfounded claims to Yehovah and wholly BELIEVE them to be true—for they lived their lives *sincerely* believing they worked miracles and did wonderful works in the name of Jesus and fully expect and are convinced they are deserving and worthy of the resultant eternal rewards. But Yeshua tells them not only that He "NEVER KNEW" them, but in an even more disconcerting manner, declares to them, "Depart from Me, you who work lawlessness!"

How is it possible for so many that profess to be His true followers to be so deceived? Is it *really true* what the Bible says on this—that it's entirely possible those who speak so often of the Lord to others, are deceived as to the "lord" they are actually serving?! Are you serving the lord Satan who appears as an "angel of light" and who loves to be mistaken for the Messiah Himself or are you serving the *actual* Messiah—Yeshua Ha'Mashiach? How can you tell the difference and how do you know? Do you "talk the talk" but fail to "walk the walk?" Which brings us to the real crux of the matter—*will* you obey His Commandments—*or not*?

Careful examination of this critical subject will, no doubt, offend many who claim to be "believers," "deliverers" and "healers." But is it not better to face the truth *now*, while there is still time to repent and obtain forgiveness and correction from Yehovah the Most High, with regard to any delusions Satan has you believing, than to have Yehshua look you in the eye one fateful day and say, "I NEVER KNEW YOU: Depart from Me, you who work lawlessness?!"

Is it possible there are those among us who *appear* to be doing the Lord's works that are actually NOT of Him? The Word of Yehovah not only says it's possible, but clearly predicts it *WILL* happen:

> **13** For such are false emissaries, deceptive workers, masquerading as emissaries of Messiah. **14** And no wonder! For Satan himself masquerades as a messenger of light! **15** It is not surprising, then, if his servants also masquerade as servants of righteousness, whose end shall be according to their works! (**II Corinthians 11:13-15**)

> **1** But there also came to be false prophets among the people, as also among you there shall be false teachers, who shall secretly bring in destructive heresies, and deny the Master who bought them, bringing swift destruction on themselves. **2** And many shall follow their destructive ways, because of whom the way of truth shall be evil spoken of, **3** and in greed, with fabricated words, they shall use you for gain. From of old their judgment does not linger, and their destruction does not slumber. (**II Peter 2:1-3**)

> **17** Now I call upon you, brothers, watch out for those who cause divisions and stumbling, contrary to the teaching which you learned, and turn away from them. **18** For such ones do not serve our Master יהושע Messiah, but their own stomach, and by smooth words and flattering speech they deceive the hearts of the innocent. (**Romans 16:17-18**)

> **6** I marvel that you are so readily turning away from Him who called you in the favor of Messiah, to a different 'Good News,' **7** which is not another, only there are some who are troubling you and wishing to pervert the Good News of Messiah. **8** However, even if we, or a messenger out of heaven, bring a 'Good News' to you beside what we announced to you, let him be accursed. **9** As we have said before, and now I say again, if anyone brings a 'Good News' to you beside what you have received, let him be accursed. (**Galatians 1:6-9**)

They were hearing another gospel from a false preacher.

The only faith that is true is that which originates from Yehovah and is born of His Word and not the teachings of man.

> 3 Beloved ones, making all haste to write to you concerning our common deliverance, I felt the necessity to write to you urging you to earnestly contend for the belief which was once for all delivered to the set-apart ones. 4 For certain men have slipped in, whose judgment was written about long ago, wicked ones perverting the favor of our Elohim for indecency, and denying the only Masterיהוה and our Master יהושע Messiah. (**Jude 1:3-4**)

Do not be ignorant. Instead, heed the warning found in II Corinthians:

> 11 "... lest Satan should take advantage of us, for we are not ignorant of his thoughts." (**II Corinthians 2:11**)

Satan appears as an angel of light, and so do false preachers of whom Yehovah says, "their ends will be according to their works." Yet, on the surface it appears they are doing good works for Yehovah, as they will profess to Him as much in that day. Were they just deceiving themselves?

> 13 For such are false emissaries, deceptive workers, masquerading as emissaries of Messiah. 14 And no wonder! For Satan himself masquerades as a messenger of light! 15 It is not surprising then, if his servants also masquerade a servants of righteousness, whose end shall be according to their works! (**II Corinthians 11:13-15**)

Another Bible translation of the excerpt quoted on the previous page and directly above of one of Paul's Epistles to those at Corinth, states that Satan's ministers will be transformed into, or appears as, "ministers of righteousness."

> 3 "Let no one deceive you in any way, because the falling away is to come first, and the man of lawlessness[1] is to be revealed, the son of destruction ..." [**II Thessalonians 2:3** | Footnote: [1]Some texts read sin instead of lawlessness. This man might be the same one we read of in the prophecy in **Isaiah 14:12**—Hĕlĕl ("Heileil"), meaning "the shining one," the sovereign of Baḇel]
>
> 4 "... who opposes and exalts himself above all that is called Elohim or that is worshipped, so that he sits as Elohim in the Dwelling Place of Elohim, showing himself that he is Elohim." (**II Thessalonians 2:4**)

7 "For the secret of lawlessness is already at work—only until he who now restrains comes out of the midst. 8 And then the lawless one shall be revealed, whom the Master shall consume with the Spirit of His mouth and bring to naught with the manifestation of His coming. 9 The coming of the *lawless one* is according to the working of Satan, with all power and signs and wonders of falsehood, 10 and with all deceit of unrighteousness in those perishing, because they did not receive the love of the truth, in order for them to be saved. 11 And for this reason Elohim sends them a working of delusion, for them to believe the falsehood ..."[1] (**II Thessalonians 2:7-11**| Footnote: [1]**Ezekiel 20:25**; **John 9:39, 12:40; Acts 7:42; Romans 1:24-28**)

12 "... in order that all should be judged who did not believe the truth, but have delighted in the unrighteousness." (**II Thessalonians 2:12**)

Are you in that group? Should we forgo following Paul's advice to the church at Corinth?

5 Examine yourselves whether you are in the belief—prove yourselves. Or do you not know yourselves, that יהושע Messiah is in you,[1] unless you are disapproved? (**II Corinthians 13:5** | Footnote: [1]**Romans 8:10, Galatians 2:20, Ephesians 3:17, Colossians 1:27, I John 4:4**)

This is *still valid* for all of us today. It is the quicksand and quagmire of "cheap grace" that has given rise to such deceptions and caused those who are "in ministry" to be operating under the false assumption they are, in truth, saved and in all actuality, serving Yehovah.

How, then, are we to "DISCERN" truth from error?

20 To the Torah and to the witness! If they do not speak according to this Word, it is because they have no daybreak (*light*). (**Isaiah 8:20**)

14 Blessed are those doing His commands, so that the authority shall be theirs unto the Tree of Life, and to enter through the gates into the city. (**Revelation 22:14**)

15 But outside are the dogs and those who enchant with drugs, and those who whore, and the murderers, and the idolaters, and all who love and do falsehood.[1] (**Revelation 22:15** | Footnote: [1]See also, **Revelation 21:27, II Thessalonians 2:11**)

Yehshua then asks His disciples a very thought-provoking question:

8 "I say to you that He shall do right to them speedily. But when the Son of Adam comes, shall He find the belief on the earth?" (**Luke 18:8**)

8 shall He find faith on the earth? (**Luje18:8 NKJV**)

Next, Paul issues a warning below:

3 "For there shall be a time when they shall not bear sound teaching, but according to their own desires, they shall heap up for themselves teachers tickling the ear..."[1] (**II Timothy 4:3** | Footnote: [1]**Isaiah 30:10, Jeremiah 5:31, Romans 16:18**)

4 "... and they shall indeed turn their ears away from the truth, and be turned aside to myths. **5** But you be sober in all *matters*, suffer hardships, do the work of an evangelist, accomplish your service completely." (**II Timothy 4:4-5**)

We also should now look at the parable of the Ten Virgins.

1 "Then the kingdom of heaven shall be likened to ten virgins who took their lamps and went out to meet the bridegroom.2 Now five of them were wise, and five were foolish.3 Those who were foolish took their lamps and took no oil with them,4 but the wise took oil in their vessels with their lamps.5 But while the bridegroom was delayed, they all slumbered and slept.6 And at midnight a cry was heard: 'Behold, the bridegroom is coming; go out to meet him!'7 Then all those virgins arose and trimmed their lamps. 8 And the foolish said to the wise, 'Give us some of your oil, for our lamps are going out. 9 'But the wise answered, saying, 'No, lest there should not be enough for us and you; but go rather to those who sell, and buy for yourselves. 10 'And while they went to buy, the bridegroom came, And those who were ready went in with him to the wedding; and the door was shut. 11 Afterward the other virgins came also, saying, 'Lord, Lord, open to us! 12 'But he answered and said, 'Assuredly, I say to you, I do not know you. 13 'Watch therefore, for you know neither the day nor the hour in which the Son of Man is coming. (**Mathew 25:1-13**)

In verse 12 Yehshua says, "I do not know you" in the exact same why He says to those in Mathew 7 that He "NEVER KNEW" them, but in chapter 7 He declares to them, "Depart from Me, you who work lawlessness!" "Never Knew" and "workers of lawlessness"; very strong words to be told for those who do not and will not keep the Commandments.

When all is said and done, Yehshua should always have the last word on *any* subject. Here is *that* word:

24 "For false messiahs and false prophets shall arise, and they shall show great signs and wonders, so as to lead astray, if possible, even the chosen ones. 25 See, I have forewarned you." (**Matthew 24:24-25**)

- **The Law is *not* done away with**
- **The soul who sins shall die**
- **Sin *is* the transgression of The Law**
- **The Law *is* the Ten Commandments**

If you're not keeping The Commandments—and this means *all* ten, then you will be told by Yehshua on Judgment Day: "I never knew you, depart from Me, you who work lawlessness!"

10 For whoever shall guard all the Torah, and yet stumble in one point, he is guilty of all. (**James 2:10**)

That being said, which commandment will you justify not keeping? For if you break one commandment, you break them all. We have already shown you where Yehshua said that if you loved Him, you would keep and guard the commandments.

So do you? Do you love the Messiah as you say you do and as He says how to do it? By keeping the commandments! Do you keep all Ten Commandments? Are you one of those who will say LORD, LORD and never knew Him? Are you one of those 5 foolish virgins?

KEEP THE COMMANDMENTS!

Chapter 12 | Why Does Satan Want To Hide the Fourth Commandment?

The answer is found in the Book of Daniel:

> **25** "… and it (Satan) speaks words against the Most High, and it wears out the set-apart ones of the Most High, and it intends to change appointed times[1] and law[2], and they are given into its hand for a time and times and half a time. (**Daniel 7:25** | Footnotes: [1]This is another word for festivals. [2]Changing the law amounts to lawlessness)

We read in II Thessalonians 2:3-12 about "the lawless one" and the "lawlessness" which is prophesied to take over (indeed, it has already taken over!) in the set-apart place, and we also read about Messiah's judgment upon the lawless "prophets" in Matthew 7:23, and the lawless "believers" in Matthew 13:41!

> **3** Let no one deceive you in any way, because the falling away is to come first, and the man of lawlessness is to be revealed, the sone of destruction, **4** who opposes and exalts himself above all that is called Elohim or that is worshipped, so that he sits as Elohim in the Dwelling Place of Elohim, showing himself that he is Elohim. **5** Do you not rememnber that I told this while I was still with you?
>
> **6** And now you know what restrains, for him to be revealed in his time. **7** For the secret of lawlessness is already at work-only until he who now retrains comes out of the midst. **8** And then the lawless one shall be revealed, whom the Master shall consume with the spirit of His mouth and bring to naught with the manifestation of His coming.
>
> **9** The coming of the Lawless one is according to the working of Satan, with all power and signs and wonders of falsehood, **10** and with all deceit of unrightesouness in those perishing, because they did not receive

the love of the truth, in order for them to be saved. 11 And for this reason Elohim sends them a working delusion, for them to believe the falsehood, 12 in order that all should be judged who did not believe the truth, but have delighted in unrighteousness. (2 Thessalonians 2:3-12)

41 The Son of Adam shall send out His messengers, and they shall gather out of His reign all the stumbling-blocks, and those doing lawlessness 42 and shall throw them into the furnace of fire-there shall be wailing and gnashing of teeth. (Mathew 13:41-42)

23 "And I shall declare to them, 'I never knew you, depart from me, you who work lawlessness!' (Mathew 7:23)

Satan's goal is to change the Appointed Times (Holy Days) and The Law. This is his intention. Why? So you will not know or understand the plan of Yehovah or when these things are to happen. Yet, it's critical that we all know Yehovah's plan for mankind and how it is foreshadowed (with regard to what is still yet to come) and laid out, in its entirety, in the Holy Days. But if you do not start keeping them, then you can't understand their significance.

Burying your head in the sand and pretending to ignore these truths only places you in the group of lawless workers, whom Yehshua said He does not know. It puts you in opposition to those who are obeying those laws and living by them.

How would Satan set out to prevent us from coming into this kind of understanding? I have already shown you how Judah has done this unknowingly. The Jewish scribes have changed each of the Holy Days, except Passover, by changing the start of the month, and then compounding this error by employing the Rules of Postponements for the Fall Feast Days.

Not to mention how Satan, who, through the Catholic Church, changed the weekly Sabbath from Saturday to Sunday and did away with the Holy Days altogether, has also deceived the Christian world.

Let me quote a number of reputable sources below so you can see this for yourself.

Sunday[63] was the first day of the week according to the Jewish method of reckoning, but for Christians it began to take the place of the Jewish Sabbath in Apostolic times as the day set apart for the public and solemn worship of God. The practice of meeting together on the first day of the week for the celebration of the Eucharistic Sacrifice is indicated in: Acts,

---

63 http://www.catholic.org/encyclopedia/view.php?id=11155

20:7 (and) I Corinthians 16:2. In Revelation 1:10, it is called the Lord's Day. In the Didache (p.14) the injunction is given: "On the Lord's Day come together and break bread. And give thanks (offer the Eucharist), after confessing your sins that your sacrifice may be pure." St. Ignatius (Ep. ad Magnes. ix. p.324) speaks of Christians as:

> We no longer keep the Sabbath, but we live a new life on the Lord's Day, on which also our life arose with him.[64]

In the Epistle of Barnabas (xv) we read: "Wherefore, also, we keep the eighth day (i.e., the first of the week) with joyfulness, the day also on which Jesus rose again from the dead.

Sabbath Confessions[65]

The Church ... after changing the day of rest from the Jewish Sabbath, or seventh day of the week, to the first, made the Third Commandment refer to Sunday as the day to be kept holy as the Lord's Day.

But since Saturday, not Sunday, is specified in the Bible, isn't it curious that non-Catholics who profess to take their religion directly from the Bible and not the Church, observe Sunday instead of Saturday? Yes, of course, it is inconsistent; but this change was made about fifteen centuries before Protestantism was born, and by that time the custom was universally observed. They have continued the custom, even though it rests upon the authority of the Catholic Church and not upon an explicit text in the Bible. That observance remains as a reminder of the Mother Church from which the non-Catholic sects broke away—like a boy running away from home but still carrying in his pocket a picture of his mother or a lock of her hair.

The Faith of Millions

> 5 "... and upon her forehead a name written, a secret: BABEL (BABYLON) THE GREAT, THE MOTHER OF THE WHORES (HARLOTS) AND OF THE ABOMINATIONS OF THE EARTH. (**Revelation 17:5**)

Perhaps the boldest thing, the most revolutionary change The Church ever did, happened in the 1st-century. The holy day, the Sabbath, was changed from Saturday to Sunday. "The Day of the Lord" (dies Dominica) was chosen, not from any directions noted in the Scriptures, but from the Church's sense of its own power. The day of resurrection, the day

---

64 http://tinyurl.com/9gzlj3j
65 *Roman Catholic Confessions*, http://www.scribd.com/doc/20509321/Sabbath-Confessions-Roman-Catholic-Confessions-Catholic-Encyclopedia-Vol-4-Pg, Vol.4; p.153

of Pentecost, fifty days later, came on the first day of the week. So this would be the new Sabbath. People who think that the Scriptures should be the sole authority, should logically become Seventh-Day Adventists, and keep Saturday holy.[66]

If Protestants would follow the Bible, they would worship God on the Sabbath Day. In keeping the Sunday, they are following a law of the Catholic Church.[67]

Nowhere in the Bible[68] is it stated that worship should be changed from Saturday to Sunday.... Now the Church ... instituted, by God's authority, Sunday as the day of worship. This same Church, by the same divine authority, taught the doctrine of Purgatory long before the Bible was made. We have, therefore, the same authority for Purgatory as we have for Sunday.

The observance of Sunday by the Protestants is homage they pay, in spite of themselves, to the authority of the (Catholic) Church.[69]

What Important Question Does the Papacy Ask Protestants?[70]

Protestants have repeatedly asked the papacy, "How could you dare to change God's law?" But the question posed to Protestants by the Catholic Church is even more penetrating. Here it is officially:

"You will tell me that Saturday was the Jewish Sabbath, but that the Christian Sabbath has been changed to Sunday. Changed! But by whom? Who has authority to change an express commandment of Almighty God? When God has spoken and said, Thou shalt keep holy the seventh day, who shall dare to say, Nay, thou mayest work and do all manner of worldly business on the seventh day; but thou shalt keep holy the first day in its stead?"

"This is a most important question, which I know not how you can answer. You are a Protestant, and you profess to go by the Bible and the Bible only; and yet in so important a matter as the observance of one day in seven as a holy day, you go against the plain letter of the Bible, and put another day in the place of that day which the Bible has commanded."

---

66 *Sentinel*, Pastor's Page, Saint Catherine Catholic Church, Algonac, Michigan, May 21st, 1995
67 Albert Smith, Chancellor of the Archdiocese of Baltimore, February 10th, 1920
68 *Things Catholics Are Asked About* by Martin J. Scott, 1927, p.136
69 *Plain Talk About the Protestantism of Today* by Monsignor Louis Segur, p.213
70 Library of Christian Doctrine: *Why Don't You Keep Holy the Sabbath-Day?* (London: Burns & Oates, Ltd.), pp. 3-4.

"The command to keep holy the Seventh Day is one of the Ten Commandments; you believe that the other nine are still binding; who gave you authority to tamper with the fourth? If you are consistent with your own principles, if you really follow the Bible and the Bible only, you ought to be able to produce some portion of the New Testament in which this Fourth Commandment is expressly altered."

"I have repeatedly offered $1,000 to anyone who can prove to me from the Bible alone that I am bound to keep Sunday holy. There is no such law in the Bible. It is a law of the holy Catholic Church alone.[71] The Bible says 'Remember the Sabbath day to keep it holy.' The Catholic Church says, 'No. By my divine power I abolish the Sabbath day and command you to keep holy the first day of the week.' And lo! The entire civilized world bows down in reverent obedience to the command of the Holy Catholic Church."

Again I ask the question, "Why would Satan want to hide or obscure the Fourth Commandment?"

After all, all Christians will maintain they try to keep all the other nine commandments. It is just the fourth one they will not do. And yet you have just read how the Catholic Church changed the Seventh Day Saturday Sabbath to Sunday and how it had no scriptural grounds by which to do so.

So why does Satan want to hide the Sabbath or cause it to be changed? Because the Sabbath (and the keeping of it) shows you the truth! ""What truth?" you ask": Let us now look and see exactly what truth it is Satan is hiding from you.

We read in Exodus a very important piece of information about the Sabbath. Moses is speaking to the Israelites about the Days of Unleavened Bread and Passover.

9 And it shall be as a sign to you on your hand and as a reminder between your eyes, that the Torah of יהוה is to be in your mouth, for with a strong hand יהוה has brought you out of Mitsrayim (Egypt). (**Exodus 13:9**)

13 "And you, speak to the children of Yisra'ĕl, saying, 'My Sabbaths you are to guard, by all means, for it is a sign between Me and you throughout your generations, to know that I, יהוה, am setting you apart.'" (**Exodus 31:13**)

The *only* sign of Yehovah setting us apart—the only sign of His everlasting

71 *American Sentinel* (New York Roman Catholic Journal) by Priest Thomas Enright, C.S.S.R., February 18th, 1884; June 1893, p.173

covenant—is His Sabbaths—one of them being the Seventh Day Sabbath. This is repeated in the following passages in Ezekiel:

> 12 And I also gave them My Sabbaths, to be a sign between them and Me, to know that I am יהוה who sets them apart. (**Ezekiel 20:12**)

> 19 I am יהוה your Elohim. Walk in My laws, and guard My right-rulings, and do them. 20 And set apart My Sabbaths, and they shall be a sign between Me and you, to know that I am יהוה your Elohim. (**Ezekiel 20:19-20**)

What is the sign between Yehovah and those who *truly* obey Him and know Him? It is the Sabbaths. Notice how this is plural—which means there is more than one. I am not just talking about the weekly Sabbath here. All the Appointed Times (Holy Days or Feast and Festival Days) are also called High Sabbaths. These are found as we have shown you in Leviticus 23.

It is when we keep the Sabbaths, that we are being set apart by Yehovah as Holy unto Him.

> 21 But the children rebelled against Me. They did not walk in My laws, and My right-rulings they did not guard to do them, which, if a man does, he shall live by them. They profaned My Sabbaths, so I resolved to pour out My wrath on them to complete My displeasure against them in the wilderness. (**Ezekiel 20:21**)

This verse above is speaking of you today. It is talking of those who *today* will not keep Yehovah's Sabbaths. Yet, we are told in the verse below we *are* to keep Yehovah's Sabbaths in every generation forever! In the previous chapter we read of how those who do not keep The Commandments, of which the fourth is one of them, will be called lawless and will be told, in no uncertain terms, to depart from Yehshua's presence. This is a very serious thing I am showing you.

> 16 And the children of Yisra'ĕl shall guard the Sabbath, to observe the Sabbath throughout their generations as an everlasting covenant 17 Between Me and the children of Yisra'ĕl it is a sign forever. For in six days יהוה made the heavens and the earth, and on the seventh day He rested and was refreshed. (**Exodus 31:16-17**)

Now I want you to notice something else—something that will shake you to the core once you see it. I have left out verse seven below on purpose to show you this truth. You can go and read it in your own Bible so you know I am not pulling the wool over your eyes or just giving you my own interpretation.

> **6** "And these Words which I am commanding you today shall be in your heart ..." (**Deuteronomy 6:6**)

> **8** "... and (you) shall bind them as a sign on your hand, and they shall be as frontlets between your eyes." (**Deuteronomy 6:8**)

Notice below what is said in Deuteronomy again about your heart, your hand and between your eyes.

> **18** "And you shall lay up these Words of Mine in your heart and in your being, and shall bind them as a sign on your hand, and they shall be as frontlets between your eyes." (**Deuteronomy 11:18**)

What was written in stone (literally) by Yehovah in Exodus 20, is reiterated by Moses in Deuteronomy below.

> **1** And Mosheh (Moses) called all Yisra'ĕl, and said to them, "Hear, O Yisra'ĕl, the laws and right-rulings which I speak in your hearing today. And you shall learn them, and guard to do them. **2** יהוה our Elohim made a covenant with us in Ḥorĕḇ. **3** יהוה did not make this covenant with our fathers, but with us, those who are here today, all of us who are alive. **4** יהוה spoke with you face to face on the mountain from the midst of the fire. **5** I stood between יהוה and you at that time, to declare to you the Word of יהוה—for you were afraid because of the fire, and you did not go up the mountain—saying: **6** 'I am יהוה your Elohim who brought you out of the land of Mitsrayim (Egypt), out of the house of bondage.'" (**Deuteronomy 5:1-6**)

> **7** "You have no other mighty ones against My face." (**Deuteronomy 5:7**)

> **8** "You do not make for yourself a carved image, any likeness of which is in the heavens above, or which is in the earth beneath, or which is in the waters under the earth, **9** you do not bow down to them nor serve them. For I, יהוה your Elohim, am a jealous Ĕl, visiting the crookedness of the fathers upon the children to the third and fourth generations of those who hate Me, **10** but showing kindness to thousands, to those who love Me and guard My commands." (**Deuteronomy 5:8-10**)

> **11** "You do not bring¹ the Name of יהוה your Elohim to naught, for יהוה does not leave him unpunished who brings His Name to naught." (**Deuteronomy 5:11** | Footnote: ¹Or lift up, or take)

12 "Guard the Sabbath day, to set it apart, as יהוה your Elohim commanded you. **13** Six days you labor, and shall do all your work, **14** but the seventh day is a Sabbath of יהוה your Elohim. You do not do any work—you, nor your son, nor your daughter, nor your male servant, nor your female servant, nor your ox, nor your donkey, nor any of your cattle, nor your stranger who is within your gates, so that your male servant and your female servant rest as you do. **15** And you shall remember that you were a slave in the land of Mitsrayim (Egypt), and that יהוה your Elohim brought you out from there by a strong hand and by an outstretched arm. Therefore, יהוה your Elohim commanded you to observe the Sabbath day." **(Deuteronomy 5:12-15)**

16 "Respect your father and your mother, as יהוה your Elohim has commanded you, so that your days are prolonged, and so that it is well with you on the soil which יהוה your Elohim is giving you." **(Deuteronomy 5:16)**

17 "You do not murder." **(Deuteronomy 5:17)**

18 "You do not commit adultery." **(Deuteronomy 5:18)**

19 "You do not steal." **(Deuteronomy 5:19)**

20 "You do not bear false witness against your neighbor." **(Deuteronomy 5:20)**

21 "You do not covet your neighbor's wife, nor do you desire your neighbor's house, his field, nor his male servant, nor his female servant, his ox, nor his donkey, or whatever belongs to your neighbor." **(Deuteronomy 5:21)**

22 "These Words (Commands) יהוה spoke to all your assembly, in the mountain from the midst of the fire, of the cloud, and of the thick darkness, with a loud voice, and He added no more. And He wrote them on two tablets of stone and gave them to me." **(Deuteronomy 5:22)**

Deuteronomy 6 and 11 command you to write The Commandments on your hand, on your heart, and in your mind (between your eyes). Now let us compare this to what Yehshua is found saying in the Gospel of Matthew below.

36 "Teacher, which is the great command in the Torah?" **37** And יהושע said to him, "You shall love יהוה your Elohim with all your heart, and with all your being, and with all your mind. **38** This is the first and great command." **(Matthew 22:36-38)**

The Greatest Commandment, which tells us how to love Yehovah—with all our heart, all our being and all our mind—is the First Commandment. Deuteronomy 6 and 11 closely mirror the First Commandment and mutually reinforce how we are to keep The Commandments.

> **18** "And you shall lay up these Words (Commands) of Mine in your heart and in your being, and shall bind them as a sign on your hand, and they shall be as frontlets between your eyes." **(Deuteronomy 11:18)**

Yehovah seeks to place His mark and His sign of the Sabbaths upon your hand, in your mind and to write them on your heart. That is, if you have chosen to be counted amongst those who will obey Him? This is His sign between Him and us as mentioned previously in Ezekiel as well as below in Ezekiel.

> **12** "And I also gave them My Sabbaths, to be a sign between them and Me, to know that I am יהוה who sets them apart." **(Ezekiel 20:12)**

Yehovah's mark sets us apart from the world and identify us as His set-apart and peculiar people.

But what has Satan done? He has hidden the Sabbath and done away with it so that those who want to follow Yehovah are not identified as His, but instead are identified as belonging to Satan. How? He has created a "holy day" that looks like the Sabbath but is not the Sabbath. It is called Sunday or any day that is not the Sabbath. It is any hallowed day *not found* in Leviticus 23. This includes Christmas, Easter, Thanksgiving, Chanukah, Good Friday, Lent, Halloween, Kwanzaa and any other day not written down in Leviticus 23.

> **16** And he causes all, both small and great, and rich and poor, and free and slave, to be given a mark upon their right hand or upon their foreheads. **(Revelation 13:16)**

Notice that Satan's mark is in the *same place* Yehovah's mark is. It is on the hand, which signifies the way you earn a living. Will you work on the Sabbath or not? Most Christians *will* work and play on the Saturday Sabbath and think nothing of the importance of this day. This is the mark of Satan on your hand—how you etch out a living and if you make a conscious choice to do those things in keeping with doing your own pleasure on the Sabbath.

Satan's mark is *also* between the eyes. This has to do with the way you think and also, how you choose to spend your time. Will you study and meditate on Yehovah's Word on the Sabbath or are you going to do your own pleasure on that day? Are you going to spend that day going to the movies or shopping? Or will you spend it watching pro-football, golfing or playing video games? Will you spend it cleaning the house, going to the car wash and doing laundry? Satan's mark is similar to Yehovah's mark and for some it is hard to tell the difference but there is a *huge* difference.

Again, the way in which you make a living is the mark on your hand. Satan's mark, however, has no regard for the Sabbath and will, for example, work on it and/or shop on it, engaging in both business and/or pleasure on the Sabbath. Yehovah's mark, on the other hand, demonstrates an immense level of regard for the Seventh Day Saturday Sabbath and does not engage in business of *any kind* on the Sabbath. It does not seek its own. But if Yehovah places someone in your path who is in a life or death predicament or has an urgent, pressing need, we are not at all weighed in the balance and found wanting for helping someone in need.

Yehovah's mark between the eyes then would include things like: studying Torah, teaching your children foundational Torah precepts, attending Sabbath services, praying, worshipping and praising Yehovah, doing no servile or mundane work of any kind, breaking bread together with family and friends (including the stranger among you if applicable), refraining from buying and selling.

The question being—now that you know this—*which* mark is on your hand and between your eyes? Whom will you serve from this day forward? Satan or Yehovah? This is the mark of Satan as mentioned in your bible. It looks like Yehovah's Sabbaths but it perverts them and has already changed them to other days not found in your bible.

Chapter 13 | The Appointed Times of Yehovah

> **1** And **יהוה** spoke to Mosheh (Moses), saying, **2** "Speak to the children of Yisra'ĕl, and say to them, 'The appointed times of **יהוה**, which you are to proclaim as set-apart gatherings, My appointed times, are these …'" (**Leviticus 23:1-2**)

You are about to read when Yehovah's Feast Days are. These are the days that mark us and set us apart as His and His alone. Therefore, it is important for us to know *when* they are and *how* to keep them. These days positively identify us as His as we obey Him and strive, to the best of our ability and level of understanding, to keep them. They MARK US! This is Yehovah's mark or His sign upon us.

I also will explain the meaning of each of these Holy Days as we go.

> **3** "Six days work is done, but the seventh day is a Sabbath of rest, a set-apart gathering. You do no work, it is a Sabbath to **יהוה** in all your dwellings." (**Leviticus 23:3**)

The very first Holy, Set Apart Feast of time mentioned in the passage above is the weekly Sabbath. It is from sunset to sunset, from Friday evening to Saturday evening when the sun sets. During this time, there is a special window of opportunity to spend quality time with Yehovah by reading His Word, studying teachings online, listening to teaching tapes, cds and audio files (e.g., mp3s), and possibly attending a local Sabbath service near you. It is also a time to pray and engage in a two-way discourse with you and the Creator. Prayer, of course is how we speak to Him. But we can only actively listen to Him and have ears to hear what He is saying to us when we read and meditate upon His Word. And it's only in actively reading and meditating upon His Word (which always must include obeying or doing His Word) that we even know how to pray or what to ask Him for without asking amiss.

Keeping the Sabbath on Saturday, the day Yehovah commands us to keep it, is not legalism but is something we do out of reverence, love and respect for Him and also, out of respect for ourselves—for if Yehovah, who is omnipotent, needed to rest after all of His work, all the more so do we. That being said, we might do well to look more deeply into what legalism *really is*—based on truth-versus popular opinion.

> A dictionary definition of legalism is, "a strict, literal or excessive conformity to the law or to a religious or moral code."A popular (underlying) meaning attached to the word today (however), is that *any form* of biblical law-keeping is legalism and therefore to be avoided. The word is used pejoratively, especially against such practices as keeping the Sabbath or adhering to other laws given in the Old Testament.

> However, this use of the word is incorrect. It is *not* legalistic to obey God's Laws correctly. To obey God's biblical commands in a proper attitude, such as His command to remember the Sabbath and keep it holy, is not legalism. To be legalistic is to *misuse* God's Laws in a way never intended.[72-73]

The weekly Sabbath as the day of rest is symbolic of the Seventh Millennial Day of Rest. We are currently in the Sixth Millennium and the seventh one is nearly upon us. It is during the Seventh Millennium that the Messiah will rule over the Earth and Satan will finally be locked away. There is much more you can learn about this day if you read what the footnote link mentioned #72 & #73 has to say on this.

Leviticus provides us with some specific details about each of our Appointed Times with Yehovah. The weekly Saturday Sabbath is our first scheduled appointment to meet with our Creator. Just consider this simple fact. You have an appointment with Yehovah, the Creator of the whole universe, the One in whom you live, move and have your being—just like you would have an important appointment to keep with your doctor or dentist, only with much farther reaching and serious implications involving cancellations, arriving late and no-shows. We come together each week on the Sabbath to learn about Yehovah.

---

72 http://www.ucg.org/booklet/sunset-sunset-gods-sabbath-rest/jesus-christ-and-sabbath/just-what-legalism/

73 http://www.ucg.org/booklet/sunset-sunset-gods-sabbath-rest/

Passover

As we continue to read Leviticus 23 we are shown other important appointments that we have each year annually to meet with Yehovah. The following are special times He has set up in advance and told us that on these days He will bring to pass special events that will change the face of history forever.

> **4** "These are the appointed times of יהוה, set-apart gatherings which you are to proclaim at their appointed times. **5** In the first month, on the fourteenth day of the month, between the evenings, is the Passover to יהוה." (**Leviticus 23:4-5**)

It is important to know when we are to begin our count to the 14th day of the First Month. This is when the Feast of Passover falls which is the next Feast/Holy Day that I will share with you. That is why I explained to you about the necessity of knowing when the month begins. It begins when the New Moon is first sighted after sunset. I also explained to you about the necessity of the barley being ripe in order for the first month to be declared. Once this is done, then we can begin the count to the fourteenth day.

From the same Sighted New Moon you then count fourteen days until the evening, which begins this special fourteenth day—sunset-to-sunset. On this fourteenth day, the special, without blemish, sacrificial male Passover Lamb is killed at 3pm in the afternoon. As we learn of the events of this day as they are recorded in the Bible, we shall then be able to see how everything that happened to Yehshua was also indicative of that which was done unto sacrificial lambs each year ever since this 'shadow' or 'type' was established by Yehovah through Moses at Mount Sinai and at the Exodus in the case of the Passover.

The sacrifice of the Passover Lamb ceremony depicts the exact events that were to happen in the future to Yehshua in precise detail. This is *why* it is so important for us to keep each of these Holy Days—so we can know when these events took place and are to take place (so that we might know *when* to be on the lookout for them) and most importantly, to learn what these events signify and their meaning, both in the past and in the future.

The Passover reminds us of the time at the end of the ten plagues of The Exodus and how the last one was when all the firstborn of Egypt died before Pharaoh finally let all of Yehovah's people go. It then later speaks to us concerning all the events the Messiah would suffer as He was put to death for our sins. The Passover Lamb was a sin offering for our sins.

The unblemished male animal represented (the Son) as the perfect, sinless sacrifice who died in our place, His death paying the penalty for our sins and reconciling us to (the Father). (The Son), who lived a perfect life as the unblemished Lamb of God, substituted His death for ours. In fact, His death was the only possible substitution for ours. His sacrifice became the payment for our sins.[74]

Each and every detail that took place on the 14th day of Nisan (the first month of the year) to both the lamb and the barley was lived out at the exact same time in the life of Yehshua. The lamb was inspected from the 10th day until the 14th. The lamb was killed at 3 P.M. on the 14th day. Yehshua died at 3 P.M. on the 14th. So was Yehshua and there are many others you can find and learn about.

The Days of Unleavened Bread

After the Passover sacrifice, we are told of the Days of Unleavened Bread.

> 6 "And on the fifteenth day of this month is the Festival of Unleavened Bread to יהוה—seven days you eat unleavened bread. 7 On the first day you have a set-apart gathering, you do no servile work. 8 And you shall bring an offering made by fire to יהוה for seven days. On the seventh day is a set-apart gathering, you do no servile work." (**Leviticus 23:6-8**)

That being said, now that Yehshua has long since paid the price for our sins as the Passover Lamb, how then do we continue to avoid sin or keep from sinning? This is what is exemplified by the removing of leaven out of our homes. Leaven is symbolic of that which puffs up, which is what sin does.

> The Days of Unleavened Bread remind us that with God's help we must remove and avoid all types of sin (symbolized by leaven) in all areas of our life.[75]

Paul warns us about leaven in Corinthians:

> 6 Your boasting is not good. Do you not know that a little leaven leavens the entire lump? 7 Therefore cleanse out the old leaven, so that you are

74 http://www.ucg.org/booklet/gods-holy-day-plan-promise-hope-all-mankind/passover-why-did-jesus-christ-have-die/
75 http://www.ucg.org/booklet/gods-holy-day-plan-promise-hope-all-mankind/feast-unleavened-bread-lesson-leaving-sin/

a new lump, as you are unleavened. For also Messiah, our Passover, was offered for us. **8** So then let us observe the festival, not with old leaven, nor with the leaven of evil and wickedness, but with the unleavened bread of sincerity and truth. (**I Corinthians 5:6-8**)

9 A little leaven leavens all the lump. (**Galatians 5:9**)

Below we find Yehshua admonishing His disciples:

11 "How is it that you do not understand that I did not speak to you concerning bread? But beware of the leaven of the Pharisees and Sadducees." **12** Then they understood that He did not say to beware of the *leaven of bread,* but of *the teaching* of the Pharisees and Sadducees. (**Matthew 16:11-12**)

6 And יהושע said to them, "Mind! And beware of the leaven of the Pharisees and Sadducees." (**Matthew 16:6**)

It was *during* this seven day Week of Unleavened Bread that Israel was granted safe passage through the Red Sea by the miracle of Yehovah; and the Egyptians, who represented sin, were removed from the picture with regard to pursuing Israel any further.

The Wave Sheaf Day

Most Christians would be quick to assume Pentecost to be the next Holy Day in line after Passover but they are mistaken. Yet it is very important that this next event in Yehovah's timeline be celebrated and observed. The ripe barley is a prerequisite for both Passover and this next event and must *already be in place* for the head of the year (or New Year) to be declared, providing one other condition is met—the New Crescent of the Moon having been sighted. Once both are in place, then one can fulfill the obligations of celebrating this event.

In other words, once the First Visible Sliver of the Moon is sighted and the barley is ripe (or almost ripe), *then* we count the fourteen days to Passover. We then count to the fifteenth day for the next event—the first day of the Feast of Unleavened Bread. This fifteenth day can land on any day of the week. It is important to know this because we are given a very specific command in this regard:

9 And יהוה spoke to Mosheh (Moses), saying, **10** "Speak to the children of Yisra'ĕl, and you shall say to them, 'When you come into the land which I give you, and shall reap its harvest, then you shall bring a sheaf of the first-fruits of your harvest to the priest. **11** And he shall wave the sheaf before יהוה, for your acceptance. On the morrow after the Sabbath the priest waves it. **12** And on that day when you wave the sheaf, you shall prepare a male lamb a year old, a perfect one, as a burnt offering to יהוה, **13** and its grain offering: two-tenths of an ĕphah of fine flour mixed with oil, an offering made by fire to יהוה, a sweet fragrance, and its drink offering: one-fourth of a hin of wine. **14** And you do not eat bread or roasted grain or fresh grain until the same day that you have brought an offering to your Elohim—a law forever throughout your generations in all your dwellings.'" **(Leviticus 23:9-14)**

On the morrow (or the Sunday) after the weekly Sabbath, we are to take the ripe barley and make a Wave Offering to Yehovah. Yehshua was the Passover Lamb and was killed on a Wednesday.[76-77] All of this information is crucial and treated with so little regard, if not altogether overlooked, by the Christian world. Yet, it is this very information that provides us with some very compelling information about the plan of Yehovah. Notice how there are two Wave Offerings. What does the Wave Offering in and of itself represent? What does the first Wave Offering symbolize?

It was on this day that Yehshua ascended to the Father to present the Wave Offering to Yehovah. The first Wave Offering were those saints who had risen from the grave the same time Yehshua did late that Sabbath afternoon—three days and three nights after He was laid in the tomb the Wednesday before.[78] These are the "First-Fruits" Yehshua took with Him and presented before Yehovah in the same way as the barley is presented as the first Wave Offering on that Sunday morning.

> **20** "... raised from the dead, and ... the first-fruit of those having fallen asleep." **(I Corinthians 15:20)**

In addition, the Wave-Sheaf Offering represented Yeshua who is, according to Scripture:

> **15** "... the likeness of the invisible Elohim, the firstborn of all creation." **(Colossians 1:15)**

---

76 The only years that had a Crescent Moon with the fourteenth day being on a Wednesday was A.D. 28 and A.D. 31 This leaves no room for *any other year* for the crucifixion.
77 *THE GLORY OF YAHWEH AND THE GLORY OF KINGS*
http://www.sightedmoon.com/?page_id=23
78 *The Sign of Jonah*: http://www.sightedmoon.com/?page_id=19 & http://www.ucg.org/doctrinal-beliefs/son-man-will-be-three-days-and-three-nights-heart-earth/

18 "… the Head of the body, the assembly, Who is the beginning, the firstborn from the dead." (**Colossians 1:18**)

The Holy Days have meanings that build upon each other. Together, they progressively reveal how Yehovah works with humanity.

Passover symbolizes the Messiah's giving of Himself for us so our sins could be forgiven. Whereas the Days of Unleavened Bread teach us that we must remove and avoid sin, whether in our actions or attitudes. The Wave offering shows us that those who lived before and obeyed have now ascended to heaven.

The Feast of Pentecost

The next festival and Holy Day, Pentecost, builds on this important foundation. This festival is known by several names that derive from its meaning and timing. Also known as the Feast of Harvest:

> **16** "… and the Festival of the Harvest, the first-fruits of your labors which you have sown in the field; and the Festival of Ingathering (Sukkot) at the outgoing of the year, when you have gathered in the fruit of your labors from the field." (**Exodus 23:16**)

Pentecost also represents the First-Fruits in a similar fashion as the Wave Sheaf did during the Days of Unleavened Bread.

> **26** "And on the day of the first-fruits, when you bring a new grain offering to יהוה at your Festival of Weeks, you have a set-apart gathering, you do no servile work." (**Numbers 28:26**)

It is also called the Feast of Weeks:

> **22** "And perform the Festival of Weeks for yourself, of the first-fruits of wheat harvest, and the Festival of Ingathering (Sukkot) at the turn of the year." (**Exodus 34:22**)

This name comes from the seven weeks plus one day (fifty days in all) that are counted to determine when to celebrate this festival:

> **16** "Until the morrow after the seventh Sabbath you count fifty days, then you shall bring a new grain offering to יהוה." (**Leviticus 23:16**)

The most popular name for this festival is the Feast of Weeks, or Shavuot, in Hebrew. When celebrating this festival, it is one of the greatest events in history—Yehovah's revealing of The Law at Mount Sinai.

Similarly, in the New Testament, which was written in Greek, this festival is known as Pentecost (*Pentekostos* in the original), which means "50ᵗʰ."[79] But Pentecost (isn't) just (a) picture (o)f the giving of The Law; it also shows—through a great miracle that occurred (during) the very first Pentecost in the early church—how to keep the *spiritual intent* of God's Laws. God chose the first Pentecost after (the Messiah's) resurrection to pour out His Holy Spirit on 120 believers.[80]

15 "And in those days Kĕpha (Peter), standing up in the midst of the taught ones—and there was a gathering of about a hundred and twenty ..." (**Acts 1:15**)

1 And when the Day of the Festival of Weeks had come, they were all with one mind in one place. 2 And suddenly there came a sound from the heaven, as of a rushing mighty wind, and it filled all the house where they were sitting. 3 And there appeared to them divided tongues, as of fire, and settled on each one of them. 4 And they were all filled with the Set-Apart Spirit and began to speak with other tongues, as the Spirit gave them to speak. (**Acts 2:1-4**)

But the Feast of Weeks or Pentecost has another teaching enshrouded in it. As the second Wave Offering, it shows us when the next group of saints will be raised up in the near future.[81] This is the importance of the second Wave Offering. Just as the first Wave Offering during the Days of Unleavened Bread represented the raising up of the saints who had lived and died up to the time of Yehshua's first coming, Pentecost represents the day and time when those who have lived *since* the first Wave Offering will meet Him in the heavens during His Second Coming.

The Feast of Trumpets

The next appointment and set apart gathering you would do well to learn more about is the Feast of Trumpets or Yom Teruah.[82] Remember, learning

79 *Vine's Complete Expository Dictionary of Old & New Testament Words* by W.E. Vine, 1985, "Pentecost"
80 http://www.ucg.org/booklet/gods-holy-day-plan-promise-hope-all-mankind/feast-pentecost-firstfruits-gods-harvest/
81 *Pentecost's Hidden Meaning* http://www.sightedmoon.com/?page_id=21
82 http://www.ucg.org/booklet/gods-holy-day-plan-promise-hope-all-mankind/feast-trumpets-turning-point-history/

about the "what" of any given Feast helps you to better understand the "Who" of Yehovah; the Father of all humanity and the author of all the Appointed Times.

> **23** And יהוה spoke to Mosheh (Moses), saying, **24** "Speak to the children of Yisra'ĕl, saying, 'In the seventh month, on the first day of the month, you have a rest, a remembrance of blowing of trumpets, a set-apart gathering. **25** You do no servile work, and you shall bring an offering made by fire to יהוה.'" (**Leviticus 23:23-25**)

It was on this day Yehshua was born on September 11th, 3 B.C.[83] and it will be on this day He will come again to begin the judgment of the rest of mankind.

VII. The Day of Christ's Birth[84]

A. The key is symbolically hidden in Revelation:

> **1** "A great sign (astrological) appeared in heaven: a woman (constellation Virgo the Virgin which is the only sign of a Woman which exists along the ecliptic) clothed with the Sun (the Supreme Father is mid-bodied in Virgo), and the Moon (also a symbol for a Woman; see Genesis 37:9-10) under her feet, and on her head, a crown of twelve stars (in *Norton's Star Atlas* there are twelve visible stars around Virgo's head). (**Revelation 12:1**)

(1) Pi, (2) Nu, (3) Beta (near the ecliptic), (4) Sigma, (5) Chi, (6) Iota –these six stars form the Southern Hemisphere around the head of Virgo. Then there are (7) Theta, (8) Star 60, (9) Delta, (10) Star 93, (11) Beta (the 2nd magnitude star), (12) Omicron—these last six form the Northern Hemisphere around the head of Virgo. All these stars are visible ones that could have been seen by observers).

> **2** "... and she was with child (Virgin Mary pregnant with God's only begotten Son); and she cried out, being in labor and in pain to give birth." (**Revelation 12:2**)

> **3a.** "And another sign (astrological) appeared in heaven: and behold, a great red dragon ..." (**Revelation 12:3**)

(This) is represented by one of the Decans of Leo; "... whose length

---

83 *Conjunction or Sighted Which?* http://www.sightedmoon.com/?page_id=22
84 http://www.versebyverse.org/doctrine/birthofchrist.html

stretches 1/3 of the way around the whole zodiacal sphere, completely expelled from the places into which he had intruded, fleeing now for his life, and the great Lion, with claws and jaws extended, bounding in terrific fury and seizing the foul monster's neck.")[85]

> **3b.** "... having seven heads and ten horns, and on his heads were seven diadems." **(Revelation 12:3)**

> **4** And his tail swept away 1/3 of the stars of heaven, (fall of angels) and threw them to the earth. And the dragon stood before the woman who was about to give birth (in person of Herod the Great), so that when she gave birth he might devour her. **5** And she gave birth to a Son (Messiah), a male child, who is to rule all the nations with a rod of iron; and her child was caught up to God (ascension) and to His throne. **(Revelation 12:4-5)**

B. **The astronomical synchronism of this sign in the year of (the Messiah's) birth in 3 B.C.**

1. Virgo occupies, in (bodily) form, a space of about 50° along the ecliptic (The head of the Woman actually bridges some 10° into the previous sign of Leo and her feet overlap about 10° into the following sign of Libra the Scales).
2. In the year of (the Messiah's) birth, the Sun entered the head-position of the Woman about August 13th, and exited her feet about October 2nd.
3. But the apostle John saw the (configuration in which) the Sun "clothed" the Woman (to be mid-bodied), and this happens between ... 150° and 170° along the ecliptic, which occurs over about a 20-day period each year, which in 3 B.C. was from about August 27th–September 15th.
4. If John in the Book of Revelation (was) associating the birth of (the Messiah) with the period when the Sun is mid-bodied to the Woman, then (the Messiah) would have been born within this 20-day period. From the point of view of the Magi back in their homes in Babylon, this would have been the only logical sign under which the Jewish Messiah might be born. Especially if He were to be born of a virgin (Even today, astrologers recognize that the sign of Virgo is the one which has reference to a messianic world ruler to be born of a virgin).[86]

C. **The key to the very day of Jesus' birth is the words, "and the moon under her feet."**

1. The word "under" signifies that the Woman's feet were positioned just over the Moon.
2. Since the feet of Virgo represent the last 7° of the constellation (in

---

85 *The Gospel In the Stars* by Seiss, p. 135
86 Encyclopedia of Astrology by Devore, p. 366).

the time of Christ this would have been between about 180° and 187° along the ecliptic), the Moon has to be positioned somewhere under the 7° arc.

3. But the Moon also has to be in that exact location when the Sun is mid-bodied to Virgo.

4. In the year 3 B.C., these two factors came to precise agreement for less than two hours, as observed from Palestine, on September 11th.

5. The precise arrangement began about 6:15p.m. (sunset), and lasted until 7:45p.m. (moonset). This is the only day in the whole year that this could have taken place.

6. One day before (September 10th) the Moon was located mid-calf, while one day beyond (Sept. 11th) the Moon had moved so far beyond the feet of the Virgin that it was positioned at least 25 diameters (middle widths) of the Moon to the east of her feet.

7. This then, was the situation that prevailed in the heavens on the evening of the nativity when the angel announced (the Messiah's) birth to the shepherds out under the evening sky (Luke 2:8-11).

8. Apparently (the Messiah) was born in the evening, and Revelation 12 shows that it was a New Moon Day (the day the Moon first appears as a thin crescent. (Each) of the twelve months began with a New Moon).

VIII. The Birth of Christ & the Day of Trumpets

A. The further significance of September 11th, 3 B.C.

1. It was Tishri 1 on the Jewish Calendar.

2. Tishri 1 is none other than the Jewish New Year's day (Nisan 1 was the beginning of the Jewish Ecclesiastical Year. In 3 B.C. this fell on March 18th).

3. Otherwise known as Rosh sha'shanah, or as the Bible calls it, the Day of Trumpets (Leviticus 23:23-25).

4. This is amazing. Almost too amazing! What a significant day for the appearance of the Messiah on earth! To (the) Jewish people this would have been a profound occasion indeed!

5. There could have hardly have been a better day in the calendar of the Jews to introduce the Messiah to the world than the first day of the civil year.

6. Sundown on September 11th, 3 B.C. (6p.m.), was the beginning of Rosh sha'shanah (The Messiah was born very soon after 6p.m. when the day changed from Elul 30 to Tishri 1).

Interestingly enough, this is also the first day of the Ten Days of Awe.[87] This does not come as a coincidence to me at all. Unfortunately, this is the day so many Christians talk about but never contextually understand what they

---

87 *Understanding the 10 Days Of Awe* http://www.sightedmoon.com/?page_id=255

are saying because they do not keep this day. Last, but not least, this is the day that is spoken of in Scriptures as the day and hour "no man can know."

> 36 "But concerning that day and the hour no one knows, not even the messengers of the heavens, but My Father only." (**Matthew 24:36**)

The reason no one can know the day or the hour of the Messiah's triumphant return is because of how the Feast of Trumpets is determined. It is on the first day of the seventh month. The first day of any month, as I have shown you in the chapter on the New Moon, is based on the *actual sighting* of the New Moon. It can only come on the twenty-ninth day or on the thirtieth day of each month. No one knows for sure until it is actually seen. It could be obscured by clouds or haze or set too quickly after the sun has already set in order to see it. There are many variables that factor in as to why it might not be seen on a given day or hour, therefore, this first day of the seventh month is also known in Hebrew as "the day and hour no one knows."

No one knows this day except the Father. And now you know why no one can know this day. But as Paul said we can know the season of His return. The Feast of Trumpets is the day that the Messiah will come on. Whether it is on one day or the next will only be determined once the New Crescent moon is sighted.

The Ten Days of Awe

The feast of Trumpets begins what is known as the Ten Days of Awe. The Ten Days, starting with the Feast of Trumpets and ending with Yom Kippur or the Day of Atonement, are commonly known as the Days of Awe (Yamim Noraim) or the Days of Teshuvah (Repentance). This is a time for serious introspection, a time to take into account the sins of the previous year and repent ("do teshuvah") before the Day of Atonement or Yom Kippur, a High Holy Day, is upon you.

One primary theme of the Days of Awe is the concept that Yehovah has "books" He writes our names in, writing down who will live and who will die, as well as those who will have a good life and who will have a bad life and, for better or worse, be inscribed for another year. These books are written in on The Feast of Trumpets (the first day of the seventh month) but our actions during the Days of Awe are presumed to alter Yehovah's decree. The actions that change the decree are "teshuvah, tefilah and tzedekah," (repentance, prayer, and good deeds—namely, charity). These "books" are then sealed on

Yom Kippur. This concept of writing in books is where the greeting originates that is commonly associated with this time. The greeting is as follows:

May you be inscribed and sealed for a good year.[88]

Shabbat Shuva

It is during the Ten Days of Awe that we come to that juncture which has become known as Shabbat Shuvah.[89]

Shabbat Shuvah literally means "Sabbath of Return," but it is also a play on the phrase "Shabbat Teshuvah" (Sabbath of Repentance). It is the Shabbat that occurs between Rosh Hashanah and Yom Kippur and is a time for reflection leading up to the atonement of Yom Kippur. Shabbat Shuvah has two special haftarah readings, one dealing with the importance of heartfelt repentance (Hosea 14:2-10) and one praising the Creator's mercy (Micah 7:18-20).[90]

1 O Yisra'ĕl, return to יהוהyour Elohim, for you have stumbled by your crookedness. 2 Take words with you, and return to יהוה. Say to Him, "Take away all crookedness, and accept what is good, and we render the bulls of our lips."[1] (**Hosea 14:1-2** | Footnote: [1]**Hebrews 13:15**—bulls, referring to offerings)

3 "Ashshur does not save us. We do not ride on horses, nor ever again do we say to the work of our hands, 'Our mighty ones.' For the fatherless finds compassion in You." 4 "I shall heal their backsliding, I shall love them spontaneously, for My displeasure has turned away from him. 5 I shall be like the dew to Yisra'ĕl. He shall blossom like the lily, and cast out his roots like Leḇanon. 6 His branches shall spread, and his splendor shall be like an olive tree, and his fragrance like Leḇanon. 7 Those who dwell under his shadow shall return. They shall revive like grain, and blossom like the vine, and become as fragrant as the wine of Leḇanon. 8 What more has Ephrayim (Ephraim) to do with idols? It is I who answer and look after him. I am like a green cypress tree, your fruit comes from Me." 9 Who is wise and understands these *words*, discerning and knows them? For the ways of יהוה are straight, and the righteous walk in them, but the transgressors stumble in them. (**Hosea 14:3-9**)

19 He shall turn back, He shall have compassion on us, He shall trample

---

88 *Days of Awe* http://www.jewfaq.org/holiday3.htm
89 *States & Countries Going Bankrupt & Shabbat Shuva, The Year of Return,* http://www.sightedmoon.com/?page_id=278
90 *Special Shabbatot* http://www.jewfaq.org/special.htm

upon our crookednesses! And You throw all our sins into the depths of the sea! **20** You give truth to Ya'aqob (Jacob), kindness to Abraham, which You swore to our fathers from the days of old! (**Micah 7:19-20**)

We are commanded to return and to bring the Torah scrolls with us. It is in understanding Shabbat Shuva that we are able to accurately perceive when all 12 tribes of Israel[91] will return to the Land of Israel. It will be during a Sabbatical Year during the ten years of judgment on the earth.[92]

The Day of Atonement

The next appointed day is called the Day of Atonement and is the *most sacred day* on the Biblical Calendar. It is a High Holy Day.

> **26** And יהוה spoke to Mosheh (Moses), saying, **27** "On the tenth day of this seventh month is the Day of Atonement. It shall be a set-apart gathering for you. And you shall afflict your beings, and shall bring an offering made by fire to יהוה. **28** And you do no work on that same day, for it is the Day of Atonement, to make atonement for you before יהוה your Elohim. **29** For any being who is not afflicted on that same day, he shall be cut off from his people. **30** And any being who does any work on that same day, that being I shall destroy from the midst of his people. **31** You do no work—a law forever throughout your generations in all your dwellings. **32** It is a Sabbath of rest to you, and you shall afflict your beings. On the ninth day of the month at evening, from evening to evening, you observe your Sabbath." (**Leviticus 23:26-32**)

(You) have already seen—through the symbolism involved in the Passover—that (the Messiah's) shed blood atones for our sins. In fact, atonement means reconciliation. The Day of Atonement symbolizes the reconciliation of God (to) all humanity, (through His Son).

(Therefore), if we are reconciled to God through (the Messiah's) sacrifice, why do we (then) need another Holy Day to teach us about reconciliation? If we are already reconciled, why do we need to fast, as commanded on the Day of Atonement? (Leviticus 23:27; Acts 27:9) What is this day's specific significance in God's master plan for the salvation of mankind?

The Day of Atonement and Passover *both* teach us about the forgiveness of

---

91 Israel is today made up of the United States and United Kingdom, as well as Canada, Australia, South Africa and many other countries of Anglo Saxon descent. See Yair Davidiy at http://hebrewnations.com/ & http://www.britam.org/ Judah today makes up the State of Israel

92 *The Prophecies of Abraham*, pp. 117-122

sin and our reconciliation with God through (His Son's) sacrifice. However, Passover (primarily) concerns the redemption of the firstborn and thus applies most directly to (believers) whom Yehovah has called in this age, while (the Day of) Atonement carries *universal* implications.

Moreover, the Day of Atonement reveals to us an essential additional step in God's salvation plan not found in the symbolism of The Passover. This step *must take place* before humanity can experience true peace on earth. All people suffer from the tragic consequences of sin. But sin doesn't happen without an (underlying) cause, and God makes this underlying cause clear in the symbolism associated with the Day of Atonement.[93]

It is these Ten Days of Awe that include the Feast of Trumpets and Shabbat Shuva and The Day of Atonement that we are able to understand the order of the events for the seven years preceding the Great Tribulation, which comes at the end of these ten years represented by the Ten Days of Awe. The last 3 ½ years or the tribulation concluding with the Day of Atonement, which represents when Satan is locked away.

The Feast of Tabernacles

The next Appointed Time on Yehovah's divine timeline is the Feast of Sukkot (aka, The Feast of Booths, The Feast of Tabernacles, The Festival or Feast Of the Ingathering). It is a commanded Holy Day by Yehovah for you to take seven days and enjoy it with your family to eat and do what is pleasing with your family. Yes, you *are* commanded to celebrate a holiday at the same time you are keeping a Holy Day.

> 33 And יהוה spoke to Mosheh (Moses), saying, 34 "Speak to the children of Yisra'ĕl, saying, 'On the fifteenth day of this seventh month is the Festival of Booths for seven days to יהוה. 35 On the first day is a set-apart gathering, you do no servile work. 36 For seven days you bring an offering made by fire to יהוה.'" (**Leviticus 23:33-36**)

God's plan for mankind involves *restoration*. The Feast of Tabernacles symbolizes the restoration process, which will start with 1) the return of (the Messiah, illustrated) by the Feast of Trumpets and 2) the banishment of Satan, depicted by the Day of Atonement. Once these events have taken place,

---

93 http://www.ucg.org/booklet/gods-holy-day-plan-promise-hope-all-mankind/ atonement-removal-sins-cause-and-reconciliation-/

as represented by the previous Holy Days, the foundation is in place for the restoration of the creation of peace and harmony with God.

The Seven-Day Feast of Tabernacles, which begins with an annual Holy Day (Leviticus 23:34-35), depicts the 1,000 year reign of (the Messiah) over the Earth after His Second Coming (Revelation 20:4). This period is often called *The Millennium*, which simply means "1,000 years."

That age to come—a wonderful "rest" following the hardships of (this) present age—is symbolized 1) every seven days (in our keeping of) the weekly Sabbath (Hebrews 4:1-11) and 2) every year by (our observing of) the Feast of Tabernacles. Also called the Feast of Ingathering (Exodus 23:16), it celebrates the great harvest of humanity when all people who are alive on earth will learn of God's ways. Humanity will at last be restored to a right relationship with God (Isaiah 11:9-10).[94]

We also find evidence of this phenomenon in the following passages:

> 34 "And no longer shall they teach, each one his neighbor, and each one his brother, saying, 'Know יהוה,' for they shall all know Me, from the least of them to the greatest of them, declares יהוה. For I shall forgive their crookedness, and remember their sins no more." (**Jeremiah 31:34**)

> 13 "... and all your children taught by יהוה, and the peace of your children great." (**Isaiah 54:13**)

This seven day Feast represents the Marriage of the bride of Israel to the Messiah. It is what the whole of the bible is teaching. Again you learn these things by keeping these Holy Days at their appointed times.

But it doesn't end here. At the end of these seven days of The Feast of Tabernacles is yet another festival or appointment with Yehovah.

The Eighth Day Feast

> 36 "For seven days you bring an offering made by fire to יהוה. On the eighth day there shall be a set-apart gathering for you, and you shall bring an offering made by fire to יהוה. It is a closing festival, you do no servile work." (**Leviticus 23:36**)

This Eighth Day Feast Day represents the Great White Throne Judgment that is to come upon all mankind who have ever lived. Right before the Eighth

94 http://www.ucg.org/booklet/gods-holy-day-plan-promise-hope-all-mankind/feast-tabernacles-jesus-christ-reigns-over-all-e/

Millennium begins, all those who ever lived are brought back to life to live under Yehshua's rule and in His Kingdom. After a time, they are then judged once they have had their first opportunity to know the truth. This day will clear up any and all false teachings for all those who sincerely and in earnest wish to understand what it all means.[95]

> **37** "These are the appointed times of יהוה which you proclaim as set-apart gatherings, to bring an offering made by fire to יהוה, a burnt offering and a grain offering, a slaughtering and drink offerings, as commanded for every day—**38** besides the Sabbaths of יהוה, and besides your gifts, and besides all your vows, and besides all your voluntary offerings which you give to יהוה. **39** On the fifteenth day of the seventh month, when you gather in the fruit of the land, observe the festival of יהוה for seven days. On the first day is a rest, and on the eighth day a rest. **40** And you shall take for yourselves on the first day the fruit of good trees, branches of palm trees, twigs of leafy trees, and willows of the stream, and shall rejoice before יהוה your Elohim for seven days. **41** And you shall observe it as a festival to יהוה for seven days in the year—a law forever in your generations. Observe it in the seventh month. **42** Dwell in booths for seven days; all who are native Yisra'ëlites dwell in booths, **43** so that your generations know that I made the children of Yisra'ël dwell in booths when I brought them out of the land of Mitsrayim (Egypt). I am יהוה your Elohim." **44** Thus did Mosheh (Moses) speak of the appointed times of יהוה to the children of Yisra'ël. (**Leviticus 23:37-44**)

This is the conclusion of Leviticus 23. These are the *only* Holy Days you are to keep. There are no, "Yeah, buts …" here. You now know and therefore, will be held accountable for what you know. These are the *only* days Yehovah has set aside for us to observe and/or celebrate. You will notice that not even the "Hebrew Holidays" like Purim,[96] Rosh Hashanah or Chanukah[97] are listed here—nor is Christmas,[98] Easter,[99] New Year's, Halloween, Valentine's Day, St. Patrick's Day, Kwanzaa, etc. And as 'biblical' as Lent, Ash Wednesday, Good Friday, and Palm Sunday may sound, if Yehovah has not specified these as His Holy Days, then we are not to be found observing them. We are to be

---

95 http://www.ucg.org/booklet/gods-holy-day-plan-promise-hope-all-mankind/eighth-day-eternal-life-offered-all/

96 http://www.seekgod.ca/hr/hrfaqs4a1.htm

97 http://www.seekgod.ca/hr/hrfaqs4a2.htm#1, http://www.seekgod.ca/hr/hrfaqs4a2.htm#2 & http://www.seekgod.ca/hr/hrfaqs4a2.htm#3

98 http://www.lasttrumpetministries.org/tracts/tract3.html, & Jeremiah 10:2-4

99 http://www.lasttrumpetministries.org/tracts/tract1.html by David J. Meyer

His peculiar people and His set-apart ones. We are not to be like everyone else. We are "aliens and strangers" (I Peter 2:11). This world is not our home.

If it is not found in Leviticus 23 then why on earth are you rebelling against the most high by keeping other holidays that celebrate demons and false gods? You cannot mix bad seed with good seed and say you are doing it "as unto Yehovah." You cannot draw fresh water from a saltwater spring. Yehovah detests mixing. You cannot serve two masters without hating one and loving the other.

The issue of traditions transgressing The Commandments of Yehovah was a key teaching of Yehshua:

> 1 Then there came to יהושע scribes and Pharisees from Yerushalayim (Jerusalem), saying, 2 "Why do Your taught ones transgress the tradition of the elders? For they do not wash their hands when they eat bread." (**Matthew 15:1-2**)

> 3 But He answering, said to them, "Why do you also transgress the command of Elohim[1] because of your tradition?" (**Matthew 15:3** | Footnote: [1]See **Matthew 5:20**)

> 7 "Hypocrites! Yeshayahu rightly prophesied about you, saying, 8 'This people draw near to Me with their mouth, and respect Me with their lips, but their heart is far from Me. 9 But in vain do they worship Me, teaching as teachings the commands of men.'"[1] (**Matthew 15:7-9** | Footnote: [1]**Isaiah 29:13; Mark 7:7; II Kings 17:19**)

> 10 And calling the crowd near, He said to them, "Hear and understand: 11 'Not that which goes into the mouth defiles the man, but that which comes out of the mouth, this defiles the man.'" (**Matthew 15:10-11**)

> 29 "When יהוה your Elohim does cut off from before you the nations which you go to dispossess, and you dispossess them and dwell in their land, 30 guard yourself that you are not ensnared to follow them, after they are destroyed from before you, and that you do not inquire about their mighty ones, saying, 'How did these nations serve their mighty ones? And let me do so too.'"[1] (**Deuteronomy 12:29-30** | Footnote: [1]See also **18:9; Leviticus 18:3; Jeremiah 10:2; Ezekiel 11:12 & 20:32; Ephesians 4:17; I Peter 4:3**)

> 31 "Do not do so to יהוה your Elohim, for every abomination which יהוה hates they have done to their mighty ones, for they even burn their sons and daughters in the fire to their mighty ones. 32 All the words I am commanding you, guard to do it—do not add to it nor take away from

it."[1] (**Deuteronomy 12:31-32** | Footnote: [1]See also **4:2**; **Proverbs 30:6**; **Revelation 22:18-19**)

We are not to add to or subtract from Torah any holiday and say we are doing it to the glory of Yehovah. Be cautioned:

> **31** "... for every abomination which יהוה hates they have done to their mighty ones ..." (**Deuteronomy 12:31**)

> **19** "Guard My laws. Do not let your livestock mate with another kind. Do not sow your field with mixed seed. And do not put a garment woven of two sorts of thread upon you." (**Leviticus 19:19**)

We are not to mix the truths of Torah with false teachings and confuse what is holy with what is profane. This is now what is going on in most of the Christian churches today. They have some truths and a lot of false pagan teachings mixed together.

> 23 And they are to teach My people the difference between the set-apart and the profane, and make them know what is unclean and clean. (Ezekiel 44:23)

As I have now shown you, each of the Holy Days of Yehovah, as found in Leviticus 23, reveal critical things to us about Yehovah's plan of salvation. They are "Shadow Pictures" of future events—of things that are still to come. However, when we fail to keep them and do not make it our aim to know what they entail and represent, then we cannot know or accurately discern false prophecy from sound biblical prophecy or rightly predict *what* is to come or *when*. It really is *that* simple.

> **1** "For the Torah, having a shadow of the good *matters* to come, and not the image itself of the matters ..." (**Hebrews 10:1**)

> **16** Let no one therefore judge you in eating or in drinking, or in respect of a festival or a new moon or Sabbaths—**17** which are a shadow of what is to come—but the Body of the Messiah. **18** Let no one deprive you of the prize, one who takes delight in false humility and worship of messengers, taking his stand on what he has not seen, puffed up by his fleshly mind, **19** and not holding fast to the Head, from whom all the Body—nourished and knit together by joints and ligaments—grows with the growth of Elohim. (**Colossians 2:16-19**)

The Torah and the Holy Days are **Shadow Pictures** of future events yet to come. We need to make an earnest effort to learn all there is to know about them.

Chapter 14 | The First Time the Sabbatical Years Are Mentioned

Leviticus 23, which thoroughly lays out each one of the Holy Days Yehovah commanded us to keep, is then followed by Leviticus 25, which tells us about the Sabbatical Years and how to keep those as well. But this is not the first time the Sabbatical Years are mentioned in the Bible.

The first mention of the Sabbatical Years can be found in Genesis:

> 3 And יהוה said, "My Spirit shall not strive with man forever in his going astray. He is flesh, and his days shall be one hundred and twenty years." (**Genesis 6:3**)

The word for years here is "shaneh."

> **H8141** הנש הנש shâneh shânâh shaw-neh', shaw-naw'
>
> (The first form being in plural only, the second form being feminine); from **H8138**; a year (as a revolution of time): whole age, X long, old, year (X -ly).

So this first mention tells us that man will have 120 periods of time. It is the *only* place this is said. Many people use this to then jump to the following conclusion:

$$120 \times 50 = 6,000 \text{ Years}$$

I will explain to you shortly why this is *not* the case. Others conclude that Noah must have preached for 120 years. Let's put that old dog to rest right here:

> 9 This is the genealogy of Noaḥ. Noaḥ was a righteous man, perfect in

his generations. Noaḥ walked with Elohim. **10** And Noaḥ brought forth three sons: Shĕm, Ḥam, and Yepheth (Japheth). **11** And the earth was corrupt before Elohim, and the earth was filled with violence. **12** And Elohim looked upon the earth and saw that it was corrupt—for all flesh had corrupted their way on the earth—**13** and Elohim said to Noaḥ, "The end of all flesh has come before Me, for the earth is filled with violence through them. And see, I am going to destroy them from the earth. **14** Make yourself an ark of gopherwood. Make rooms in the ark, and cover it inside and outside with tar." **(Genesis 6:9-14)**

In the passage above we see Noah had three sons in verse 10. In verse 14 we are told Yehovah spoke with Noah and told him to build an ark. So this was *after* his sons were born. In Genesis 11 we read:

10 This is the genealogy (the generations) of Shem: Shem was an hundred years old, and brought forth (begat) Arpakshad (Arphaxad) two years *after* the flood: **(Genesis 11:10)**

So Shem was already ninety-eight years old when The Flood happened.

Just by doing the math, you can quickly see Noah had *not* preached for 120 years as some like to maintain in their sermons. From the time Yehovah told Noah of the coming flood until it actually took place was 98 years, *or less* because we are told of the birth Noah's three sons and then we are told of the coming destruction that is to come. So the Genesis 6:3 account of 120 years is not speaking about the number of years until The Flood. It has to be *something else*. Noah could not have preached for 120 years. Although it is not entirely outside the realm of possibility, the chronology of his sons strongly suggests it was closer to 100 years or less.

It appears Genesis 6:3 is speaking of 120 periods of time or more likely of 120 Jubilee Cycles of time.

The next time we are told of the Sabbatical Years in the Bible is in Exodus. This is part of the very first "Ketubah" or marriage contract (or marriage covenant) Yehovah instituted with Israel.

1 "These are the right-rulings which you are to set before them: **2** When you buy a Hebrew servant, he serves six years, and in the seventh he goes out free, for naught. **3** If he comes in by himself, he goes out by himself; if he comes in married, then his wife shall go out with him. **4** If his master has given him a wife, and she has borne him sons or daughters, the wife and her children are her master's, and he goes out by himself. **5** And if the servant truly says, 'I love my master, my wife, and my children, let me not go out free,' **6** then his master shall bring him before Elohim, and shall bring him to the door, or to the doorpost, and his master shall pierce his ear with an awl. And he shall serve him forever." (**Exodus 21:1-6**)

So right here you know they kept the Sabbatical Years even *before* they entered the Promised Land. This is *extremely important* to realize.

One of the arguments people often present to me in objection to the practice of keeping the Sabbatical and Jubilee Years is that it is only intended for when you are in the Land of Israel and not for anywhere else. I will address this point a bit later. But for now I want to show you that the nation of Israel kept the Sabbatical Year laws before they even so much as entered the Promised Land or crossed the Jordan River.

The next instance where we read of the Sabbatical Year Laws is in Exodus 23. Again, this is still while they are at Mount Sinai and before they even embark on their journey to the Land of Milk and Honey and before they had arrived in the Wilderness of Paran where they received the curse from Yehovah and had to wander in the wilderness for forty years.

> **10** "And for six years you are to sow your land, and shall gather its increase, **11** but the seventh year you are to let it rest, and shall leave it, and the poor of your people shall eat. And what they leave, the beasts of the field eat. Do the same with your vineyard and your olive yard. **12** Six days you are to do your work, and on the seventh day you rest, in order that your ox and your donkey might rest, and the son of your female servant and the sojourner be refreshed. (**Exodus 23:10-12**)

The Seventh Year Sabbatical Year is now compared to the weekly Sabbath in that the very same way in which we keep the weekly Sabbath every Seventh Day is the exact same way we reckon the Sabbatical Years. Every Seventh Year is a Sabbatical Year and there are no exceptions to this rule. You just count seven years and keep on doing so on a yearly basis to arrive at the next Sabbatical Year.

This is why we had to deal with the weekly Sabbath in such detail in the previous chapters. Understanding that the Sabbath comes every seven days is crucial to understanding that the Sabbatical years come every seven years repeatedly. No exceptions! Which is what the Lunar Sabbath theory would have you believe; that there are exceptions.

Again, all of this was well in place even before the Israelites set foot in the Promised Land.

I will now present to you the fourth time the Sabbatical and Jubilee Years are mentioned in Scripture. We find the next instance of this in Leviticus 25.

This is still part of the marriage covenant that is being spelled out in these chapters starting with Exodus and now comes to a close in Leviticus:

> **46** These are the laws and the right-rulings and the Torot[1] which יהוה made between Himself and the children of Yisra'ël on Mount Sinai by the hand of Mosheh (Moses). (**Leviticus 26:46** | Footnote: [1]Torot—plural of Torah)

The marriage contract between Israel and Yehovah includes the Holy Days of Leviticus 23, the Sabbatical and Jubilee Years of Leviticus 25, and has now been concluded at the end of Leviticus 26. The marriage contract between Yehovah and Israel had originally been stated and recorded in Exodus and is expanded and concluded in Leviticus.

> **3** And Mosheh (Moses) came and related to the people all the Words of יהוה and all the right-rulings. And all the people answered with one voice and said, "All the Words which יהוה has spoken we shall do." (**Exodus 24:3**)

This same marriage contract is repeated in Leviticus and it concludes with Leviticus 26:46. In *both cases* it includes the Sabbatical Years.

Moses knew that when the Israelites entered into the Promised Land it would be a Jubilee Year. Because of this, he had to explain the Jubilee Year Laws to them. And Moses knew that the year they entered The Land it would be the fiftieth year.

How did he know this?

All you have to do is to add up all the years from the creation of Adam to the time of the forty years curse of wandering in the wilderness coming to a close and you too can see it would most definitely have to be a Jubilee Year when the Israelites are given permission by Yehovah to set their sights on entering The Land again.

I will do the math for you shortly so you can see where most people make some all too simple mistakes. Below is the event that indicated to Moses what year they would enter The Land.

> **28** "Say to them, 'As I live,' declares יהוה, 'as you have spoken in My hearing, so I do to you: **29** The carcasses of you who have grumbled against Me are going to fall in this wilderness, all of you who were registered (numbered), according to your entire number, from twenty years old and above. **30** None of you except for Kaleb (Caleb) the son of Yephunneh (Jephunneh) and Yehoshua (Joshua) son of Nun, shall

enter the land which I swore I would make you dwell in. **31** But your little ones, whom you said would become a prey, I shall bring in, and they shall know the land which you have reject (despised). **32** But as for you, your carcasses are going to fall in this wilderness. **33** And your sons shall be wanderers (shepherds) in the wilderness forty years, and shall bear your whorings (the brunt of your infidelity), until your carcasses are consumed in the wilderness.'" (**Numbers 14:28-33**)

34 "'According to the number of the days in which you spied out the land, forty days, for each day you shall bear your guilt one year, *namely* forty years, and you shall know My rejection. **35** I יהוה have spoken this. I will surely do so to all this evil congregation who are gathered together against Me. In this wilderness they shall be consumed, and there they shall die.'" **36** Now the men whom Mosheh (Moses) sent to spy out the land, who returned and made all the congregation complain against him by bringing a bad report of the land, **37** those very men who brought the evil report about the land, died by the plague before יהוה. **38** But Joshua the son of Nun and Caleb the son of Yephunneh (Jephunneh) remained alive, of the men who went to spy out the land. **39** Then Mosheh (Moses) told these words to all the children of Yisra'ël, and the people mourned greatly. (**Numbers 14:34-39**)

It was not too long after this event that Moses also learned that He Himself would not be allowed to enter the Promised Land.

1 And the children of Yisra'ël, all the congregation, came into the Wilderness of Tsin (Zin) in the first month, and the people stayed in Qadesh (Kadesh). And Miryam died there and was buried there. **2** Now there was no water for the congregation and they assembled against Mosheh (Moses) and against Aharon (Aaron). **3** And the people contended with Mosheh (Moses) and spoke, saying: "If only we had died when our brothers died before יהוה! **4** Why have you brought up the assembly of יהוה into this wilderness, that we and our livestock should die here? **5** And why have you brought us up out of Mitsrayim (Egypt), to bring us to this evil place? Not a place of grain or figs or vines or pomegranates, and there is no water to drink." **6** Then Mosheh (Moses) and Aharon (Aaron) went from the presence of the assembly to the door of the Tent (Tabernacle) of Meeting, and they fell on their faces. And the esteem (glory) of יהוה appeared to them. (**Numbers 20:1-6**)

7 Then יהוה spoke to Mosheh (Moses), saying, **8** "Take the rod and assemble the congregation, you and your brother Aharon (Aaron). And you shall speak to the rock before their eyes, and it shall give its water. And you shall bring water for them out of the rock and give drink to the congregation and their livestock." **9** And Mosheh (Moses) took the rod from before יהוה as He commanded him. **10** And Mosheh (Moses) and Aharon (Aaron) assembled the assembly before the rock. And he said to them, "Hear now, you rebels, must we bring water you water out of this rock?" **11** Then Mosheh (Moses) lifted his hand and struck the rock twice with his rod. And much water came out, and the congregation and their livestock drank. **12** But יהוה spoke to Mosheh (Moses) and to Aharon (Aaron), "Because you did not believe Me, to set me apart (hallow) Me in the eyes of the children of Yisra'ĕl, therefore you do not bring this assembly into the land which I have given them." **13** These were the waters of Meribah (strife), because the children of Israel contended with יהוה, and He was set apart (hallowed) among them. (**Numbers 20:7-13**)

What did Moses do that warranted such a severe penalty from Yehovah? First, Moses disobeyed a direct command. Yehovah had commanded Moses to *speak* to the rock. Instead, Moses struck the rock with his staff. Second, Moses took the credit for bringing forth the water. Notice how in verse ten Moses said, "Must we (referring to himself and Aaron) bring you water out of this rock?" Moses took the credit for the miracle himself, instead of attributing it to Yehovah and giving Yehovah all the glory. Third, Moses did this in front of *all* the Israelites. Such a public example of direct disobedience could not go unpunished. Moses' punishment was that he would not be allowed to enter the Promised Land.

As a result of Moses not being able to enter the Promised Land and because Moses was now able to know when they would enter it, Moses then set forth for them all the rules for the Jubilee Years. He had already shared with them on the other side of the Jordan the rules they needed to know for keeping the Sabbatical Years, but they had never kept a Jubilee Year and would not be doing so until they actually crossed *over* the Jordan.

As I mentioned earlier in this chapter, both the Sabbatical and Jubilee Years, as well as the rules for keeping them, were written out for us in Leviticus 25.

In the following chapter I will provide you with all the variables that must be taken into consideration to arrive at the right conclusions mathematically with regard to keeping Yehovah's Appointed Times.

Chapter 15 The Chronology From Adam To Entry Into the Promised Land

In order to understand how Moses knew that Israel would enter the Promised Land on a Jubilee Year all we have to do is add up all the years from Adam until that time. It seems simple enough, but many people come to an impasse (or even several) or take wrong turns along the way and because of that, I will go point by point to give you all the information you need to get it right and come away with a much more complete understanding of things.

It is important to understand and keep in mind that the single act of the Israelites crossing the Jordan River and entering into The Promised Land of what is now Israel (as we know it) coincided with a Jubilee Year. If there did not appear to be a strong case for this, then our chronology would be in error and we would have to go back and double-check our math.

The creation of Adam to the birth of Abram will be the first section I elaborate on to lay a sound foundation biblically and historically and to ensure you get off to the right start. The numbers from Genesis that should be of the greatest interest to you are the ages of the patriarchs at the time the next generation came to be.

For example, Adam was 130 years old when Seth was born, so we record 130 years from the onset of creation to the birth of Seth. We do this all the way to the birth of Abram. Do your own homework and double-check it against the table that follows below. I will provide you with a running total so you can crosscheck as well.

The Chronology From Adam until Israel Crosses the Jordan		
Patriarchs	Age of Patriarchs at birth Son	The Year From the Creation of Adam up to that Time in Total
Adam	130 Years	130
Seth	105 Years	235
Enosh	90 Years	325
Cainan	70 Years	395
Mahalal'el	65 Years	460
Jared	162 Years	622
Enoch	65 Years	687
Methusaleh	187 Years	874
Lamech	182 Years	1,056

When Noah was born, the year was 1,056 years *after* the creation of Adam. Double-check your math and compare. Most people do not get this part wrong.

Next, we read that Noah was 600 years old when The Great Flood came.

> 6 Now Noaḥ was six-hundred years old when the flood-waters were on the earth. (**Genesis 7:6**)

We now add 600 years to 1,056 years and the year of The Flood is 1,656 years *after* the creation of Adam.

I am now about to show you where many people make the first chronological "leap of logic," or error, so pay attention. Having now summed up the years in Genesis and arriving at 1,656 years for The Flood, they then jump to the passage in Genesis below and conclude that Shem was born when Noah was 500 years old.

> 32 And Noah was five-hundred years old, and Noah brought forth (begat) Shem, Ham, and Yepheth (Japheth). (**Genesis 5:32**)

Is this correct? Let's read on in Genesis to find out. What most people neglect or do not consider is what is told to us in Genesis 11.

> 10 This is the genealogy of Shem: Shem was a hundred years old, and brought forth (begat) Arpakshad (Arphaxad), two years after the flood. (**Genesis 11:10**)

The verse in Genesis 11 is important because it states that Shem was 100 when Arphaxad was born and Arphaxad was born two years *after* The Flood.

I have just done the math for you. If you have double-checked it, you now know The Flood took place 1,656 years *after* the creation of Adam. You also should now know The Flood only lasted five months.

> 1 And Elohim remembered Noah, and all the beasts and all the cattle that were with him in the ark. And Elohim made a wind to pass over the earth, and the waters subsided. 2 And the fountains of the deep and the windows of the heavens were stopped, and the rain from the heavens was withheld. 3 And the waters receded steadily from the earth, and at the end of the hundred and fifty days the waters diminished. 4 And in the seventh month, the seventeenth day of the month, the ark rested on the mountains of Ararat. 5 And the waters decreased steadily until the tenth month. In the tenth month, on the first day of the month, the tops of the mountains became visible. (**Genesis 8:1-5**)

> 13 And it came to be in the six-hundred and first year, in the first month, the first day of the month, that the waters were dried up from the earth. And Noah removed the covering of the ark and looked, and saw the surface of the ground was dry. 14 And in the second month, on the twenty-seventh day of the month, the earth was dry. (**Genesis 8:13-14**)

What this means is that Shem was *not* born when Noah was 500 years old as we are told in general terms in Genesis 5:32, but that Noah was *502* years old when Shem was born. We now have 1,056 years to the birth of Noah. The table on the following page then, is a continuation of the previous table.

It was 1,948 years *after* the creation of Adam that Abram was born. But some take issue with Terah being either seventy years of age or a hundred and thirty years of age. The big question is, "Was Terah seventy years old or a hundred and thirty years old when Abram was born?"

> 26 And Terah lived seventy years, and brought forth (begat) Abram, Nahor and Haran. (**Genesis 11:26**)

> 32 And the days of Terah came to be two-hundred and five years, and Terah died in Haran. (**Genesis 11:32**)

4 And Abram left (Ur) as יהוה had commanded him, and Lot went with him. And Abram was seventy-five years old when he set out from Haran. **(Genesis 12:4)**

The Chronology From Adam until Israel Crosses the Jordan		
Patriarches	**Age of Patriarchs at birth Son**	**The Year From the Creation of Adam up to that Time in Total**
Noah	502 Years	1,056 + 502 = 1,558
Shem	100 Years	1658
Arphaxad	35 Years	1693
Salah	30 Years	1723
Eber	34 Years	1757
Peleg	30 Years	1787
Reu	32 Years	1819
Serug	30 Years	1849
Nahor	29 Years	1878
Terah	70 Years	1948

By using this logic of subtracting 75 from 205; 205 - 75 = 130, many conclude Terah was 130 years old and not seventy years old when Abram was born.[100]

Let's look at the following two texts first:

26 When Terah had lived seventy years, he became the father of Abram, Nahor, and Haran. 27 Now these are the descendants of Terah. Terah was the father of Abram, Nahor, and Haran; and Haran was the father of Lot. 28 Haran died before his father Terah in the land of his birth, in Ur of the Chaldeans. 29 Abram and Nahor took wives; the name of Abram's wife was Sarai, and the name of Nahor's wife was Milcah. She was the daughter of Haran the father of Milcah and Iscah. 30 Now Sarai was barren; she had no child. 31 Terah took his son Abram and his grandson Lot son of Haran, and his daughter-in-law Sarai, his son Abram's wife, and they went out together from Ur of the Chaldeans to go into the land of Canaan; but when they came to Haran, they settled

100 http://christianthinktank.com/abebirth.html

REMEMBERING THE SABBATICAL YEARS OF 2016

there. **32** The days of Terah were two-hundred and five years; and Terah died in Haran. **(Genesis 11:26-32)**

2 The God of glory appeared to our ancestor Abraham when he was in Mesopotamia, before he lived in Haran, **3** and said to him, "Leave your country and your relatives and go to the land that I will show you." **4** Then he left the country of the Chaldeans and settled in Haran. After his father died, God had him move from there to this country in which you are now living. **(Acts 7:2-4)**

There are three (but they boil down to two) ways to understand this: 1) Terah was 70; or 2) Terah was 130. And both are 'reasonable' approaches, although I personally side with Bruce Waltke[101] and F. Bruce[102] (i.e., that Terah was 70 and that "205" is a textual error, on the evidence of Philo Judaeus/Samaritan Pentateuch):

Three suggestions have been made to deal with Stephen's (Book of Acts) understanding of early events in the life of the patriarch. One explanation appeals to the Samaritan Pentateuch, which has Terah dying not at 205 (as in the Masoretic Text and the LXX—aka, The Septuagint or Greek O.T.)[103] but at 145. This, we are told, is the source that Stephen was using, and thus the inconsistencies disappear. Terah was seventy when Abram was born. Seventy-five years later Terah died, and Abram left Haran for Canaan. This fact is then presented, with others, as evidence that Stephen's speech in Acts 7 is Samaritan in its interpretation of O.T. history. A second suggestion is a variation of the above. Rather than limiting Stephen's source to the S.P., we are told that at this time a plurality of textual families or traditions existed, and the S.P. is but a representative of an expanded and reworked Palestinian text that differed from the M.T. and the LXX. Certainly Philo, who also gave Terah's age at death as 145, did not rely on the S.P., for he would not use a sectarian Torah. A third approach harmonizes the Genesis data and Acts 7:4 without appealing to a text other than the M.T. or the LXX The basic tenet of this approach is that (Genesis) 11:26 does not say that Terah was seventy years old when he fathered Abram. Rather, it says that Terah was seventy years old when he began to beget. Perhaps Abram is mentioned first because he is the most important of the three. Thus Terah was 130 years old, near the end of his life, when Abram was born! (NICOT)

F. Bruce favors the "textual" solution:

---

101 http://en.wikipedia.org/wiki/Bruce_Waltke
102 http://tinyurl.com/9hh56kf
103 http://en.wikipedia.org/wiki/Septuagint#The_LXX_and_the_NT

The chronological data of Genesis 11:26, 32; (Genesis) 12:4 would suggest that Terah's death took place sixty years after Abraham's departure from Haran. J. Ussher and other chronolog(ists) of an earlier day harmonized the present statement of Stephen with the evidence of Genesis by the improbable expedient of supposing that Terah was seventy years old when his oldest son (Haran) was born, and that Abraham was not born until Terah was 130. That Abraham did not leave Haran until his father was dead is asserted also by Philo [*On the Migration of Abraham*[104], XXXII (177)], and is implied by the Samaritan Pentateuch, which in Genesis 11:32 gives Terah's age at death as 145, not 205 (M.T., LXX). It would follow that Abraham, who left Haran at the age of 75 (Genesis 12:4), did so as soon his father had died. … Possibly Stephen (or Luke) and Philo relied on a Greek version (no longer extant) which agreed with the Samaritan Pentateuch reading of Genesis 11:32. P. E. Kahle says with greater assurance that "not a single M.S. of the Christian 'Septuagint' has preserved in Genesis 11:32 a reading which Philo and Luke read in their Greek Tora(h) in the 1ˢᵗ Christian century." [*The Cairo Geniza* (London, 1947), p. 144] (NICNT, "Acts")

As does Waltke, in his commentary on Genesis:

"205 years. **The original text probably read '145 years**.'" This reading is attested in the Samaritan Pentateuch, which preserves an early text type and informs Acts 7:2-4. If the Masoretic Text is original, Terah was 130 when Abram (Abraham) was born (see Genesis 11:26; 12:4). This seems unlikely for three reasons: 1) it accords badly with the rest of the genealogy from Shem to Terah, who have their firstborn in their early thirties; 2) there would be nothing exceptional in Abraham fathering Isaac at 100 years of age; 3) Stephen could not have known that Abraham left Haran after his father's death, for Abraham could have left Haran before his father's death (see Acts 7:2-4).

Now, normally, if the M.T. and LXX agreed, that would be strong data, but in this case they actually DON'T agree (with regard to) the passage itself. The LXX says "and all the days of Terah in Haran were 205 years, and Terah died in Haran"—making Terah live another 205 years in Haran! But the M.T. (states): "And they were, the days of Terah, five and two-hundred years; and Terah died in Haran." So there is some definite textual confusion in our existing sources.

Additionally, we might note that an ancient, rabbinic source even noted

---

104 http://www.earlychristianwritings.com/yonge/book16.html

a possible 'dislocation' in the text—suggesting that (the) sequence of events in Genesis was uncertain. Tov explains (OT:TCHB2,54f):

> In the printed editions one finds inverted nunin ... the original meaning of these signs in Greek sources was that the section enclosed by the sigma and antisigma did not suit its present place in the text ... An additional case, not attested in the (printed) manuscripts, is mentioned in Minhat Shay and the Mp of the second Rabbinic Bible on Genesis 11:32 ('in Haran') ... It is possible that the inverted nun in this place showed that the verse did not occur in its correct place, for a chronological calculation reveals that the death of Terah mentioned here ought to have occurred after what is recorded in the following sections (cf. Rashi).

So, given the textual problems in our modern M.T./LXX and the specific references/indications of 145 (age of Terah's death; Genesis 11:32) in Philo, Stephen (Luke), and the S.P., I have to go with the "70 years old" conclusion.

What has just been put forth above was the conclusions arrived at by the author, Glenn Miller (aka, Glenn, Little Glenn & "The Man Behind the Curtain")[105] at:

http://www.christianthinktank.com/abebirth.html

The *Book of Jasher*[106] also states the following:

> **50** And Terah took a wife and her name was Amthelo the daughter of Cornebo; and the wife of Terah conceived and bare him a son in those days. **51** Terah was SEVENTY YEARS OLD when he begat him, and Terah called the name of his son ABRAM, because the king had raised him in those days, and dignified him above all his princes. (**Jasher 7:50-51**)

So who is right and how do we prove it? The answer is that the sum total of all the chronological calculations we make must add up to a Jubilee Year at the point in history Joshua crosses the Jordan River.

In order to prove which is right, we must now have two columns; one representing the age of Terah at 70 and another representing the age of Terah at 130. From Adam to the birth of Abram with Terah being seventy is 1,948

---

105 http://christianthinktank.com/letter2007apr11.html, http://christianthinktank.com/Letter2readersJAN2012.html, http://christianthinktank.com/postpassion.html, http://christianthinktank.com/curtains.html
106 http://www.ccel.org/a/anonymous/jasher/7.htm

years, whereas from Adam to the birth of Abram with Terah being 130 is 2,008 years or, List "A" & List "B" *respectively.*

Our next clue is also a difficult one to figure out and the mystery it holds will take some doing to unravel.

In Genesis 12:4 we are told that Abram was seventy-five when he left Haran. We then read about events after this date in Genesis, chapter 13, where Abram goes down to Egypt and how Sarah was taken to be the wife of Pharaoh. We then read of how they left Egypt, how the sheep grew and how Abram and Lot had to part ways because there was not enough room for the both of them. All of this transpired over the course of a number of years.

In Genesis, chapter 14, we read how Lot was taken prisoner and how Abram then went and rescued Lot out of captivity. This event developed over a period of one year and then came to a close with Abram's appointment with Melchizedek, King of Salem.

In chapter 15, we read of how Yehovah made a covenant with Abram.

Next we read about Abram going into Hagar in Genisis chapter 16 and how Hagar conceives and gives birth to Ishmael.

In Genesis, chapter 17, we read about Abraham turning ninety-nine, Yehovah changing his name from Abram to Abraham[107] and also, Ishmael turning thirteen and how they both were to be circumcised.

Based on these biblical accounts, we can correctly conclude that thirteen years before chapter 17, Abram was eighty-six and that the year before the birth of Ishmael, when he went into Hagar, he was eighty-five, allowing for the nine months of Hagar being pregnant.

> Abraham at 99 – 13 years for the birth of Ishmael – 1 year for Hagar's pregnancy = 85.

We now have two fixed ages for Abraham. We now know that somewhere between age seventy-five and age eighty-five Yehovah made a covenant with Abraham and within the construct of that ten-year span we have our next set of clues to work with.

We are also given another clue in Genesis 15. The descendants of Abraham will be mistreated 400 years in a country not their own.

---

107 Genesis 17:1,5 "when Abram was ninety-nine years old, that Yehovah appeared to Abram and said to him, "I am Yehovah – walk before Me and be perfect. No longer is your name called Abram, but your name shall be Abraham, because I shall make you a father of many nations.

13 Then He said to Abram: "Know certainly that your descendants will be strangers in a land that is not theirs, and will serve them, and they will afflict them four-hundred years." (**Genesis 15:13**)

Isaac was born when Abraham was 100 years old. This was 2,048 years after creation according to List "A" with Abraham being born in the year 1948 after creation with Terah being seventy years of age; or 2,108 years after creation according to List "B using Terah being one hundred and thirty at Abarhams birth.

8 And the child grew, and was weaned: and Abraham made a great feast the same day that Isaac was weaned. 9 And Sarah saw the son of Hagar the Egyptian, which she had born unto Abraham, mocking. (**Genesis 21:8-9**)

The 430 years from Yehovah forging a covenant with Abraham ends at the same time the 400 years of affliction on Abraham's descendants ends—in the year of the Exodus.

40 And the sojourn of the children of Yisra'ĕl who lived in Mitsrayim (Egypt) was four hundred and thirty years. 41 And it came to be at the end of the four hundred and thirty years, on that same day it came to be that all the divisions of יהוה went out from the land of Mitsrayim (Egypt). (**Exodus 12:40-41**)

15 Brothers, as a man I say it: a covenant, even though it is man's, yet if it is confirmed, no one sets it aside, or adds to it. 16 But the promises were spoken to Aḅraham, and to his Seed. He does not say, "And to seeds," as of many, but as of one, "And to your Seed," who is Messiah. 17 Now this I say, "Torah, that came four hundred and thirty years later, does not annul a covenant previously confirmed by Elohim in Messiah, so as to do away with the promise." (**Galatians 3:15-17**)

In order to determine the year the covenant was made, we must try each of the ten year intervals between the time Abraham was seventy-five up to the time when we know he went into Hagar when he was eighty-five. Again, the year that adds up to the Jubilee Year when the Israelites crossed the Jordan River will prove to be the correct year.

This then means we will have multiple lists to check. So let me do all the work for you here below so you can check and see which one works.

List I

- 1948 to Abram's birth
- 75: Abram's age when the Covenant is made
- 430 years to the Exodus
- 2,453 years total

List II

- 1948 to Abram's birth
- 76: Abram's age when the Covenant is made
- 430 years to the Exodus
- 2,454 years total

List III

- 1948 to Abram's birth
- 77: Abram's age when the Covenant is made
- 430 years to the Exodus
- 2,455 years total

List IV

- 1948 to Abram's birth
- 78: Abram's age when the Covenant is made
- 430 years to the Exodus
- 2,456 years total

List V

- 1948 to Abram's birth
- 79: Abram's age when the Covenant is made
- 430 years to the Exodus
- 2,457 years total

List VI

- 1948 to Abram's birth
- 80: Abram's age when the Covenant is made
- 430 years to the Exodus
- 2,458 years total

List VII

- 1948 to Abram's birth
- 81: Abram's age when the Covenant is made
- 430 years to the Exodus
- 2,459 years total

List VIII

- 1948 to Abram's birth
- 82: Abram's age when the Covenant is made
- 430 years to the Exodus
- 2,460 years total

List IX

- 1948 to Abram's birth
- 83: Abram's age when the Covenant is made
- 430 years to the Exodus
- 2,461 years total

List X

- 1948 to Abram's birth
- 84: Abram's age when the Covenant is made
- 430 years to the Exodus
- 2,462 years total

List XI

- 1948 to Abram's birth
- 85: Abram's age when the Covenant is made
- 430 years to the Exodus
- 2,463 years total

The preceding list has all the possible years using list "A" with Terah being seventy. To use list "B" all you have to do is tack on sixty more years to any of the totals you wish to investigate further.

You now have the age of Abram when the Covenant with Yehovah was made using the age of Terah being seventy years old when Abram was born. This now provides you with all ten potential years as to when the covenant was made. You then add on the 430 years to arrive at the year of the Exodus.

I will come back to the 400 years with you in a moment, but for now, let me finish this line of thinking with you before you get too confused.

Most people will now just tack on the forty years the Israelites wandered in the wilderness to arrive at the year they entered the Promised Land.

But far too many people fail to factor in the following verse:

> **11** And it came to be on the twentieth day of the second month, in the second year, that the cloud was taken up from above the Dwelling Place of the Witness. **12** And the children of Yisra'ĕl departed, setting out from

the Wilderness of Sinai. And the cloud dwelt on it in the Wilderness of
Paran. **13** Thus they departed the first time, according to the command
of יהוה by the hand of Mosheh (Moses). (**Numbers 10:11-13**)

It was two years after the Exodus that the Israelites left Mount Sinai
for the very first time. And then, in the fifth month on the ninth day of that
month, Israel rebelled against Yehovah and would not be allowed entry into
the Promised Land. It was from this point forward that the forty-year's curse
in Numbers 14:33 begins.

We now must attach two years plus another forty years on to each of
the lists on the previous page to see where we end up—keeping in mind, as
always, that we must end up at a Jubilee Year.

Of all the lists I presented you with previously, the only one that adds up
to a Jubilee Year when you add the two years the Israelites were at Mount Sinai
and also, the forty years they wandered in the wilderness is List VI.

List VI

- 1948 to Abram's birth
- 80: Abram's age when the Covenant is made
- 430 years to the Exodus
- 2,458 years total

You then add two years to the above 2,458 total for their time spent at
Mount Sinai, which equals 2,460. Finally, you add forty years to the 2,460
total for their years spent wandering in the wilderness. This comes to 2,500
years total. **This *is* a Jubilee Year!**

There are 2,458 years from the creation of Adam to the Exodus plus
two years, which is the time spent at Mount Sinai followed by the curse in
the Wilderness of Paran, which entailed forty years of wandering until they
entered the Promised Land. This comes to 2,500 years total.

When we take 2,499 and divided it by forty-nine we have fifty-one Jubilee
Cycles. Each Jubilee Cycle is forty-nine years as we are about to learn in the
following chapters. This then makes the year 2500 A.C.[108] (After Creation)
the fiftieth Year of Jubilee.

If you use the date for Terah being 130, then you must add on sixty more
years to the running tally. When you do this and then add up all the rest of the
known chronology down to our time, you will see how this would then give

---

108 http://www.sightedmoon.com/?page_id=319

too many years. It would mean that we are already in the Seventh Millennium and the Messiah would have to have returned already. His Second Coming has not happened yet, so this is obviously incorrect. That being said, one must conclude Terah was *indeed* seventy years old and *not* 130 years old when Abraham was born.

When I say the *known* chronology, I mean the time spanning from the Exodus (2,458 years) until the fourth year of King Solomon's reign (967 B.C.), which totalled 480 years (I Kings 6:1) + 967 years down to the year "0" and then to our current year of 2012. All of which equals 5,917 years. We still have thirty-three more years to get to the next Jubilee Year in 2045, however, so this would be a grand total of 5,950 years. And if we add on the extra 60 years for Terah being 130 at the birth of Abraham, then the total of 6010 years is too many. Some groups promote that we are in the year 6012 in the Gregorian year of 2012. Again this is too many years into the 7th Millennium and the Messiah has not yet come. So this usage of Terah being one hundred and thirty when Abraham was born just does not work out chronologically.

And, as I still intend to illustrate to you, there are only 5,880 years in these 120 Jubilee Cycles. We then have a huge error here and we have seventy years too many. Or using Terah at age 130 then we have 130 years too many. But we are getting ahead of ourselves on this.

Let us now go back to the 400 years of mistreatment I previously made mention of. Earlier, I stated that Isaac was weaned at the age of ten. I also would like to point out that the party Abraham threw for Isaac was the very first Bar Mitzvah in human history. And it was from the age of ten onward that Ishmael began to persecute Isaac and his descendants.

> **8** And the child grew and was weaned, and Abraham made a great feast on the day that Yitsḥaq (Isaac) was weaned. **9** And Sarah saw the son of Haḡar the Mitsrite (Egyptian), whom she had borne to Abraham, mocking. **10** So she said to Abraham, "Drive out this female servant and her son, for the son of this female servant shall not inherit with my son, with Yitsḥaq (Isaac)." **(Genesis 21:8-10)**

We have Isaac born 2,048 years after the creation of Adam. He is only ten years old when the mistreatment begins. We were told that they would be mistreated for 400 years and that would end at the Exodus, the same as the 430 years of Abraham. 2,048 (birth of Isaac) + 10 (age when weaned) + 400 (years for persecution) = 2,458 (the same total as we calculated for Abraham).

The entire math is adding up correctly.

What's more, Joshua tells of how they ate of the produce of the land, the day after Passover—on the very same day the Wave Sheaf was offered—a Sunday, no less.

> 10 And the children of Yisra'ĕl camped in Gilgal, and performed the Passover on the fourteenth day of the month at evening on the desert plains of Yeriḥo (Jericho). 11 And they ate of the stored grain of the land on the morrow after the Passover, unleavened bread and roasted grain on this same day. 12 And the manna ceased on the day after they had eaten the stored grain of the land. And the children of Yisra'ĕl no longer had manna, but they ate the food of the land of Kena'an (Canaan) that year. (**Joshua 5:10-12**)

The year 2500 A.C. was the Jubilee Year and all of Yehovah's Commandments fit perfectly into this scenario.

The year Joshua entered the Promised Land was a Jubilee Year and it took place 2,500 years after the creation of Adam.

Chapter 16 | How To Count the Sabbatical & Jubilee Years

Some people will tell you that the Jubilee Cycles are spaced precisely fifty years apart from one from another. They are convinced that every fifty years is a Jubilee. And as such, they also think that all you have to do is count in increments of fifty.

But is this right? And if so, how do we prove or disprove it?

Each year we have an annual reminder of how to count the Sabbatical and Jubilee Years. It is during this annual reminder that we are reminded exactly where we are in the Jubilee Cycle. This annual reminder is called Shavuot (aka, Pentecost, the Feast of Weeks and the Feast of Shabua). Shabua is Hebrew for seven and there are seven days in a week.

> 15 And from the morrow after the Sabbath, from the day that you brought the sheaf of the wave offering, you shall count for yourselves: seven completed Sabbaths. 16 Until the morrow after the seventh Sabbath you count fifty days, then you shall bring a new grain offering to יהוה.
> (Leviticus 23:15-16)

These two verses command us to count seven weeks from the time that the omer, the new barley offering, was brought to the Temple, (i.e., from the Sunday after the weekly Sabbath).

Inasmuch and insofar as we are to count the Omer to Pentecost, we are commanded in Leviticus 25 *in the very same way* to count to the Jubilee Year. Compare the two sections in scripture and see.

> 10 "Speak to the children of Yisra'ĕl, and you shall say to them, 'When you come into the land which I give you, and shall reap its harvest, then you shall bring a sheaf of the first-fruits of your harvest to the priest."
> (Leviticus 23:10)

149

11 "And he shall wave the sheaf before יהוה, for your acceptance. On the morrow after the Sabbath the priest waves it." **(Leviticus 23:11)**

15 "And from the morrow after the Sabbath, from the day that you brought the sheaf of the wave offering, you shall count for yourselves: seven completed Sabbaths." **(Leviticus 23:15)**

16 "Until the morrow after the seventh Sabbath you count fifty days, then you shall bring a new grain offering to יהוה." **(Leviticus 23:16)**

The first Wave Offering of barley is made on the Sunday during the Days of Unleavened Bread. The second Wave Offering of two leavened loaves is then made fifty days later and is called Shavuot and it too, is on a Sunday; the first day of the week.

Now let's read about the Sabbatical and Jubilee Years and compare. Keep in mind what I have already shown you in Exodus:

10 And six years thou shalt sow thy land, and shalt gather in the fruits thereof: **11** But the seventh year thou shalt let it rest and lie still; that the poor of thy people may eat: and what they leave the beasts of the field shall eat. In like manner thou shalt deal with thy vineyard, and with thy olive yard. **12** Six days thou shalt do thy work, and on the seventh day thou shalt rest: that thine ox and thine ass may rest, and the son of thy handmaid, and the stranger, may be refreshed. **(Exodus 23:10-12)**

Right here Yehovah is showing you that the way you count for the weekly Sabbath, which is always, without exception, on the seventh day, you also count for the Sabbatical Years, which is always, without exception, on the seventh year—the former occurring every seven days and the latter occurring every seven years, but both in multiples of seven.

3 "Six years you sow your field, and six years you prune your vineyard, and gather in its fruit, **4** but in the seventh year the land is to have a Sabbath of rest, a Sabbath to יהוה. Do not sow your field and do not prune your vineyard." **(Leviticus 25:3-4)**

The Sabbatical Year is just like the weekly Sabbath. It comes every Seventh Year, like clockwork and without a break.

8 "And you shall count seven Sabbaths of years for yourself, seven times seven years. And the time of the seven Sabbaths of years shall be to you forty-nine years. **9** You shall then sound a ram's horn to pass through on the tenth day of the seventh month, on the Day of Atonement cause a ram's horn to pass through all your land. **10** And you shall set the fiftieth year apart, and proclaim release throughout all the land to all its inhabitants, it is a Jubilee for you. And each of you shall return to his possession, and each of you return to his clan. **11** The fiftieth year is a Jubilee to you. Do not sow, nor reap what grows of its own, nor gather from its unpruned vine. **12** It is a Jubilee, it is set-apart to you. Eat from the field its crops. **13** In the Year of this Jubilee let each one of you return to his possession. (**Leviticus 25:8-13**)

The Jubilee Year comes on the first year in the next count to seven or the first year in the count to the next Sabbatical Year. So we count like this:

1, 2, 3, 4, 5, 6, 7—which is the Sabbath Day and the Sabbatical Year, for they are identical.

And we repeat this seven times as we are commanded in both Leviticus 23 and 25:

1, 2, 3, 4, 5, 6, 7	Total of 7
1, 2, 3, 4, 5, 6, 7	Total of 14
1, 2, 3, 4, 5, 6, 7	Total of 21
1, 2, 3, 4, 5, 6, 7	Total of 28
1, 2, 3, 4, 5, 6, 7	Total of 35
1, 2, 3, 4, 5, 6, 7	Total of 42
1, 2, 3, 4, 5, 6, 7	Total of 49

And as we then begin the count again toward the next Sabbath or the next Sabbatical Year we count '... 47, 48, 49, 50...' Which is also the first year or '1,' followed by '2, 3, 4...' so that from one Sabbath or one Sabbatical Year to the next is just seven years. In the exact same context, Pentecost Sunday is the fiftieth day and also it is the first day of the week in our count toward the next weekly Sabbath.

1, 2, 3, 4, 5, 6, 7	Total of 7
1, 2, 3, 4, 5, 6, 7	Total of 14
1, 2, 3, 4, 5, 6, 7	Total of 21
1, 2, 3, 4, 5, 6, 7	Total of 28
1, 2, 3, 4, 5, 6, 7	Total of 35
1, 2, 3, 4, 5, 6, 7	Total of 42
1, 2, 3, 4, 5, 6, 7	Total of 49
50, 2, 3, 4, 5, 6, 7	Total of 7

When people insert '50' and then begin to count from '1' after that, they errantly succeed in turning a seven-day week into an actual eight-day week, when it should only ever be seven:

1, 2, 3, 4, 5, 6, 7	Total of 7
1, 2, 3, 4, 5, 6, 7	Total of 14
1, 2, 3, 4, 5, 6, 7	Total of 21
1, 2, 3, 4, 5, 6, 7	Total of 28
1, 2, 3, 4, 5, 6, 7	Total of 35
1, 2, 3, 4, 5, 6, 7	Total of 42
1, 2, 3, 4, 5, 6, 7	Total of 49
50, 1, 2, 3, 4, 5, 6, 7	Total of 8

Notice how it now is a total of eight and *not* seven. And yet, it should only total seven each week. So by counting '... 48, 49, 50, 1, 2...' you have erred.

When you count from the Wave Offering of the barley to Pentecost it is called the counting of the Omer. You are to count each day up to the fiftieth day. We are to count the Omer as a reminder of where we are in the Jubilee Cycle. You can see the *entire* count, along with the Psalms that are tradtionaly read for each day during the counting of the Omer until Pentecost, in Appendix C at the end of this book.

For example, the year 2014 would be the fifth year of the third Sabbatical Cycle. There are seven years in each Sabbatical Cycle. Doing the math *correctly* then looks like this:

> 7 for 1st Sabbatical Cycle + 7 for 2nd Sabbatical Cycle + 5 years which is 2014 in the 3rd Sabbatical Cycle=19 years

Using the "Day-Year Principle," "Year-Day Principle" or "Year-For-A-Day Principle" is a method of interpretation of Bible prophecy in which the word 'day' in apocalyptic prophecy is symbolic for a year of actual time and vice-versa.

> 34 "According to the number of the days in which you spied out the land, forty days—a day for a year, a day for a year—you are to bear your crookedness forty years." (**Numbers 14:34**)

In addition, the prophet Ezekiel is commanded to lie on his left side for

390 days, followed by his right side for forty days, to symbolize the equivalent number of years of punishment on Israel and Judah respectively:

> **4** "And lie on our left side, and you shall put the crookedness of the house of Yisra'ĕl on it. As many days as you lie on it, you shall bear their crookedness. **5** For I Myself have laid on you the years of their crookedness, according to the number of the days, three hundred and ninety days. And you shall bear the crookedness of the house of Yisra'ĕl. **6** And when you have completed them, you shall lie again on your right side and you shall bear the crookedness of the house of Yehudah (Judah) forty days, a day for a year. I have laid on you a day for a year. (**Ezekiel 4:4-6**)

Each year as we approach the Feast of Pentecost or the counting towards this day of Pentecost we have an annual reminder of where we are in the Jubilee cycle. It is an annual reminder of where we are in Yehovah's chronology.

The year 2014 is the nineteenth year in the Jubilee Cycle and the nineteenth day as we count out the Omer. We count out the Omer from the day after the Sabbath during the Days of Unleavened Bread until we get to the fiftieth day, which is then Pentecost.

The nineteenth day of this count would also represent the year of 2014. The eighteenth day would be 2013. Each day of counting the Omer represents a year in the Jubilee cycle. On each individual day of counting the Omer, a different Psalm is read in keeping with that day and by extension for that year.

While I am on the subject, I must address one of the objections some of you might raise.

Judah says the count starts from the day after the High Holy Day or on the First Day of the Feast of Unleavened Bread—which consequently would make every one of the fiftieth days occur on Sivan 6.

Leviticus 23 says, however, "from the day after the Sabbath" and, in this context, "Sabbath" is **Strong's #7676** and denotes the weekly Sabbath and *not* the High Holy Day:

H7676 תבש shabbâth *shab-bawth'*

Intensive from **H7673**; *intermission*, that is, (specifically) the *Sabbath*: (+ every) Sabbath.

If this was a High Holy Day such as the First Day of Unleavened bread, the word used would have been **#7677** Sabbathown.

The command to begin to count to '50' is effectively the day *after* the weekly Sabbath and *not after* the High Holy Day. The only exception to this rule would be if that same High Holy Day fell on the weekly Sabbath like it did in Joshua 5:10—which is what some use to support their claim of it being after the High Holy Day.

But in order to do this, they must ignore Leviticus 23, which states that from the day after the seventh Sabbath shall be fifty days:

> **15** And from the morrow after the Sabbath, from the day that you brought the sheaf of the wave offering, you shall count for yourselves: seven completed Sabbaths. **16** Until the morrow after the seventh Sabbath you count fifty days, then you shall bring a new grain offering to יהוה.
> (**Leviticus 23:15-16**)

We are commanded to begin our count after the seventh day Sabbath, which makes the start of the count (and the fiftieth day) always on the first day of the week, or Sunday. The fiftieth day is the first day in the next count to the seventh day Sabbath. The fiftieth year is also the first year in the next count to the next seventh year Sabbatical Year. The fiftieth year is always going to be the same year as the 1st year in the next Jubilee cycle. This is the lesson we learn from Pentecost.

In conclusion then, each Jubilee cycle consists of 49 years. 120 Jubilee cycles is then 5880 years. The year 2012 C.E. is equal to the year 5848 After Creation. This means we have 33 years until the 120 Jubilee in 2045. The year 2045 would be the 5881st year since the creation of Adam.

Chapter 17	When You Enter the Land—Understanding the Full Context Leads To Better Understanding[109]

I have often heard the phrase "When you enter the land …" mentioned in discussions on the applicability to a specific Commandment. I have previously spoken about our logic getting in the way of our obedience. Could the use of this condition be (yet) another example of us trying to reason (away) which of the instructions of YHVH to obey? A good example of this is the Sabbatical Year. Should we or shouldn't we keep the instructions regarding the Sabbatical Year? Is it only applicable to people living in Israel or is it applicable to all? Let us do a detailed study of this all too commonly used phrase and see what conclusions we can (draw) and how (this) needs to be applied in our lives today.

The Giving of The Commandments

In order to understand the phrase, we need to make sure that we take into account the history of the nation of Israel when the instructions were given to them via Moses. Allow me to provide a short recap of the key events:

1. **Exodus**—The (citizenry of the) nation of Israel are slaves to the Egyptians in the land of Egypt. While in Egypt they are forced to follow the laws of the Pharaoh and they do not possess any land. YHVH sends Moses to lead them out of bondage and return them to the land that was promised to Abraham. During this process of The Exodus they become YHVH's people and He gives them the feast of Pesach as a reminder of this turning point.

2. **Sin In the Desert**—Israel is now turned into a free nation that is given the choice of who (it) will obey. Shortly after the victory over the

109 By Permission of Schalk & Elsa Klee http://www.setapartpeople.com/enter-landunderstanding-full-context-leads-understanding

Egyptians, the nation faces a problem with (its) water supply and YHVH provides for them via a miracle. It is during this time that they receive their first ordinances.

24 So the people grumbled at Moses, saying, "What shall we drink?" **25** Then he cried out to YHVH, and YHVH showed him a tree; and he threw it into the waters, and the waters became sweet. There He made for them a statute and regulation, and there He tested them. **26** And He said, "If you will give earnest heed to the voice of YHVH your Elohim, and do what is right in His sight, and give ear to His commandments, and keep all His statutes, I will put none of the diseases on you which I have put on the Egyptians; for I, YHVH, am your healer." **(Exodus 15:24-26)**

Shortly after this, they run out of food and Yehovah again provides for them via the manna and quails (Exodus 16:1-20). During this time, the instructions of the Sabbath (are) also explained to them and they experience firsthand what the (outcome) of disobedience is. They are told that the seventh day rest will be a test to them.

4 Then **YHVH** said to Moses, "Behold, I will rain bread from heaven for you; and the people shall go out and gather a day's portion every day, that I may test them, whether or not they will walk in My instruction. **5** On the sixth day, when they prepare what they bring in, it will be twice as much as they gather daily." **(Exodus 16:4-5)**

At Mount Sinai the people of Israel choose to obey YHVH. At Mount Sinai YHVH gives to them His Law and ordinances—including personal injury laws, property laws, (the) Sabbatical Year … the tabernacle and (the) priesthood.

8 All the people answered together and said, "All that **YHVH** has spoken we will do!" And Moses brought back the words of the people to YHVH. **(Exodus 19:8)**

However, before Moses returns with The Law, the people have already rebelled against YHVH and built the golden calf. After Moses intercedes for them, they are saved. When they reach the Promised Land, the incident with the (twelve) spies happen and they end up wandering for forty years before entering The Land due to their unbelief.

3. **Entering The Land**—Once they cross the Jordan River, they take possession of The Land and are commanded to drive out the inhabitants of The Land. The Land is divided among the tribes (Joshua 13) and now they are a free nation that owns (its) own property. They also now need to provide for their own food, shelter and safety. Joshua is given the instructions regarding the six cities of refuge from YHVH.

1 Then YHVH spoke to Joshua, saying, 2 "Speak to the sons of Israel, saying, 'Designate the cities of refuge, of which I spoke to you through Moses, 3 that the manslayer who kills any person unintentionally, without premeditation, may flee there, and they shall become your refuge from the avenger of blood.'" (**Joshua 20:1-3**)

After settling in **The Land**, YHVH gives them rest from their enemies and after an address from Joshua, the nation again confirms that they will serve YHVH (Joshua 24:14-28).

4. **Sin & Exile**—However, the nation does not keep His Commandments and soon they need to be rescued by the Judges. The cycle of sin, repentance, salvation and peace repeats itself a couple of times. Eventually, the nation chooses to have a king rule over them. After three kings, this leads to a split of the nation. This setup eventually leads them (in)to idolatry and due to the fact that they sin (including not keeping His Sabbatical Years) they end up in exile and The Land receives its rest.

5. **Return To The Land**—They return to The Land of YHVH, but not as a free nation. They are a vessel nation that is ruled over by many different nations. However, in the period they again discover the Book of The Law and choose to implement the Laws of YHVH, including The Feasts.

Ezekiel 20

Why is all of this important? When the elders of the nation in exile come to inquire of Ezekiel, Yehovah tells Ezekiel not to answer them. In the explanation to them Yehovah recounts this history to them. He explains that He had given His statutes and ordinances to them on several occasions.

- Sojourn in Egypt (Ezekiel 20:5-10)
- 1st Period in The Wilderness (Ezekiel 20:11-17)
- 2nd Period in The Wilderness (Ezekiel 20:18-26)
- Settlement in The Land (Ezekiel 20:27-29)
- Exilic Period & (the) Future (Ezekiel 20:30-44)

Here we have confirmation from Yehovah that He gave them His ordinances more than once:

> 11 "I gave them My statutes and informed them of My ordinances, by which, if a man observes them, he will live. 12 Also I gave them My sabbaths to be a sign between Me and them, that they might know that I am YHVH who sanctifies them." (Ezekiel 20:11-12)

> 19 "I am YHVH your Elohim; walk in My statutes and keep My ordinances and observe them. 20 Sanctify My sabbaths; and they shall be a sign between Me and you, that you may know that I am YHVH your Elohim." (Ezekiel 20:19-20)

Why did He have to do this? Due to the fact that the fathers did not teach their children His statutes ... Yehovah taught them the statutes again.

> 18 "I said to their children in the wilderness, 'Do not walk in the statutes of your fathers or keep their ordinances or defile yourselves with their idols.'" (Ezekiel 20:18)

This portion in Ezekiel is the key to understanding why certain laws are repeated in the Books of Moses. What did Moses say, why did he explain these Commandments to the nation during the second period in The Wilderness as described by Ezekiel?

> 5 See, I have taught you statutes and judgments just as YHVH my Elohim commanded me, that you should do thus in the land where you are entering to possess it. (Deuteronomy 4:5)

"When you enter the land ..."

The first use of the phrase is actually given before the start of The Exodus. It is then used in reference to the Feast of Pesach (Passover).

> 25 "When you enter the land which YHVH will give you, as He has promised, you shall observe this rite. 26 And when your children say to you, 'What does this rite mean to you?' 27 you shall say, 'It is a Passover sacrifice to YHVH who passed over the houses of the sons of Israel in Egypt when He smote the Egyptians, but spared our homes.'" And the people bowed low and worshipped. (Exodus 12:25-27)

Most occurrences of this phrase occur in the book of Leviticus (with regard to) the first generation in The Wilderness before the counting or the incident with the twelve spies. (Leviticus 14:34-35, 19:23-25, 23:10, 25:2) It also appears in Numbers (15:2, 34:2) and Deuteronomy (18:9-11, 26:1-2).

This phrase can be used in Scripture to denote two different things:

- What laws (to) follow as a free nation that owns (its) own land.
- Laws that YHVH felt He needed to repeat.

Let us now compare all the Scripture for The Commandments that are preceded with ... "**When You Enter the Land.**"

Reference	Instruction	New	Landowner	Previous Reference
Exodus 12:25-27	"**When you enter the land** which **YHVH** will give you, as He has promised, you shall observe this rite. And when your children say to you, 'What does this rite mean to you?' you shall say, 'It is a Passover sacrifice to **YHVH** who passed over the houses of the sons of Israel in Egypt when He smote the Egyptians, but spared our homes.'"	Yes	No	
Leviticus 14: 34–35	"**When you enter the land** of Canaan, which I give you for a possession, and I put a mark of leprosy on a house in the land of your possession, then the one who owns the house shall come and tell the priest, saying, 'Something like a mark of leprosy has become visible to me in the house.'"	Yes	Yes	
Leviticus 19:23-25	"**When you enter the land** and plant all kinds of trees for food, then you shall count their fruit as forbidden. Three years it shall be forbidden to you; it shall not be eaten. But in the fourth year all its fruit shall be holy, an offering of praise to **YHVH**. In the fifth year you are to eat of its fruit, that its yield may increase for you; I am **YHVH** your Elohim."	Yes	Yes	
Leviticus 23:10	"**When you enter the land** which I am going to give to you and reap its harvest, then you shall bring in the sheaf of the first-fruits of your harvest to the priest."	No	Yes	Exodus 23:16

Leviticus 25:2-7	"**When you come into the land** which I shall give you, then the land shall have a Sabbath to **YHVH**. Six years you shall sow your field, and six years you shall prune your vineyard and gather in its crop, but during the seventh year the land shall have a Sabbath Rest, a Sabbath to **YHVH**; you shall not sow your field nor prune your vineyard."	No	Yes	Exodus 23:10
Numbers 15:2	"**When you enter the land** where you are to live, which I am giving you, then make an offering by fire to **YHVH**, a burnt offering or a sacrifice to fulfill a special vow, or as a freewill offering or in your appointed times, to make a soothing aroma to **YHVH**, from the herd or from the flock."	No	No	Leviticus 1:2
Numbers 15:18-19	"Speak to the sons of Israel and say to them, '**When you enter the land** where I bring you, then it shall be, that when you eat of the food of the land, you shall lift up an offering to **YHVH**.'"	No	Yes	Leviticus 2:1
Numbers 34:2	"Command the sons of Israel and say to them, '**When you enter the land** of Canaan, this is the land that shall fall to you as an inheritance, even the land of Canaan according to its borders.'"	Yes	Yes	
Deuteronomy 17:14-17	"**When you enter the land** which **YHVH** your Elohim gives you, and you possess it and live in it, and you say, 'I will set a king over me like all the nations who are around me,' you shall surely set a king over you whom **YHVH** your Elohim chooses, one from among your countrymen you shall set as king over yourselves; you may not put a foreigner over yourselves who is not your countryman. Moreover, he shall not multiply horses for himself, nor shall he cause the people to return to Egypt to multiply horses, since **YHVH** has said to you, 'You shall never again return that way.'"	Yes	Yes	

Deuteronomy 18:9-11	"**When you enter the land** which **YHVH** your Elohim gives you, you shall not learn to imitate the detestable things of those nations."	No	No	Deuteronomy 12:29-31
Deuteronomy 26:1-2	"Then it shall be, **when you enter the land** which **YHVH** your Elohim gives you as an inheritance, and you possess it and live in it, that you shall take some of the first of all the produce of the ground which you bring in from your land that the **YHVH** your Elohim gives you, and you shall put it in a basket and go to the place where **YHVH** your Elohim chooses to establish His name."	No	Yes	Deuteronomy 16:10

Based on these facts, what are the logical conclusions we can (draw)?

- New Commandments are not always given after the phrase.
- Not all (of the) Commandments given after the phrase (pertain to) land or property ownership (Pesach celebration and making the offer).
- (Over) half the Commandments (containing) the phrase (were) given earlier without the phrase.

Thus, the conclusion must simply be that the Commandments following this phrase could have wider application than simply when you live in the land of Israel. Turning the argument the other way, are all the Commandments that require land ownership preceded (by) this phrase? No, some verses regarding planting, sowing and harvesting (do) not (make) any reference to this phrase:

9 Now when you reap the harvest of your land, you shall not reap to the very corners of your field, nor shall you gather the gleanings of your harvest. 10 Nor shall you glean your vineyard, nor shall you gather the fallen fruit of your vineyard; you shall leave them for the needy and for the stranger. I am the YHVH your Elohim. (**Leviticus 19:9-10**)

19 You are to keep My statutes. You shall not breed together two kinds of your cattle; you shall not sow your field with two kinds of seed, nor wear a garment upon you of two kinds of material mixed together. (**Leviticus 19:19**)

Are we to keep these instructions?

15 If you love Me, you will keep My commandments. (**John 14:15**)

Every single instruction in the Torah was given to Israel—a free nation—for when they are in The Land. All Torah is given as instructions in righteousness. Some instructions can be followed more easily than others. We even have some instruction that we cannot follow at all at the moment. For example, instructions pertaining to the Temple and Levitical Priesthood are not applicable at the moment, because there is no Temple.

We should do as we are able and as best we can. This simply means we must do all that is physically possible for us to do. Can you celebrate Sabbath anywhere? Yes of course. Should you go to Jerusalem for the three pilgrimage festivals? Yes. It is commanded. Is it possible for every believer to do so? No. Due to financial constraints it would not be possible for every believer, but that does not nullify the Commandment.

Yehovah knows our hearts and tests our hearts. He will know if it was physically possible for you to do (and if) you willfully chose to disobey or make His Commandments your second or third priority (instead).

We should not try to reason The Commandments away but rather to use this (same) energy to find the best way for us to keep The Commandments. We should ask ourselves if we are able and if the answer is yes, then we should do it. If not, what can I do to get me closer to the place or position where I can? Maybe I cannot go for all three of the feasts, but if I save my "holiday" (Holy Day—His Set-Apart days) money, I can go once a year or once every second year. We can save money to go to nice warm and sunny beach resorts (most likely not holy or set apart) but we reason that Israel during The Feasts is just too expensive. This type of reasoning exposes the true intention of our hearts.

Do I need to keep the Sabbatical Year? Yes, Exodus 23:10 and Leviticus 25:2 tells you that you should. It does not mean that it is easy to do it, but still you need to find the best way. You need to start to study and prepare. If you know what The Commandments are, you can study ways to survive for a year without eating anything produced from the land. You may be surprised by the other interesting things you learn along the way. Just like we plan our week in such a way that we do not have to work or shop on Sabbath, so we can plan for six years that the land can rest for one year. It is all about (your level of) commitment and the intentions of (your) heart. How much do you love Yehovah? Remember, John 14:15 does not refer to "some of My Commandments."

Changing (your) attitude does not change The Commandment but does get (you) closer to it.

It is really simple. If you are in any way able to do a Commandment, you should. Yehovah will know your heart and your effort, or the lack thereof. Do not reason away Yehovah's instructions. Do what He requires of you as best you possibly can and to the best of your ability!

> 10 "I, YHVH, search the heart, I test the mind, Even to give to each man according to his ways, According to the results of his deeds." (**Jeremiah 17:10**)

> 3 For this is the love of YHVH, that we keep His commandments; and His commandments are not burdensome. (**I John 5:3**)

> 21 "He who has My commandments and keeps them is the one who loves Me; and he who loves Me will be loved by My Father, and I will love him and will disclose Myself to him." (**John 14:21**)

> 3 By this we know that we have come to know Him, if we keep His Commandments. (**I John 2:3**)

I want to now take the time to stop and thank Schalk and Elsa for the above teaching and for their support of Yehovah's Commandments, of which the keeping of the Sabbatical Year is one. "Thank you!"

I also want to ask you all a question: How many Torahs are there?

Judah says you need only keep the Noahide Laws and do not have to keep the Ten Commandments. Some even go so far as to say we do not have to keep the Sabbatical Years unless we are in the land of Israel.

Yet, in Leviticus we are told:

> 2 Speak to the children of Yisra'ĕl, and say to them, 'When you come into the land which I give you, then the land shall observe a Sabbath to יהוה.' (**Leviticus 25:2**)

As Schalk and Elsa so clearly and insightfully just explained, this is not just for when you are in The Land, it is for everybody, everywhere.

If one were to use the same argument the people who teach against keeping the Sabbatical years outside the Land of Israel, are using, and how they say they are for keeping the Sabbatical and Jubilee Years *only* when you're in The Land, then this same reasoning would also invariably apply to:

23 "And when you come into the land ..." (**Leviticus 19:23**)

And then, a few verses later, we are instructed:

26 "Do not eat *meat* with the blood. Do not practice divination or magic." (**Leviticus 19:26**)

That being said, if one were to follow this line of reasoning to its inevitable conclusion, one would not only be forced to conclude one does *not* have to keep the Sabbatical Years outside of The Land, but also, that when one is not in The Land, it is considered permissible in Yehovah's sight to eat meat with the blood still in it and to consult with diviners and sorcerers while you're at it. Surely we can plainly see the folly that would come from adhering to this line of logic. All we need do is recall how Yehovah dealt with Saul when he consulted with the Witch of Endor (I Samuel 28). Yet this *is* their logic. Sliding still further down this slippery slope we find:

27 Do not round the corner of your head, nor destroy the corner of your beard. (**Leviticus 19:27**)

Which means when we are not in the land of Israel, we *can* round the corners of our heads and beards which is done for the worship of the dead.

28 And do not make any cuttings in your flesh for the dead, nor put tattoo marks on you. I am יהוה. (**Leviticus 19:28**)

Again using this *same* argument, we can cut our flesh for the dead and do all the tattoos we want when not in The Land.

29 Do not profane your daughter by making her a whore, so that the land does not whore, and the land becomes filled with wickedness. (**Leviticus 19:29**)

But when we are not in The Land we can turn our daughters into prostitutes and it is OK because we are not in The Land and this command only applies to those who are in The Land of Israel.

30 Guard My Sabbaths and reverence My set-apart place. I am יהוה. (**Leviticus 19:30**)

And since we are not in The Land we do not have to keep the Sabbath or the Holy Days.

31 Do not turn to mediums, and do not seek after spiritists to be defiled by them. I am יהוה your Elohim. (**Leviticus 19:31**)

Is Yehovah only our Elohim when we are in the land of Israel?

It is my hope that by now you can, on a scale far more grand than ever before, clearly see the foolishness of this argument, which alleges you do not have to keep the Sabbatical and Jubilee Years because it is "only" for when you are in the land of Israel.

Again I ask you—how many Torahs are there?

There is only but one Torah for *both* the Israelite *and* the stranger. One Torah! One Torah for Asians, Indians, Afro-Americans, Hispanics and those of Caucasian European heritage—just to name a few. There has only ever been one Torah for all the peoples of the earth and it is the same Torah. Period.

49 There is one Torah for the native-born and for the stranger who sojourns among you. (**Exodus 12:49**)

Chapter 18 | How To Reckon the Sabbatical & Jubilee Years To Our Chronology

I have been speaking to you about the Sabbatical Years the duration of this entire book. But you are most likely wondering when the ones that have come and gone were, when the *next one* is going to occur and *how* to know or how to *prove* it, as this is what we *all* must do.

There is a great deal of confusion out there about the Sabbatical Years and it is due to this confusion that most of us today are unable to figure it out. I will expose the false teachers and their false teachings shortly, but in order to find the truth before it was adulterated, one must go back in time to a source that is sure and true. One must go back to Scripture itself and to Yehovah's very own words spoken by Himself. From this point on, we can *then* go forward (and backward) to know *when* the Sabbatical and Jubilee Years were and which ones are still to come.

Respected Chronologist, Edwin R. Thiele wrote the book, *The Mysterious Numbers of the Hebrew Kings*.[110] In it he states how there are *only* two dates in all of Hebrew chronology that can be confirmed by outside sources.

In the Old Testament, no absolute dates are given for the Hebrew kings and it becomes a true Berean's task to establish, if he or she can, an absolute date in the history of Israel that can be used as a starting place to establish other dates in the desired chronological scheme. One's only hope of doing this in the instances where there exists historical gaps which cannot be accounted for, is to isolate an intersecting principal point of contact where Hebrew history correlates with certainty to the history of another nation whose chronology, for a given space and time, is more well-known.

In the early history of the Hebrew monarchies, the two most well

---

110 http://www.amazon.com/Mysterious-Numbers-Hebrew-Kings/dp/082543825X

documented examples of this were the Assyrians first and the Babylonians second. Fortunately for us, the chronologies of these two nations as they pertain to the time periods we will be concerning ourselves with the most have been very thoroughly established.[111]

One is the battle of Qarqar in 853 B.C. in which King Ahab died. This story is found in I Kings 22. The reason this date is important is because of *who* Ahab is fighting against. He and his regiment were fighting against Assyria.

Assyrian chronology dating back to the beginning of the 9th century B.C. rests on a highly dependable and exceptionally solid foundation. All the essentials for a sound chronology are present. Therefore, scholars have been able to come up with a sound chronological system for the nation of Assyria.[112]

The only other date that ties into other chronologies is 701 B.C. when King Sennacherib attacks Judah in the fourteenth year of King Hezekiah's reign.

A solid synchronism between Judah and Assyria in which our pattern of Hebrew dates could begin is 701 B.C. is a definitely fixed date in Assyrian history and is the year in which King Sennacherib, in his third campaign, "went against the Hittite-land" (Aram), and shut up King Hezekiah the Jew... like a caged bird in Jerusalem, his royal city. This took place in the fourteenth year of King Hezekiah's reign (II Kings 18:13), that is, in the year 701 B.C.[113]

The Assyrians adhered to a practice of appointing to the office of Eponym, or Limmu, some high official of the court such as the governor of a province or the king himself. The Limmu held office for a calendar year and to that year was given the name of the individual then occupying the position of Limmu.[114]

From the ruins of Nineveh we have four Assyrian Chronologies called *Eponym* with which we can date from 911 B.C.–701 B.C.—each of which overlap the others.

We also have seven Assyrian Chronologies called *Limmu Lists* which cover the years from 891 B.C.–648 B.C. and they too have astronomical

---

111 Edwin R. Thiele, *The Mysterious Numbers of the Hebrew Kings*; p.67
112 Edwin R. Thiele, *The Mysterious Numbers of the Hebrew Kings*; p.67
113 Edwin R. Thiele, *The Mysterious Numbers of the Hebrew Kings*; p.78
114 Edwin R. Thiele, *The Mysterious Numbers of the Hebrew Kings*; p.68

events that can be used to pinpoint the exact time in history that an event itself took place and the King that existed at that time.

There are also two other documents known as the *Khorsabad King List* from Sargon and the *SDAS King List* which not only are in agreement with each other, but are also in agreement with the *Eponym* and *Limmu Lists* previously mentioned.

And if the above isn't enough, to all of this we can then add *Ptolemy's Canon* which is a chronology of Babylonian, Persian and Grecian kings dating from 747 B.C.–161 C.E. But even this is not the end of it. Ptolemy also authored over eighty astronomical recordings (aka, observations)—including their dates and their relationship to the rulers at that time. These astronomical recordings can then be used to double-check the accuracy of the list of Kings and confirm when they ruled in human history.

It is *only* with these lists of chronologies, recovered from the ruins of Nineveh, that we are able to have a reliable chronological record of *any* of the Hebrew Kings.

Having the lists of Assyrian rulers at our disposal only matters, however, when we can connect one or more Israelite kings to it and, remarkably, this has been done with the Battle of Qarqar *and* the Assyrian attack on King Hezekiah. Except for these two events tying directly into the known Assyrian chronology, we would have *no* date by which to reckon the Kings of Israel to, for they left no records to us.

Why, you may ask, is any of this important?

For one, the reference above with regard to King Sennacherib's attack on King Hezekiah is recorded in the Assyrian chronologies. This recording is an absolute benchmark year and from that year we can determine when all the other kings of Israel reigned. We could also use the Battle of Qarqar, but the one for Hezekiah is much more important to us in the context of the Sabbatical and Jubilee Years.

In this well-documented account, of which I cited earlier, King Sennacherib, in his third campaign, "went against the Hittite-land Aram, and shut up Hezekiah the Jew ... like a caged bird in Jerusalem, his royal city." This took place in the fourteenth year of King Hezekiah's reign (II Kings 18:13). This is the year 701 B.C.

As I also stated earlier, but in more general terms, 701 B.C. is an absolute chronological benchmark date in history. It is irrefutable. It is provable beyond scrutiny. Knowing this, let us now read about the events that led up to this dramatic event.

1 And it came to be in the third year of Hoshĕa (Hosea) son of Ĕlah, sovereign of Yisra'ĕl, that Ḥizqiyahu (Hezekiah) son of Aḥaz, sovereign of Yehudah (Judah), began to reign. **2** He was twenty-five years old when he began to reign, and he reigned twenty-nine years in Yerushalayim (Jerusalem). And his mother's name was Abi, daughter of Zekaryah (Zechariah). **3** And he did what was right in the eyes of יהוה, according to all that his father Dawid (David) did. **4** He took away the high places and broke the pillars, and cut down the Ashĕrah, and broke in pieces the bronze serpent which Mosheh (Moses) had made, for until those days, the children of Yisra'ĕl burned incense to it, and called it Neḥushtan (a bronze trifle). **5** He put his trust in יהוה Elohim of Yisra'ĕl, and after him was none like him among all the sovereigns of Yehudah (Judah), nor who were before him, **6** and he clung to יהוה. He did not turn away from following Him, but guarded His commands, which יהוה had commanded Mosheh (Moses). **7** And יהוה was with him—wherever he went, he acted wisely. And he rebelled against the sovereign of Ashshur (Assyria) and did not serve him. **8** He smote the Philistines, as far as Azzah (Gaza) and its borders—from watchtower unto the walled city. **(II Kings 18:1-8)**

13 And in the fourteenth year of Sovereign Ḥizqiyahu (Hezekiah), Sanḥĕrib (Sennacherib) sovereign of Ashshur (Assyria) came up against all the walled cities of Yehudah (Judah) and captured them. **14** And Ḥizqiyahu (Hezekiah) sovereign of Yehudah (Judah) sent to the sovereign of Ashshur (Assyria) at Lakish (Lachish), saying, "I have done wrong, turn away from me. I shall bear whatever you impose on me." And the sovereign of Ashshur (Assyria) imposed upon Ḥizqiyahu (Hezekiah), the sovereign of Yehudah (Judah), three hundred talents of silver and thirty talents of gold. **15** And Ḥizqiyahu (Hezekiah) gave him all the silver that was found in the House of יהוה and in the treasuries of the sovereign's house. **(II Kings 18:13-15)**

16 At that time Ḥizqiyahu (Hezekiah) cut off the doors of the Hĕkal (Temple) of יהוה, and the doorposts which Ḥizqiyahu (Hezekiah) sovereign of Yehudah (Judah) had overlaid (with gold), and gave it to the sovereign of Ashshur (Assyria). **17** And the sovereign of Ashshur (Assyria) sent the Tartan, and the Rabsaris, and the Rabshaqĕh (Rabshakeh) from Lakish (Lachish), with a great army against Yerushalayim (Jerusalem), to Sovereign Ḥizqiyahu (Hezekiah). And they went up and came to Yerushalayim (Jerusalem). And when they had come up, they came and stood by the channel of the upper pool, which was on the highway to the Launderer's (Fuller's) Field. **(II Kings 18:16-17)**

18 And they called to the sovereign. And Elyaqim (Eliakim) son of Ḥilqiyahu (Hilkiah), who was over the household, and Shebnah

(Shebna) the scribe, and Yo'aḥ (Joah) son of Asaph, the recorder, came out to them. **19** And the Raḇshaqëh (Rabshakeh) said to them, "Please say to Ḥizqiyahu (Hezekiah), 'Thus said the great sovereign, the sovereign of Ashshur (Assyria),' "What is this trust in which you have trusted? **20** You have spoken of having counsel and strength for battle, but they are only words of the lips! And in whom do you trust, that you rebel against me? **21** Now look! You have put your trust in the staff of this crushed reed, Mitsrayim (Egypt), on which if a man leans, it shall go into his hand and pierce it. So is Pharaoh, sovereign of Mitsrayim (Egypt) to all who trust in him. **22** But when you say to me, 'We trust in יהוה our Elohim,' is it not He whose high places and whose altars Ḥizqiyahu (Hezekiah) has taken away, and said to Yehuḏah (Judah) and Yerushalayim (Jerusalem), 'Bow yourselves before this altar in Yerushalayim (Jerusalem)?' **23** And now, I urge you, give a pledge to my master the sovereign of Ashshur (Assyria), then I give you two thousand horses, if you are able to put riders on them!" **(II Kings 18:18-23)**

24 "And how do you turn back the face of one commander of the least of my master's servants, and trust in Mitsrayim (Egypt) for chariots and horsemen? **25** Have I now come up without יהוה against this place to destroy it? יהוה said to me, 'Go up against this land, and you shall destroy it.'" **26** Then said Elyaqim (Eliakim) son of Ḥilqiyahu (Hilkiah), and Sheḇnah (Shebna), and Yo'aḥ (Joah) to the Raḇshaqëh (Rabshakeh), "Please speak to your servants in Aramaic, for we understand it. And do not speak to us in the language of Yehuḏah (Judah), in the ears of the people on the wall." **27** And the Raḇshaqëh (Rabshakeh) said to them, "Has my master sent me to your master and to you to speak these words, and not to the men sitting on the wall to eat their own dung and drink their own urine, with you?" **(II Kings 18:24-27)**

28 And the Raḇshaqëh (Rabshakeh) stood and called out with a loud voice in the language of Yehuḏah (Judah), and spoke and said, "Hear the word of the great sovereign, the sovereign of Ashshur (Assyria)!" **29** Thus said the sovereign, "Do not let Ḥizqiyahu (Hezekiah) deceive you, for he is unable to deliver you out of his hand, **30** and do not let Ḥizqiyahu (Hezekiah) make you trust in יהוה, saying, 'יהוה shall certainly deliver us, and this city is not given into the hand of the sovereign of Ashshur (Assyria).' **31** "Do not listen to Ḥizqiyahu (Hezekiah)," for thus said the sovereign of Ashshur (Assyria), "Make peace with me by a present and come out to me, and let each of you eat from his own vine and each from his own fig tree, and each of you drink the waters of his own cistern, **32** until I come. Then I shall take you away to a land like your own land, a land of grain and new wine, a land of bread and vineyards, a land of olive trees and honey, and live, and not die. But do not listen to Ḥizqiyahu (Hezekiah), when he misleads you, saying, 'יהוה shall deliver us.' **33** Has any of the mighty ones of the nations at all delivered its land from the hand of the sovereign of Ashshur (Assyria)?" (II Kings 18:29-33)

34 "Where are the mighty ones of Ḥamath and Arpaḏ? Where are the mighty ones of Sepharwayim (Sepharvaim) and Hěna and Iwwah (Ivvah)? Did they deliver Shomeron (Samaria) from my hand? 35 'Who among all the mighty ones of the lands have delivered their land out of my hand, that יהוה should deliver Yerushalayim (Jerusalem) from my hand?'" 36 But the people were silent and did not answer him a word, for the command of the sovereign was, "Do not answer him." 37 And Elyaqim (Eliakim) son of Ḥilqiyah (Hilkiah), who was over the household, and Sheḇnah (Shebna) the scribe, and Yo'aḥ (Joah) son of Asaph, the recorder, came to Ḥizqiyahu (Hezekiah) with their garments torn, and they reported to him the words of the Raḇshaqěh (Rabshakeh). (II Kings 18:34-37)

1 And it came to be, when Sovereign Ḥizqiyahu (Hezekiah) heard it, that he tore his garments, and covered himself with sackcloth, and went into the House of יהוה, 2 and sent Elyaqim (Eliakim), who was over the household, and Sheḇnah (Shebna) the scribe, and the elders of the priests, covering themselves with sackcloth, to Yeshayahu (Isaiah) the prophet, son of Amots (Amoz). 3 And they said to him, "Thus said Ḥizqiyahu (Hezekiah), 'This day is a day of distress and rebuke and scorn, for the children have come to birth but there is no power to bring forth. 4 It could be that יהוה your Elohim does hear all the words of the Raḇshaqěh (Rabshakeh), whom his master the sovereign of Ashshur (Assyria) has sent to reproach the living Elohim, and shall rebuke the words which יהוה your Elohim has heard. Therefore lift up your prayer for the remnant that is left.'" (II Kings 19:1-4)

5 And the servants of Sovereign Ḥizqiyahu (Hezekiah) came to Yeshayahu (Isaiah), 6 and Yeshayahu (Isaiah) said to them, "Say this to your master," 'Thus said יהוה,' "Do not be afraid of the words which you have heard, with which the servants of the sovereign of Ashshur (Assyria) have reviled Me. 7 See, I am putting a spirit upon him, and he shall hear a report and return to his own land. And I shall cause him to fall by the sword in his land." 8 And the Raḇshaqěh (Rabshakeh) returned and found the sovereign of Ashshur (Assyria) fighting against Liḇnah, for he had heard that he had left Laḵish (Lachish). 9 And when the sovereign heard concerning Tirhaqah (Tirhakah) sovereign of Kush (Cush), "See, he has come out to fight against you," he again sent messengers to Ḥizqiyahu (Hezekiah), saying, 10 "Speak to Ḥizqiyahu (Hezekiah) sovereign of Yehuḏah (Judah), saying," 'Do not let your Elohim in whom you trust deceive you, saying,' "Yerushalayim (Jerusalem) is not given into the hand of the sovereign of Ashshur (Assyria)." (II Kings 19:5-10)

11 "See, you have heard what the sovereigns of Ashshur (Assyria) have done to all lands by putting them under the ban. And are you going to be delivered? **12** 'Have the mighty ones of the nations delivered those whom my fathers have destroyed: Gozan and Ḥaran (of Mesopotamia) and Retseph (Rezeph), and the sons of Ěḏen who were in Telassar (Thelasar)? **13** Where is the sovereign of Ḥamath, and the sovereign of Arpaḏ, and the sovereign of the city of Sepharwayim (Sepharvaim), Hěna, and Iwwah (Ivah)?'" **14** And Ḥizqiyahu (Hezekiah) received the letters from the hand of the messengers, and read them, and went up to the House of יהוה. And Ḥizqiyahu (Hezekiah) spread it before יהוה. **15** And Ḥizqiyahu (Hezekiah) prayed before יהוה, and said, "O יהוה Elohim of Yisra'ěl, the One who dwells between the kerubim (cherubim), You are Elohim, You alone, of all the reigns of the earth. You have made the heavens and earth. **16** Incline Your ear, O יהוה, and hear. Open Your eyes, O יהוה, and see. And hear the words of Sanḥěrib (Sennacherib), which he has sent to reproach the living Elohim. **17** Truly, יהוה, the sovereigns of Ashshur (Assyria) have laid waste the nations and their lands, **18** and have put their mighty ones into the fire, for they were not mighty ones, but the work of men's hands, wood and stone, and destroyed them. **19** And now, O יהוה our Elohim, I pray, save us from his hand, so that all the reigns of the earth know that You are יהוה Elohim, You alone." **(II Kings 19:11-19)**

21 Then Yeshayahu (Isaiah) son of Amots (Amoz) sent to Ḥizqiyahu (Hezekiah), saying, "Thus said יהוה Elohim of Yisra'ěl, 'Because you have prayed to Me against Sanḥěrib (Sennacherib) sovereign of Ashshur (Assyria), **22** this is the word which יהוה has spoken concerning him,' "The maiden, the daughter of Tsiyon (Zion), has despised you, mocked you; the daughter of Yerushalayim (Jerusalem) has shaken her head behind you! **23** Whom have you reproached and reviled? And against whom have you raised your voice, and lifted up your eyes in pride? Against the Set-Apart One of Yisra'ěl! **24** By the hand of your servants you have reproached יהוה, and said, 'With my many chariots I have come up to the height of the mountains, to the limits of Lebanon. And I cut down its tall cedars and its choice cypress trees. And I enter its farthest height, its thickest forest. **25** I have dug and drunk water, and with the soles of my feet I have dried up all the streams of defense.' **26** Have you not heard long ago how I made it, from days of old, that I formed it? Now I have brought it about, that you should be for crushing walled cities into heaps of ruins." **(Isaiah 37:21-26)**

27 "And their inhabitants were powerless, they were overthrown and put to shame. They were as the grass of the field and as the green plant, as the grass on the house-tops and as grain blighted before it is grown. **28** But I know your sitting down, and your going out and your coming in, and your rage against Me. **29** Because your rage against Me and your pride have come up to My ears, I shall put My hook in your nose and My bridle in your lips, and I shall turn you back by the way which you came. **30 And this shall be the sign for you: This year you eat such as grows of itself, and the second year what springs from that, and in the third year sow and reap, plant vineyards, and eat the fruit of them. 31** And the remnant who have escaped of the house of Yehuḏah (Judah) shall again take root downward, and bear fruit upward. **32** For out of Yerushalayim (Jerusalem) comes forth a remnant, and those who escape from Mount Tsiyon (Zion)—the ardor of יהוה of hosts does this. **33** Therefore thus said יהוה concerning the sovereign of Ashshur (Assyria), 'He does not come into this city, nor does he shoot an arrow there, nor does he come before it with shield, nor does he build a siege mound against it. **34** By the way that he came, by the same he turns back. And into this city he does not come,' declares יהוה. **35** 'And I shall defend this city, to save it for My own sake and for the sake of My servant Dawiḏ (David).'" **36** And a messenger of יהוה went out, and killed in the camp of Ashshur (Assyria) one hundred and eighty-five thousand. And they arose early in the morning, and saw all of them, dead bodies. **37** And Sanḥĕriḇ (Sennacherib) the sovereign of Ashshur (Assyria) broke camp and went away, and turned back, and remained at Ninewĕh (Ninevah). **(Isaiah 37:27-37)**

What Isaiah has just told is repeated and confirmed in II Kings 19:29-30.

29 And this is the sign for you: This year you eat what grows of itself, and in the second year what springs from that, and in the third year sow and reap and plant vineyards and eat their fruit. 30 And the remnant who have escaped of the house of Yehuḏah (Judah) shall again take root downward, and bear fruit upward. (II Kings 19:29-30)

1 In those days Ḥizqiyahu (Hezekiah) was sick unto death. And Yeshayahu (Isaiah) the prophet, son of Amots (Amoz) went to him and said to him, "Thus said יהוה, 'Set your house in order, for you are going to die, and not live.' " **2** And he turned his face toward the wall, and prayed to יהוה, saying, **3** "I pray to You, O יהוה, remember how I have walked before You in truth and with a perfect heart, and have done what was good in Your eyes." And Ḥizqiyahu (Hezekiah) wept bitterly. **4** And it came to be, before Yeshayahu (Isaiah) had gone out into the middle court, that the word of יהוה came to him, saying, **5** "Return and say to Ḥizqiyahu (Hezekiah) the leader of My people, 'Thus said יהוה, the Elohim of Dawiḏ (David) your father,' "I have heard your prayer, I have seen your tears. See, I am going to heal you. On the third day go up to the House of יהוה. **6** And I shall add to your days fifteen years, and deliver you and this city from the hand of the sovereign of Ashshur (Assyria), and shall defend this city for My own sake, and for the sake of Dawid̲ (David) My servant." **(II Kings 20:1-6)**

7 And Yeshayahu (Isaiah) said, "Take a cake of figs." And they took and laid it on the boil, and he recovered. 8 And Ḥizqiyahu (Hezekiah) said to Yeshayahu (Isaiah), "What is the sign that יהוה does heal me, and that I shall go up to the House of יהוה the third day?" 9 And Yeshayahu (Isaiah) said, "This is the sign for you from יהוה, that יהוה does the word which He has spoken: shall the shadow go forward ten degrees or go backward ten degrees?" 10 And Ḥizqiyahu (Hezekiah) said, "It would be easy for the shadow to go down ten degrees; no, but let the shadow go backward ten degrees." 11 And Yeshayahu (Isaiah) the prophet cried out to יהוה, and He brought the shadow ten degrees backward, by which it had gone down on the sundial of Aḥaz. **(II Kings 20:7-11)**

This is the full account of the events surrounding King Hezekiah and the attack of Judah by the Assyrians.

The most important passage of Scripture in this section we just read was in II Kings 19:29 I will now encourage you to look at this verse point by point with me to get a much closer look at it's meaning.

And this is the sign for you:

- This year you eat what grows of itself,
- And in the second year what springs from that,
- And in the third year sow and reap and plant vineyards and eat their fruit.

We are given a very large clue in the first line. "This is the sign for you."

You will read in the next chapter what the sign of Yehovah is. For now, just know that Yehovah's sign is His Sabbaths and He is intimating here to King Hezekiah that His sign to him has something to do with the Sabbaths. Keep in mind that we have already discussed the sign or mark of Yehovah, which are His weekly and Annual Sabbaths and Holy Days. The Sabbatical years are also part of those signs that identify those who keep them as His. We also shared with you what Satans sign or mark was. They are any other days or holi-days that are not listed in Lev 23.

Yehovah is telling Hezekiah that this sign has something to do with these Holy Appointments that we have learned about in Levitcus 23 and 25.

"This year you eat what grows of itself" is telling us that *no one* has planted or harvested in this first year.

"... and in the second year, what springs from that" is showing us that for two years in a row we do *not* plant or harvest crops. To most people this is very peculiar unless—well, unless you are familiar with the Sabbatical Cycles of Yehovah.

"… and in the third year, sow and reap and plant vineyards and eat their fruit." With this closing line in Yehovah's promise to Hezekiah we see they can now plant, sow and harvest crops.

What you have just read is Yehovah's injunction that for two years they were commanded not to plant or harvest and there are only two years in a Sabbatical Cycle when you cannot plant or harvest and that is the forty-ninth and fiftieth years of the Jubilee Cycle.

But as to the II Kings 19:29 opener, "And this is the sign for you," this is speaking about the Sabbatical and Jubilee Years, which are part of the Sabbaths and Holy Days that go into keeping the Fourth Commandment—a sign that we are His.

But as to how what follows the opener pertains to any kind of timeline or chronology, I will now explain:

"This year you eat what grows of itself."

The year Sennacherib attacked Jerusalem and Hezekiah, was as I have shown you, one of the most documented and undisputable years in history. It was 701 B.C.

"… and in the second year what springs from that."

Knowing what year Sennacherib attacks then makes this second line the year 700 B.C.

"… and in the third year sow and reap and
plant vineyards and eat their fruit."

So the logical conclusion is that this third year is 699 B.C.

As I have reiterated already, these are proven historical years which match up with other known chronological histories.

701 B.C. is a proven historical date that can be successfully corroborated with a proven Assyrian date. We now can tie the succession of Hebrew kings in with a *known* chronology. Even more importantly, we can also use this exact same date to know when a Sabbatical Year was, which was followed by another Sabbatical Year, which was, in fact, a Jubilee Year.

This information is truly *ground breaking* and so pivotal, yet no one wants to look at it or acknowledge it. Very few seem to be operating under the conviction of just *how paramount* the Sabbatical and Jubilee Years are with regard to biblical history and prophecy, yet their importance is not to be denied and they can be found throughout the Bible if you know how to look for them and where.

Just *how* important are the Sabbatical and Jubilee Years to Yehovah? Do they even matter? Did anyone even keep them? We do not read of them in the Bible, do we? But *if* we do, *why* do they matter?

The passages below (and the answers contained therein) are central to gaining an understanding of and insight into the pointed questions I have just asked.

> **19** And they burned the House of Elohim, and broke down the wall of Yerushalayim (Jerusalem), and burned all its palaces with fire, and destroyed all its valuable utensils. **20** And those who escaped from the sword he exiled to Babel, where they became servants to him and his sons until the reign of the reign of Persia, **21** in order to fill the word of יהוה by the mouth of Yirmeyahu (Jeremiah), until the land had enjoyed her Sabbaths. As long as she lay waste she kept Sabbath, until seventy years were completed. (**II Chronicles 36:19-21**)

> **11** "And all this land shall be a ruin and a waste, and these nations shall serve the sovereign of Babel seventy years. **12** And it shall be, when seventy years are completed, that I shall punish the sovereign of Babel and that nation, the land of the Chaldeans, for their crookedness," declares יהוה, "and shall make it everlasting ruins. **13** And I shall bring on that land all My words which I have pronounced against it, all that is written in this book, which Yirmeyahu (Jeremiah) has prophesied concerning all the nations." (**Jeremiah 25:11-13**)

> **10** For thus said יהוה, "When seventy years are completed, at Babel I shall visit you and establish My good word toward you, to bring you back to this place. **11** For I know the plans I am planning for you," declares יהוה, "plans of peace and not of evil, to give you a future and an expectancy. **12** Then you shall call on Me, and shall come and pray to Me, and I shall listen to you. **13** And you shall seek Me, and shall find Me, when you search for Me with all your heart."[1] (**Jeremiah 29:10-13** | Footnote: [1]**Deuteronomy 4:29, Joel 2:12**)

So again I ask you, *DO* the Sabbatical and Jubilee Years even matter? Jeremiah warned them they would be captives seventy years and II

Chronicles explains why—for *not* keeping seventy Sabbatical Years prior to this outcome.

This captivity took place in 586 B.C. You must be mindful to factor in the Jubilee Years when you count the Sabbatical Years—the seventy Sabbatical Years being no different. So seventy Sabbatical Years from 586 B.C. takes you back far enough, at the very least, to the time when David became king in 1010 B.C.[115] If the Israelites kept some of the Sabbatical Years and not others, then we can speculate they never kept them from the time of Joshua, which was fifty-three Sabbatical Years *before* King David.

What we are seeing here is the fact that, if no one else kept track of the Sabbatical and Jubilee years, Yehovah did. He kept track of precisely how many Sabbatical Years the Earth was owed. One might think it strange that the Earth would be "owed" anything. Yet, this is what Yehovah is impressing upon us in His Word, even though it keeps falling on deaf ears. Yet, the simple truth of the matter is this: each year the Earth has to work while it grows your food on the Sabbath while you are resting. It misses fifty-two Shabbats a year as a result. Unlike us, it is not possible for the Earth to cease and desist from growing your food once a week to observe the weekly Sabbath rest.

When you multiply 52 weeks x 7 years you get 364 Sabbath Days that the Earth misses, or:

$$52 \times 7 = 364$$

The Sabbatical Year is when the Earth finally is allowed to rest from and make up for all the Sabbaths it had to work growing your food on the weekly Sabbath.

Do these years which are so vital to the Earth's ongoing, overall well-being matter to Yehovah? You bet your life they do. And if you wish to keep benefiting from the Earth being in a position to continue to yield its sustenance, then these years should matter to you too—every bit as much.

It is after Judah returned to the land of Israel that we begin to see the Jews getting on board with observing and keeping the Sabbatical Years—along with the other Holy Days and the weekly Sabbath—something they did not do *before* their captivity. They are now becoming zealous about obeying them. And it is only *after* this time that we are actually able to find references to the Sabbatical Years in biblical history.

After Judah went into captivity for seventy years, the Jews returned to

115 http://www.aboutbibleprophecy.com/e8.htm

The Land and were more zealous than ever to keep the Sabbatical Years, the weekly Sabbath and the Holy Days than before their captivity when they made little or no effort to keep them. So again, it is only *after* their captivity we find artefacts and records of Judah keeping the Sabbatical Years. But you will notice also that after the Bar Koch bah Revolt we do not have any records. We will explain this in the following chapters.

> 17 And the entire assembly of those who had come back from the captivity made booths and sat under the booths, for since the days of Yehoshua (Joshua) son of Nun until that day the children of Yisra'ël had not done so. And there was very great rejoicing. 18 And day by day, from the first day until the last day, he read from the Book of the Torah of Elohim. And they performed the festival seven days. And on the eighth day there was an assembly, according to the right-ruling. (**Nehemiah 8:17-18**)

The following are historically recorded Sabbatical Years, with the last four being artifacts that mention a Sabbatical Year.

Historically Recorded Sabbatical Years	
701 B.C.	Sennacherib attack Judah 2 Kings 19:29
700 B.C.	2 Kings 19:29 A Jubilee year
456 B.C.	Nehemiah 8:18
162 B.C.	I Maccabees 16:14 & Josephus Antiquities
134 B.C.	I Maccabees & Josephus Antiquities
43 B.C.	Julius Caesar & Josephus Antiquities
36 B.C.	Josephus Antiquities 14:16:2
22 B.C.	Josephus Antiquities 15:9:1
42 C.E.	Josephus Antiquities 18
56 C.E.	A note of Indebtedness in Nero's time.
70 C.E.	The Sabbath year of 70/71 C.E.
133 C.E.	Rental contracts before Bar Koch bah Revolt
140 C.E.	Rental contracts before Bar Koch bah Revolt

From the Days of Joshua until Nehemiah they had not kept the Feast of Booths. If they never kept Sukkot then, how would they know or remember to keep the Sabbatical Years and the Jubilee Years?

10 And Mosheh (Moses) commanded them, saying, "At the end of seven years, at the appointed time, the year of release, at the Festival of Booths, **11** when all Yisra'ĕl comes to appear before יהוה your Elohim in the place which He chooses, read this Torah before all Yisra'ĕl in their hearing. **12** Assemble the people, the men and the women and the little ones, and your sojourner who is within your gates, so that they hear, and so that they learn to fear יהוה your Elohim and guard to do all the Words of this Torah. **13** And their children, who have not known it, should hear and learn to fear יהוה your Elohim as long as you live in the land you are passing over the Yardĕn to possess." **(Deuteronomy 31:10-13)**

Moses commanded the Israelites to read the Torah every seventh year during Sukkot. And this is also what Nehemiah was doing. This was the "Year of Release."

Qadesh La Yahweh Press in their book, *The Sabbath and Jubilee Cycle*[116] examine the theories stemming from the Zuckermann-Schurer school of thought and the Marcus-Wacholder interpretation method, as well as others in extreme detail. This book is 445 pages and is free to download and read from their website. I highly recommend this book. We will begin to look at some of the theories these men have put forward and show where they have erred in their understanding of the Sabbatical and Jubilee years.

---

116 http://www.yahweh.org/yahweh2.html

Chapter 19 | The Mark of the Beast

In the preceding chapter I cited II Kings 19:29, "And this is the sign for you" is a reference to the Sabbath and the mark of Yehovah. I shall now lead you further along on this path and show you *precisely* how this is the sign of Yehovah and how His Sabbaths are a sign between Him and us.

Let us do a simple Bible study.[117] First go to a concordance and look up: "mark of". I use Crosswalk.com and the NKJV in this chapter. I make sure however to keep The Name sacred.

Notice in the Book of Job how we are marked by Yehovah if we sin:

> **14** If I sin, then you mark me, and will not acquit me of my iniquity.
> (**Job 10:14**)

Notice in the Psalms how the upright man is also marked:

> **37** Mark the blameless man, and observe the upright; for the future of that man is peace. (**Psalm 37:37**)

Next, in Ezekiel we find:

> **4** "... and YHVH said to him, "Go through the midst of the city, through the midst of Jerusalem, and put a mark on the foreheads of the men who sigh and cry over all the abominations that are done within it." (**Ezekiel 9:4**)

Notice again a mark on the forehead by Yehovah placed on those who mourn over all the evil being done.

---

117 Taken from the article, *The Mark of the Beast,* http://www.sightedmoon.com/ ?page_id=17

In Revelation we hit pay dirt concerning the mark:

17 "... and that no one may buy or sell except one who has the mark or the name of the beast, or the number of his name." **(Revelation 13:17)**

11 And the smoke of their torment ascends forever and ever; and they have no rest day or night, who worship the beast and his image, and whoever receives the mark of his name. **(Revelation 14:11)**

2 And I saw something like a sea of glass mingled with fire, and those who have the victory over the beast, over his image and over his mark and over the number of his name, standing on the sea of glass, having harps of Elohim. **(Revelation 15:2)**

2 So the first went and poured out his bowl upon the earth, and a foul and loathsome sore came upon the men who had the mark of the beast and those who worshipped his image. **(Revelation 16:2)**

20 Then the beast was captured, and with him the false prophet who worked signs in his presence, by which he deceived those who received the mark of the beast and those who worshipped his image. These two were cast alive into the lake of fire burning with brimstone. **(Revelation 19:20)**

4 And I saw thrones, and they sat on them, and judgment was committed to them. Then I saw the souls of those who had been beheaded for their witness to Yehshua and for the word of Elohim, who had not worshipped the beast or his image, and had not received his mark on their foreheads or on their hands. And they lived and reigned with Yehshua for a thousand years. **(Revelation 20:4)**

Next we are going to look up the word 'signs.' There were eighty-three Bible verse search results and out of those eighty-three, I looked for signs that related to strictly hands and foreheads.

In Exodus Yehovah is found saying:

1 Then YHVH spoke to Moses, saying, 2 "Consecrate to Me all the firstborn, whatever opens the womb among the children of Israel, both of man and beast; it is Mine." 3 And Moses said to the people: "Remember this day in which you went out of Egypt, out of the house of bondage; for by strength of hand YHVH brought you out of this place. No leavened bread shall be eaten. 4 On this day you are going out, in the month Abib. 5 And it shall be, when YHVH brings you into the land of the Canaanites and the Hittites and the Amorites and the Hivites and the Jebusites, which He swore to your fathers to give you, a land flowing

with milk and honey, that you shall keep this service in this month. **6** Seven days you shall eat unleavened bread, and on the seventh day there shall be a feast to YHVH. **7** Unleavened bread shall be eaten seven days. And no leavened bread shall be seen among you, nor shall leaven be seen among you in all your quarters. **8** And you shall tell your son in that day, saying, 'This is done because of what YHVH did for me when I came up from Egypt.' **9** It shall be as a sign to you on your hand and as a memorial between your eyes, that YHVH's law may be in your mouth; for with a strong hand YHVH has brought you out of Egypt. **10** You shall therefore keep this ordinance in its season from year to year. (**Exodus 13:1-10**)

Here we have a sign that would be on our hand and a memorial on our forehead (between our eyes). What is that sign? It is the keeping of Passover as referenced in chapters 12 and 13 of the Book of Exodus. It is the keeping of the Days of Unleavened Bread—a sign that we are to keep from year to year.

Also in Exodus, Yehovah then continues by saying:

12 And YHVH spoke to Moses, saying, **13** "Speak also to the children of Israel, saying: 'Surely My Sabbaths you shall keep, for it is a sign between Me and you throughout your generations, that you may know that I am YHVH who sanctifies you. **14** You shall keep the Sabbath, therefore, for it is holy to you. Everyone who profanes it shall surely be put to death; for whoever does any work on it, that person shall be cut off from among his people. **15** Work shall be done for six days, but the seventh is the Sabbath of rest, holy to YHVH. Whoever does any work on the Sabbath day, he shall surely be put to death. **16** Therefore the children of Israel shall keep the Sabbath, to observe the Sabbath throughout their generations as a perpetual covenant. **17** It is a sign between Me and the children of Israel forever; for in six days YHVH made the heavens and the earth, and on the seventh day He rested and was refreshed.'" **18** And when He had made an end of speaking with him on Mount Sinai, He gave Moses two tablets of the Testimony, tablets of stone, written with the finger of Elohim. (**Exodus 31:12-18**)

1 "Now this is the commandment, and these are the statutes and judgments which YHVH your Elohim has commanded to teach you, that you may observe them in the land which you are crossing over to possess, **2** that you may fear YHVH your Elohim, to keep all His statutes and His commandments which I command you, you and your son and your grandson, all the days of your life, and that your days may be prolonged. **3** Therefore hear, O Israel, and be careful to observe it, that it may be well with you, and that you may multiply greatly as YHVH Elohim of your fathers has promised you–'a land flowing with milk and honey.'" (**Deuteronomy 6:1-3**)

4 "Hear, O Israel: YHVH our Elohim, YHVH is one! 5 You shall love YHVH your Elohim with all your heart, with all your soul, and with all your strength. 6 And these words which I command you today shall be in your heart. 7 You shall teach them diligently to your children, and shall talk of them when you sit in your house, when you walk by the way, when you lie down, and when you rise up. 8 You shall bind them as a sign on your hand, and they shall be as frontlets between your eyes. 9 You shall write them on the door posts of your house and on your gates." (**Deuteronomy 6:4-9**

1 "Therefore you shall love YHVH your Elohim, and keep His charge, His statutes, His judgments, and His commandments always ... 18 Therefore you shall lay up these words of mine in your heart and in your soul, and bind them as a sign on your hand, and they shall be as frontlets between your eyes. 19 You shall teach them to your children, speaking of them when you sit in your house, when you walk by the way, when you lie down, and when you rise up. 20 And you shall write them on the door posts of your house and on your gates, 21 that your days and the days of your children may be multiplied in the land of which YHVH swore to your fathers to give them, like the days of the heavens above the earth. 22 For if you carefully keep all these commandments which I command you to do—to love YHVH your Elohim, to walk in all His ways, and to hold fast to Him 23 then YHVH will drive out all these nations from before you, and you will dispossess greater and mightier nations than yourselves. 24 Every place on which the sole of your foot treads shall be yours: from the wilderness and Lebanon, from the river, the River Euphrates, even to the Western Sea, shall be your territory. 25 No man shall be able to stand against you; YHVH your Elohim will put the dread of you and the fear of you upon all the land where you tread, just as He has said to you." (**Deuteronomy 11:1, 18-25**)

10 "Therefore I made them go out of the land of Egypt and brought them into the wilderness. 11 And I gave them My statutes and showed them My judgments, 'which, if a man does, he shall live by them.' 12 Moreover, **I also gave them My Sabbaths, to be a sign between them and Me,** that they might know that I am YHVH who sanctifies them. 13 Yet the house of Israel rebelled against Me in the wilderness; they did not walk in My statutes; they despised My judgments, 'which, if a man does, he shall live by them;' and they greatly defiled My Sabbaths. Then I said I would pour out My fury on them in the wilderness, to consume them. 14 But I acted for My name's sake, that it should not be profaned before the Gentiles, in whose sight I had brought them out. 15 So I also raised My hand in an oath to them in the wilderness, that I would not bring them into the land which I had given them, 'flowing with milk and honey,' the glory of all lands, 16 because they despised My judgments and did

not walk in My statutes, but profaned My Sabbaths; for their heart went after their idols. **17** Nevertheless, My eye spared them from destruction. I did not make an end of them in the wilderness. **18** But I said to their children in the wilderness, 'Do not walk in the statutes of your fathers, nor observe their judgments, nor defile yourselves with their idols.'" **(Ezekiel 20:10-18)**

19 "I am YHVH your Elohim: 'Walk in My statutes, keep My judgments, and do them; **20** hallow My Sabbaths, and they will be a sign between Me and you, that you may know that I am YHVH your Elohim.' **21** Notwithstanding, the children rebelled against Me; they did not walk in My statutes, and were not careful to observe My judgments, 'which, if a man does, he shall live by them;' but they profaned My Sabbaths. Then I said I would pour out My fury on them and fulfill My anger against them in the wilderness. **22** Nevertheless I withdrew My hand and acted for My name's sake, that it should not be profaned in the sight of the Gentiles, in whose sight I had brought them out. **23** Also I raised My hand in an oath to those in the wilderness, that I would scatter them among the Gentiles and disperse them throughout the countries, **24** because they had not executed My judgments, but had despised My statutes, profaned My Sabbaths, and their eyes were fixed on their fathers' idols. **25** Therefore I also gave them up to statutes that were not good, and judgments by which they could not live; **26** and I pronounced them unclean because of their ritual gifts, in that they caused all their firstborn to pass through the fire, that I might make them desolate and that they might know that I am YHVH." **(Ezekiel 20:19 -26)**

With the preceding verses, you can easily see that the mark of Yehovah is the keeping of His Laws, Sabbaths and Holy Days. When we keep them, they become a sign on our hand and a sign between our eyes, or in our mind, which is also that which is written on our heart. 'The hand' signifies the way we live—our way of life, the way we work or conduct ourselves. 'Between our eyes' signifies the way we think and how we treat others. It is our heart, our innermost being, and our thoughts.

Those who will not keep The Laws and Sabbaths of Yehovah, have the mark of the beast as a sign on their hands and on their foreheads.

Returning to Revelation we read:

3 Do not harm the earth, the sea, or the trees till we have sealed the servants of our Elohim on their foreheads. **(Revelation 7:3)**

4 They were commanded not to harm the grass of the earth, or any green thing, or any tree, but only those men who do not have the seal of Elohim on their foreheads. (**Revelation 9:4**)

16 He causes all, both small and great, rich and poor, free and slave, to receive a mark on their right hand or on their foreheads. (**Revelaton 13:16**)

1 Then I looked, and behold, a Lamb standing on Mount Zion, and with Him one hundred and forty-four thousand, having His Father's name written on their foreheads. (**Revelation 14:1**)

4 And I saw thrones, and they sat on them, and judgment was committed to them. Then I saw the souls of those who had been beheaded for their witness to Yehshua and for the word of Elohim, who had not worshipped the beast or his image, and had not received his mark on their foreheads or on their hands. And they lived and reigned with Yehshua for a thousand years. (**Revelation 20:4**)

4 They shall see His face, and His name shall be on their foreheads. (**Revelation 22:4**)

1 Now, brethren, concerning the coming of Yehshua and our gathering together to Him, we ask you, 2 not to be soon shaken in mind or troubled, either by spirit or by word or by letter, as if from us, as though the day of Yehshua had come. 3 Let no one deceive you by any means; for that day will not come unless the falling away comes first, and the man of sin is revealed, the son of perdition, 4 who opposes and exalts himself above all that is called Elohim or that is worshipped, so that he sits as Elohim in the temple of Elohim, showing himself that he is Elohim. 5 Do you not remember that when I was still with you I told you these things? 6 And now you know what is restraining, that he may be revealed in his own time. 7 For the mystery of lawlessness is already at work; only He who now restrains will do so until He is taken out of the way. 8 And then the lawless one will be revealed, whom the (Master) will consume with the breath of His mouth and destroy with the brightness of His coming. 9 The coming of the lawless one is according to the working of Satan, with all power, signs, and lying wonders, 10 and with all unrighteous deception among those who perish, because they did not receive the love of the truth, that they might be saved. 11 And for this reason Elohim will send them strong delusion, that they should believe the lie, 12 that they all may be condemned who did not believe the truth but had pleasure in unrighteousness. (**II Thessalonians 2:1-12**)

Notice here in Thessalonians that the "mystery of lawlessness" (not keeping Yehovah's Laws) is at work. The lawless one is Satan performing miraculous signs, lying wonders, and unrighteous deceptions on those who would not love the truth of Yehovah and keep His Laws. On them Yehovah will send a powerful delusion that they should continue to believe upon a lie.

What lie? Satan, who is the "father of *all* lies."

> 44 You are of your father the devil, and the desires of your father you want to do. He was a murderer from the beginning, and does not stand in the truth, because there is no truth in him. When he speaks a lie, he speaks from his own resources, for he is a liar and the father of it. (**John 8:44**)

If you are not keeping The Commandments, then you are a liar if you, in the same breath, claim to obey Yehovah.

> 4 He who says, "I know Him," and does not keep His commandments, is a liar, and the truth is not in him. (**I John 2:4**)

But again, just what *is* the "mark of the beast?" I have clearly shown you using passages in Scripture what the mark of Yehovah is and how it is on our **HAND** and **BETWEEN OUR EYES** or on our foreheads. So I'm sure you have a pretty good idea by now what I am going to finger as being the mark of the beast. But I need to prove it to you without leaving any wiggle room for doubt.

This year (2012) the world population is not only predicted to reach but exceed the seven billion mark. Throughout the past 6,000 years of human history there have been multiples of billions of people.

Today, as in the past, the vast majority of Europe and both North and South America are either Catholic or Protestant. The Middle East has been predominantly Muslim for the greater part of the last 1,500 years. Asia is both Muslim and Hindu with a mixture of Buddhism and Confucianism. Russia is part of Europe and predominantly Catholic. Which part of the world is comprised primarily of Sabbath keepers? Up until 1948, none … believe it or not. Then, the State of Israel was re-born. There has also been a significantly infinitesimal number of Jews and other Sabbath-keepers scattered throughout Europe and North America by way of comparison. I think we can all agree upon this.

It is even written that one of the primary reasons YHVH chose Abraham and his descendants now called Israel, to be His "chosen ones" were because they were the fewest in number:

7 YHVH did not set His love on you nor choose you because you were more numerous than any other people, for you were the least of all peoples. (**Deuteronomy 7:7**)

Continuing on in Revelation we find:

9 So the great dragon was cast out, that serpent of old, called the Devil and Satan, who deceives the whole world; he was cast to the earth, and his angels were cast out with him. (**Revelation 12:9**)

John said that Satan deceives the whole world. The *WHOLE WORLD*. Not just a few. Yehshua Himself warned the apostles and us in Matthew:

4 "Take heed that no one deceives you. **5** For many will come in My name, saying, 'I am Yehshua,' and will deceive many." (**Matthew 24:4-5**)

We now know that Satan deceives the whole world, and Yehshua warns His disciples and anyone who has ears to hear how many will come in His name and deceive many.

Notice in Revelation where it says:

2 And I looked, and behold, a white horse. He who sat on it had a bow; and a crown was given to him, and he went out conquering and to conquer. (**Revelation 6:2**)

You should make note of the fact that; Yehshua in Matthew 24 interprets the Four Horsemen of the Apocalypse in Revelation. The first horse, although white and representative of religion, is *not* Yehshua, nor is it representative of the one true religion the Father accepts which is pure, undefiled religion. Instead, it symbolizes false religion. These false religions conquered their way by force.

The verses contained in the following chapter of Matthew most believers are very familiar with:

7 "Ask, and it will be given to you; seek, and you will find; knock, and it will be opened to you. **8** For everyone who asks receives, and he who seeks finds, and to him who knocks it will be opened. **9** Or what man is there among you who, if his son asks for bread, will give him a stone? **10** Or if he asks for a fish, will he give him a serpent? **11** If you then, being evil, know how to give good gifts to your children, how much more will your Father who is in heaven give good things to those who ask Him! **12** Therefore, whatever you want men to do to you, do also to them, for this is the Law and the Prophets. **13** Enter by the narrow gate; for wide is the gate and broad is the way that leads to destruction, and there are many who go in by it. **14** Because narrow is the gate and difficult is the way which leads to life, and there are few who find it. **15** Beware of false prophets, who come to you in sheep's clothing, but inwardly they are ravenous wolves. **16** You will know them by their fruits. Do men gather grapes from thorn bushes or figs from thistles?" (**Matthew 20:7-16**)

17 "Even so, every good tree bears good fruit, but a bad tree bears bad fruit. **18** A good tree cannot bear bad fruit, nor can a bad tree bear good fruit. **19** Every tree that does not bear good fruit is cut down and thrown into the fire. **20** Therefore by their fruits you will know them. **21** Not everyone who says to Me, '(Master, Master),' shall enter the kingdom of heaven, but he who does the will of My Father in heaven. **22** Many will say to Me in that day, '(Master, Master), have we not prophesied in Your name, cast out demons in Your name, and done many wonders in Your name?' **23** And then I will declare to them, 'I never knew you; depart from Me, you who practice lawlessness!' **24** Therefore whoever hears these sayings of Mine, and does them, I will liken him to a wise man who built his house on the rock: **25** and the rain descended, the floods came, and the winds blew and beat on that house; and it did not fall, for it was founded on the rock. **26** But everyone who hears these sayings of Mine, and does not do them, will be like a foolish man who built his house on the sand: **27** and the rain descended, the floods came, and the winds blew and beat on that house; and it fell. And great was its fall." **28** And so it was, when Yehshua had ended these sayings, that the people were astonished at His teaching, **29** for He taught them as one having authority, and not as the scribes. (**Matthew 7:17-29**)

Now, concerning the mark of the beast, we should be looking for a mark that would cause us to not obey the Laws of Yehovah. If Yehovah's mark is the Sabbath and the Feast Days as shown to us in Leviticus 23, and the Sabbatical years of Lev 25, then Satan's mark is the one that causes us to rest on another day besides the Sabbath and to worship on other holy days other than the Feast Days Yehovah has ordained in Leviticus 23 and to keep other land rest years that do not match up with those known and provable Sabbatical years. In short, this is the mark of the beast: keeping other days holy that are not set apart by Yehovah and doing our own pleasure on the Sabbath or any of the other Appointed Times and not letting the land to rest are in effect placing the mark of Satan upon us.

9 The coming of the lawless one is according to the working of Satan, with all power, signs, and lying wonders, **10** and with all unrighteous deception among those who perish, because they did not receive the love of the truth, that they might be saved. (**II Thessalonians 2:9-10**)

Here, we see Satan is altogether lawless and anything but a keeper of Yehovah's Laws. He demonstrates his power through lying wonders and unrighteous deceptions.

25 He shall speak pompous words against the Most High, (he) shall persecute the saints of the Most High, and (he) shall intend to change times and law. (**Daniel 7:25**)

Here again, we have Satan changing the mark of Yehovah by changing the times and Yehovah's Laws. The days we are to worship Yehovah are changed to other days and then we are told to worship Yehovah on these new days. The days Yehovah called Holy are done away and new holidays are put in place. The Sabbatical years Yehovah told us to keep are not and then people stop keeping them at all or at the wrong time or let parts of the land rest one year and another part the next, which is not what we are told to do.

I have inquired of others many times, and even right up to this late date, to show me a single passage in Scripture which supports any of the following: Sunday worship, Christmas, Easter, Lent, Good Friday, Palm Sunday, or any other day that the "Christian" or "Moslem" world makes a point to keep or celebrate. Not one person, no matter how learned, has been able to provide me with any kind of scriptural basis for any of the above. Does it not then go without saying that these are clearly days which draw their sole inspiration from the mark of the beast and Satan himself?! They are the days the whole world keeps in honor of its gods, making it a mark on their hands and a sign between their eyes or on their foreheads.

Yet, the mark of Yehovah is none other than *His* Sabbaths and *His* Holy Days. Satan, however, who has deceived the entire world, has already long since succeeded in changing the times and Yehovah's Laws for the expressed purpose of causing the entire world to believe in, observe, and partake in pagan religious beliefs while grossly missing the mark when it comes to believing in, observing, and partaking in those things which constitute worshipping Yehovah in spirit and in truth as He has taken great pains to outline for us in His Word. Yet, in keeping *His* Sabbaths, Holy Days, Sabbatical Years and Jubilee Cycles, we worship Yehovah in a way that is pleasing to Him, that Satan can't touch, and in a manner in which we never would be capable of otherwise, apart from keeping Yehovah's Appointed Times. By doing this we are marked by Yehovah and sealed by Him.

As it stands, however, and as I have already indicated, Satan has successfully deceived the entire world and the entire world has believed the lie. How about you? I can provide for you many proofs attesting to how Christmas, Easter and other so-called "holy days" are pagan, but you may not believe me. But to those who want the truth, look each holiday up in any reputable encyclopaedia and you'll soon see. Satan has deceived the entire world (and you too) by changing Yehovah's Holy Days (as laid out in Leviticus) to other days and then getting those in a position of power and influence to convince the world they are Yehovah's set-apart days.

Listen to what Yehovah has to say in the Book of Amos:

> **21** "I hate, I despise your feast days, and I do not savor your sacred assemblies. **22** Though you offer Me burnt offerings and your grain offerings, I will not accept them, nor will I regard your fattened peace offerings. **23** Take away from Me the noise of your songs, for I will not hear the melody of your stringed instruments. **24** But let justice run down like water, and righteousness like a mighty stream. **25** Did you offer Me sacrifices and offerings in the wilderness forty years, O house of Israel? **26** You also carried Sikkuth (Sakkuth) your king and Chiun (Kaiwan, Kiyyun), your idols, the star of your gods (star-god, astral mighty ones), which you made for yourselves. **27** Therefore I will send you into captivity beyond Damascus," says YHVH, whose name is Elohim of hosts. (**Amos 5:21-27**)

Do a study on Sikkuth and Chiun. They are Molech (the god which babies were sacrificed to) and Ishtar, or Christmas and Easter. As a point of interest, it may behove you to know that Israel was worshipping these gods long before Yehshua was ever born.

Alexander Hislop exposes all these lies of Satan with many multiple proofs in his book, *The Two Babylons*. In closing then, I highly recommend you read not only *The Two Babylons*[118], but also, *The Papal Worship Proved To Be the Worship of Nimrod and His Wife*—both of which were written by the late Reverend Alexander Hislop.

---

118 http://www.biblebelievers.com/babylon/

Chapter 20	**"One Day Is Like A Thousand Years"** **& Its Prophetic Significance**[119]

What Does This Mean?

What is implied when Peter writes, "one day is like a thousand years" (II Peter 3:8)? Is this a literal (1,000) years? We have been taught to believe that. I, for one, have never questioned it before. We also have to determine the context and how broadly we can apply it. This study started out as a quick look-up of this phrase but, as I studied, I realized that it is a key to understanding some of the Bible prophecies.

> **3** Know this first of all, that in the last days mockers will come with their mocking, following after their own lusts, **4** and saying, "Where is the promise of His coming? For ever since the fathers fell asleep, all continues just as it was from the beginning of creation." **5** For when they maintain this, it escapes their notice that by the word of YHVH the heavens existed long ago and the earth was formed out of water and by water, **6** through which the world at that time was destroyed, being flooded with water. **7** But by His Word the present heavens and earth are being reserved for fire, kept for the Day of Judgment and destruction of ungodly men. **8** But do not let this one fact escape your notice, beloved, that _with YHVH one day is like a thousand years, and a thousand years like one day_. **9** YHVH is not slow about His promise, as some count slowness, but is patient toward you, not wishing for any to perish but for all to come to repentance. **10** But the day of YHVH will come like a thief, in which the heavens will pass away with a roar and the elements will be destroyed with intense heat, and the earth and its works will be burned up. **(II Peter 3:3-10)**

The discussion in this passage is about the coming of the Messiah at the

---

119 By Permission of Schalk & Elsa Klee
http://www.setapartpeople.com/day-thousand-years-prophetic-significance-2

end of the age. People were expecting it to be in their time. Since it has not occurred yet; they are now mocking it. A. Robertson explains it well when he says:

> Peter applies the language of Psalm 90:4 about the eternity of YHVH and shortness of human life to 'the impatience of human expectations' (Bigg) about the Second Coming of Christ. 'The Day of Judgment' is at hand (I Peter 4:7). It may come tomorrow; but *what is* tomorrow? What does YHVH mean by a day? It may be a thousand years. Precisely the same argument applies to those who argue for a literal interpretation of the thousand year (timeframe) mentioned in Revelation 20:4-6. It may be a day or a day may be a thousand years. YHVH's clock does not run by our timepieces. The scoffers scoff ignorantly.[120]

To explain it further, we must look at the meaning of the word "like." The Greek word "hos" means an approximation of time.

> 4. **hos** (ὡς, 5613) usually means "as." **Used with numerals it signifies "about,"** (e.g., Mark 5:13, 8:9; John 1:40, 6:19, 11:18; Acts 1:15; Revelation 8:1).

> 5. **hosei** (ὡσεί, 5616), "as if," before numerals, denotes "about, nearly, something like," with perhaps an indication of greater indefiniteness than No. 4 (e.g., Matthew 14:21; Luke 3:23, 9:14, 28; Acts 2:41; with a measure of space, Luke 22:41, "about a stone's cast." See LIKE.[121]

If we look at all the other passages where this word was used with numerals it was translated as "about."

(I do not include John 1:40 in the examples below, as it uses a different Greek word "heis").

> 13 Y'shua gave them permission. And coming out, the unclean spirits entered the swine; and the herd rushed down the steep bank into the sea, about (hos) two thousand of them; and they were drowned in the sea. **(Mark 5:13)**

> 9 About (hos) four thousand were there; and He sent them away. **(Mark 8:9)**

---

120 Robertson, A (1997). *Word Pictures In the New Testament* (II Peter 3:8). Oak Harbor: Logos Research Systems.
121 Vine, W.E., Unger, M.F., & White, W. (1996). Vol. 2: *Vine's Complete Expository Dictionary of Old & New Testament Words*. Nashville, TN: T. Nelson.

19 Then, when they had rowed about (hos) three or four miles, they saw Y'shua walking on the sea and drawing near to the boat; and they were frightened. (**John 6:19**)

18 Now Bethany was near Jerusalem, about (hos) two miles off. (**John 11:18**)

15 At this time Peter stood up in the midst of the brethren [a gathering of about (hosei) one hundred and twenty persons was there together]. (**Acts 1:15**)

1 When the Lamb broke the seventh seal, there was silence in heaven for about (hos) half an hour. (**Revelation 8:1**)

10 But the day of YHVH will come like (hos) a thief, in which the heavens will pass away with a roar and the elements will be destroyed with intense heat, and the earth and its works will be burned up. (**II Peter 3:10**)

I have included the last passage to illustrate to you that the word "like" (hos), is meant as a comparative phrase. It does not mean that Y'shua will literally come as a thief to steal, but it means that He will come unexpectedly. The phrase "as a thousand years" is equally not meant in a literal sense. It alludes to a time period, likened to "a thousand years." There is a similar passage comparing "a thousand years" with a day in (the following Psalm):

4 For a thousand years in Your sight are like yesterday when it passes by, or as a watch in the night. **5** You have swept them away like a flood, they fall asleep; in the morning they are like grass which sprouts anew. **6** In the morning it flourishes and sprouts anew; toward evening it fades and withers away. (**Psalm 90:4-6**)

In this passage "a thousand years" is compared to two things:

- Yesterday
- A Night Watch

Yesterday

919 לוֹמְתֶא (’ĕṯ·môl): adv.; **Strong's 865; TWOT 2521—1. LN 67.201–67.208** yesterday, [i.e., the day before today (**Psalm 90:4+**)], see also **9453; 2. LN 67.17–67.64** lately, before, heretofore, [i.e., a period of time prior to another time, either short or long (**Isaiah 30:33; Micah 2:8+**)]; **3. LN 67.17–67.64** unit: שׁ לוֹמְתֶא שֶׁלֹ שׁוֹמ (’ĕṯ·môl šil·šôm) formerly, before, in the past, i.e., formally, yesterday and day before, [i.e., pertaining to a point in time prior to another time (**I Samuel 4:7, 10:11, 14:21, 19:7+**)]; **4. LN 67.17–67.64** unit: גַ‌ ם‌ אֶ‌ ת‌ מוֹל גַ‌ ם (**găm 'ĕṭ·môl găm šil·šôm**) formerly, before, in the past, [i.e., formally, yesterday and day before, i.e., pertaining to a point in time prior to another time (**II Samuel 5:2+**)]][122]

The word "yesterday" can refer to either a period of time prior to another time (short or long), or to the past.

A Night Watch

A watch in the night was approximately four hours (Jude 7:19 refers to a middle watch, suggesting three periods). Such a portion of the night, when man sleeps, is brief.[123]

We can conclude the same for this passage in Psalms as for the passage in II Peter. **These time periods do not have to be a literal (1,000) years,** although (they) could be.

How Do We Apply This To the Interpretation of Bible Prophecy?

In order for us to (further) apply this prophetic principle of "one day is like a thousand years," we must first find proof in Scripture. In the second book of Genesis, we (find) a good example of the prophetic application and fulfillment of this principle:

> **17** "... but from the tree of the knowledge of good and evil you shall not eat, for in the day that you eat from it you will surely die." (**Genesis 2:17**)

It is no coincidence that those who lived before The Flood died just short of 1,000 years of age. Thus, figuratively speaking, Adam and all his offspring before The Flood, died within a "day"—that is, within (1,000) years.[124]

Can we assume that whenever the word "day" is used, it could mean (1,000) years? I don't think so. It is more complex than that. As always,

---

122 *Dictionary of Biblical Languages with Semantic Domains: Hebrew (Old Testament)* (electronic ed.) by Swanson, J. (1997). Oak Harbor: Logos Research Systems, Inc.
123 *The Bible Knowledge Commentary: An Exposition of the Scriptures* (Psalm 90:1-6) by Walvoord, J.F., Zuck, R.B., & Dallas Theological Seminary. (1983-). Wheaton, IL: Victor Books.
124 http://www.1260-1290-days-bible-prophecy.org/day-year-principle.html

context is king when interpreting Scripture. Let's look at some verses (that better) illustrate this point.

The Scripture says that the world was created in six days. Was the world actually created in 6,000 years? I would not go so far as to say that. Plants were created before the sun and (wouldn't) be able to survive for 1,000 years without photosynthesis. Therefore, I support a literal six-day creation.

Another example would be the time Y'shua spent in the grave. Those were a literal three days and three nights. We can find many more examples.

Both verses Psalm 90 and II Peter 3 speak about the return of our Messiah. Therefore, we can conclude: the phrase "one day is like a thousand years" can only be applied in a prophetic context.

It is often said that Genesis 6:3 points to a prophetic time period. It refers to the period of man on earth before Y'shua returns. The calculation is as follows:

$$120 \times 50 = 6,000$$

The '50' refers to the number of years (in) a Jubilee Cycle.

> 3 Then YHVH said, "My Spirit shall not strive with man forever, because he also is flesh; nevertheless his days shall be one hundred and twenty years." (Genesis 6:3)

The (main) problem (with this) is a Jubilee Cycle is, (in truth), only forty-nine years. Shall we investigate this further?

How Long Is A Jubilee?

> 10 "You shall thus consecrate the fiftieth year and proclaim a release through the land to all its inhabitants. It shall be a Jubilee for you, and each of you shall return to his own property, and each of you shall return to his family. 11 You shall have the fiftieth year as a Jubilee; you shall not sow, nor reap its aftergrowth, nor gather in from its untrimmed vines." (Leviticus 25:10-11)

From the above Scripture, clearly the fiftieth year is the Jubilee. Why do I say forty-nine years?

How Do We Calculate A Jubilee?

We calculate the Jubilee Year in the same way we calculate the fifty days for Shavuot.

15 "You shall also count for yourselves from the day after the Sabbath, from the day when you brought in the sheaf of the wave offering; there shall be seven complete Sabbaths. **16** You shall count fifty days to the day after the seventh Sabbath; then you shall present a new grain offering to YHVH." (**Leviticus 23:15-16**)

- We are to count from the day after the weekly Sabbath—the first day of the week.
- There shall be seven complete Sabbaths.
- You shall count fifty days to the day after the seventh Sabbath—the first day of the week.

It is very important to follow the instructions carefully. We are to commence counting on the first day of the week and end the count on the first day of the week. Take note: the fiftieth day is also the first day of the weekly cycle. This is a pattern for us for the calculation of the Jubilee Years. Thus, the fiftieth year—the Jubilee Year—is also the first year of the next Sabbatical Cycle. Don't you think it's awesome to see how YHVH uses the same pattern?

I would just like to add this for clarification: If a Jubilee Cycle is fifty years, then between the last year of the first cycle and the first Sabbatical Year of the next cycle, (that) would (constitute a total of) eight years to (make) a Jubilee Year. This *cannot be* as we are told in Scripture that a Sabbath Cycle is to be seven years.

How Do We Apply All We Have Learned In This Study?

We have just proven from Scripture the Jubilee Cycle is forty-nine years instead of fifty years. We also have the prophetic Scripture in Genesis 6:3. If we apply what we have learned, our calculation of prophetic years would be as follows:

$$120 \times 49 = 5,880$$

We can conclude in saying that, "(a) day is like 980 years."

12 So teach us to number our days, that we may present to You a heart of wisdom. **13** Do return, O YHVH; how long will it be? And be sorry for Your servants. (**Psalm 90:12-13**)

We can only ask YHVH for His wisdom to live our lives according to His plan. Time is short. We have to number our days.

Chapter 21 | How Do We Keep the Sabbatical Year Today?

Just before the Israelites entered the Promised Land, which consequently, *was* a Jubilee Year, Moses laid down the rules they were to obey during a Sabbatical and a Jubilee Year.

These *same* rules apply to us today. Far too many however, to this day, remain totally ignorant of these Commandments, whereas many, who *do* know of them, do not even *try* to obey these Commandments and then miss out on the inherent blessings that come from keeping these Commandments as a result.

Yet, in keeping the Sabbaths, the Appointed Times, the Sabbatical Years and the Jubilee Years, we not only will be blessed ourselves by Yehovah but will be a blessing to others as well. For I believe the more Commandments we keep of His, the more His blessings are bestowed upon us pressed down and shaken together.

I have already shown you when the Sabbatical and Jubilee Years are so you can know (and prepare for) when they are coming.

The last Jubilee Year was 1996 from Abib to Abib. Since then, two Sabbatical Years have transpired—one in 2002 and one in 2009 from Abib to Abib. At the time of this writing, there is an upcoming Sabbatical Year that will occur in 2016. The remaining Seventh Year Sabbatical Years of Rest in this Jubilee Cycle are 2023, 2030, 2037 and 2044—with 2045 as the *next* Jubilee Year.

Let us now look at *how* we are to keep the Sabbatical and Jubilee Years when they come upon us.

1 And יהוה spoke to Mosheh (Moses) on Mount Sinai, saying, 2 "Speak to the children of Yisra'ĕl, and say to them, 'When you come into the land which I give you, then the land shall observe a Sabbath to יהוה. 3

Six years you sow your field, and six years you prune your vineyard, and gather in its fruit, **4** but in the seventh year the land is to have a Sabbath of rest, a Sabbath to יהוה. Do not sow your field and do not prune your vineyard. **5** Do not reap what grows of its own of your harvest, and do not gather the grapes of your unpruned vine, for it is a year of rest for the land. **6** And the Sabbath of the land shall be to you for food, for you and your servant, and for your female servant and your hired servant, and for the stranger who sojourns with you, **7** and for your livestock and the beasts that are in your land. All its crops are for food. **8** And you shall count seven Sabbaths of years for yourself, seven times seven years. And the time of the seven Sabbaths of years shall be to you forty-nine years. **9** You shall then sound a ram's horn to pass through on the tenth day of the seventh month, on the Day of Atonement cause a ram's horn to pass through all your land.'" **(Leviticus 25:1-9)**

10 "And you shall set the fiftieth year apart, and proclaim release throughout all the land to all its inhabitants; it is a Jubilee for you. And each of you shall return to his possession, and each of you return to his clan. **11** The fiftieth year is a Jubilee to you. Do not sow, nor reap what grows of its own, nor gather from its unpruned vine. **12** It is a Jubilee, it is set-apart to you. Eat from the field its crops. **13** In the year of this Jubilee let each one of you return to his possession. **14** And when you sell whatever to your neighbor or buy from the hand of your neighbor, do not exploit one another. **15** According to the number of years after the Jubilee you buy from your neighbor, and according to the number of years of crops he sells to you. **16** According to the greater number of years you increase its price, and according to the fewer number of years you diminish its price, because he sells to you according to the number of the years of the crops. **17** And do not oppress one another, but you shall fear your Elohim. For I am יהוה your Elohim. **18** And you shall do My laws and guard My right-rulings, and shall do them. And you shall dwell in the land in safety, **19** and the land shall yield its fruit, and you shall eat to satisfaction, and shall dwell there in safety." **(Leviticus 25:10-19)**

20 "And since you might say, 'What do we eat in the seventh year, since we do not sow nor gather in our crops?' **21** Therefore I have commanded My blessing on you in the sixth year, and it shall bring forth the crop for three years. **22** And you shall sow in the eighth year, and eat of the old crop until the ninth year. Eat of the old until its crop comes in. **23** And the land is not to be sold beyond reclaim, for the land is Mine, for you are sojourners and settlers with Me. **24** And provide for a redemption for the land, in all the land of your possession. **25** When your brother becomes poor, and has sold some of his possession, and his redeemer, a close relative comes to redeem it, then he shall redeem what his brother sold. **26** And when the man has no one to redeem it, but he himself becomes able to redeem it, **27** then let him count the years since its sale, and return the remainder to the man to whom he sold it, that he shall return to his possession. **28** And if his hand has not found enough to give back to him, then what was sold shall remain in the hand of him who bought it until the Year of Jubilee. And it shall be released in the Jubilee, and he shall return to his possession." **(Leviticus 25:20-28)**

29 "And when a man sells a house in a walled city, then his right of redemption shall be at the end of the year after it is sold. His right of redemption lasts a year. **30** But if it is not redeemed within a complete year, then the house in the walled city shall be established beyond reclaim to the buyer of it, throughout his generations. It is not released in the Jubilee. **31** The houses of villages, however, which have no wall around them are reckoned as the field of the country. A right of redemption belongs to it, and they are released in the Jubilee. **32** As for the cities of the Lĕwites (Levites), and the houses in the cities of their possession, the Lĕwites (Levites) have a right of redemption forever. **33** And that which is redeemed from the Lĕwites (Levites), both the sale of a house and the city of his possession shall be released in the Year of Jubilee, because the houses in the cities of the Lĕwites (Levites) are their possession in the midst of the children of Yisra'ĕl. **34** But the field of the open land of their cities is not sold, for it is their everlasting possession." **(Leviticus 25:29-34)**

35 "And when your brother becomes poor, and his hand has failed with you, then you shall sustain him, and he shall live with you, like a stranger or a sojourner. **36** Take no interest from him, or profit, but you shall fear your Elohim, and your brother shall live with you. **37** Do not lend him your silver on interest, and do not lend him your food for profit. **38** 'I am יהוה your Elohim, who brought you out of the land of Mitsrayim (Egypt), to give you the land of Kena'an (Canaan), to be your Elohim. **39** And when your brother who dwells by you becomes poor, and sells himself to you, do not make him serve as a slave. **40** But as a hired servant, as a settler he is with you, and serves you until the Year of Jubilee. **41** And then he shall leave you, he and his children with him, and shall return to his own clan, even return to the possession of his fathers. **42** For they are My servants, whom I brought out of the land of Mitsrayim, they are not sold as slaves. **43** Do not rule over him with harshness, but you shall fear your Elohim.'" **(Leviticus 25:35-43)**

44 "And your male and female slaves whom you have from the nations that are around you, from them you buy male and female slaves, **45** and also from the sons of the strangers sojourning among you, from them you buy, and from their clans who are with you, which they shall bring forth in your land, and they shall be your property. **46** And you shall take them as an inheritance for your children after you, to inherit them as a possession, they are your slaves for all time. But over your brothers, the children of Yisra'ël, you do not rule with harshness, one over another. **47** Now when a sojourner or a settler with you becomes rich, and your brother with him becomes poor, and sells himself to the settler or sojourner with you, or to a member of the sojourner's clan, **48** after he has been sold, there is a right of redemption to him—one of his brothers does redeem him, **49** or his uncle or his uncle's son does redeem him, or anyone who is a close relative to him in his clan does redeem him, or if he is able, then he shall redeem himself." **(Leviticus 25:44-49)**

50 "And he shall reckon with him who bought him: The price of his release shall be according to the number of years, from the year that he was sold to him until the Year of Jubilee; as the days of a hired servant it is with him. **51** If there are yet many years, according to them he repays the price of his redemption, from the silver of his purchase. **52** And if few years are left until the Year of Jubilee, then he shall reckon with him, and according to his years he repays him the price of his redemption. **53** He is with him as a yearly hired servant, and he does not rule with harshness over him before your eyes. **54** And if he is not redeemed in these years, then he shall be released in the Year of Jubilee, he and his children with him. **55** Because the children of Yisra'ël are servants to Me, they are My servants whom I brought out of the land of Mitsrayim (Egypt). I am יהוה your Elohim." **(Leviticus 25:50-55)**

In Leviticus 25, I feel it imperative to re-emphasize the following:

4 "... but in the seventh year the land is to have a Sabbath of rest, a Sabbath to יהוה. Do not sow your field and do not prune your vineyard. **5** Do not reap what grows of its own of your harvest, and do not gather the grapes of your unpruned vine, for it is a year of rest for the land." **(Leviticus 25:4-5)**

During the Sabbatical Year, from Abib to Abib (Abib being the first month of the year when Passover occurs), we are *not* to plant, harvest or reap anything from the land. But whatever the land produces on its own we *can* eat. We just cannot harvest, store up or freeze anything at the summer's end to see us through the winter. But when we do find food growing in our garden we have not planted ourselves, we may pick it and eat of it. When our fruit trees bear fruit, we can pick what we need to eat *that day* or *that week*. But we can't pick, can or freeze anything for storing away for extended periods of time, for that is considered harvesting.

We *can* eat what we find, however, and that is OK. All that grows without any effort on our part is for *anybody* to eat. It is during this time, your neighbors, as well as the foreigner (alien) and the stranger are allowed to forage on your land and, by the same token, you are allowed to forage on other people's land. Also, during this time, you are *not* to lock up any garden you have planted and thus prohibit your own animals or wild animals from partaking of its produce. You need to leave your garden open and accessible to all living things so they might enjoy the fruits of the land during any given Sabbatical Year.

> **6** "And the Sabbath of the land shall be to you for food, for you and your servant, and for your female servant and your hired servant, and for the stranger who sojourns with you, **7** and for your livestock and the beasts that are in your land. All its crops are for food." (**Leviticus 25:6-7**)

So what do we do then for food during the Sabbatical Year?

> **20** "And since you might say, 'What do we eat in the seventh year, since we do not sow nor gather in our crops?' **21** Therefore I have commanded My blessing on you in the sixth year, and it shall bring forth the crop for three years. **22** And you shall sow in the eighth year, and eat of the old crop until the ninth year. Eat of the old until its crop comes in." (**Leviticus 25:20-22**)

We are told in this verse that we must store up food in the sixth year. In fact, we must store up enough food to last us until the new crop comes in the ninth year.

I kept the Sabbatical Year in 2009. It was the first time I had done it. I was also going to have to do this alone as my wife was not going to help me at all. So I did some simple math. I calculated that I was going to eat 365 breakfasts, 365 lunches and 365 suppers. I then tacked on another 180 days to get me through to the following fall when the next crop of food would then be harvested and available in the local stores.

I bought cases of the following: soup, beans, sauces, spices and canned fruits of as many different fruits as I could find. I also purchased bags of the following: spaghetti noodles, rice, and frozen vegetables. I also bought the condiments I thought I would need and even stored away the junk food I wanted to eat throughout the year.

But there was another situation I had to plan for. I was going to go to Israel three times this given year and had to make provision for what I was going to eat while I traveled on the planes and while I was in the land of Israel, because I had made a solemn vow to Yehovah I would not eat anything from any store or restaurant that would have food grown from the land during that

Sabbatical Year. All I could and would eat would only be that which I had stored away in the sixth year as I was commanded.

I could eat meat anywhere as meat is *not* produced by the land and being we are not commanded to store away meat. This command applies only to refraining from the consumption of, harvesting of and storing away of the fruits and vegetables that would be grown from the land during a given Sabbatical Year.

This would also mean that any farmers seeking to obey Yehovah in like manner would have to store away enough hay and crops for their animals not only for the Sabbatical Year, but up until the new crop ready to be harvested the following year, or in some cases, two years after.

I planned on having fifty-two loaves of bread for my lunches, so I bought and froze them right *after* the Days of Unleavened Bread, which is during Passover when you are to have *no leaven* in your home. One week after the Days of Unleavened Bread I bought bread and froze it. The following year when the Days of Unleavened Bread came around again, I had to throw out only two loaves of bread. But from that point on, I had to eat matzos until Pentecost when the wheat harvest would then be taken in. So, after Pentecost I could again begin to eat bread. But I also had to have a two-year supply of matzos.

I had stir-fry and rice many a night, but alternated with soups and stews. Through it all, I never lacked the entire year, nor did anything go bad on me even once, apart from the two loaves of bread I had to throw out. In fact, this food has lasted well into 2012 since the year of 2008 when I stored it away. Again, not only for the intended year, but in the years that followed right up to the present, the food I stored away in advance in 2008 never went bad. We ate most of it and even had some leftover to give away. At this late date even, we *still* have food from 2008 and we still eat it. I do hope it will be thoroughly consumed before the year is out. But none of it has spoiled.

I am sharing this with you so that you know it *is* possible to do. All it takes is some careful, thoughtful planning and faith. And it is your faith that is being tested here.

Below is another Command during the Sabbatical Year we are to be aware of and do:

> **1** "At the end of every seven years you make a release *of debts*. **2** And this is the word of the release: Every creditor is to release what he has loaned to his neighbor; he does not require it of his neighbor or his

brother, because it is called the release of יהוה. **3** Of a foreigner you could require it, but your hand is to release whatever is owed by your brother. **4** Only, there should be no poor among you. For יהוה does greatly bless you in the land which יהוה your Elohim is giving you to possess as an inheritance, **5** only if you diligently obey the voice of יהוה your Elohim, to guard to do all these commands which I am commanding you today. **6** For יהוה your Elohim shall bless you as He promised you. And you shall lend to many nations, but you shall not borrow. And you shall rule over many nations, but they do not rule over you. **7** When there is a poor man with you, one of your brothers, within any of the gates in your land which יהוה your Elohim is giving you, do not harden your heart nor shut your hand from your poor brother, **8** for you shall certainly open your hand to him and certainly lend him enough for his need, whatever he needs. **9** Be on guard lest there be a thought of Beliya'al (a base thought) in your heart, saying, 'The seventh year, the year of release, is near,' and your eye is evil against your poor brother and you give him naught. And he shall cry out to יהוה against you, and it shall be a sin in you."
(Deuteronomy 15:1-9)

10 "You shall certainly give to him, and your heart should not be grieved when you give to him, because for this reason יהוה your Elohim does bless you in all your works and in all to which you put your hand. **11** Because the poor one does not cease from the land. Therefore I am commanding you, saying, 'You shall certainly open your hand to your brother, to your poor and to your needy one, in your land.' **12** When your brother is sold to you, a Hebrew man or a Hebrew woman, and shall serve you six years, then let him go free from you in the seventh year. **13** And when you send him away free from you, let him not go away empty-handed. **14** You shall richly supply him from your flock, and from your threshing-floor, and from your winepress. With that which יהוה has blessed you with, give to him. **15** And you shall remember that you were a slave in the land of Mitsrayim (Egypt), and יהוה your Elohim redeemed you. Therefore I am commanding you this word today. **16** And it shall be, when he says to you, 'I do not go away from you,' because he loves you and your house, because it is good for him with you, **17** then you shall take an awl and thrust it through his ear to the door, and he shall be your servant forever. Do the same to your female servant. **18** Let it not be hard in your eyes when you send him away free from you, for he has been worth a double hired servant in serving you six years. And יהוה your Elohim shall bless you in all that you do." **(Deuteronomy 15:10-18)**

I must admit that this Commandment I did not like. And this is the one I did not want to obey. If someone owes you a few hundred dollars then it is not too difficult to carry out, but I was owed thousands of dollars and had been trying to collect it for some time.

It was with this Commandment in mind that I wrote those who owed me and told them their debts to me were canceled in full. They were stunned, to put it mildly, as no one had ever done that for them before. They then insisted they would pay me immediately, and I had to tell them I could not accept payment from them under any terms *even if* they did pay up. Like I said, I *did not like* this command.

In addition to setting aside food in 2008 for the 2009 Sabbatical Year, in my *The Chronological Order of Prophecy*[125] DVD, which came out in March of 2008, I made a specific point to illustrate very clearly that going back in time—Industrial Revolution included—one can readily see the recessions and depressions occurring very closely alongside of all the Sabbatical and Jubilee Years throughout history. I believe there was a definite cause and effect dynamic at work there; a definite correlation, to be certain.

On the following two charts (the first one below and the second one on the following page), I present to you again the charts I featured in my March of 2008 DVD showing the rise in debt *at that time* along with the recession years *before* this date. I also show how the year 2009 was indeed another recession year, as well as being a Sabbatical Year.

Again, what I have come to understand from all this is that many of the Sabbatical Years have recessions or depressions that occur back-to-back or more or less simultaneously even. I have been of the conviction for some time now this happens because we will not forgive our neighbors the debts they have accumulated. If we were to do that, then everyone would be granted a fresh start and these economic recessions and depressions we see would not occur—nor would hyperinflation, for that matter.

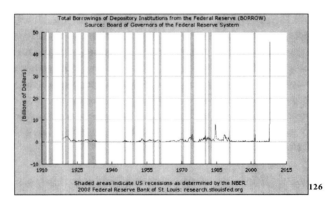

---

125 You can order this DVD at: http://www.sightedmoon.com
126 http://research.stlouisfed.org/fred2/series/BORROW

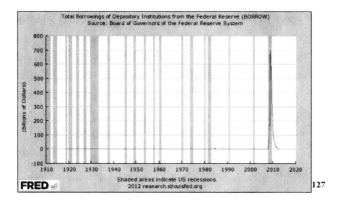

These charts attest to the fact that during this recession of 2008-2011, I was kept employed and busy in the housing industry, in new construction no less—the very industry that was hurt *the most*. I cannot help but wonder what would have happened had I *not* obeyed this Commandment and forgiven those who owed me thousands. Yes, I believe Yehovah looked after me for being obedient.

But there is still one other Commandment I would have you take a close look at and strongly urge you to obey and not defer or neglect during the Sabbatical Year.

> **10** And Mosheh (Moses) commanded them, saying, "At the end of seven years, at the appointed time, the year of release, at the Festival of Booths, **11** when all Yisra'ĕl comes to appear before יהוה your Elohim in the place which He chooses, read this Torah before all Yisra'ĕl in their hearing. **12** Assemble the people, the men and the women and the little ones, and your sojourner who is within your gates, so that they hear, and so that they learn to fear יהוה your Elohim and guard to do all the Words of this Torah. **13** And their children, who have not known it, should hear and learn to fear יהוה your Elohim as long as you live in the land you are passing over the Yardĕn (Jordan) to possess." (**Deuteronomy 31:10-13**)

At the Feast of Tabernacles, which is the weeklong festival in the fall, we are commanded to read the Torah out loud so that everyone can hear it and understand what it says during a given Sabbatical Year. Three other men and

---

127 http://research.stlouisfed.org/fred2/series/BORROW The Federal Reserve Bank of St. Louis holds copyrights for all other content published in the Review and grants permission free of charge to reprint these articles. No written permission is necessary if articles are reprinted in full and without modification.

I went to Gihon Spring in the city of David and proceeded to read the entire Law out loud as thousands of tourists passed by on their way to Hezekiah's Tunnel. It took us about four hours to do in all and each man read one chapter and then the next man took over as we all listened.

We did as we were commanded. We may not have understood exactly *how* to do what we were told, but we did the best we could with the understanding we had at that time. My understanding has grown so much more since then, however, and I am very excited to be sharing with you the new things I have been shown since then in this book.

In short, I implore you to do the best you can with what you have, obey Yehovah in full with regard to what He requires of you, and in those instances when you can only obey in part at best, trust wholly on Yehovah to take care of the rest.

Chapter 22	Rise of the False Teachings; Where It All Began

I have just shown you all the historically recorded Sabbatical Years. Nearly everyone agrees these *are* the correct years. What they cannot seem to agree upon is when a given Sabbatical Year begins and because of this, they try to twist the historical records to match their own errors—even to the point of omitting critical information (like that found in II Kings 19:29) in order to continue to propagate their own teaching.

According to these teachers, the next Sabbatical Year will be from Tishri 2014–Tishri 2015. But, this presumed Sabbatical Year does *not* match up with any of the known ones I have brought to your attention, nor does it match with II Kings 19:29.

We are commanded by the Holy One to "Walk before Him, and be perfect."

1 "I am El Shaddai—walk before Me and be perfect." (**Genesis 17:1**)

A walk may be deemed perfect according to the standards of a council of men, but when that walk is not, in truth, according to the standard of The Word of the Holy One, it does not esteem or please the Holy One. That kind of walk only esteems "self," vanity and falsehood.

It is upon this premise I will be building upon for the next few pages. I am going to expose the very foundation upon which Judaism bases their Sabbatical Year reckonings upon.

How did the Sabbatical and Jubilee Years get lost and why are they so hard to correctly determine and pin down now?

Today's Rabbis teach that the next Shmita Year will occur during 2014–2015. As a result, they keep a Shmita Year an entire year earlier than the restored Sabbatical Year/Jubilee Year schedule would have them do. The question we all should be asking is, *"Why?"*

I am going to go over with you when these things began (and with whom), and provide you with a few of the key reasons why. In order for all these things to make sense to you, one must go back to the source of where and/or with whom it all started. In this case, the "whom" being more searchable than the "where." The "whom" were the Tannaim.

Just who exactly were the Tannaim and what role have they played in Judaism?

The Making Of the Mishnah & the Talmud [128]

> The very (word), "tanna," is Aramaic for a memorizer and reciter of traditions.

Tanna also means "to teach," and other sources maintain it means "to repeat." Either way, the Tannaim were a group of teachers (aka, sages) of the *Mishnah*, or the "oral law" who existed during a specific time in history (40 B.C.E.–220 C.E). In the 1st-century of this Common Era, there were religious men who much of the believing community now likens to and associates with the Sadducees or Pharisees of the Bible who were teachers of a kind of law which was handed down to successive generations orally. This was something very different from the *written law* given to Moses by Yehovah. Later, the oral teachings of these religious men were written down and became known as the *Mishnah* and the *Baraita*. The oral traditions propagated by these men during this time became known as Rabbinic Judaism. These teachers of the oral traditions persisted throughout the 1st-century all the way up to the present age.

These teachers were known under the following titles during the time periods shown:

Zugot—515 B.C.E.–70 C.E. (Pairs of Tannaim)

> In Hebrew, the word "Zugot" indicates a plural of two identical objects. (In English: "pairs.") The name was given to the two leading teachers of the Law during each successive generation during the period. According to tradition, two of them always stood at the head of the Sanhedrin; one

---

128 http://printingthetalmud.org/essays/1.pdf, The Making of the Mishnah & the Talmud by Lawrence H. Schiffman

as president ("Nasi") and the other as vice-president or father of the
court ("Av Beit Din"; see Sanhedrin).[129]

Tannaim—10–220 C.E. (Sages of the Mishnah)

The *Mishnah* or *Mishna* [Hebrew: הנשמ, "repetition," from the verb
'shanah' הנש, or "to study and review," also "secondary" (derived from
the adj. 'shani' ינש)] is the first major written redaction of the Jewish
oral traditions called the "Oral Torah." It is also the first major work of
rabbinic Judaism.

It was redacted (in) 220 C.E. by Rabbi Yehudah haNasi when, according
to the *Talmud*, the persecution of the Jews and the passage of time raised
the possibility that the details of the oral traditions dating from Pharisaic
times (536 B.C.E.–70 C.E.) would be forgotten. It is thus named for
being both the one written authority (codex) secondary (only) to the
Tanakh as a basis for the passing of judgment, a source and a tool for
creating laws, and the first of many books to complement the Bible
in a certain aspect. The *Mishnah* is also called *Shas* (an acronym for
Shisha Sedarim—the "six orders"), in reference to its six main divisions.
Rabbinic commentaries on the *Mishnah* over the next three centuries
were redacted as the *Gemara*, which, coupled with the *Mishnah*, comprise
the *Talmud*.

The *Mishnah* reflects debates from 1ˢᵗ-century B.C.E–2ⁿᵈ-century C.E.
by the group of rabbinic sages known as the Tannaim.[130]

The Tannaim [Hebrew: םיאנת (plural)], and Tanna [Hebrew: אנת
(singular)] (or) "repeaters," "teachers" were the rabbinic sages whose
views were recorded in the *Mishnah* ... The period of the Tannaim, also
referred to as the Mishnaic period ... came after the period of the Zugot
("pairs"), and was immediately followed by the period of the Amoraim
("interpreters").

The root 'tanna' (אנת) is the Aramaic equivalent for the Hebrew root
'shanah' (הנש), which also is the root-word of Mishnah. The verb shanah
(הנש) literally means "to repeat (what one was taught)" and is used to
mean "to learn."[131]

Amoraim—220 C.E.–500 C.E. (Sages of the Talmud)

129 http://en.wikipedia.org/wiki/Zugot
130 http://en.wikipedia.org/wiki/Mishnah#cite_note-0
131 http://en.wikipedia.org/wiki/Tannaim

Amoraim ("expounders"): Refers to the sages of the Talmud who were active during the end of the era of the sealing of the *Mishnah*, and until the times of the sealing of the *Talmud* (220 C.E.–500 C.E.). The Amoraim sages were active in two areas, the Land of Israel, and Babylon. In addition to the *Babylonian Talmud* and the *Jerusalem Talmud*, their writings were also preserved in Midrashes such as *Midrash Rabba*.[132]

Savoraim—500 C.E.–650 C.E. (Reasoners of the Torah study places in Babylon)

Savoraim ("reasoners"): Refers to the sages of Beth Midrash (Torah study places) in Babylon from the end of the era of the Amoraim (5th-century) and until the beginning of the era of the Geonim (From the end of the 6th-century or into the midst of the 7th-century).[133]

Geonim—650 C.E.–1050 C.E.

"... were the presidents of the two great Babylonian, Talmudic Academies of Sura and Pumbedita, in the Abbasid Caliphate, and were the generally accepted spiritual leaders of the Jewish community worldwide in the early medieval era, in contrast to the Resh Galuta (Exilarch) who wielded secular authority over the Jews in Islamic lands."

Geonim is the plural of וראג (Gaon'), which means "pride" or "splendor" in biblical Hebrew and since the 19th-century "genius" as in modern Hebrew. As a title of a Babylonian college president it meant something like, "His Excellency."[134]

Rishonim—1050 C.E.–1500 C.E. (The first ones)

Rishonim or Rishon (Hebrew: רשאור ;םינושאר‎; sing. רשאור)

"... were the leading Rabbis and Poskim who lived approximately during the 11th-15th centuries, in the era before the writing of the *Shulkhan Arukh* (Hebrew: שולח ן ךורע‎, "Set Table," a code of Jewish law, 1563 C.E.) and following the Geonim (589 C.E.-1038 C.E.). Rabbinic scholars subsequent to the *Shulkhan Arukh* are generally known as Acharonim ("the latter ones").[135]

---

132 http://en.wikipedia.org/wiki/Chazal
133 http://en.wikipedia.org/wiki/Chazal
134 http://en.wikipedia.org/wiki/Geonim
135 http://en.wikipedia.org/wiki/Rishonim

Acharonim—1500 C.E. to present (The last or latter ones)

Acharonim (Hebrew: **אחרונים** Aharonim‎; sing. **אחרון**, Aharon; lit.)

"… is a term used in Jewish law and history, to signify the leading Rabbis and Poskim (Jewish legal decisors) living from roughly the 16th-century to the present, and more specifically since the writing of the *Shulkhan Arukh* (Hebrew: **שֻׁלְחָן עָרוּךְ**‎, "Set Table." A code of Jewish law.) in 1563 C.E.[136]

From the *Jewish Encyclopedia*

The period of the Tannaim, which lasted about 210 years (10 C.E.–220 C.E.), is generally divided by Jewish scholars into five or six sections or generations, the purpose of such division being to show which teachers developed their principal activity contemporaneously. Some of the Tannaim, however, were active in more than one generation. The following is an enumeration of the first three generations and of the more prominent Tannaim respectively belonging to them:

First Generation (10 C.E.–80 C.E.)

Principal Tannaim: The Shammaites and the Hillelites, Akabya b. Mahalaleel, Rabban Gamaliel the Elder, Hanina, chief of the priests ("segan ha-kohanim"), Simeon b. Gamaliel, and Johanan b. Zakkai.

Second Generation (80 C.E.–120 C.E.)

Principal Tannaim: Rabban Gamaliel II. (of Jabnesh), Zadok, Dosa b. Harkinas, Eliezer b. Jacob, Eliezer b. Hyrcanus, Joshua b. Hanaiah, Eleazar b. Azariah, Judah b. Bathvra.

Third Generation (120 C.E.–140 C.E.)

Principal Tannaim: Tarfon, Ishmael, Akiba, Johanan b. Nuri, Jose ha-Gelili, Simeon b. Nanos, Judah b. Baba, and Johanan b. Baroka. Several of these flourished in the preceding period.[137]

So now you know who you are reading about in the Messianic writings concerning the Pharisees in the 1st-century. They were responsible for authoring voluminous traditions as "commandments," and exacting numerous detailed regulations upon people that went far above and beyond what had

---

136 http://en.wikipedia.org/wiki/Acharonim
137 http://www.jewishencyclopedia.com/articles/14240-tannaim-and-amoraim

been written in stone by Yehovah and given to Moses. Some had it in mind to "protect" the people from breaking commandments, but by doing this, the Pharisees actually went against the written Torah Yehovah commanded us not to add to or take away from and put oral Torah in a place of importance on par with written Torah. The Tannaim also placed a heavy burden upon the people—a burden of which they did not lift a finger to lighten.

I will now get to the crux of the matter and provide you with a brief history as to how current Judaism developed as we know it, how many things were changed and why.

Keep in mind the Temple of Herod had been destroyed in 70 C.E.

> After the destruction of the Second Temple in 70 C.E., the Sanhedrin was re-established in Yavneh with reduced authority. The imperial government and legislation of Rome recognized it as the Palestinian Patriarchate, the ultimate authority in Jewish religious matters. The seat of the P.P. moved to Usha under the presidency of Gamaliel II in 80 C.E. In 116 C.E. it moved back to Yavneh, and then again back to Usha. It then moved to Shefaram in 140 C.E. under the presidency of Shimon ben Gamaliel II, and to Beit Shearim and Sephoris in 163 C.E. under the presidency of Judah I. Finally, it moved to Tiberias in 193 C.E., under the presidency of Gamaliel III (193 C.E.–230 C.E.), eldest son of Simeon[138] ben Judah ha-Nasi and renowned editor of the *Mishnah*,[139] where it became more of a consistory, but still retained, under the presidency of Judah II (230 C.E.–270 C.E.), the power of excommunication.

> During the presidency of Gamaliel IV (270 C.E.–290 C.E.), due to Roman persecution, it dropped the name Sanhedrin; and its authoritative decisions were subsequently issued under the name of Beth HaMidrash.

> As a reaction to Julian's pro-Jewish stance, Theodosius I forbade the Sanhedrin to assemble and declared ordination illegal. Capital punishment was prescribed for any rabbi who received ordination and complete destruction of the town where the ordination occurred.[140]

> However, since the Hebrew Calendar was determined by observations based on eyewitness testimony that had become far too dangerous to undertake, Hillel II recommended the change to a mathematically based

138 http://www.jewishencyclopedia.com/articles/13700-simeon-ben-judah-ha-nasi-i
139 http://www.britannica.com/EBchecked/topic/224739/Gamaliel-III
140 A History of the Jewish People, by Hayim Ben-Sasson, Harvard University Press (October 15th, 1985), ISBN 978-0-674-39731-6

calendar that was adopted (during) a clandestine, and perhaps, final meeting in 358 C.E. This marked the last authoritative decision made by that body.

Gamaliel VI (400 C.E.–425 C.E.) was the Sanhedrin's last president. With his death in 425 C.E.,[141] executed by Theodosius II for erecting new synagogues contrary to the imperial decree, the title Nasi, the last remains of the ancient Sanhedrin, became illegal. An imperial decree in 426 C.E. diverted the patriarchs' tax (post excessum patriarchorum) into the imperial treasury.[142]

Prior to this date, you would be wise to be mindful of what other dynamics were at work.

Constantine became ... a Roman Emperor (and issued) the Edict of Milan in 313 C.E., which *fully legalized* Christianity in the Roman Empire for the first time and the Council of Nicaea in 325 C.E. which he chaired. (His) actions completely changed the conditions under which Christians lived.

Christians prior to this date subscribed to a mixture of pagan religions while also, in part, embracing the one true Nazarene faith. The Nazarenes, however, were those who followed Torah in spirit and in truth and were, in all respects, adherents of the Jewish faith—the only difference being, they followed Yehshua.

Constantine brought to an end 300 years of persecution, during which Christians had to worship in secret ... faced arbitrary arrest and (lived under the constant threat of) martyrdom in the coliseums. He inaugurated a new era in which Christians enjoyed the power and patronage of the Roman state.

Constantine's reputation as the "first Christian emperor" has been promulgated by historians from Lactantius and Eusebius of Caesarea to the present day; although there has been debate over the sincerity of his faith since he was baptized only on his death bed. It has been argued that he conflated the Sun God with the Christian God. His support for Christianity, however, was sincere and reflected in his policies. The church could now own land, Christians could worship openly, and imperial patronage resulted in the affirmation of a single creed. However, now that bishops had imperial support, those who dissented

---

141 http://tinyurl.com/bp2kcet ("C.E." verified)
142 http://en.wikipedia.org/wiki/Sanhedrin

from the dominant or prevailing concept of orthodoxy or othopraxis [a term derived from Greek (ὀρθοπραξις) meaning "correct action/ activity"] could be punished. Thus, Christianity was changed from a fairly loose and diverse body of believers into an orthodoxy based on a uniform faith with a disciplined hierarchical institution based on the Roman pattern.

Christians, previously reluctant to engage in military action, now joined the army and incorporated violence into their faith. Once Christianity became established as the state religion in the years following Constantine, the state began to impose Christianity on everyone and to persecute dissent, just as it had once persecuted Christians before Constantine's conversion. Christian leaders quickly took advantage of their power to punish all perceived heretics, pagans, and Jews, now backed by the coercive power of the state.[143]

It is critical and ironic to note that right about the time the persecution of Christians began to dissipate (both in frequency and intensity), the persecution of the Jews or anti-semitism came into full play. This was no small matter, for the Sanhedrin had to cease to exist in any kind of official capacity for fear of being killed.

You can read in Scripture how thousands of Jews during this transitional phase began to follow Yehshua. This was because most of His teachings brought them back to the truth of Torah. Afterward, when Christianity became the dominant religion, you do not see Jewish converts at all. Why? Because Christianity gradually devolved into a pagan religion that led people away from the very Torah that Yehshua embodied, exemplified, upheld and made come alive to the people.

After Yehshua died, there were Jews who went around killing and stoning those who were following and preaching about Yehshua. The Apostle Paul was one. Yet, Jewish converts were taking place in the thousands.

Apart from Paul, the killing of Stephen in Acts 6:8-8:1 was one of the innumerable martyrdoms one can read about. *Foxe's Book of Martyrs* can provide you with a much more in depth treatment of the subject of martyrdom, if you wish to know more on this. This hatred for all followers of Yehshua was one of the contributing factors to endorse and promote Simon Bar Kochba as the Jewish Messiah 100 years later.

Another contributing factor that would cause some to consider Simon the

---

143 http://www.newworldencyclopedia.org/entry/Constantine_I

Messiah was a book published in 101 C.E. entitled the *Book of Elchasai*, which prophesied that the years at that time were the last 3 ½ years.

> Origin and dissemination: according to his own account ... Elchasai came forward with his message in the third year of Trajan; he seems to have composed his book during the reign of the same emperor, as is suggested by the prophecy ... but not fulfilled, of a universal conflict blazing up three years after the Parthian war ... but still under Trajan's rule.[144]

> Against the Judean Christians who lived in Judea, Simon Bar (Kochba) proceeded with hostility since they were regarded as apostates and especially as inform(ants) and spies. The hatred against the Judean Christians was enhanced when they refused to participate in the national war, and remained indifferent spectators of this fearful (historical) drama. In the restored State where all the laws came into force again, the Judean tribunals felt justified in summoning to judgment those members of their nation who not only denied The Law but even scorned it. The death penalty, however, was never imposed upon them, as later Christian chroniclers maintained. (But), in order to excite hatred against the Judeans, they were scourged. However, even among the Nazarenes there were patriots who embraced the national cause and who delivered up to the tribunals those members of their (own) sect(s) who were guilty of treason. A few statements in The Gospels, which were composed at this time, (convey) the discord which prevailed among the Christians of Palestine during the course of this war, and the anxiety under which they labored.[145]

All of the following found their full expression in the Simon Bar Kochba Revolt—Simon the anticipated (albeit false) Messiah due to the false prophesy of Elchasai of it being the last 3 ½ years, the hatred of those who were Nazarenes who already claimed to have known the Messiah Yehshua, and the state of warring in Judea with Rome.

The first revolt began in 66 C.E. and ended with the Temple being destroyed in 70 C.E. A little later, the Romans took the fortress Masada in 74 C.E. ending in the suicides of the last members of the revolt.

Forty-one years later in 115 C.E., the Levantine Jews revolted against the Emperor Trajan:

> The Roman Emperor Trajan had decided to bring peace to the eastern borders of his empire for once and for all. Therefore, in 115 C.E., he attacked Armenia and the kingdom of the Parthians. His operations were

---

144 http://www.earlychristianwritings.com/elchasai.html
145 http://www.globalsecurity.org/military/world/israel/akiva-ben-joseph.htm

a brilliant success, and he was to be the only Roman emperor to sail on the Persian Gulf. However, after he had created new provinces—Armenia, Mesopotamia and Assyria—and believed he had been victorious; several Messianic revolts broke out simultaneously. The reasons are unclear to us, but the appearance of a comet, a Messianic symbol, may be the explanation; it is referred to in Chinese sources (and perhaps Juvenal, Satires, 6.407). The diasporic Jews of Egypt, Cyrenaica and Cyprus were among the rebels, but the newly conquered region of Mesopotamia was unquiet too.

Cyrenaica

Their revolt started in Cyrene, where one Lukuas—sometimes called Andreas—ordered the Jews to destroy the pagan temples of Apollo, Artemis, Hecate, Demeter, Isis and Pluto, and to assail the worshippers. The latter fled to Alexandria, where they captured and killed many Jews. (With a population of some 150,000 Jews, Alexandria was the largest Jewish city.) In 116 C.E., the Jews organized themselves and had their revenge. The temples of gods like Nemesis, Hecate and Apollo were destroyed; the same fate befell the tomb of Pompey, the Roman general who had captured Jerusalem almost two centuries before.

Meanwhile, the Cyrenaican Jews plundered the Egyptian countryside, reaching Thebes, 600 kilometers upstream. The future historian Appian of Alexandria records that he made a providential escape from a party of Jews pursuing him in the Nile marshes. There was nothing the Roman Governor, Marcus Rutilius Lupus could do, although he sent a legion (III Cyrenaica or XXII Deiotariana) to protect the inhabitants of Memphis.

Trajan sent out two expeditionary forces. One, consisting of VII Claudia, restored order on Cyprus; the other was to attack Lukuas' rebels and was commanded by Quintus Marcius Turbo. The Roman general sailed to Alexandria, defeated the Jews in several pitched battles and killed thousands of enemies, not only those in Egypt but also those of Cyrene. It is unclear what became of Lukuas, except for the fact that according to our Greek source Eusebius he had styled himself 'king' (Messiah?). After this war, much of northern Africa had to be repopulated. The Emperor Trajan and his successor Hadrian confiscated Jewish property to pay for the reconstruction of the destroyed temples.

Trajan was afraid that this revolt would spread to the Jews in the rebellious eastern provinces. Perhaps, there was some cause for his anxiousness. After the end of the revolt in Mesopotamia, someone had written the *Book of Elchasai*, in which the end of the world was predicted within (roughly) three years. Of course, Trajan did not read this book, but he may have sensed that the Jews remained restless.

Therefore, he ordered the commander of his Mauritanian auxiliaries, Lusius Quietus, to purge the suspects out of these regions. Quietus organized a force and killed many Cypriote, Mesopotamian and Syrian Jews—in effect wiping them out. As a reward, he was appointed governor of Judea. (He is one of the few blacks known to have made a career in Roman service.) He was responsible for a forced policy of hellenization. In response, the rabbis ordered the Jewish fathers not to teach their sons Greek.[146]

Meanwhile, Trajan had achieved his military objectives and returned home. On his way back, he fell ill, and not much later, he died (August 8th, 117 C.E.). His successor, Hadrian, gave up the newly conquered countries and dismissed Lusius Quietus, who was killed in the Summer of 118 C.E.[147]

When the emperor Hadrian forbade circumcision in 132 C.E., Simon Bar Kochba started a Messianic war.

Simon Bar Kochba Revolt

The First Revolt lasted 5 years and was led by Simon Bar Giora. The Second Revolt lasted 2 ½ years and was led by Simon Bar Kochba during the 2nd-century C.E. Simon Bar Kochba was a militant figure and proclaimed restoration and deliverance of the Jewish people from Roman rule by military resistance and revolt.

Let's start by going back to the First Revolt and look at something I did not make a point to discuss with you earlier. The First Revolt began in the twelfth year of Nero and lasted five years. Printed coins and the writings of Josephus bear evidence of this fact for both the length of the revolt and the dating of it's rule with the standard Nisan-Aviv reckoning, which in turn, reveals the revolt began in the Hebrew month of Iyar (April-May):

The 1st Revolt	
Year 1	66 C.E.
Year 2	67 C.E.
Year 3	68 C.E.
Year 4	69 C.E.
Year 5	70 C.E.

---

146 Mishna Sota 9.14
147 http://www.livius.org/ja-jn/jewish_wars/jwar06.html

In addition to printed coinage and Josephus—who was actually living in Judea at the very time these things took place (which makes his writings not hearsay, but firsthand eyewitness accounts)—there was another witness named Publius Cornelius Tacitus.

Tacitus lived circa 56 C.E.—circa 117 C.E. and was *also* an eyewitness to these matters. He was one of the important historians of Roman antiquity. Two of his major works entitled *Annals* and *Histories* survive him. In *Histories*, chapter 4:39-5:13, Tacitus wrote of how the Judean Revolt persisted for five years. He also went on to say:

> "... the first of January of the year that Vespasian assumed the consular office was 70 C.E., chosen by his father Titus to complete the subjugation of Judea and (how) later that same year, 70 C.E.—Jerusalem fell."

So here you can see at least three eyewitnesses to the account of the First Revolt—all of which confirm the dates and duration of this revolt. Why is this important for our correct observance of a Sabbath Year in 2016 and *not* 2014? For one, chronology and the proper dating of this revolt now enables me to confirm to you that a Sabbath Year did indeed occur during 56 C.E.–57 C.E.! I will explain this to you in the next paragraphs.

Furthermore, the first year of the First Revolt occurred in the year 66 C.E. and it was the twelfth year of the reign of Nero. Knowing that the year 66 C.E. was the twelfth year of Nero's reign allows one to deduce a known Sabbatical Year as recorded on an artifact found in a Judean cave. The *Note of Indebtedness* was also found in a cave at Wadi Murabba, which records that year as being a Sabbath Year for the Jews.

Here is the inscription on the note written in Hebrew, but typed below in English:

> (Y)ear two of Nero Caesar, in Tzyah; declared by Abshalom bar Khanin of Tzyah, in his presence, of my own free will, that I, Zachariah bar Yahukhanan ... dwelling in Keslon, silver money pieces twenty ... acquiring ... I ... not sell until the time this, I will pay you in five and possibly in its entirety this Year of Shemitah (Shmita), and if not so, I will make a payment to you from my properties, and those (things) that I will buy later will be pledged to you as mortgage.[148]

Doing some simple math, if the twelfth year reign of Nero was 66 C.E.,

---

148 http://yahweh.org/publications/sjc/sj23Chap.pdf; p.287

then year two of Nero's reign was ten years earlier than 66 C.E., which proves a Shmita (Sabbatical Year) Year of 56 C.E. Simply moving forward in history, counting by seven year intervals, will bring you to the time we are in now which brings us to the next Shmita Year occurring in 2016, *not 2014.*

But if you were to go back in time again by sevens then you could prove (to yourself) each and every Sabbatical or Shmita Year I have already shown you. Counting by seven, you will find yourself arriving upon each of these historically recorded Sabbatical Years.

A Land Rest Year occurred in 701 B.C. as written in the Bible in II Kings 19:29, Isaiah 37, and II Chronicles 32. The table below breaks it down even more:

Historically Recorded Sabbatical Years	
701 B.C.	Sennacherib attack Judah 2 Kings 19:29
700 B.C.	2 Kings 19:29 A Jubilee year
456 B.C.	Nehemiah 8:18
162 B.C.	I Maccabees 16:14 & Josephus Antiquities
134 B.C.	I Maccabees & Josephus Antiquities
43 B.C.	Julius Caesar & Josephus Antiquities
36 B.C.	Josephus Antiquities 14:16:2
22 B.C.	Josephus Antiquities 15:9:1
42 C.E.	Josephus Antiquities 18
56 C.E.	A note of Indebtedness in Nero's time.
70 C.E.	The Sabbath year of 70/71 C.E.
133 C.E.	Rental contracts before Bar Koch bah Revolt
140 C.E.	Rental contracts before Bar Koch bah Revolt

The Second Revolt

The years that followed the First Revolt were riddled with smaller resistances to the ever-increasing Roman rule over the land of Judea and the Romans certainly did not want a repeat of what happened leading up to 70 C.E. Hadrian ruled over the people during this time. Obviously the Temple had been destroyed and the Jewish religious leaders had started the "era of the rabbinical teachings." This time is also known as the Mishnaic Period, when the "oral traditions and teachings were written down." The Mishnaic Period lasted for about 130 years and began in 70 C.E. with the Taanaim.

The prominent rabbi of the Taanaim during the time and era of the Simon Bar Kochba Revolt was Rabbi Akiva. Whenever Rabbi Akiva would see Simon Bar Kochba, he would proclaim:

"Bar Kochba, son of the Star."

He was proclaiming the prophecy that was well known to the people found in the Book of Numbers:

17 There shall come a star out of Jacob. (**Numbers 24:17**)

When Rabbi Aqiba beheld Bar Kozeba (aka, Kochba, Kosiba, Cocheba), he exclaimed: "This is the king Messiah!" Rabbi Johanan ben Torta retorted: "Aqiba, grass will grow (on) your cheeks and he will still not have come!"

This famous exchange can also found in the Talmud where Rabbi Simeon ben Yohai taught:

"Aqiba, my master, used to interpret a star goes forth from Jacob as Kozeba goes forth from Jacob." Rabbi Aqiba, when he saw Bar Kozeba, said: "This is the king Messiah!" Rabbi Johanan ben Torta said to him: "Aqiba! Grass will grow on your cheeks and still the son of David does not come!"[149] (*Palestine Talmud* | Ta'anit 4.5)

Simon Bar Kochba ran with this notion and did nothing to dispel the proclamation that he, in fact, *was* the Promised Messiah chosen to deliver and restore the Kingdom.

One of Rabbi Akiva's disciples was a Rabbi Yose (aka, Jose).[150] During their ongoing efforts to have Simon Bar Kochba fit into their prophetic construct, several dates in history were altered in order for Daniel, chapter 9 to line up with Simon Bar Kochba.

Given the fact Rabbi Akiva was the head of the *Mishnah* (oral tradition) writers during this time and he adamantly maintained Simon Bar Kochba was the "promised Messiah"—these ideas became part of the *Mishnah* to aid

---

149 *Midrash Rabbah Lamentations* 2.2§4
150 http://en.wikipedia.org/wiki/Jose_ben_Halafta

them in interpretation of Bible prophecy to in fact "prove" Simon Bar Kochba was the "Messiah."

The reason this misinformation is so popular today is because of the work of Benedict Zuckermann[151] in 1857 and Emil Schürer with regard to his work entitled, *History of the Jewish People* (1901).

> When scrutinized, their arguments are found to rest almost entirely upon a statement from the mid to late 2nd-century C.E. Jewish work entitled, *Seder Olam* (chapter 30), written by the chronographer Rabbi Jose (Yose) ben Khalaphta. Jose (attests) that the year prior, both to the destruction of the First Temple to the destruction of the Second Temple, was a Sabbath (Sabbatical) Year. The opinions voiced in Rabbi Jose's text became the opinion of numerous Talmudic writers (who) followed him. It was the tradition of the Geonim and it was the considered opinion of, among others, Moses Maimonides, a well respected Talmudist of the 12th-century C.E.[152]

> "...all of the opinions held by Talmudic Jewish writers from late 2nd-century C.E. and beyond are further colored (with) some flagrant and basic chronological errors. Using a distorted interpretation of the prophecy in Daniel 9:24-27 (seventy weeks being understood to mean seventy weeks of years—i.e., 490 years), their chronology was built upon the supposition that the Second Temple stood for 420 years, being destroyed in the 421st year.

> Under this construction, the Second Temple began to be constructed in 351 B.C.E. It is obvious from reading the *Seder Olam* (pg. 29-30) that Rabbi Jose's chronology is based entirely upon the rabbinical interpretation of this prophecy from Daniel and that he purposely makes the destruction of the temples built by Solomon and Herod (the First and Second Temples) conform to this premise.

> According to the prophecy of Daniel, 69 weeks (seven weeks plus sixty-two weeks) would pass before the appearance of the Messiah, which was understood to mean 483 years (i.e., the Messiah would appear in the 484th year). The 421st year of this chronology brings us to the destruction of the Second Temple in 70 C.E. The 484th year becomes 133 C.E., the actual beginning of the Bar Kochba Revolt. During this revolt, some of the prominent rabbis of that period declared Simeon (Simon) Bar Kochba to be the "messiah." The drift of this evidence

---

151 *Ueber Sabbatjahrcyclus and Jobelperiode*, Jahresbericht des juedisch-theologischen Seminars Fraenckelscher Stiftung (Breslau, 1857).
152 Qadesh La Yahweh Press http://yahweh.org/publications/sjc/sj01Chap.pdf; p.9

leads one to suspect that the chronology advocated by Rabbi Jose was, in truth, originally devised to support the claim of Bar Kochba as the messiah. After Bar Kochba failed, his claim as the messiah died, but the chronology which had been made popular at that time continued, (taking) on a life all its own.[153]

Unfortunately, Rabbi Jose's arrangement is impossible since the book of Ezra places the completion of the Second Temple in the sixth year of King Darius of Persia (515 B.C.E.)

14 And the elders of the Yehudim (Jews) were building, and they were blessed through the prophesying of Haggai the prophet and Zekaryah (Zechariah) son of Iddo. And they built and finished it, according to the decree of the Elah (God) of Yisra'ël, and according to the decree of Koresh (Cyrus) and Dareyawesh (Darius), and Artahshashta (Artaxerxes), sovereign of Persia. **15** And this House was completed on the third day of the month of Adar, which was in the sixth year of the reign of Sovereign Dareyawesh (Darius). **16** Then the children of Yisra'ël, the priests and the Lëwites (Levites) and the rest of the sons of the Exile, did the dedication of this House of Elah (God) with joy. **(Ezra 6:14-16)**

Ezra and Nehemiah, noted for their involvement in the activities of the Second Temple lived in the 5th-century B.C.E., long before 351 B.C.E. Further, as history reveals, Bar Kochba was *not* the Messiah, as many other rabbis of that time had themselves argued. Nevertheless, the chronology continued *as if* it had been valid.[154]

I have already shared with you all the known Sabbatical Years in history. When you put what I've shown you to the test and work it out for yourself, you will discover the year 586 B.C. (when the First Temple fell) was, in fact, the third year of the third Sabbatical Cycle. It was *not* a Sabbatical Year—nor was the year before, as Rabbi Yose erroneously claimed, or the year after.

Again, using the same *known* Sabbatical Years, you can also count by sevens from one known Sabbatical Year to the next to see how the year 70 C.E., when King Herod's Temple was destroyed was, in fact, a Sabbatical Year and *not* the year before as Rabbi Yose alleged. But this only solves part of the problem.

Today, Judah and many Messianics will keep the Sabbatical Year because of Rabbi Yose's misinformation, which is not just one year early. They will

---

153 Qadesh La Yahweh Press http://yahweh.org/publications/sjc/sj01Chap.pdf; pp.10-11
154 Qadesh La Yahweh Press http://yahweh.org/publications/sjc/sj01Chap.pdf; p.11

keep it 1 ½ years early! This is because they begin the year in the seventh month of Tishri and not Abib.

> **2** This month is the beginning of months for you, it is the first month of the year for you. (**Exodus 12:2**)

Yehovah has clearly stated that the beginning of the year is to take place when the month of Passover is, that is, the month of Abib—also known as Nisan (March-April). Nowhere does He say to start the year in the seventh month.

One cannot just dismiss this obvious error, but if you look into this more deeply, you will see how this error also came about in the 2nd-century and because of the Sabbatical Years.

Read again what Qadesh La Yahweh Press has to say on this subject:

> Next, beginning in the latter part of the 2nd-century C.E., Jewish writers incorrectly established the first of Tishri of the seventh month in the sixth year of the Sabbatical Cycle as the start of the Sabbath Year. In so doing, they abandoned the first of Abib (called "Nisan" by the Babylonians and post-exilian Jews), as being the first month (March-April) in the calendar originally used among the Israelites.[155] This arrangement was the outgrowth of centuries of tradition intent upon building "a fence around the Law."[156] By putting into place Sabbath Year precepts during the months just prior to the actual start of the Sabbath Year, the religious leaders of Judea believed they were preventing their followers from inadvertently breaking the Law. This interpretation at first created a Sabbath Year that extended from Tishri of year six until the last day of Adar, the twelfth month (February-March), of year seven. In the 2nd-century C.E., even this was shortened so that the year ended with the arrival of Tishri in the seventh year. The eighth year (or first year of the next cycle) was, in turn, made to begin on the first day of Tishri of year seven.[157]
>
> Modern day chronologists have assumed that this first of Tishri beginning was used as the official start of the Sabbath Year not only from the time

---

155 See for example R.Sh., 1:1 and B. A. Zar., 10a.

156 Ab., 1:1-5. As C. K. Barrett points out, the Jews understood that by this fence making they were to, "make additional commandments in order to safeguard the original commandments; for example, certain acts should be avoided towards the approach of evening on Friday lest one forget and inadvertently continue to do them on the Sabbath" (TNTB,p.149).

157 Eg. Sot., 7:

of the *Mishnah*, when the oral laws of the Talmudists were first put into writing (about 200 C.E. forward) but in the *Halakoth* (oral laws) period, which started in about the mid-2nd-century B.C.E. and continued until around 200 C.E. Indeed, many apply it not only to the Sabbath Year, but to every year in the post-exilian period. Yet ... evidence from the pre-destruction era (i.e., before Jerusalem was destroyed in 70 C.E.) and even as late as the Bar Kochba Revolt (133 B.C.E.-135 B.C.E.) proves that the early Jews of Judea observed an Abib (Nisan) 1 beginning for all of their years, including the Sabbath Year.[158]

Another issue or argument used to justify the beginning of the year in the seventh month is the Jubilee Year. There is evidence that many Jews continued to keep the Jubilee Years long after the fall of Jerusalem in 70 C.E.—a fact clearly indicated by the *Babylonian Rosh Hashanah*:

> (A)s if he fasted on both the ninth and the tenth days. **1** Our Rabbis taught: It is a Jubilee **2**—'A Jubilee' **3** even though they did not observe the release of fields, even though they did not observe the blowing of the trumpet. **4** I might say (that it is still a Jubilee) even though they did not observe the dismissal of slaves. Therefore it says, 'it is.' **5** So R. Judah. R. Jose said: 'It is a Jubilee,'—'A Jubilee' **3** even though they did not release fields, even though they did not dismiss slaves. I might think (that it is still a Jubilee) even if they did not blow the trumpet. It therefore says, 'it is.' Now **6** since one text brings some cases under the rule and another text excludes others from it, why should I expound: 'A Jubilee,' **7** even though they did not dismiss, but it is not a Jubilee unless they blew the trumpet?' Because it is possible that there should be no (opportunity for) **8** dismissing slaves, but it is not possible that there should be no (opportunity for) blowing the trumpet. **9** Another explanation is that the performance of the latter depends on the Beth Din, but the performance of the former does not depend on the Beth Din. **10** What need is there for the alternative explanation?—**Because you might argue that it is impossible that there should not be someone in some part of the world who has not a slave to dismiss.** Therefore, I say that the one depends on the Beth Din but the other does not depend on the Beth Din.[159]

The *Babylonian Rosh Hashanah* not only gives opinions on how a Jubilee Year should be kept, but argues that, "... it must be kept outside Palestine."[160]

---

158 Qadesh La Yahweh Press http://yahweh.org/publications/sjc/sj01Chap.pdf; p.12
159 *Talmud*—Masoretic Rosh HaShana 9b, http://juchre.org/talmud/rosh/rosh1.htm#8b
160 Qadesh La Yahweh Press, http://yahweh.org/publications/sjc/sj01Chap.pdf, p.17

As I have stated before, the supposition that the Sabbath Year officially began on Tishri 1 originated from the teachings of Rabbi Akiva and through the writings of Rabbi Yose during 2nd-century C.E. and persevered through space and time with the help of other proponents of the Talmudic teachings.

The Talmudists misinterpreted Leviticus 25:8-13 to mean that the observances of Jubilee rituals designated for the seventh month belonged to the forty-ninth year in the cycle. Nevertheless, a careful reading proves that the seventh month spoken of actually belongs to the fiftieth year, *not* the forty-ninth.

This Bible passage clearly states that forty-nine years had *already been counted* before one was to consider the seventh month, thereby placing the seventh month in the fiftieth year. Furthermore, this same passage attaches to the duties of the seventh month the phrase, "... and you shall make sacred this year, the fiftieth year, and you shall proclaim liberty in the land to all its dwellers." Also, on the tenth day of the seventh month, the Day of Atonement, a ram's horn or trumpet was to be sounded. This passage in no way implies the trumpets were to be sounded *because* it announced the coming of the Jubilee, which was still six months off. Rather, it was to be sounded because one was in the seventh month of the Jubilee Year and the nation was proclaiming "liberty." In addition, the very fact that the seventh month is mentioned without a qualifying statement, such as, "... being the first month of the Sabbatical Year ..." demonstrates that this seventh month belonged to a year *already in progress.*

The Jubilee (Hebrew yovel יובל) Year literally means, "... the blast of a horn (from its continuous sound)." In Strong's we find:

H3104 יבל יובל
yôbêl yôbêl yo-bale', yo-bale'

The Year of Jubilee, therefore, is named after the year in which the trumpets are blown. It would make no sense if the trumpets were blown in the middle of the forty-ninth year, for in that case, the forty-ninth year would be the Year of Jubilee (trumpet blowing).

Josephus accordingly pronounced that:

"... the fiftieth year is called by the Hebrews 'Jubil.' During that season, debtors are absolved from their debts and slaves are set at liberty."

Josephus then goes on to say:

> And truly Moses gave them all these precepts, being such as were
> observed during his own lifetime; but though he lived now in the
> wilderness, yet did he make provision how they might observe the same
> laws when they should have taken the Land of Canaan.

> He gave them rest to the land from ploughing and planting every seventh
> year, as he had prescribed to them to rest from working every seventh
> day; and ordered, that then what grew of its own accord out of the
> earth should in common belong to all that pleased to use it, making
> no distinction in that respect between their own countrymen and
> foreigners: and he ordained, that they should do the same after seven
> times seven years, which in all are fifty years; and that fiftieth year is
> called by the Hebrews the Jubilee, wherein debtors are freed from their
> debts, and slaves are set at liberty; which slaves became such, though
> they were of the same stock, by transgressing some of those laws the
> punishment of which was not capital, but they were punished by this
> method of slavery.

> This year also restores the land to its former possessors in the manner
> following: When the Jubilee is come, which name denotes liberty, he
> that sold the land, and he that bought it, meet together, and make an
> estimate, on one hand, of the fruits gathered; and, on the other hand,
> of the expenses laid out upon it. If the fruits gathered come to more
> than the expenses laid out, he that sold it takes the land again; but if the
> expenses prove more than the fruits, the present possessor receives of
> the former owner the difference that was wanting, and leaves the land to
> him; and if the fruits received, and the expenses laid out, prove equal to
> one another, the present possessor relinquishes it to the former owners.
> Moses would have the same law obtain as to those houses also which
> were sold in villages; but he made a different law for such as were sold
> in a city; for if he that sold it tendered the purchaser his money again
> within a year, he was forced to restore it; but in case a whole year had
> intervened, the purchaser was to enjoy what he had bought. This was the
> constitution of the laws which Moses learned of God when the camp lay
> under Mount Sinai, and this he delivered in writing to the Hebrews.[161]

Philo adds clarification by noting how Yehovah:

> "… consecrated the whole of the fiftieth year."[162]

---

161 *Josephus Antiquities* 3:12:3 3.
162 *Philo Special Laws* 2:22

Nothing is said about consecrating the last six months of the forty-ninth year as the beginning of the Jubilee.

The awkwardness created by the explanation that the Jubilee Year began with the seventh month of the forty-ninth year in the cycle is further compounded by the fact that many of the Talmudic Jews actually started this year not with the first day of the seventh month but with the tenth day—the day the trumpets of the Jubilee were actually sounded.

The *Babylonian Rosh Hashanah*, for example, argues:

> "… (is the New Year for) Jubilees on the first of Tishri?" Surely (the New Year for) Jubilees is on the tenth of Tishri, as it is written, on the Day of Atonement shall (you) make proclamation with the horn.[163]

Qadesh La Yahweh Press, however, has this to say:

> It is clear that the original scheme of the Jubilee and Sabbath Cycles came to be obscured by the inventive over-interpretations of subsequent, ill-informed theologians.[164]

In the following quote you are about to read how Benedict Zuckermann and then later, Emil Schürer, read Rabbi Yose's *Seder Olam* and concluded that Tishri (September-October) 1, 68 C.E.–Tishri 1, 69 C.E. was the Sabbatical Year before the Temple fell. You will also read where Ralph Marcus and Zion Wacholder propose the same thing and come up with a one year difference— that difference being Tishri 1, 69 C.E.–Tishri 1, 70 C.E. But both continue to mistakenly operate on the faulty premise the year begins with Tishri—which I have just shown you didn't even begin until *after* the 2ⁿᵈ-century C.E.

> There are two possible sets of dates for Sabbatical Years in the Second Temple Period, one advanced by Benedict Zuckermann in 1857 and the other by Ben Zion Wacholder in 1973. Zuckermann translated a line *Seder Olam Rabbah* 30, ומוצאי שביעית (we-motsa'e shebi'it; see also b. Arakin 11b, t. Taanit 3:9), to mean that the two destructions of Jerusalem, first in biblical times and then again in the summer of A.D. 70, was "after a seventh year" (i.e., a Sabbatical Year). Thus, the year beginning in the fall of A.D. 68 was a Sabbatical Year; the year beginning the fall of A.D. 69 and continuing through the following summer was a post-Sabbatical Year. From A.D. 68, therefore, one can count backward or forward in multiples of seven years to find other Sabbatical Years.

163 *Talmud*—Masoretic Rosh HaShana 8b, http://juchre.org/talmud/rosh/rosh1.htm#8b
164 Qadesh La Yahweh Press, http://yahweh.org/publications/sjc/sj02Chap.pdf, p.20

> A hundred years later, Wacholder took this phrase to mean instead that Jerusalem fell to the Romans "at the end" of a Sabbatical Year. Thus, Wacholder came up with dates one year later than Zuckermann's, based on the year beginning in the fall of A.D. 69 as a Sabbatical Year. The Zuckermann dates are considered conventional or "orthodox"—they are the basis for the Sabbatical Year count in use in Israel today. Wacholder's dates, however, enjoy broad acceptance among scholars.[165]

Not only have these leading scholars on the Sabbatical and Jubilee Years in our modern times based their theories upon the false premise of Rabbi Yose, they also have done something else that should fill anyone seeking truth with righteous indignation. When they did find some historical facts that proved their own theory wrong, they did not modify their assertions in the least to accommodate the new facts. No, what they did was hide the facts or dismiss them while they continued to propagate their own theories.

Advocates of these various theories have often been forced to harshly criticize ancient records, like those from Josephus and the Maccabean books, because the historical data is inconsistent with present theory. Robert North, for example, takes Josephus to task by challenging his historical year as exhibiting:

> "... internal inconsistencies which invalidate their use for chronology."

North concludes by maintaining:

> It should be abundantly clear that the Sabbath Year dates of Josephus are either palpably incommensurate, or else insolubly obscure.

According to a study entitled, *The Sabbath & Jubilee Cycle* from Qadesh La Yahweh Press we see just how flagrant those who wish to perpetuate the lie truly are:

> This study disagrees. It is not Josephus or any other ancient report (predating) 2nd-century C.E. that is the source of confusion. Indeed, we find them all remarkably accurate. Rather, it is the attempt to force these early records to conform (to) one of the three erroneous Sabbath Cycle theories now prevalent which has created an illusion of historical error.[166]

---

165 http://pursiful.com/2010/05/sabbatical-years-in-the-second-temple-period/
166 Qadesh La Yahweh Press, http://www.yahweh.org/yahweh2.html, Introduction

I will now have you look at two clear examples, of which tampering with the truth by leading modern day chronologists are undoubtedly the case.

The Seige of Bethzura (Beth-Zur) & Jerusalem 162 B.C.–161 B.C.

The 150th Seleucid Year will simply not fit the proposed Sabbath Cycles offered by (these) systems. As a result, the first effort of the advocates of these systems has been to claim that the records dealing with the events surrounding the siege of Bethzura and Jerusalem by Antiochus (V) Eupator and associated with the 150th Seleucid Year are in conflict with one another, are misinformed, or are just plain wrong. Wacholder, for example, argues:

> I and II Maccabees differ, however, as to the date of Antiochus V's march into Judea. II Maccabees 13:1 dates the march in the 149th year of the Seleucian Era, I Maccabees 6:20, repeated by Josephus, in the 150th year.[167]

Wacholder then declares I Maccabees and Josephus to be in error and that the 149th Seleucid Year was the real Sabbath Year. Zuckermann goes as far as to retranslate I Maccabees, 6:53, so that it implies, "There had been a Sabbatical Year in the preceding 149th Seleucian Year" rather than in the stated 150th year.[168] North reads I Maccabees, 6:53, to mean, "... because the effects of the Sabbath Year were then being felt,"[169] and concludes the dates found in Josephus, "... are either palpably incommensurate or else insolubly obscure."[170]

Based upon the inability of these chronologists to make all the evidence fit their desired Sabbath Cycle systems, they extrapolate that the 149th Seleucid Year is the correct figure and that the 150th (Seleucid) Year somehow must have been introduced as a mistake, is misunderstood, or simply reflects a poor form of Greek grammar used in the source texts (theorizing that the true intent of these authors was to express that the 149th year was a Sabbath Year).

Contrary to these opinions, close examination of these records proves that the relevant accounts found in I & II Maccabees, the *Antiquities* of Josephus, are all very much in harmony and that the Greek of these texts is quite precise in its meaning. The belief that the sources are in conflict is a forced interpretation, based up a spurious claim that the Jewish

---

167 HUCA, 44, p.161
168 TSCJ, pp.47f.
169 Bib., 34, p.507
170 Ibid., p.511.

year in this early period began with the month of Tishri (September-October). It is built upon a longing to have some justification to make the 149th Seleucid Year encompass the Sabbath Year intended by the story rather than the 150th year.[171]

You can read the rest of the proof at Qadesh La Yahweh Press.[172]

Before I present to you the next proof that clearly exposes the schemes of these modern day chronologists, I would like you to read something else from:

Sabbatical Years (Shemitot) In the Second Temple Period[173]

The first modern treatise devoted to the Sabbatical (and Jubilee) Cycles was that of Benedict Zuckermann.[174] Zuckermann insisted that for Sabbatical Years after the Exile, "it is necessary to assume the commencement of a new starting-point, since the laws of Sabbatical Years and Jubilees fell into disuse during the Babylonian captivity, when a foreign nation held possession of the Land of Canaan ...We therefore cannot agree with chronologists who assume an unbroken continuity of septennial Sabbaths and Jubilees."[175]

This is a profound statement made by Zuckermann. I hope you understand what he has just done. He knows for a fact that the Sabbatical Cycles after the 2nd-century C.E. do not line up with those before that time. Yet, he proceeds to make any of those before the error of Rabbi Yose line up with those after the presumed destruction in 68 C.E.–69 C.E. to justify his own theory and that of Rabbi Yose's. Make sure you understand this point because he will, as I have just shown and will again, blur the line of truth to persist in his own theory.

Continuing:

The first instance of a Sabbatical Year treated by Zuckermann was Herod the Great's siege of Jerusalem, as described by Josephus.[176] Zuckermann

---

171 Qadesh La Yahweh Press http://yahweh.org/publications/sjc/sj13Chap.pdf; p.181
172 Qadesh La Yahweh Press http://yahweh.org/yahweh2.html
173 http://en.wikipedia.org/wiki/Historical_Sabbatical_Years
174 Benedict Zuckermann, *Treatise On the Sabbatical Cycle & the Jubilee*, trans. A Löwy; (New York: Hermon, 1974); originally published as "Ueber Sabbatjahrcyclus und Jobelperiode," in Jarhesbericht des jüdisch-theologischen Seminars "Fraenckelscher Stiftung" (Breslau, 1857).
175 Zuckermann, *Treatise.*, p.31.
176 *Antiquities* 14.16.2; 15.1.2.

assigned this to (the year of) 38 B.C.E.–37 B.C.E. (i.e. he considered that a Sabbatical Year started in Tishri of 38 B.C.E.). Next, he considered John Hyrcanus's siege of Ptolemy in the fortress of Dagon, which is described both in Josephus (*Antiquities* 13:8:1; *Wars of the Jews* 1:2:4) and I Maccabees (16:14-16), and during which a Sabbatical Year started; from the chronological information provided in these texts, Zuckermann concluded that 136 B.C.E.–135 B.C.E. was a Sabbatical Year.

Again, this is a huge statement that most would just skim right over. "Zuckermann concluded ..." meaning because he could not make the information fit his theory, he now changes history to make it line up. I will present to you this information shortly. But for now, suffice it to say both Zuckermann and Wacholder take issue with this part of history and with the 162 B.C.E.–161 B.C.E. and 134 B.C.E.–133 B.C.E. Sabbatical Years because they persist in maintaining they began in the month of Tishri and refuse to acknowledge they actually began in Nisan—also known as Abib (March-April).

Continuing further:

The next event ... (given their treatment) was Antiochus Eupator's siege of the fortress Beth-Zur (*Antiquities* 12.9.6; I Maccabees 6:53), dated by Zuckermann (as the year) 163 B.C.E.–162 B.C.E. However, he also remarked on the difficulties presented to this figure by the text in I Maccabees, which would seem to date the siege one year later, and so he decided to leave it out of consideration.[177] The final text considered by Zuckermann was a passage in the *Seder Olam* that relates the destruction of the Second Temple to a Sabbatical Year, an event that is known from secular history to have happened in the summer of 70 C.E. Zuckermann interpreted the *Seder Olam* text as stating that this happened in a year after a Sabbatical Year, thus placing a Sabbatical in 68 C.E.–69 C.E.

At this juncture, Zuckermann has now taken history, set it aside and dismissed it, if not discarded it altogether to continue to justify the pursuit and endorsement of his own theory and reinforce what Rabbi Yose put forth, which is, consequently, what all the sages of Judaism have agreed to since Yose's time up until now. But in order to do this, they all must turn a blind eye to that which is a matter of established historical record, including the Second Temple destruction in 70 C.E.

Reading further we find:

---

177 Zuckermann, *Treatise*, pp.47-48.

All (of) these dates as calculated by Zuckermann are separated by an integral multiple of seven years, except for the date associated with the siege of Beth-Zur. Furthermore, his chronology is consistent with that accepted by the Geonim (medieval Jewish scholars) and the calendar of Sabbatical Years used in present-day Israel.

I have just shown you how this siege of Beth-Zur is correctly stated by Josephus and accurately described in I and II Maccabees. I have also just shown you how Zuckermann refuses to factor in the destruction of the Second Temple in 70 C.E. Zuckermann then opts to dismiss what Josephus and I and II Maccabees have to say on the matter and would rather favor his own theory in order to have it line up with and echo what all the renowned sages and Geonim have intimated the past 2,000 years all based on the false teachings of Rabbi Jose and the Seder Olam. I am emphasizing this so you get it. Do not just read over these statements without thinking.

All of this would seem to be strong evidence in favor of Zuckermann's scheme. Nevertheless, some problems have been recognized, beyond just the question of the siege of Beth-Zur, which was one year too late for Zuckermann's Calendar. A consistent problem has been the ambiguity alleged in some of the passages, notably of Josephus, where it has been questioned, for example, when Josephus started the regnal (reigning) years of Herod. Therefore, many modern scholars have adopted a Sabbatical Year Calendar for the Second Temple period that is one year later, though there are many prominent scholars who still maintain a cycle consistent with Zuckermann's conclusion of a 38 B.C.E.–37 B.C.E. Sabbatical Year, which the Josephus text, in coordination with Appian, Dio Cassius, Plutarch, and Velleius Paterculus, would demonstrate to be more likely. Among those who have advocated an adjustment, the most extensive studies in its favor have been those of Ben Zion Wacholder.[178] Wacholder had access to legal documents from the time of the Bar Kochba Revolt that Zuckermann did not. The arguments of Wacholder and others to support the calendar one year later than that of Zuckermann are rather technical and will not be presented here, except for one item to which Zuckermann, Wacholder, and other scholars have given great weight: the testimony of the *Seder Olam* relating the destruction of the Second Temple to a Sabbatical Year.

---

178 Ben Zion Wacholder, *The Calendar of Sabbatical Cycles During the Second Temple & the Early Rabbinic Period*, Hebrew Union College Annual (HUCA) 44 (1973), pp.53-196; *Chronomessianism: The Timing of Messianic Movements & the Calendar of Sabbatical Cycles*, HUCA 46 (1975), pp.201-218; *The Calendar of Sabbath Years During the Second Temple Era: A Response*, HUCA 54 (1983), pp.123-133.

I have now shown you what Wacholder concludes from the same reading that Zuckermann read in Rabbi Yose's work, the *Seder Olam*, and how Wacholder concluded it was one year later. Zuckermann says the Second Temple was destroyed in 68 C.E.–69 C.E. going from Tishri to Tishri. Wacholder then says no, it was from 69 C.E.–70 C.E., going again from Tishri–Tishri. Wacholder gets part of the year right and is able to line up some of the historically recorded Sabbatical Years correctly, but they both have trouble with the history of John Hyrcanus because they hold to the same view (which only began in the 2nd-century) that the year began with Tishri and ended with Tishri.

And so it is today, that you will find groups of people, along with most of Judah, who will keep the next Sabbatical Year in 2014; from Tishri 2014–Tishri 2015. And then you will find others who will keep 2015 as the Sabbatical Year and they also will do so from Tishri 2015–Tishri 2016. And just so you know, I am strongly advocating that the year begins as I have shown you—from Abib to Abib and that the next Sabbatical Year is from Abib 2016–Abib 2017. Abib or Aviv being from March/April.

Now let us take a close look at the one historical document that gave *both* Wacholder and Zuckermann a considerable amount of trouble—the history of John Hyrcanus.

I would love to quote the entire chapter of Qadesh La Yahweh Press's book *The Sabbath and Jubilee Cycle*,[179] but you can go and read chapter 14[180] yourself and be blessed for doing so. It does throw out at you a lot of dates, so it is best to read it there. But let me summarize it for you here:

(During the Maccabean days), the High Priest Simon came to power after the capture and death of his brother Jonathan by the Syrian Greek Empire.

We are then told in I Maccabees 16:14 that Simon is killed by Ptolemy (aka, Ptolemaeus) in the month of Shebat. Take note: Shebat is the eleventh month, (i.e., January-February). This eleventh month is confirmed in Zechariah 1:7 on the twenty-fourth day of the eleventh month, which is the month Shebat.

After killing Simon, Ptolemy imprisoned Simon's wife and two sons, Mattathias and Judas, and then sent men to kill his third son, John Hyrcanus.

---

179 Qadesh La Yahweh Press http://yahweh.org/yahweh2.html
180 Qadesh La Yahweh Press http://yahweh.org/publications/sjc/sj14Chap.pdf

John escaped and then made plans to attack Ptolemy in Dagon, a city just north of Jericho.

I will now let the late Josephus explain what happened next:

(230) So Ptolemaeus (aka, Ptolemy) retired to one of the fortresses that was above Jericho, which was called Dagon. But Hyrcanus having taken the high priesthood that had been his father's before, and in the first place propitiated יהוה by sacrifices, he then made an expedition against Ptolemaeus; and when he made his attacks upon the place, in other points he was too hard for him, but was rendered weaker than he, by the commiseration he had for his mother and brethren, and by that only; (231) for Ptolemaeus brought them upon the wall, and tormented them in the sight of all, and threatened that he would throw them down headlong, unless Hyrcanus would leave off the siege. And as he thought that so far as he relaxed as to the siege and taking of the place, so much favor did he show to those that were dearest to him by preventing their misery, his zeal about it was cooled.

(232) However, his mother spread out her hands, and begged of him that he would not grow remiss on her account, but indulge his indignation so much the more, and that he would do his utmost to take the place quickly, in order to get their enemy under his power, and then to avenge upon him what he had done to those that were dearest to himself; for that death would be to her sweet, though with torment, if that enemy of theirs might but be brought to punishment for his wicked dealings to them. (233) Now when his mother said so, he resolved to take the fortress immediately; but when he saw her beaten, and torn to pieces, his courage failed him, and he could not but sympathize with what his mother suffered, and was thereby overcome. (234) And as the siege was drawn out into length by this means, that year on which the Jews used to rest came on; for the Jews observe this rest every seventh year, as they do every seventh day; (235) so that Ptolemaeus being for this cause released from the war, he slew the brethren of Hyrcanus, and his mother; and when he had so done, he fled to Zenon, who was called Cotylas, who was then the tyrant of the city Philadelphia.[181]

John Hyrcanus could not save his mother and brothers because a Sabbatical Year was approaching. It was the eleventh month and so the siege had to be broken off. It was the eleventh month of Shebat, not the sixth month called Elul and not one month before the seventh month of Tishri. The twelveth month being Adar and the first month being Aviv.

John Hyrcanus tried to avenge the death of his father and brothers before the

---

181 Josephus Antiquities 13.8.

Sabbatical Year arrived in just one month's time. He was emotional as his mother and two other brothers were tortured on the wall in front of the entire Jewish army. But John failed to take the fort and because the Sabbath Year was now approaching, he had to withdraw and in so doing his mother was then killed.

Jewish law forbids them from conducting military expeditions in a Sabbatical Year, the same as it is forbidden to do so on a Sabbath Day.

I have been unable to find the actual law that states you are not to go to war in a Sabbatical Year. It was just not done during the Maccabean times. Yet we can read how Joshua who arrived in a Jubilee Year in the Promised Land did go to war repeatedly and this was indeed a Jubilee Year. I am led to believe this law of not warring during a Sabbatical Year is a tradition more so than it is a binding law.

Zuckermann conveniently fails to incorporate this date into his calculations because it shows the year beginning in Nisan/Aviv and not Tishri. So you can now see how these renowned chronologists leave out relevant and pertinent historical information that proves when the year begins—at Abib. They do so to justify their own predisposed theories.

Wacholder uses it, which is why his calculations are one year different than Zuckermann, but Wacholder still holds to Tishri being the beginning of the year and not Abib.

Starting with a faulty foundation, they both have arrived at faulty conclusions

We have Rabbi Akiba endorsing Simon Bar Kochba to prove that Yehshua was not the Messiah and had Rabbi Yose write the *Seder Olam* with faulty chronology and falsified historical dates used to justify their position—all of which were proven false. We later have the respected Geonim (the sages) dismiss the false messiah, Simon Bar Kochba, but hold to the faulty chronology and Rabbi Yose's false teaching about Daniel's 70 Weeks.

Zuckermann would again base his research upon the supposed facts of the *Seder Olam*. Wacholder would also use the *Seder Olam* as his starting point but change it by one year based on a different translation of chapter 30. The *Seder Olam* gives the year that both Temples were destroyed as *ve-motsae sheviit* (תיעבש יאצומו). Guggenheimer's recent translation[182] renders this phrase as "… at the end of a Sabbatical Year," thus unambiguously supporting the Wacholder Calendar that starts a Sabbatical Year in the fall of 69 C.E.

---

182 *Seder Olam*, chapter 30, translation by Heinrich W. Guggenheimer, *Seder Olam: The Rabbinic View of Biblical Chronology* (Lanham, MD: Rowman and Littlefield, 2005).

The problem, however, is that many translations of the *Seder Olam* render the phrase as "… in the year after a Sabbatical Year" or its equivalent. This was the sense adopted by Zuckermann when citing the *Seder Olam* as supportive of *his* calendar of Sabbatical Years.

So you have all the researchers basing their research, to one extent or another, upon Rabbi Yose who rewrote history to support Rabbi Akiba and the Simon Bar Kochba Revolt.

Historically Recorded Sabbatical Years	
701 B.C.	Sennacherib attack Judah 2 Kings 19:29
700 B.C.	2 Kings 19:29 A Jubilee year
456 B.C.	Nehemiah 8:18
162 B.C.	I Maccabees 16:14 & Josephus Antiquities
134 B.C.	I Maccabees & Josephus Antiquities
43 B.C.	Julius Caesar & Josephus Antiquities
36 B.C.	Josephus Antiquities 14:16:2
22 B.C.	Josephus Antiquities 15:9:1
42 C.E.	Josephus Antiquities 18
56 C.E.	A note of Indebtedness in Nero's time.
70 C.E.	The Sabbath year of 70/71 C.E.
133 C.E.	Rental contracts before Bar Koch bah Revolt
140 C.E.	Rental contracts before Bar Koch bah Revolt

You can know, however, from II Kings 19:29, when the Sabbatical and Jubilee Years were recorded in the Bible and you can also accurately determine what year this was based on Assyrian records. Next, all you have to do is count by sevens from 701 B.C. to arrive at any known and/or not yet known Sabbatical Years. Above are all the *known* Sabbatical Years. The years we know to be Land Rest Years and Jubilee Years are as indicated in the chart on the previous page. Taken from Qadesh La Yahweh Press.[183]

Qadesh La Yahweh Press goes to great lengths to prove these dates are correct and takes great pains to demonstrate how the other theories go astray. Prove all things! For they have done this.

---

183 Qadesh La Yahweh Press, http://yahweh.org/yahweh2.html

Chapter 23 | Another Teaching Known As Daniel's Timeline

This is not Daniel, the biblical prophet, but a modern teaching used today and known as Daniel's Timeline[184] amongst Messianic believers.

The many Messianic believers found embracing this false teaching have never crosschecked the years in question to make sure they are in fact, Jubilee Years. The man spearheading this is doing so in all sincerity, I believe and most likely is an honest man—as I'm sure all the other teachers are who continue to espouse this teaching, which fortunately, is easily proven false.

I have now established with you that a Jubilee Year is forty-nine years and the fiftieth year is the *same as* the first year. This is the exact same way in which we count to Pentecost or Shavuot. The fiftieth day is the *same as* the first day of the week.

I have also shown you in *The Prophecies of Abraham*[185] all the known and recorded Sabbatical Years, and I am not going to duplicate those charts in this book. If you have a burning desire within you to know more, I urge you to get a copy of that book and delve into the Sabbatical subject more deeply. You can read the reviews for The Prophecies of Abraham at Amozon.com[186]

Revisiting a familiar II Kings passage we are reminded:

> 29 "And this is the sign for you: This year you eat what grows of itself, and in the second year what springs from that, and in the third year, sow and reap and plant vineyards and eat their fruit." **(II Kings 19:29)**

---

184 http://www.danielstimeline.com/
185 http://bookstore.authorhouse.com/Products/SKU-000366309/The-Prophecies-of-Abraham.aspx
186 http://www.amazon.com/The-Prophecies-Abraham-Declaring-beginning/product-reviews/1449047521/ref=cm_cr_dp_see_all_btm?ie=UTF8&showViewpoints=1&sortBy=bySubmissionDateDescending

That first year in II Kings ran from 701 B.C. to 700 B.C. and along with that year, I have since shown you the other known Sabbatical Years, which were recorded throughout history. The good news being—you can now know *every* Sabbatical and Jubilee Year throughout history.

The teaching of Daniel's Timeline begins with the Balfour Declaration in 1917 as a Jubilee Year. Those promulgating this errant doctrine have never checked to see if it was *truly* a Jubilee Year. Instead, they just speculated this was indeed the case and based on this presumption, they began the wrong teaching.

This guess was literally taken out of thin air, and so many others, like "sheeple" gone astray have just assumed it was true, never once checking to find out—anymore than those who teach this did—if, in fact, 1917 *was* an actual Jubilee Year. It was not. 1917 is, instead, the sixth year of the third cycle.

Fifty years after 1917 is 1967. It is the year of the Six Days War. It is *not* a Jubilee Year as Daniel's Timeline suggests. But it *is* a Sabbatical Year. But because of these two important world events—the Balfour Declaration and the Six Day War being fifty years apart—these well meaning, yet misinformed teachers and those who, out of sheer ignorance, adhere to this teaching assume it *has* to be true; that 1917 and 1967 *must* be Jubilee Years. Adding on another fifty years to 1967 brings you to 2017 and this is when they assume the Messiah is to come—during this false Jubilee Year. 2017 is *not* a Jubilee Year, however. So, why is this year of 2017 the year the Messiah must come back and not the next Jubilee year according their method of calculating which would make it 2067? They do not know. They just insist this must be the time of the Messiah's Second Coming and they base this on Daniel's Timeline, which I have just described to you. It has no other logic or fact than what we have just stated.

They have not figured out how many Jubilee years or cycles have come and gone. They have not figured out where we are in those Jubilee cycles to know if indeed this is the last one. They have done none of this work. All they have done is speculated and everyone else has fallen in line with it because it looks good. But no one has done any research, none!

Also, none of those teaching this false doctrine ever suggest you keep the year 2016 as a Sabbatical Year to begin with. Instead, they focus on the potential return in 2017 and not on being obedient to keeping the Sabbatical Years Holy in 2016. If the fiftieth year, or the Jubilee Year were 2017, then the forty-ninth Sabbatical Year would be 2016. Yet, they have no deliberate intention of keeping it holy based on how Yehovah would have them keep it holy as outlined in Torah.

Daniel's Timeline automatically is found to be false just knowing when the true Jubilee Years are (that Yehovah requires us to keep)—as I already cited in II Kings 19:29. When you count forward from 700 B.C. by 49's, you will end up at 1996 for the last Jubilee Year, 1947 as the Jubilee Year before that, 1898 as the Jubilee Year before that, and so on. It is not rocket science. All you have to do is add and also to be able to have the proper starting point. II Kings 19:29 is that starting point.

Because the teaching of Daniel's 70 Weeks is such a big teaching, we will address this in our next book that should be ready very soon. Look for "**The 70 Shabua of Daniel**", the most terrifying prophecy in the entire bible, which can only be unveiled in the last days; we are now in those last days and this book should be published in 2013.

Chapter 24 | The II Kings 17 & 18 Controversy

Thus far, we have hinged the fullness of our understanding of the Sabbatical and Jubilee Years on the timeframe of 701 B.C.–700 B.C. as the forty-ninth and fiftieth years in a Jubilee Cycle in accordance with II Kings 19:29 and how this lines up with the known chronology of Assyria.

Based on the research of Qadesh La Yahweh Press in their book *The Sabbath and Jubilee Cycle*,[187] Edwin R. Thiele's *The Mysterious Numbers of the Hebrew Kings*[188] and Jack Finegan's *The Handbook of Biblical Chronology*,[189] we can safely conclude we have absolute benchmark years by which to tie in the Israelite kings with a known and acceptable chronology that we can trace down through the years to our present day.

I have shown you in this book how those years of 701 B.C.–700 B.C. match up perfectly with all the other known historically recorded Sabbatical Years. If you do not believe 701 B.C.–700 B.C. are the benchmark years I have determined them to be, then you must empirically prove how each of the other Sabbatical Years as recorded in history are also false which would be next to impossible to do—although some *have* tried as I have previously pointed out.

Yet, there are some today who will still claim King Hezekiah ruled twelve years earlier than what I have been saying. And they will base this on II Kings 17-18. They will then proceed to quote the famous and much overused Scripture in II Timothy, "All Scripture is breathed by Elohim and profitable for teaching."

---

187 http://yahweh.org/PDF_index2.html

188 http://www.amazon.com/The-Mysterious-Numbers-Hebrew-Kings/dp/082543825X

189 http://www.chapters.indigo.ca/books/Handbook-Biblical-Chronology-PRINCIPLES-TIME-Jack-Finegan/9781565631434-item.html?cookieCheck=1

14 But you, stay in what you have learned and trusted, having known from whom you have learned, **15** and that from a babe you have known the Set-apart Scriptures, which are able to make you wise for deliverance through belief in Messiah יהושע. **16** All Scripture is breathed by Elohim and profitable for teaching, for reproof, for setting straight, for instruction in righteousness, **17** that the man of Elohim might be fitted, equipped for every good work. (**II Timothy 3:14-17**)

We read the following from *Clarke's Commentary*[190] about this verse:

16 All Scripture is given by the inspiration of God. (**II Timothy 3:16**)

This sentence is not well translated; the original πασα γραφη θεοκνευστος ωφιλιμος προς διδασκαλιαν, κ. τ. λ. should be rendered: *Every writing divinely inspired is profitable for doctrine* ... (the particle και or "and") is omitted by almost all the versions and many of the fathers, and certainly does not agree well with the text. The apostle is here, beyond all controversy, speaking of the writings of the *Old Testament*, which, because they came by Divine inspiration, he terms the *Holy Scriptures*, II Timothy 3:15; and it is of them *alone* that this passage is to be understood; and although all the New Testament came by as direct an inspiration as the Old, yet, as it was not collected at that time, not indeed complete, the apostle could have no reference to it.

Even Yehshua tells us *precisely* what those scriptures are in Luke; they are the Torah, the first five books, The Prophets, and the Psalms. It is not and was not what is today called the New Testament, nor does this include the historical books of Kings and Chronicles.

> **44** And He said to them, "These are the words which I spoke to you while I was still with you, that all have to be filled that were written in the Torah of Mosheh (Moses) and the Prophets and the Psalms concerning Me." **45** Then He opened their minds to understand the Scriptures. (**Luke 24:44-45**)

Knowing this, we can then look at the Books of Chronicles and Kings strictly as historical documents—documents of which all renowned chronologists recognize and acknowledge there are some contextual as well as general errors in these texts—one of which I will have you take a closer look at while I explain the part which is errant.

---

190 http://www.godrules.net/library/clarke/clarke2tim3.htm

We read in II Kings how King Hoshea reigned in the twentieth year of Jotham:

> **30** And Hoshea the son of Elah made a conspiracy against Pekah the son of Remaliah (of Ishmael), and smote him, and slew him, and reigned in his stead, in the twentieth year of Jotham, the son of Uzziah (king of Judah). **(II Kings 15:30)**

But we also read in II King 17 that King Hoshea began his reign in the twelfth year of Ahaz:

> **1** In the twelfth year of Ahaz, king of Judah, began Hoshea, the son of Elah, to reign in Samaria over Israel nine years. **(II Kings 17:1)**

If II Kings 17:1 is correct, then who ruled over Israel in the interval between the fourth and twelfth years of Ahaz? How can this latter synchronism be made to harmonize with the previous synchronism of Hoshea's accession in the twelfth year of Jotham when the latter reigned only sixteen years?[191]

Edwin R. Thiele in his book, *The Mysterious Number of the Hebrew Kings*[192] answers this very question. His book is a reconstruction of the chronology of the Kingdoms of Israel and Judah. The book was originally his doctoral dissertation and is widely regarded as the definitive work on the chronology of the Hebrew kings. The book is considered the classic and comprehensive work in reckoning the accession of kings, calendars, and co-regencies, based on biblical and extra-biblical sources.

David Rohl[193] is a world renowned Egyptologist having written numerous books on the ancient history of the Middle East and a leading figure in ancient chronology. He is most known for having shortened the Egyptian chronology by 300 years to match up more precisely with the narrative of the bible.

I wrote to David Rohl and asked him just how reliable he felt Edwin R. Thiele's book to be. He responded and said that all reputable chronologists agree with Thiele and have found his work impeccable.

---

191 *The Mysterious Numbers of the Hebrew Kings* by Edwin Thiele, p.38
192 *The Mysterious Numbers of the Hebrew Kings* by Edwin Thiele, (1st ed.; New York: Macmillan, 1951; 2nd ed.; Grand Rapids: Eerdman's, 1965; 3rd ed.; Grand Rapids: Zondervan/Kregel, 1983). ISBN 0-8254-3825-X, 9780825438257
193 *The Lost Testament* by David Rohl (published in the UK in 2002, republished as *From Eden To Exile* in the USA in 2009) and other chronology books of ancient Egypt.

To solve the problem of II Kings 17-18, I have turned to Edwin R. Thiele's book *The Mysterious Number of the Hebrew Kings.*

A correct understanding of Hoshea (Hosea) is vital to a correct understanding of the Hebrew history of this important time.

This understanding is based on the recognition of dual dating for Pekah. Unless this is understood, and unless it is seen that Pekah began his twenty years in 752 B.C., then this misunderstanding throws Hoshea twelve years beyond his true position in history and twelve years out of line with the rulers of Judah.

When the editors of Kings were nearing the final form of the two volumes, they did not understand dual dating for Pekah; and this dynamic was responsible for the synchronisms of II Kings 17-18. In II Kings 17:1, the accession of Hoshea is placed in the twelfth year of Ahaz. That, however, is twelve years out of line with II Kings 15:30, where we are told that Hoshea assassinated Pekah and "... then succeeded him as King in the twentieth year of Jotham." The synchronism of II Kings 17:1, which places the accession of Hoshea in the twelfth year of Ahaz, reveals this twelve year misplacement of Hoshea.

Hoshea did not begin to rule in 720 B.C. but in 732 B.C., which was the twentieth year of Jotham and the commencement of the sixteen years of Ahaz. In the pivotal year of 752 B.C., two kings began their reign in Israel; Menahem in Samaria and Pekah in Gilead. The first twelve of Pekah's twenty years, from 752 B.C.–740 B.C., overlapped the ten years of Menahem and the two years of Pekahiah. From 740 B.C.–732 B.C. Pekah had a sole reign of eight years. That began in the fifty-second and last year of Azariah in accord with the synchronism of II Kings 15:27. All of this is in accord with dual dating for Pekah and with the picture given in Hosea 5:5.

Only in keeping with this arrangement does the accession of Hoshea come in the twentieth year of Jotham in accord with II Kings 15:30. And therefore, this is the only true historical reckoning and correct representation of that period.

The twentieth year of Jotham's reign was 732 B.C.—twelve years before 720 B.C. And the beginning of Pekah's reign was 752 B.C.—twelve years before the fifty-second year of Azariah's reign, 740 B.C. Thus, also the commencement of Hoshea's reign was 732 B.C.—twelve years before 720 B.C. and his end came in 723 B.C. There was no overlap with Hezekiah, however, who began in 716 B.C.

A careful survey of the account of Hezekiah's reign shows that when he began his reign, Hoshea and the nation of Israel were gone. Samaria fell in 723 B.C., thus during the reign of Shalmaneser V (727 B.C.–722 B.C.). But Sargon II (722 B.C.–705 B.C.) claims that he took Samaria. Because of this, the year of 722 B.C. came to be looked upon as the date of Samaria's fall.

As mentioned earlier, a number of outstanding scholars have carefully studied the subject and concluded that Samaria fell in 723 B.C. Among these are the renowned Assyriologist Professor A.T. Olmstead of the University of Chicago and Professor Hayim Tadmor of the Hebrew University of Jerusalem.[194]

We have pointed this error in II Kings 17-18 out to you, as some will use this to move the reign of Hezekiah by 12 years. In so doing they will also move the year of II Kings 19:29 from 701 B.C. to 713 B.C. Once you do this you have changed the year Yehovah tells us is a 49th year and the year Yehovah tells us in a Jubilee year.

If we then use the year of 713 B.C. as the 49th year as some are saying it should be, then none of the known Sabbatical years in history line up with it. Again look at the chart below, which has all the known and proven Sabbatical years in it and change the first two to 713B.C., 712 B.C. and count by 7 from 713 B.C. to the next Sabbatical year of 456 B.C.

Historically Recorded Sabbatical Years	
701 B.C.	Sennacherib attack Judah 2 Kings 19:29
700 B.C.	2 Kings 19:29 A Jubilee year
456 B.C.	Nehemiah 8:18
162 B.C.	I Maccabees 16:14 & Josephus Antiquities
134 B.C.	I Maccabees & Josephus Antiquities
43 B.C.	Julius Caesar & Josephus Antiquities
36 B.C.	Josephus Antiquities 14:16:2
22 B.C.	Josephus Antiquities 15:9:1
42 C.E.	Josephus Antiquities 18
56 C.E.	A note of Indebtedness in Nero's time.
70 C.E.	The Sabbath year of 70/71 C.E.
133 C.E.	Rental contracts before Bar Koch bah Revolt
140 C.E.	Rental contracts before Bar Koch bah Revolt

194 *The Mysterious Numbers of the Hebrew Kings* by Edwin Thiele, pp. 134-135, 137

When you do the math you will see that none of the known Sabbatical years line up. You must then conclude that something is wrong, and that something is exactly what we have just explained to you about II King 17 and 18 with the misunderstanding of Hoshea's reign.

Hezekiah's 14th year was 701 B.C. This was the year Senacherib comes to attack Jeruasalem as we have shown to you from the Limmu lists. Again as we have said this year of 701 B.C. is the most undisputed date in chronology by all renowned Chronologists. But because some will try to show you this other theory that Hezekiah reigned 12 years earlier in order to disprove what we are sharing with you, we have brought this to your attention.

Chapter 25 | The 480 Years Explained

At the 2012 writing of this book, when you add up all the *known* chronology, you will realize we are in the 119ᵗʰ Jubilee Cycle. When this Jubilee Cycle comes to a close we will be in the 120ᵗʰ Jubilee Cycle and the start of the Seventh Millennium—the one in which the Messiah is to rule over all the Earth.

It is only after you have added up all the years in history *correctly* that you will be able to declare what year we are in since the creation of Adam. I have already summed up the years for you from Adam to The Exodus and on into the entrance of the Israelites into the Promised Land in chapter 15 of this book. Feel free to review that chapter if you like. The timeframe spanning from Adam up to The Exodus and from Adam up to the entrance of the Israelites into the Promised Land is 2,458 years and 2,500 years respectively.

Moreover, I have covered Assyrian chronology with you and indicated how it is the *only way* to fill in the blanks with regard to a known and trustworthy chronology of the Hebrew Kings. Edwin R. Thiele,[195] as I have said already, has done a truly remarkable job of this.

In knowing this, you also know King Solomon died in the year 930 B.C. and that he reigned for forty years prior to his death.[196] This gives us 970 B.C. as the year he came to the throne.

There is only one remaining verse I have determined must still be woven in with the ancient history and chronology from Adam to The Exodus to the reign of King Solomon. From King Solomon, one can then calculate down to our present time. This verse is found in I Kings:

---

195 *The Mysterious Numbers of the Hebrew Kings* by Edwin Thiele
196 I Kings 11:42 | And the days that Shelomoh (King Solomon) reigned in Yerushalayim (Jerusalem) over all Yisra'ĕl was forty years.

1 And it came to be, in the four hundred and eightieth year after the children of Yisra'ĕl had come out of the land of Mitsrayim (Egypt), in the fourth year of the reign of Shelomoh (Solomon) over Yisra'ĕl, in the month of Ziw (Ziv), which is the second month, that he began to build the House of יהוה. (**I Kings 6:1**)

So from the year 2458 after creation A.C., when the Exodus took place until the fourth year of Solomon was 480 years. You now take away four years from the year 970 B.C., when Solomon began his reign and you can then accurately conclude King Solomon's 4ᵗʰ year after he came to the throne in 966 B.C. Now, all you need to do is simple addition to know where we are in the history of the world.

2458 + 480 + 966 + 2012 (current year) = 5,916 Grand Total

Now many will look at this and exclaim we have just eighty-four more years to go until the year 6000, which is the start of the Seventh Millennium. But they would be wrong.

How so? I have already explained to you that each Sabbatical Cycle is made up forty-nine years. The fiftieth year is then the first year of the following cycle. The numbers '50' and '1' are the same year—just as Pentecost is the fiftieth day and yet is also the first day of the week counting towards the next Sabbath. I have proven this to you a number of times in this book already.

The first time the Sabbatical Years are mentioned is in Genesis. We already looked at the passage below, but this is a refresher:

3 And יהוה said, "My Spirit shall not strive with man forever in his going astray. He is flesh, and his days shall be one hundred and twenty years." (**Genesis 6:3**)

The word for years here is "shaneh."

H8141 שׁנה הנשׁ shâneh shânâh shaw-neh', shaw-naw'

(The first form being in plural only, the second form being feminine); from **H8138**; a year (as a revolution of time): + whole age, X long, + old, year (X -ly).

So this first mention should tell you that man will be allotted 120 "periods of time." It is the *only* place this is said. Many people use this to then jump to the erroneous conclusion that:

$$120 \times 50 = 6{,}000 \text{ Years}$$

I will explain a little later why this is *not* the case. Others conclude that Noah must have preached for 120 years. We have already explained why this was not the case in a previous chapter.

The 120 periods of time or, 120 Jubilee Cycles as shown above is not 6000 years, although the above total is what most people mistakenly believe, it is instead and in truth:

$$120 \times 49 = 5{,}880 \text{ Years}$$

You know for certain the timeframe from:

$$\text{Adam to The Exodus} = 2{,}458 \text{ Years}$$

You also now know it is not 6,000 years but, again:

$$120 \times 49 = 5{,}880 \text{ Years}$$

This is with regard to the total number of years that will have already elapsed before the Seventh Millennium begins with the Messiah as our ruler. And you know for certain the number of years from Solomon down to our time.

But when we add all of this up we have a total that exceeds 5,880. Why? Well something is obviously wrong, but *what*?

$$2458 + 480 + 966 + 2012 \text{ (current year)} = 5{,}916 \text{ Years Grand Total}$$

Something else we definitely need to be mindful of is that II Kings 19:29 refers to when a Jubilee Year took place and this just so happens to be the most undisputed year in chronology, believe it or not! That is, the year Sennacherib came up against King Hezekiah. That year was 701 B.C. and the Jubilee Year was 700 B.C! In counting forward to our time, you will discover that 1996 C.E. was the last Jubilee. And the next Jubilee year will be 2045. This now means we have to add an additional 33 years on to our sum total of 5916 to get us to the Jubilee year and the 7th Millennium. Our total is now 5949, but do not forget the year zero. When you go from 1 B.C. to 1 C.E. there is no year zero. This means we must add one more year to get a grand total of 5950. This is 70 years more than the 5880 we should have. And if you remember, if we added on the other 60 years for Terah being 130 at the birth of Abraham we would be that much more out of date.

If you count back from this date of 1996, you must do so in such a way that the year Joshua enters The Land of Israel *matches* one of the Jubilee Years.

You know now that 2,458 is right and does not need to be changed or refigured. You also know now that the 966 B.C. year is right and the current year 2012 is obviously right. This leaves the one figure of *480* as the potential problem.

Again, I am going to repeat what I said in chapter 23, given the fact I am about to call into question again a scriptural passage in the Bible that many people, more than likely, will be up in arms over me having done so. As I said previously, the tendency to quote the famous and all too liberally applied Scripture in II Timothy, "All Scripture is breathed by Elohim and profitable for teaching," is still alive and well.

> **14** But you, stay in what you have learned and trusted, having known from whom you have learned, **15** and that from a babe you have known the Set-apart Scriptures, which are able to make you wise for deliverance through belief in Messiah יהושע. **16** All Scripture is breathed by Elohim and profitable for teaching, for reproof, for setting straight, for instruction in righteousness, **17** that the man of Elohim might be fitted, equipped for every good work. (**II Timothy 3:14-17**)

But again, you would do well to be reminded of *Clarke's Commentary* on this verse.

II Timothy 3:16

> All Scripture is given by inspiration of God—This sentence is not well translated; the original πασα γραφη θεοκνευστος ωφιλιμος προς διδασκαλιαν, κ. τ. λ. should be rendered: Every writing Divinely inspired is profitable for doctrine, etc. The particle και, and, is omitted by almost all the versions and many of the fathers, and certainly does not agree well with the text. The apostle is here, beyond all controversy, speaking of the writings of the Old Testament, which, because they came by Divine inspiration, he terms the Holy Scriptures, II Timothy 3:15; and it is of them *alone* that this passage is to be understood; and although all the New Testament came by as direct an inspiration as the Old (Testament), yet, as it was not collected at that time, not indeed complete, the apostle could have no reference to it.

Even Yehshua tells us precisely which Scriptures these are in the Gospel of Luke. They are the Torah (the first five books), the Prophets, and the Psalms.

They are not and were not what is today called the New Testament, nor does this include the historical books of I and II Kings or I and II Chronicles.

> **44** And He said to them, "These are the words which I spoke to you while I was still with you, that all have to be filled that were written in the Torah of Mosheh (Moses) and the Prophets and the Psalms concerning Me." **45** Then He opened their minds to understand the Scriptures. **(Luke 24:44-45)**

Knowing this, we can then look at *both* books of Kings simply as historical documents, of which all renowned chronologists agree there are some existing contextual errors regarding chrononlogy—another one of which I am about to point out and explain to you.

That being said let us now look at the 480 year block of time that is in question more closely. First of all, we have just one witness. There is no other verse in the Bible to support this particular verse.

Joshua began to serve Israel just before he crossed the Jordan when Moses died, but Joshua's first year would be the Abib that occurred after he crossed over the Jordan. We have shown this year in which he crossed over the Jordan to be 2,500 After Creation A.C. or 1337 B.C.—which, consequently, is both a Jubilee Year *and* the first year of the next Jubilee Cycle.

In Judges, chapter 3 we are told how some of the Canaanites lived *alongside of* Israel. And then, in verse 6, we are told how Israel began to intermarry with the Canaanites and, as a result, began to serve their gods. We are then told over and over of how Yehovah, in His hot displeasure, gave Israel into the hands of this king or that king and then raised up Judges on different occasions to free them from their captivity.

But it is during this time period from the time Joshua died until the time King Saul was chosen as king that has many chronologists in a quandary. I have already pointed out that Joshua crossed over the Jordan 2,500 A.C., which is 1337 B.C. In contrast, the fourth year of Solomon is 2,870 A.C. or 967 B.C., a difference of 370 years. However, we are told in Acts:

> 20 And after that He gave judges for about four hundred and fifty years, until Shemu'ĕl (Samuel) the prophet. (Acts 13:20)

We are also told in Kings:

> 1 And it came to be, in the four hundred and eightieth year after the children of Yisra'ĕl had come out of the land of Mitsrayim (Egypt), in

the fourth year of the reign of Shelomoh (Solomon) over Yisra'ĕl, in the month of Ziw (Ziv), which is the second month, that he began to build the House of יהוה. (I Kings 6:1)

Concerning this verse Clarkes commentary has the following to say;

> In the four hundred and eightieth year - The Septuagint has the four hundred and fortieth year. It need scarcely be noticed, that among chronologists there is a great difference of opinion concerning this epocha. Glycas has 330 years; Melchior Canus, 590 years; Josephus, 592 years; Sulpicius Severus, 588; Clemens Alexandrinus, 570; Cedrenus, 672; Codomanus, 598; Vossius and Capellus, 580; Serarius, 680; Nicholas Abraham, 527; Maestlinus, 592; Petavius and Valtherus, 520. Here are more than a dozen different opinions; and after all, that in the common Hebrew text is as likely to be the true one as any of the others.

The Septuagint states there are 440 years and many other chrologist have concluded with many other totals for this period of time as you can see.

The above passage in I Kings 6:1 KJV tells us that Solomon's Temple was commenced in the 480th year after the departure of the Israelites out of Egypt. It was during the fourth year of Solomon's reign.

Josephus points out that from The Exodus to the building of the Temple was 592 years.[197] From 592, you *deduct*: two years at Mount Sinai, forty years wandering aimlessly in The Wilderness, twenty-eight years under Joshua's rule,[198] forty years under King Saul's reign (Acts 13:2), forty years under King David's reign, and finally, the first four years under King Solomon's reign (I Kings 6:1). What remains then is just 462 years—and we still do not have a diffinitive conclusion.

K.A. Kitchen[199] provides us with an extended discussion on this matter and concludes that the 480 years is:

> "... some kind of aggregate of overlapping periods which spanned (approximately) 300 years."

Once again, basing the data on my Sabbatical and Jubilee charts from my

---

197 *Antiquities* by JOSEPHUS, 8.3.1
198 *Antiquities* by JOSEPHUS, 5.1.29
199 *Ancient Orient & Old Testament*, 1966, pp.72-75

previous book,[200] look at the table on the following page. From the year Joshua entered Canaan until the fourth year of King Solomon's reign is 370 years. If you *add* to this the forty years in The Wilderness *and* the two years spent at Mount Sinai, you arrive at 412 years as the total number of years from the Exodus until the 4th year of Solomon.

This timeframe of 450 years, which you can add up from the chart on the next page, matches what is said in Acts 13:20. To calculate how much time elapsed between entry into Canaan and King Solomon's fourth year, one has to *add* to these 450 years (listed above) the following:

- The Judgeship of Joshua
- The Judgeship of Samuel
- The Kingship of Saul
- The Kingship of David
- King Solomon's 1st Four Years

While definite biblical, chronological references exist with regard to King David and King Solomon, there are only extra biblical records upon which we can rely when determining the time periods for Joshua, Samuel and Saul. These records indicate Joshua was Judge for up to twenty-eight years, Samuel was Judge for thirty years and that King Saul reigned up to twenty-two years—all of which comes to a grand total of sixty-eighty years.

This makes the 450 year grand total referenced above fall within the ballpark of 510-530 years.

To this must be *added* the forty years for King David's reign and the first four years of King Solomon's reign. This reveals that a total of 554-574 years elapsed between the entrance of the Israelites into Canaan up to the fourth year of King Solomon's reign.

If the period of the Judges was 554-574 years, then clearly, something is wrong with the reference in I Kings 6:1 to a period of 440 years as stated in the Septuagint or 480 years as stated in the Bible.

It is clear that some of the stories in the Book of Judges, like the Gospel accounts, are *not* arranged in chronological order and not all the periods are accompanied by the phrase "and after this." Overlap can be seen in Samson's twenty years that were expressly "in the days of the Philistines" (Judges 15:11, 20).

---

200 *The Prophecies of Abraham* by Joseph F. Dumond | Authorhouse | 1-25-2010 | ISBN:978-1-4490-4752-8

JUDGES	A Biblical Data Record
Judges	No timeframe for Joshua
Judges 3:8-8 Years	Years spent serving Chushan-Rishathaim
Judges 3:11-40 Years	Rest provided by Othniel
Judges 3:14-18 Years	Serving Moab
Judges 3:30-80 Years	Rest during Ehud's lifetime
Judges 4:4-20 Years	Oppression
Judges 5:31-40 Years	Deborah
Judges 6:1-7 Years	Midianite Oppression
Judges 8:28-40 Years	Gideon
Judges 9:22-23 Years	Abimelech
Judges 10:2-23 Years	Tola
Judges 10:3-22 Years	Jair
Judges 10:8-18 Years	Oppression
Judges 12:6-7 Years	Jephthah
Judges 12:7-8 Years	Ibzan
Judges 12:10-11 Years	Elon
Judges 12:13-18 Years	Abdon
Judges 13:1-40 Years	Philistine Oppression
Judges 16:31-20 Years	Samson
Judges–Samuel	No timeframe for Samuel
I Samuel 4:18-40 Years	Eli
TOTAL TIMEFRAME	**450 Years**

There is an existing view that the 480 years is accurate, but that it does not mean to include or take into account the Years of Oppression listed in the Book of Judges. This type of thinking took precedence in ancient Egyptian and Near Eastern thought. For example, Egyptian king lists would intentionally omit the dynasties and reigns of kings that were foreign-born, since these were considered a national disgrace by the indigenous Egyptians.

Adding in the 111 Years of Oppressions during the time of the Judges would raise the 480 year total to 591 years. The Book of Acts appears to support this line of reasoning. Acts 13:19-20 seems to indicate that the period of the Judges alone was 450 years (to which other periods of history would need to be incorporated to account for when King Solomon's reign comes into play). The 450 year total in Acts would correspond to the 111 Years of Oppression in Judges added to the 339 years of judgeship and peace.

I Kings 6:1 states that The Exodus was 480 years *before* the Temple of Solomon was built, yet Josephus clearly states 592 years in his book, *The Antiquity of the Jews*. The difference seems to be in the way the rule of the Judges was calculated. Josephus seems to include the Oppressions *as well as* the Judges, whereas the writer of Kings *excludes* the Rule of Oppressors, as was customary at that time.[201] This would amount to roughly a 111 year difference.

So now, all things considered, let's try this once more. I have provided you with two references to the fact that the Years of Oppression were *not* counted during this time. Let us say that the 480 years *did* include the Years of Oppression. Then one should be subtracting them and *not* adding them as these other commentators have been found doing.

Earlier, I stated that between the entrance into the Land of Canaan and the fourth year of King Solomon's reign is 370 years. (Entry into the Promised Land was in 1337 B.C. and King Solomon's fourth year reign was 967 B.C.).

If you add to this the 111 Years of Oppression as stated in the commentary above, you arrive at 481 years. This being said, I am now of the opinion this riddle has been solved, with only one year being unaccounted for.

But, I have calculated it from the time of Joshua entering The Land and *not* from The Exodus—which is what I Kings does. To go from The Exodus, tack on forty-two years and now nothing works.

The 480 years mentioned in I Kings 6:1 includes the Years of Oppression. Josephus, instead of subtracting these 111 Years of Oppression, added them and arrived at 592 years. Had he subtracted them, he would have arrived at 370 years as I do with a mere one-year discrepancy.[202]

I know I may very well be confusing you to no end at this point throwing so many numbers at you all at once, but just take your time and work them out on a piece of paper. The reason I am showing you this is because it *IS* so confusing.

---

201 Jackson & Lake, 1979, p.151

202 *The Edomites Begin To Unite & the World Financial Picture Continues To Crumble* http://www.sightedmoonnl.com/?page_id=647, June 5th, 2010

There is another way to work this all out, however. We know that in Genesis it says:

> 3 And יהוה said, "My Spirit shall not strive with man forever in his going astray. He is flesh, and his days shall be one hundred and twenty years."
> **(Genesis 6:3)**

The word "years" indicates "periods of time" and let it also be known this is not referring to the preaching of Noah. This passage is, in fact, telling us there will be 120 Jubilee Cycles or:

$$120 \times 49 = 5,880 \text{ Years}$$

I have also demonstrated to you that when Joshua entered the Promised Land, it was the 51st Jubilee Cycle. And when one adds up all the known years, one arrives at 5,916 years (which is still thirty-six years too many) and that this only is with regard to our time now, at present the year 2012. But, if you factor in the year 1996 being a Jubilee Year—meaning the next one is going to be in 2045—which is still 33 years from now, this brings us to a nearly doubled difference of sixty-nine years too many or:

$$36 + 33 = 69 \text{ Years}$$

How then do we reconcile this? Again, here is what we *do* know:

2,458 years (Adam–Exodus) + 480 (unknown variable) + 966 B.C. 4th year of Solomon + 2012 C.E. (current year) all must add up to and equal 5,880 Years (120 Jubilee Cycles from Genesis 6:3 x 49). And remember, a Jubilee Cycle is 49 years, *not* 50. From 5,880, you then *deduct* 2012 (our current year from 1 C.E.) You then *deduct* 32 years, (the difference between 2012C.E.–2044 C.E. or the same year as 5880 A.C. And ... you must *also* deduct one year for the year "0" because it goes from 1 B.C. to 1 A.D. Technically, there is no year "0." Next, you *deduct* 966 years, which is the year when King Solomon began to build the Temple in 966 B.C. Last, but not least, you *deduct* 2,458—which again, is the time from Adam–The Exodus. In the end you are left with 411 years.

The number of years from The Exodus until the fourth year of King Solomon's reign is 411 years and *not* 480 years. When you plot out all the known variables and encapsulate them in a 120 x 49 years construct or within a 5,880 years total timeframe and when you know precisely when the Jubilee Years are, you can then *much more easily* arrive at the conclusion there are 410 years between The Exodus and King Solomon's fourth year reign versus the

480 year figure. But you have to plot it all out to find this out for yourself—whether it be via a graph or a chart.

5880 A.C.	The total number of years allowed in the 6th millennium. 120 X 49 = 5880
-2458 A.C.	The Year of the Exodus, from the creation of Adam
-966 B.C.	B.C. the fourth year of Solomon when he began to build the Temple
-2044 C.E.	The 49th year in this the last Jubilee cycle. 2045 being the Jubilee year using II Kings 19:29 to determine when a Jubilee year was in 700 B.C. and counting from that year by 49's down to our time and backwards
-1	There is no year zero so we must take one year away
411	Total. This is the total amount of years left to complete the 5880 and not go over this amount of time.

The only number that works for all of this confusion is that instead of the number in 1 Kings 6:1 being 480 years it is in fact 411 years as we have just shown you. 111 years of oppression and 300 years of ruler ship and peace.

This then leave 285 years once you subtract the 4 years for Solomon and the 40 years of King David and the 40 years of King Saul, and the 2 years that Israel was at Mount Sinai and the 40 years they were in the wilderness.

This means that Joshua and the time of the judges could only be a total of 285 years.

You can read of the difficulties many others have had in sorting this out.[203] As you have just seen it is an extremely difficult subject. So instead of figuring out what most have not been able to and all agree, we have left the 480 years as a variable in our equation.

Once again let me do the math for you in another way.

120 Jubilee cycles totals 5880 years. That is 120 X 49 = 5880

5880 – 2458 from Adam to the Exodus – 966 which is the total years B.C. and the 4th years of Solomon's reign – 2044 which is the 49th year of this the last Jubilee cycle counting from year 1 of this Commom Era, C.E. – 1 for the year zero between 1 B.C. and 1 C.E.

5880 – 2458 – 966 – 2044 - 1 = 411 as the total number of years that I Kings 6:1 should be reporting.

---

203 http://www.bibleinsight.com/judges-chronology.html

Chapter 26 | The Missing 76 Years

This next Abib, which coincides with the beginning of the New Year in accordance with Yehovah's calendar, which begins in the spring of the year around March/April in the Gregorian Year of 2013, will fall on the year 5849 since the creation of Adam.

But Judah maintains it will be in the year 5773 After Creation at that time. Which calendar is right? Is it 5773 A.C. or is it 5849 A.C.?

In the Gospel of Matthew we uncover the answer:

> 7 Solomon begot Rehoboam, Rehoboam begot Abijah, and Abijah begot Asa. 8 Asa begot Jehoshaphat, Jehoshaphat begot Joram, and Joram begot Uzziah. 9 Uzziah begot Jotham, Jotham begot Ahaz, and Ahaz begot Hezekiah. (**Matthew 1:7-9**)

So do you see the answer? It is right up above in Matthew 1:8.

Actually, if you read between the lines, it is what is not there that is the answer. Between Joram (aka, Jehoram) and Uzziah (aka, Azariah) there are four missing kings.

Those four missing kings are Ahaziah who reigned one year in 841 B.C.,[204]Athaliah who reigned six years from 841 B.C.–835 B.C., Jehoash who reigned forty years from 835 B.C.–796 B.C. and Amaziah who reigned twenty-nine years from 796 B.C.–767 B.C.—all of which are missing from the chronology.

There are seventy-six years total when you add up the years they reigned. From the year 841 B.C.–767 B.C., you can see that it is only seventy-four years. But when you add up the years that each one actually ruled, you arrive at a seventy-six year total. Athaliah, queen consort to King Joram of Judah,

---

204 *The Mysterious Numbers of the Hebrew Kings* by Edwin Thiele

and later, queen regnant of Judah,[205] claimed the year Ahaziah died so she gets seven years according to some chronologists,[206] and not six. As a result you get:

$$7 + 40 + 29 = 76$$

So how is *this* the answer you may ask? We read in Deuteronomy of a strange curse, but we are not shown anywhere in the Bible any evidence of it having come to pass.

> **16** For you know how we dwelt in the land of Mitsrayim (Egypt) and how we passed through the nations which you passed through, **17** and you saw their abominations and their idols, wood and stone, silver and gold, which were with them, **18** lest there should be among you a man or woman or clan or tribe, whose heart turns away today from יהוה our Elohim, to go and serve the mighty ones of these nations, lest there should be among you a root bearing bitterness or wormwood. **19** And it shall be, when he hears the words of this curse, that he should bless himself in his heart, saying, "I have peace though I walk in the stubbornness of my heart," in order to add drunkenness to thirst. (**Deuteronomy 29:16-19**)

> **20** יהוה would not forgive him, but rather, the displeasure of יהוה and His jealousy shall burn against that man, and every curse that is written in this book shall settle on him, and יהוה shall blot out his name from under the heavens. (**Deuteronomy 29:20**)

What was it these kings did to anger Yehovah so? We read in Deuteronomy 29:20 where Yehovah threatened to blot out the names of those who served other gods. Yehovah also issues a very clear warning in the Second Commandment below:

> **3** "You have no other mighty ones against My face. **4** You do not make for yourself a carved image, or any likeness of that which is in the heavens above, or which is in the earth beneath, or which is in the waters under the earth, **5** you do not bow down to them nor serve them. For I, יהוה your Elohim am a jealous Ěl, visiting the crookedness of the fathers on the children to the third and fourth generations of those who hate Me, **6** but showing kindness to thousands, to those who love Me and guard My commands." (**Exodus 20:3-6**)

---

205 http://en.wikipedia.org/wiki/Athaliah
206 *The Mysterious Numbers of the Hebrew Kings* by Edwin Thiele, p.107

In case you missed it, in Exodus 20:5 it says how the sins of the fathers will be visited to the third and fourth generations of those who hate Him. What wicked king could this be? We read in Chronicles:

7 For the sons of Athalyahu, that wrong woman, had broken into the House of Elohim, and had also prepared all the set-apart vessels of the House of יהוה to the Ba'als. (II Chronicles 24:7)

Because of this blasphemy, the city of Libnah revolted against Joram.

22 Yet Edom has revolted from under the hand of Judah to this day. Then Libnah revolted at the same time. (II Kings 8:22)

Libnah was one of the cities of the Aaronic Priests.

13 But to the children of Aharon the priest they gave Ḥebron with its open land—a city of refuge for the slayer—and Libnah with its open land. (Joshua 21:13)

Obviously they objected violently to Joram's desecration of Solomon's temple. For Joram's blasphemy, Yehovah judged not only his wife Athaliah, but his son Ahaziah, and grandson Jehash (Joash), and great grandson Amaziah.

24 So Yoram (Jehoram, Joram) slept with his fathers, and was buried with his fathers in the City of Dawiḏ (David). And Aḥazyahu (Ahaziah) his son reigned in his place. 25 In the twelfth year of Yoram (Jehoram, Joram) son of Aḥab sovereign of Yisra'ěl, Aḥazyahu (Ahaziah) son of Yehoraḏ (Jehoram, Joram) sovereign of Yehuḏah (Judah) began to reign. 26 Aḥazyahu (Ahaziah) was twenty-two years old when he began to reign, and he reigned one year in Yerushalayim (Jerusalem). And the name of his mother was Athalyahu, the granddaughter of Omri, sovereign of Yisra'ěl. 27 And he walked in the way of the house of Aḥab, and did evil in the eyes of יהוה, as the house of Aḥab had done, for he was the son-in-law of the house of Aḥab. (II Kings 8:24-27)

1 And Athalyah was the mother of Aḥazyahu (Ahaziah). And when she saw that her son was dead, she arose and destroyed all the offspring of the reign. 2 But Yehosheba (Jehosheba), the daughter of Sovereign Yoram (Joram, Jehoram), sister of Aḥazyahu (Ahaziah) took Yo'ash (Joash) son of Aḥazyah (Ahaziah), and stole him away from among the sons of the sovereign's sons who were put to death. So they hid him and his nurse in the bedroom, from Athalyahu, and he was not put to death. 3 And

he remained with her in hiding in the House of יהוה for six years, while Athalyah was reigning over the land. (**II Kings 11:1-3**)

I am going to include this whole story here for you to read, as it is essential to obtaining a deeper and more complete understanding.

> **4** And in the seventh year Yehoyada (Jehoiada, the priest, Yehosheba's husband) sent and brought the commanders of hundreds, with the Karites and the runners, and brought them into the House of יהוה to him. And he made a covenant with them and took an oath from them in the House of יהוה, and showed them the son of the sovereign. **5** And he commanded them, saying, "This is what you are to do: One-third of you who come in on the Sabbath to be on guard in the sovereign's house, **6** and one-third at the gate of Sur, and one-third at the gate behind the runners. And you shall be on guard in the house, lest it be broken down. **7** And the two detachments of you who are going out on the Sabbath shall be on guard in the House of יהוה for the sovereign. **8** And you shall surround the sovereign on all sides, every man with his weapons in his hand. And whoever comes within the ranks, let him be put to death. And be with the sovereign as he goes out and as he comes in." (**II Kings 11:4-8**)

> **9** So the commanders of the hundreds did according to all that Yehoyada (Jehoiada) the priest commanded. And each of them took his men who were going in on the Sabbath, with those who were going out on the Sabbath, and came to Yehoyada (Jehoiada) the priest. **10** And the priest gave the commanders of hundreds the spears and shields which had belonged to Sovereign Dawid (David), that were in the House of יהוה. **11** And the runners stood, every man with his weapons in his hand, all around the sovereign, from the right side of the House to the left side of the House, by the altar and the House. **12** And he brought out the son of the sovereign and put on him the diadem (crown) and the Witness. And they set him up to reign and anointed him, and they clapped their hands and said, "Let the sovereign live!" (**II Kings 11:9-12**)

This is the same expression we use today when the King is coronated. If you listen to the recordings of the coronation of Queen Elizabeth II, they all shout, "Long live the Queen."[207]

> **13** And Athalyah heard the noise of the runners, the people, and she came to the people, into the House of יהוה, **14** and looked and saw the sovereign standing by a column, according to the ruling, and the chiefs

---

207 http://news.bbc.co.uk/onthisday/hi/dates/stories/june/2/newsid_2654000/2654501.stm

and the trumpeters were beside the sovereign, and all the people of the land rejoicing and blowing trumpets. And Athalyah tore her garments and cried out, "Treason! Treason!" **(II Kings 11:13-14)**

It is this very same column that today is found under the Throne of the Kings of Britain when they are anointed.

The Stone of Scone /ˈskuːn/; Scottish Gaelic: An Lia Fàil) ... also known as the Stone of Destiny and often referred to in England as The Coronation Stone.[208]

15 And Yehoyaḏa (Jehoiada) the priest commanded the commanders of the hundreds, the officers of the army, and said to them, "Take her outside the ranks, and slay with the sword whoever follows her." For the priest had said, "Do not let her be killed in the House of יהוה." **16** So they took hold of her, and she went by way of the horses' entrance to the sovereign's house, and was put to death there. **17** And Yehoyaḏa (Jehoiada) made a covenant between יהוה and the sovereign and the people, to be the people of יהוה—also between the sovereign and the people. **18** And all the people of the land went to the house of Ba'al, and broke it down. They completely broke up its altars and images, and slew Mattan the priest of Ba'al before the altars. And the priest appointed inspectors over the House of יהוה, **19** and took the commanders of hundreds, and the Karites, and the runners, and all the people of the land. And they brought the sovereign down from the House of יהוה, and went by way of the gate of the runners to the sovereign's house. And he sat on the throne of the sovereigns. **20** And all the people of the land rejoiced. And the city had rest, for they had slain Athalyahu with the sword in the sovereign's house. **21** Yeho'ash (Joash) was seven years old when he began to reign. **(II Kings 11:15-21)**

1 In the second year of Yo'ash (Joash), son of Yo'aḥaz (Jehoahaz), sovereign of Yisra'ĕl, Amatsyahu (Amaziah) son of Yo'ash (Joash), sovereign of Yehudah (Judah), began to reign. **2** He was twenty-five years old when he began to reign, and he reigned twenty-nine years in Yerushalayim (Jerusalem). And his mother's name was Yeho'addin (Jehoaddin) of Yerushalayim (Jerusalem). **(II Kings 14:1-2)**

19 And they made a conspiracy against him in Yerushalayim (Jerusalem), and he fled to Lakish (Lachish). And they sent after him to Lakish (Lachish) and killed him there, **20** and brought him on horses, and he was buried at Yerushalayim (Jerusalem) with his fathers in the City of Dawiḏ (David). **21** And all the people of Yehudah (Judah) took Azaryah

---

208 http://en.wikipedia.org/wiki/Stone_of_Scone

(Azariah, Uzziah), who was sixteen years old, and set him up to reign instead of his father Amatsyahu (Amaziah). (II Kings 14:19-21)

This Azaryah was also called Uzziah in II Kings 15:13 and is the very same Ozias of Matthew 1:8.

Today, in the fall of 2012, Judah has already calculated the year to be 5773 A.C. starting with the onset of Rosh Hashanah on into 2013. If we tack these 76 missing years onto this, we end up with a total of 5,849, which is exactly what the Sabbatical and Jubilee Years show us. But because Judah starts at the seventh month and Yehovah's timetable begins in the spring on Abib, for six months Judah will be slightly off. In Aviv of 2013 the year will be 5849 since the creation of Adam.

This should explain the difference between the Jewish years of 5773 and why the Sabbatical and Jubilee years are 76 years further advanced.

Chapter 27 | Why Does Any of This Matter?

For those of you who believe your soul goes to heaven or hell and lives forever, I would like you to read the passage in Ezekiel below:

The soul that sins, it shall die.[209]

> 4 "See, all beings are Mine, the being of the father as well as the being of the son is Mine. The being that is sinning shall die." (**Ezekiel 18:4**)

Just in case you missed it, it is repeated in Ezekiel as follows:

> 20 "The being who sins shall die." (**Ezekiel 18:20**)

As some of you may still not yet believe, there is no better prescription or antidote for your unbelief than the Old Testament. Take the time to become much more intimately acquainted with it than ever before and see where that takes you. In the meanwhile, Paul exhorts us in Romans:

> 23 For the wages of sin is death, but the favorable gift of Elohim is everlasting life in Messiah יהושע our Master. (**Romans 6:23**)

Whenever you read things like this, it should behoove you to ask the questions that need asking and then search out the answers. The most important question being, "What is sin?" The answer to this question is clearly stated in I John:

> 4 Everyone doing sin also does lawlessness, and sin is lawlessness. (**I John 3:4**)

---

209 *New King James*

3 And by this we know that we know Him, if we guard His commands.[1] (I John 2:3 | Footnote: [1]See 3:6.)

4 The one who says, "I know Him," and does not guard His commands is a liar and the truth is not in him. 5 But whoever guards His Word, truly the love of Elohim has been perfected[1] in him. By this we know that we are in Him.[2] (I John 2:4-5 | Footnotes: [1]Genesis 17:1; Psalms 119:1; Matthew 5:48. [2]See also, Matthew 3:24)

6 The one who says he stays in Him ought himself also to walk, even as He walked. The law is not done away. (I John 2:6)

- **The soul that sins shall die**
- **Sin is the transgression of The Law**
- **The Law is the Ten Commandments**

9 He who turns away his ear from hearing the Torah, even his prayer is an abomination. (Proverbs 28:9)

2 But your crookednesses have separated you from your Elohim. And your sins have hidden His face from you, from hearing. (Isaiah 59:2)

Ever wonder why your prayers go unanswered? Now you know. If you do not keep The Commandments; if you will not guard them in your walk, then Yehovah does not and will not hear your prayers. In fact, He will mock you in the time of your calamity.

23 "Turn at my reproof. See, I pour out my spirit on you, I make my words known to you."[1] (Proverbs 1:23 | Footnote: [1]See Psalms 33:6)

24 "Because I called and you refused, I have stretched out my hand and no one inclined, 25 and you spurned all my counsel, and would not yield to my reproof, 26 let me also laugh at your calamity, (and) mock when your dread comes. 27 When your dread comes like a storm, and your calamity comes like a whirlwind, when distress and anguish come upon you. 28 Let them then call on me, but I answer not; Let them seek me, but not find me. 29 Because they hated knowledge and did not choose the fear of יהוה, 30 They did not accept my counsel, They despised all my reproof, 31 Therefore let them eat the fruit of their own way, and be filled with their own counsels. 32 For the turning away of the simple slays them, and the complacency of fools destroys them. 33 But whoever listens to me dwells safely, and is at ease from the dread of evil." (Proverbs 1:24-33)

Most of the people in the world *do not* keep the Sabbath. Of those who keep the Seventh Day Saturday Sabbath, again, many of them do not keep the Holy Days as told to us in Leviticus 23. Finally, almost none of these keep the Sabbatical Years, or even know what or when they are.

> **29** יהוה is far from the wrong ones, but He hears the prayer of the righteous. (**Proverb 15:29**)

So what is righteousness, and how do I get it?

> **31** And we know that Elohim does not hear sinners. But if anyone fears Elohim and does His desire, He hears him. (**John 9:31**)

If we are sinning, that is not keeping The Commandments; if we will not keep the 4th Commandment, which includes the weekly Sabbath, the Holy Days and the Sabbatical and Jubilee Years; then Yehovah does not and cannot hear our prayers! But He *will hear* if we fear Him and *obey* His Commandments.

> **22** And whatever we ask we receive from Him, because we guard His commands and do what is pleasing in His sight. (**I John 3:22**)

In order to be pleasing in His sight we must be keeping The Commandments. And this includes the keeping of the Sabbatical Years. Then He will hear us, and then and *only then* can we ask in utmost confidence with the heavens no longer being as brass (aka, bronze) unto us.

> **23** And your heavens which are over your head shall be bronze, and the earth which is under you iron. (**Deuteronomy 28:23**)

For us to think we know how better to obey Yehovah *apart from* what He makes so clear to us in His Word, is the ultimate form of pride. Yet, Yehovah states in Leviticus below, as he similarly stated in Deuteronomy above:

> **19** And I shall break the pride of your power, and shall make your heavens like iron and your earth like bronze. (**Leviticus 26:19**)

But in obeying His Commandments, we not only put on righteousness, it's the *only* way we attain righteousness (or right standing) with Yehovah.

> **172** My tongue sings of Your Word, for all Your commands are righteousness. (**Psalm 119:172**)

You are considered righteous when you keep The Commandments—all of them, that is versus only the ones you *feel like* keeping. You must keep *all* ten of them.

It is this righteousness of keeping The Law that we are to have on at The Wedding Feast of the Lamb. It is who we are to be and in the process of becoming. Read the following scriptures to see exactly what you must wear at The Wedding and what the white robe is actually comprised of.

> 11 And when the sovereign came in to view the guests, he saw there a man who had not put on a wedding garment, 12 and he said to him, "Friend, how did you come in here not having a wedding garment?" And he was speechless. 13 Then the sovereign said to the servants, "Bind him hand and foot, take him away, and throw him out into the outer darkness—there shall be weeping and gnashing of teeth. 14 For many are called, but few are chosen." (**Matthew 22:11-14** | Footnote: [1]See **Matthew 20:16**)

If you do not have on this proper wedding garment, you will be forcefully removed from The Wedding Feast.

> 11 And there was given to each one a white robe, and they were told that they should rest a little while longer, until both the number of their fellow servants and their brothers, who would be killed as they were, was completed. (**Revelation 6:11**)

> 9 After this, I looked and saw a great crowd which no one was able to count, out of all nations and tribes and peoples and tongues, standing before the throne and before the Lamb, dressed in white robes, and palm branches in their hands, 10 and crying out with a loud voice, saying, "Deliverance belongs to our Elohim who sits on the throne, and to the Lamb!" 11 And all the messengers stood around the throne and the elders and the four living creatures, and fell on their faces before the throne and worshipped Elohim, 12 saying, "Amēn! The blessing, and the esteem, and the wisdom, and the thanksgiving, and the respect, and the power, and the might, to our Elohim forever and ever. Amēn." 13 And one of the elders responded, saying to me, "Who are these dressed in white robes, and where did they come from?" 14 And I said to him, "Master, you know." And he said to me, "These are those coming out of the great distress, having washed their robes and made them white in the blood of the Lamb. 15 Because of this they are before the throne of Elohim, and serve Him day and night in His Dwelling Place. And He who sits on the throne shall spread His Tent over them. 16 They shall hunger no more, neither thirst any more, neither shall the sun strike them, nor any heat, 17 because the Lamb who is in the midst of the

throne shall shepherd them and lead them to fountains of waters of life. And Elohim shall wipe away every tear from their eyes." (**Revelation 7:9-17**)

6 And I heard as the voice of a great crowd, as the sound of many waters and as the sound of mighty thunders, saying, "Halleluyah, for יהוה Ěl Shaddai reigns! 7 Let us be glad and rejoice and give Him praise, for the marriage of the Lamb has come, and His wife prepared herself." 8 And to her it was given to be dressed in fine linen, clean and bright, for the fine linen is the righteousnesses of the set-apart ones. 9 And he said to me, "Write, 'Blessed are those who have been called to the marriage supper of the Lamb!'" And he said to me, "These are the true words of Elohim." (**Revelation 19:6-9**)

The portion of the above passage I wish to emphasize to you the most is as follows:

7 "His wife prepared herself." 8 And to her it was given to be dressed in fine linen, clean and bright, for the fine linen is the righteousnesses of the set-apart ones. (**Revelation 6:7-8**)

I have already pointed out to you earlier in having cited Psalm 119:172 how *all* of His Commandments are righteousness (the sum vs. just some) and how this is what we *must* be clothed in. It must go far beyond mere mental ascent to where it is written in stone and inscribed on our hearts—to where it has become an integral part of our core personality and the very essence of who we are, as well as very much a part of the way in which we live. It must come from deep within to be evident in us from without.

As it is already so stated in the Fourth Commandment, the one that tells us to keep the Sabbath Day Holy, the same one that is expanded in Leviticus 23 to include the Sabbath and the Holy Days:

2 "Speak to the children of Yisra'ĕl, and say to them, 'The appointed times of יהוה, which you are to proclaim as set-apart gatherings, My appointed times, are these:'" (**Leviticus 23:2**)

When you read this chapter, the first appointed time we are to keep with the Holy One is the weekly Sabbath, followed by His Holy Days. Just like a doctor's appointment you might be charged for not keeping, you have appointments to meet with Yehovah, the Creator of the universe. That being said, why would you miss *any* of these appointments to end all appointments?

The Fourth Commandment Sabbath also includes the Sabbatical Years of Leviticus 25 and these are all Commandments Yehovah has put in place to test us.

4 And יהוה said to Mosheh (Moses), "See, I am raining bread from the heavens for you. And the people shall go out and gather a day's portion every day, in order to try them, whether they walk in My Torah or not." **(Exodus 16:4)**

- **The Sabbath is a test.**
- **The Holy Days are a test**
- **The Sabbatical Years are a test**.

9 And it shall be as a sign to you on your hand and as a reminder between your eyes, that the Torah of יהוה is to be in your mouth, for with a strong hand יהוה has brought you out of Mitsrayim (Egypt). **(Exodus 13:9)**

1 And יהוה spoke to Mosheh (Moses), saying, **2** "Set apart to Me all the first-born, the one opening the womb among the children of Yisra'ĕl, among man and among beast, it is Mine." **3** And Mosheh (Moses) said to the people, "Remember this day in which you went out of Mitsrayim (Egypt), out of the house of slavery. For by strength of hand יהוה brought you out of this place, and whatever is leavened shall not be eaten. **4** Today you are going out, in the month Aḇiḇ. **5** And it shall be, when יהוה brings you into the land of the Kena'anites (Canaanites), and the Ḥittites, and the Amorites, and the Ḥiwwites (Hivites), and the Yeḇusites (Jebusites), which He swore to your fathers to give you, a land flowing with milk and honey, that you shall keep this service in this month. **6** Seven days you eat unleavened bread, and on the seventh day is a festival to יהוה. **7** Unleavened bread is to be eaten the seven days, and whatever is leavened is not to be seen with you, and leaven is not to be seen with you within all your border. **8** And you shall inform your son in that day, saying, 'It is because of what יהוה did for me when I came up from Mitsrayim (Egypt).'" **(Exodus 13:1-8)**

9 And it shall be as a sign to you on your hand and as a reminder between your eyes, that the Torah of יהוה is to be in your mouth, for with a strong hand יהוה has brought you out of Mitsrayim (Egypt). **10** And you shall guard this law at its appointed time from year to year. **12** And יהוה spoke to Mosheh (Moses), saying, **13** "And you, speak to the children of Yisra'ĕl, saying, 'My Sabbaths you are to guard, by all means, for it is a sign[1] between Me and you throughout your generations, to know that I, יהוה, am setting you apart.'" **(Exodus 13:9-13)**

12 "And I also gave them My Sabbaths, to be a sign[1] between them and Me, to know that I am יהוה who sets them apart." (**Ezekiel 20:12**

19 "I am יהוה your Elohim. Walk in My laws, and guard My right-rulings, and do them. **20** And set apart My Sabbaths, and they shall be a sign between Me and you, to know that I am יהוה your Elohim." (**Ezekiel 20:19-20**)

13 And you, speak to the children of Yisra'ĕl, saying, "My Sabbaths you are to guard, by all means, for it is a sign[210] between Me and you throughout your generations, to know that I, יהוה, am setting you apart. **14** And you shall guard the Sabbath, for it is set-apart to you. Everyone who profanes it shall certainly be put to death, for anyone who does work on it, that being shall be cut off from among his people. **15** Six days work is done, and on the seventh is a Sabbath of rest, set-apart to יהוה. Everyone doing work on the Sabbath day shall certainly be put to death. **16** And the children of Yisra'ĕl shall guard the Sabbath, to observe the Sabbath throughout their generations as an everlasting covenant. **17** Between Me and the children of Yisra'ĕl it is a sign forever. For in six days יהוה made the heavens and the earth, and on the seventh day He rested and was refreshed." **18** And when He had ended speaking with him on Mount Sinai, He gave Mosheh (Moses) two tablets of the Witness, tablets of stone, written with the finger of Elohim. (**Exodus 31:13-18**)

The Mark of Yehovah is to be on your hand and on your forehead. Notice that same command in Exodus:

9 "And it shall be as a sign to you on your hand and as a reminder between your eyes." (Exodus **13:9**)

Satan's mark is in the same place and is similar to Yehovah's, but unlike Yehovah's mark, Satan's mark is to lead you astray.

16 And he causes all, both small and great, and rich and poor, and free and slave, to be given a mark upon their right hand or upon their foreheads. (**Revelation 13:16**)

If you keep The Commandments, that is, if you keep the Sabbaths and the Holy Days, then you will not work on them. This is the way you earn a living with your hands. So this is the mark on your hand revealed by the way

---

210 The only sign of Yehovah setting us apart, the only sign of the everlasting covenant, is His Sabbaths—one of them being the Seventh Day Sabbath. This is repeated in Ezekiel 20:12 & 20:14

in which you live. The way you think and what you do on these Holy Days is the mark on your head. Are you watching sports events on the Sabbath or are you studying Yehovah's Word?

This then is *the mark*. Both Yehovah's and Satan's mark are placed on your hand and on your forehead. The one for Yehovah is His test Commandment and when you keep the Fourth Commandment, you will be dressed in white, wearing the right clothes for The Wedding Feast.

To be wearing Satan's mark is to treat the true Sabbath like any other day or to treat any other day as 'holy' *in place of or in addition to* the Sabbath. Sunday is such an imposter; posing as the true Sabbath when it has been such a well known and long since established fact that Saturday is the one, true Sabbath. This is Satan's mark, to not keep the one and only true Sabbath and it can be *any day but* the true day. He does not care—just as long as you do not walk in truth and keep on observing the wrong day. If this is the path you choose, you will continue to be dressed in rags of unrighteousness instead of being clothed in Yehovah's righteousness that comes only from obeying His Commandments. In so doing, you will be removed from The Wedding Feast suddenly and without remedy.

We read how Israel, the Northern ten tribes, did not keep the laws of Yehovah in 2 Kings 17 and how Yehovah then tore them from the house of David and sent them into captivity.

> 1 In the twelfth year of Aḥaz sovereign of Yehuḏah, Hoshĕa son of Ělah began to reign over Yisra'ĕl in Shomeron, for nine years. 2 And he did evil in the eyes of יהוה, but not as the sovereigns of Yisra'ĕl who were before him.

> 3 Shalmaneser sovereign of Ashshur came up against him. And Hoshĕa became his servant, and rendered him a present. 4 But the sovereign of Ashshur found a conspiracy in Hoshĕa, for he had sent messengers to So, sovereign of Mitsrayim, and had not brought a present to the sovereign of Ashshur, as year by year. And the sovereign of Ashshur shut him up, and bound him in prison.

> 5 And the sovereign of Ashshur went through all the land, and went up to Shomeron and besieged it for three years.

> 6 In the ninth year of Hoshĕa, the sovereign of Ashshur captured Shomeron and exiled Yisra'ĕl to Ashshur, and settled them in Ḥalaḥ and Ḥaḇor, the River of Gozan, and in the cities of the Medes.

7 Now this came to be because the children of Yisra'ĕl had sinned against יהוה their Elohim – who had brought them up out of the land of Mitsrayim, from under the hand of Pharaoh sovereign of Mitsrayim – and feared other mighty ones, 8 and walked in the laws of the gentiles whom יהוה had dispossessed from before the children of Yisra'ĕl, and of the sovereigns of Yisra'ĕl that they had made. 9 And the children of Yisra'ĕl secretly did against יהוה their Elohim matters that were not right, and they built for themselves high places in all their cities, from watchtower unto the walled city, 10 and set up for themselves pillars and Ashĕrim on every high hill and under every green tree, 11 and burned incense there on all the high places, like the gentiles whom יהוה had removed from their presence. And they did evil matters to provoke יהוה, 12 and served the idols, of which יהוה had said to them, "Do not do this."

13 And יהוה warned Yisra'ĕl and Yehuḏah, through all of His prophets, and every seer, saying, "Turn back from your evil ways, and guard My commands and My laws, according to all the Torah which I commanded your fathers, and which I sent to you by My servants the prophets."

14 But they did not listen and hardened their necks, like the necks of their fathers, who did not put their trust in יהוה their Elohim, 15 and rejected His laws and His covenant that He had made with their fathers, and His witnesses which He had witnessed against them, and went after worthlessness, and became worthless, and after the gentiles who were all around them, of whom יהוה had commanded them not to do like them.

16 And they left all the commands of יהוה their Elohim, and made for themselves a moulded image, two calves, and made an Ashĕrah and bowed themselves to all the host of the heavens, and served Baʽal, 17 and caused their sons and daughters to pass through the fire, and practised divination and sorcery, and sold themselves to do evil in the eyes of יהוה, to provoke Him.

18 So יהוה was very enraged with Yisra'ĕl, and removed them from His presence – none was left but the tribe of Yehuḏah alone. (2 Kings 19:1-18)

We also read how Judah also did not keep the laws and she too was sent into captivity for 70 years.

19 Yehuḏah, also, did not guard the commands of יהוה their Elohim, but walked in the laws1 of Yisra'ĕl which they made. Footnote: 1Man-made laws. 20 And יהוה rejected all the seed of Yisra'ĕl, and afflicted them, and gave them into the hand of plunderers, until He had cast them out from His presence.

275

21 For He tore Yisra'ĕl from the house of Dawiḏ, and they made Yaroḇ'am son of Neḇat sovereign. And Yaroḇ'am drove Yisra'ĕl from following יהוה, and made them commit a great sin. 22 And the children of Yisra'ĕl walked in all the sins of Yaroḇ'am which he did. They did not turn away from them, 23 until יהוה removed Yisra'ĕl from His presence, as He spoke by all His servants the prophets. So Yisra'ĕl was exiled from their land to Ashshur, as it is to this day. (2 Kiing 17:19-23)

Jeremiah had warned them of what was coming.

1 The word that came to Yirmeyahu concerning all the people of Yehuḏah, in the fourth year of Yehoyaqim son of Yoshiyahu, the sovereign of Yehuḏah, which was the first year of Neḇukaḏretstsar sovereign of Baḇel, 2 which Yirmeyahu the prophet spoke to all the people of Yehuḏah and to all the inhabitants of Yerushalayim, saying, 3 "From the thirteenth year of Yoshiyahu son of Amon, sovereign of Yehuḏah, even to this day, this is the twenty-third year in which the word of יהוה has come to me. And I have spoken to you, rising early and speaking, but you have not listened.

4 "Moreover, יהוה has sent to you all His servants the prophets, rising early and sending them, but you have not listened nor inclined your ear to hear, 5 saying, 'Turn back now everyone from his evil way and from the evil of your deeds, and dwell on the soil which יהוה has given to you and your fathers forever and ever. 6 'And do not go after other mighty ones to serve them and to bow down to them. And do not provoke Me with the works of your hands, so that I do you no evil.' 7 "But you did not listen to Me," declares יהוה, "so as to provoke Me with the works of your hands, for your own evil.

8 "Therefore thus said יהוה of hosts, 'Because you did not obey My words, 9 see, I am sending and taking all the tribes of the north,' declares יהוה, 'and Neḇukaḏretstsar the sovereign of Baḇel, My servant, and shall bring them against this land and against its inhabitants, and against these nations all around, and shall put them under the ban, and make them an astonishment, and a hissing, and everlasting ruins.

10 'And I shall banish from them the voice of rejoicing and the voice of gladness, the voice of the bridegroom and the voice of the bride, the sound of the millstones and the light of the lamp. 11 'And all this land shall be a ruin and a waste, and these nations shall serve the sovereign of Baḇel seventy years. 12 'And it shall be, when seventy years are completed, that I shall punish the sovereign of Baḇel and that nation, the land of the Chaldeans, for their crookedness,' declares יהוה, 'and shall make it everlasting ruins. 13 'And I shall bring on that land all My words which I have pronounced

against it, all that is written in this book, which Yirmeyahu has prophesied concerning all the nations. (Jeremiah 25:1-13)

The reason Judah was going into captivity for 70 years as we were told by Jeremiah is explained to us in 2 Chronicles.

> 17 Therefore He brought against them the sovereign of the Chaldeans, and he slew their young men with the sword in the House of their set-apart place, and had no compassion on young man or maiden, on the aged or the weak – He gave all into his hand. 18 And all the utensils from the House of Elohim, great and small, and the treasures of the House of יהוה, and the treasures of the sovereign and of his leaders, all these he brought to Babel. 19 And they burned the House of Elohim, and broke down the wall of Yerushalayim, and burned all its palaces with fire, and destroyed all its valuable utensils.

> 20 And those who escaped from the sword he exiled to Babel, where they became servants to him and his sons until the reign of the reign of Persia, 21 in order to fill the word of יהוה by the mouth of Yirmeyahu, until the land had enjoyed her Sabbaths. As long as she lay waste she kept Sabbath, until seventy years were completed. (2 Chronicles 3617-21)

In order to fill the word of יהוה by the mouth of Yirmeyahu, until the land had enjoyed her Sabbaths. As long as she lay waste she kept Sabbath, until seventy years were completed.

So does Yehovah care whether or not we keep the Sabbatical years? Absolutely! The same as He does for us not keeping the Holy Days and the weekly Sabbath.

We also read in Nehemiah 8 how they read the whole law to the people during the Feast of Tabernacles and then the people learned that they were to make booths and so they did. But then the verse I want you to understand is verse 17.

For since the days of Joshua the son of Nun until that day the children of Israel had not done so. And there was very great gladness. (Nehemiah 8:17)

It is from this time after the return from the captivity that Judah is zealous in keeping the laws. And it is from this time that we have records of Sabbatical years that they kept. Before that time they were slack just as Israel was and is even until today.

If Yehovah is willing to cast the Ten Northern Tribes into captitivty in 723 B.C. and also Judah in 586 B.C.for not keeping the Laws of the Torah, which also include the Sabbatical years then He is also just as willing to do it now to those of us who still refuse to keep these same laws. This includes the Sabbatical years.

Now consider this fact; that Judah has been in the land of Israel since 1948. As of 2016 there will have been 10 Sabbatiacal years and one Jubilee year that the State of Israel will not have kept. And as we have seen from history, Yehovah will require that from them in the years just ahead of us.

Chapter 28 | What If We *Do Not* Keep the Sabbatical Years?

To truly please Yehovah and to be considered "good" according to His standards, we must keep His Commandments. We are told of the blessings we will receive if we keep The Commandments of Yehovah found in the following passage in Leviticus:

> **1** "Do not make idols for yourselves, and do not set up a carved image or a pillar for yourselves, and do not place a stone image in your land, to bow down to it. For I am יהוה your Elohim. **2** Guard My Sabbaths and reverence My set-apart place. I am יהוה. **3** If you walk in My laws and guard My commands, and shall do them, **4** then I shall give you rain in its season, and the land shall yield its crops, and the trees of the field yield their fruit. **5** And your threshing shall last till the time of the grape harvest, and the grape harvest shall last till the time of sowing. And you shall eat your bread until you have enough, and shall dwell in your land safely. **6** And I shall give peace in the land, and you shall lie down and no one make you afraid. And I shall clear the land of evil beasts, and not let the sword go through your land. **7** And you shall pursue your enemies, and they shall fall by the sword before you. **8** And five of you shall pursue a hundred, and a hundred of you pursue ten thousand. And your enemies shall fall by the sword before you. **9** And I shall turn to you and make you bear fruit, and shall increase you, and shall establish My covenant with you. **10** And you shall eat the old supply, and clear out the old because of the new. **11** And I shall set My Dwelling Place in your midst, and My being shall not reject you. **12** And I shall walk in your midst, and shall be your Elohim, and you shall be My people. **13** I am יהוה your Elohim, who brought you out of the land of Mitsrayim (Egypt), from being their slaves. And I have broken the bars of your yoke and made you walk upright." (**Leviticus 26:1-13**)

Notice the condition Yehovah places on us in order to receive His blessings:

> **3** "If you walk in My laws and guard My commands, and shall do them."
> **(Leviticus 26:3)**

Based on the conditions all around you in the area you live, are the blessings spoken of in Leviticus being poured out on you and those in your area? If not, then as I go through the curses with you for not keeping the Sabbatical Years, give careful thought to how many of these either have already taken place or are currently taking place in the area where you live.

In Leviticus, Yehovah warns us of the curses that will come upon us if we do not obey.

> **14** "But if you do not obey Me, and do not do all these commands, **15** and if you reject My laws, or if your being loathes My right-rulings, so that you do not do all My commands, but break My covenant, **16** I also do this to you: And I shall appoint sudden alarm over you, wasting disease and inflammation, destroying the eyes, and consuming the life. And you shall sow your seed in vain, for your enemies shall eat it. **17** And I shall set My face against you, and you shall be smitten before your enemies. And those who hate you shall rule over you, and you shall flee when no one pursues you." **(Leviticus 26:14-17)**

I titled the First Curse the Curse of Terror and described to you all the events that have already taken place during this first Sabbatical Cycle of this, the last Jubilee Cycle before the Seventh Millennium begins in 2045. To find out more, you can order the DVD or watch it for free on my website.[211]

This first Sabbatical Cycle began in 1996 and the seven years, which comprised it, brought you as far along as the year 2002. It was during *this time* that Osama bin Laden declared war on the U.S.A. and The West in August of 1996.[212] He then blew up the U.S. Embassies in Tanzania and Kenya[213] in 1998 and attacked a ship called the U.S.S. Cole[214] in 2000, followed by the attack on

211 *The Chronological Order of Prophecy In the Jubilees*, http://www.sightedmoon.com/?page_id=251
212 Text of Bin laden's 1996 *Declaration of Jihad Against the United States* http://middleeast.about.com/od/terrorism/a/bin-laden-jihad.htm
213 http://foxfromzim.wordpress.com/2010/05/18/the-u-s-embassy-attacks-in-kenya-and-tanzania-1998/
214 http://en.wikipedia.org/wiki/USS_Cole_bombing

the Twin Towers on September 11th, 2001 or 9/11.[215] This attack would then lead to the retaliation war declared by the U.S. on Iraq and Afghanistan or what the Bush Administration chose to call: "The War On Terror."

On October 7th, 2001, the war in Afghanistan officially began when U.S. and British forces initiated aerial bombing raids targeting Taliban and al-Qaeda camps, and then later invaded Afghanistan with ground troops of the Special Forces.[216]

> The 2003 Invasion of Iraq (March 19th—May 1st, 2003), was the start of the conflict known as the Iraq War, or Operation Iraqi Freedom, in which a combined force of troops from the United States, the United Kingdom, Australia and Poland invaded Iraq and toppled the regime of Saddam Hussein (via) twenty-one days of major combat operations.[217]
>
> On May 2nd, 2011, Osama bin Laden was shot and killed inside a private residential compound in Abbottabad, Pakistan, by members of the U.S. Naval Special Warfare Development Group (U.S. Navy Seals) and C.I.A. operatives in a covert operation ordered by the United States President, Barack Obama.[218]

On June 22nd, 2011, President Obama announced that at the end of 2011 he would withdraw 10,000 U.S. troops. It was then determined there would be an additional 23,000 troop drawdown by the summer of 2012. A September 20th, 2012 article reports, however, that the 33,000 additional U.S. troops President Obama ordered to Afghanistan to clamp down the Taliban attacks nearly two years ago have now left the country.[219] After the withdrawal of 10,000 U.S. troops, 80,000 are still left participating in the war.

The United States and its N.A.T.O. allies finalized agreements on April 18th, 2012 to wind down the war in Afghanistan by formalizing three commitments;

- To move the Afghanis gradually into a lead combat role.
- To keep some international troops in Afghanistan beyond 2014.
- To pay billions of dollars a year to help support the Afghani security forces.

---

215 September 11th Attacks http://en.wikipedia.org/wiki/September_11_attacks
216 War In Afghanistan (2001–Present)
http://en.wikipedia.org/wiki/War_in_Afghanistan_(2001%E2%80%93present)
217 2003 Invasion of Iraq: http://en.wikipedia.org/wiki/2003_invasion_of_Iraq
218 Bin Laden: http://en.wikipedia.org/wiki/Osama_bin_Laden
219 http://www.armytimes.com/news/2012/09/ap-last-surge-troops-leave-afghanistan-092012/

On May 2nd, 2012 Afghan President Hamid Karzai and U.S. President Barack Obama signed ... the "Enduring Strategic Partnership Agreement" between the Islamic Republic of Afghanistan and the United States of America. The U.S. president had arrived ... to sign the agreement ... and to address ... (America) ... about his plans to responsibly end the war in Afghanistan.

The plan called for:

- The removal of 23,000 U.S. troops at the end of September 2012.
- Afghani security forces to take the lead in combat operations by the end of 2013 while the I.S.A.F. (International Security Assistance Force) forces train, advise and assist the Afghanis and fight alongside them when needed.
- The complete removal of all U.S. troops by the end of 2014, except for trainers who will assist Afghan forces and a small contingent of troops with a specific mission to combat al-Qaeda through counterterrorism operations.

On May 21st, 2012 the leaders of the N.A.T.O.-member countries endorsed an exit strategy (to end the Afghanistan war) during the 2012 N.A.T.O. Summit in Chicago. The N.A.T.O.-led I.S.A.F. (International Security Assistance Force) will ... withdraw most of the ... foreign troops by the end of December 2014.[220]

As a result of the attacks during 9/11, many governments around the world have passed legislation to combat terrorism.[221] In the United States, the Department of Homeland Security was created to coordinate domestic anti-terrorism efforts. The U.S.A. Patriot Act gave the federal government greater powers, including the authority to detain foreign terror suspects for a week without charge, to monitor telephone communications, e-mail, and Internet usage by terror suspects, and to prosecute suspected terrorists without time restrictions.[222]

That was just the First Curse of Terror, however, and it continues to be added to each of the following curses I will be describing to you throughout the remainder of this chapter. In fact, each previous curse is compounded by any successive curse until a nation repents.

---

220 War In Afghanistan (2001–Present)
http://en.wikipedia.org/wiki/War_in_Afghanistan_(2001%E2%80%93present)
221 *In the Asia-Pacific: Threat & Response. The Journal of Asian Studies*, by Andrew Scobell. (2004). 63 (4): 1078–9. DOI:10.1017/S0021911804002463.
222 *Modern World History* by Roger Beck (2004), "20." Holt McDougal. pp. 657–8. ISBN 978-0-618-69012-1.

As we begin the second curse we remind you of the bombings on Londons Subway systems also known as 7/7.[223] Nor do we neglect the coutless terrorist attacks in the land of Israel itself.

The Second Curse of Leviticus 26 is Drought, but is also weather extremes and severity.

> **18** "And after all this, if you do not obey Me, then I shall punish you seven times more for your sins. **19** And I shall break the pride of your power, and shall make your heavens like iron and your earth like bronze. **20** And your strength shall be spent in vain and your land not yield its crops, nor the trees of the land yield their fruit." (**Leviticus 26:18-20**)

In the passage in Daniel I'm about to quote, we read that "a time and times and half a time" equals 3 ½ years. Before citing Leviticus 26 above, I had to draw your attention to the Sabbatical Cycles in Leviticus 25 which come right before. So the seven times mentioned in Leviticus 26 is, in fact, seven years of curses.

> **25** "... and it speaks words against the Most High, and it wears out the set-apart ones of the Most High, and it intends to change appointed times[1] and law,[2] and they are given into its hand for a time and times and half a time. [**Daniel 7:25** | Footnotes: [1]This is another word for festivals. [2]Changing the law amounts to lawlessness. Read also in **II Thessalonians 2:3-12** about "the lawless one" and the "lawlessness" which would take over (indeed, it has already taken over!) in the set-apart place, and also about Messiah's judgment upon the lawless "prophets" in **Matthew 7:23**, and the lawless "believers" in **Matthew 13:41!**]

The First Curse is applied to the first Sabbatical Cycle of 1996-2002. The second Sabbatical Cycle is from 2003 to 2009. The Curse of Drought is now added to the previous Curse of Terror. They are combined or compounded and these will then be added to the next one and they then to the one after that and all of them to the 5th and last one until we repent.

> January 2000 to December 2009 was the warmest decade on record. Looking back to 1880, when modern scientific instrumentation became available to monitor temperatures precisely, a clear warming trend is present.[224]

---

223 http://www.guardian.co.uk/society/2005/jul/07/terrorism.transportintheuk
224 http://www.nasa.gov/home/hqnews/2010/jan/HQ_10-017_Warmest_temps.html

Natural disasters across the globe have made 2011 the costliest on record in terms of property damage, and that was just six months into 2011, according to a report released by a leading insurer that tracks disasters.

The first six months saw $265 billion in economic losses—well above the previous record of $220 billion (adjusted for inflation) set for all of 2005 (the year Hurricane Katrina struck), according to Munich Re,[225] a multinational reinsurance company that insures insurance companies.[226]

> The summer heat wave in Europe in 2003 ... was the hottest in continental Europe since at least 1540![227]

This heat wave led to:

> "... serious health crises and droughts in many European countries with a death toll reaching almost 40,000. There (also) occurred a crop shortfall in Southern Europe due to long droughts."

Peer reviewed analysis placed the European death toll at 70,000.[228] France was hit especially hard:

> In France, almost 14,802 deaths happened because of this heat wave according to the French National Institute of Health.

> Extensive forest fires occurred in Portugal with almost 5% of the countryside and 10% of the forests being destroyed due to the temperatures reaching 48°C (118°F). In the Netherlands, there were about 1,500 heat-related deaths with temperatures reaching 37.8°C.[229]

Australia Suffers the Worst Drought In 1,000 Years[230]

> Depleted reservoirs, failed crops and arid farmland spark global warming tussle.

225 http://www.munichre.com/en/homepage/default.aspx
226 http://www.msnbc.msn.com/id/43727793/ns/world_news-world_environment/t/already-costliest-year-natural-disasters
227 http://www.preventionweb.net/english/professional/news/v.php?id=14970
228 *Toll Exceeded 70,000 In Europe During the Summer of 2003*. Robine, Jean-Marie; Siu Lan K. Cheung, Sophie Le Roy, Herman Van Oyen, Clare Griffiths, Jean-Pierre Michel, François Richard Herrmann (2008). *Comptes Rendus Biologies*, 331 (2): 171–178. DOI:10.1016/j.crvi.2007.12.001. ISSN 1631-0691. PMID 18241810.
229 http://www.tiptoptens.com/2011/03/28/10-worst-natural-disasters-of-21st-century/
230 http://www.guardian.co.uk/world/2006/nov/08/australia.drought

Australia's blistering summer has only just begun but reservoir levels are dropping fast, crop forecasts have been slashed, and great swaths of the continent are entering what scientists yesterday called a "one in a thousand years drought."

With many regions in their fifth year of drought, the government yesterday called an emergency water summit in Canberra. The meeting between the Prime Minister John Howard, and the leaders of New South Wales, Victoria, South Australia, and Queensland was told that more than half of Australia's farmland was experiencing drought.

Australia Faces Worst Plague of Locusts In 75 Years
Ideal breeding conditions for grasshoppers are expected to cost farmers billions.

Sunday 26th, September 2010

Australia's Darling River is running with water again after a drought in the middle of the decade reduced it to a trickle. But the rains feeding the continent's fourth longest river are not the undiluted good news you might expect. For the cloudbursts also create ideal conditions for an unwelcome pest—the Australian plague locust.[231]

Australia's Queensland Faces "Biblical" Flood
A senior official has described the flooding in Queensland, Australia, as a disaster of "biblical proportions."

January 1st, 2011

State Treasurer, Andrew Fraser said the economic impact would be severe, with huge costs compounded by lost income from mining, farming and tourism.

Rockhampton, where 77,000 people live, is the latest city bracing for impact, amid warnings of 30 ft. (9m) floodwaters.

More than 20 other towns have already been left cut off or flooded across a area larger than France and Germany.

The crisis has been triggered by Australia's wettest spring on record. At least six river systems across Queensland have broken their banks.

---

231 http://www.independent.co.uk/environment/nature/australia-faces-worst-plague-of-locusts-in-75-years-2089919.html

The floods have affected about 200,000 people, and many have been evacuated.[232]

April 2011 Tornadoes Break Record For Most Twisters Ever In A Day

WASHINGTON—Preliminary government estimates say there were more tornadoes in a single day last week than any other day in history.

Government analysts say there were 312 tornadoes during last week's outbreak, including a record-setting 226 in one day.[233]

May 2012 Global Temperatures Second Warmest On Record

Science Daily (June 18th, 2012)—The globally-averaged temperature for May 2012 marked the second warmest May since record keeping began in 1880. May 2012 also marks the 36th consecutive May and 327th consecutive month with a global temperature above the 20th-century average.

Most areas of the world experienced much warmer-than-average monthly temperatures, including nearly all of Europe, Asia, northern Africa, most of North America and southern Greenland. Only Australia, Alaska and parts of the western U.S.-Canadian border region were notably cooler than average.[234]

Ireland Experiences Its Wettest June On Record

June 30th, 2012—IRELAND—Ireland has been hit by torrential rain as the summer disappears again—with parts of Cork and Belfast flooded. Emergency services are struggling to cope with the flash floods across the country as homes are left without electricity. The towns of Douglas, Bandon and Clonakilty in Cork are badly flooded with some areas under three feet of water. Residents were evacuated from the Ballyvolane area of Cork city while there is no access in or out of Clonakilty. The Irish Independent reports that up to 15,000 homes in Cork are currently without electricity after the overnight storms which saw 70mm of rain

232 http://www.bbc.co.uk/news/world-asia-pacific-12102126
233 http://www.huffingtonpost.com/2011/05/02/2011-tornadoes-record-most-in-day_n_856542.html
234 http://www.sciencedaily.com/releases/2012/06/120618152733.htm

fall in a few hours. Flooding has also been reported in parts of Sligo and Tipperary and motorists have been warned to take extreme care.[235]

Temperatures In Kansas Hit 118°F: 32 Communities From Colorado To Indiana Post Highest Temperatures Ever

June 30th, 2012—CLIMATE—Norton Dam, Kansas, hit 118°F (48°C) on Thursday, and 32 communities from Colorado to Indiana just posted their highest temperatures ever. Forecasters say back-to-back La Niñas are partly to blame. These records appear to be falling into step with a longer-term trend in which record highs are being set more often than record lows for each decade since the 1970's—a trend many climate researchers have attributed to global warming. As June 2012 drew to a close, it felt more like mid-July or August to people in wide swaths of the country.[236]

U.S. Drought 2012: More Than Half Of Continental States Experiencing Extremely Dry Conditions

The United States is parched, with more than half of the lower forty-eight states experiencing moderate to extreme drought, according to a report released in July 5th.

Just under 56% of the contiguous United States is (subject to) drought conditions, the most extensive area in the twelve-year history of the U.S. Drought Monitor. The previous drought records occurred on August 26th, 2003, when 54.79% of the lower forty-eight were in drought and on September 10th, 2002, when drought extended across 54.63% of this area.[237]

Chaos In Skies Over Britain: Forecasters Describe Horrific Summer As 'the Worst Since Records Began'

July 7th, 2012—UNITED KINGDOM—Britain is facing its "worst ever" summer with cold wet weather ruining family holidays and blighting the Olympics, forecasters warned last night. August is set to be a washout

---

235 http://theextinctionprotocol.wordpress.com/2012/06/30/ireland-experiences-its-wettest-june-on-record/
236 http://theextinctionprotocol.wordpress.com/2012/06/30/temperatures-in-kansas-hit-118-f-32-communities-from-colorado-to-indiana-post-highest-temperatures-ever/
237 http://www.huffingtonpost.com/2012/07/06/us-drought-2012-heat-wave_n_1654908.html

following a miserable July and the wettest June since records began—meaning summer is effectively over. Gloomy forecasts suggest dire weather will continue as officials last night put Britain on flood alert after torrential downpours yesterday wreaked havoc. As the Environment Agency warned of a "potential danger to life" with rivers swelling to breaking point in the Midlands, Yorkshire and Wales, government forecasters were on standby to brief The Cabinet if severe floods strike. The agency last night issued fifty-one flood warnings—meaning flooding is expected—and 135 alerts. Monsoon-like downpours hit 85,000 music fans at the T In the Park festival in Kinross, Scotland, and 28,000 Formula 1 spectators camping for the British Grand Prix weekend at Silverstone.[238]

Sweltering U.S. Heat Wave Claims 30 Lives

July 7th, 2012—WASHINGTON—Americans dipped into the water, went to the movies and rode the subway just to be in air conditioning Saturday for relief from unrelenting heat that has killed thirty people across half the country. The heat (not only) sent temperatures soaring over 100°F in several cities, including a record high 105°F in Washington, 106°F in St. Louis, and 104°F in Indianapolis; (but also) buckled highways and derailed a Washington-area train even as another round of summer storms threatened. If people ventured outside to do anything, they did it early. But even then, the heat was stifling. "It was baking on the 18th green," said golfer Zeb Rogerson, who teed off at 6am at an Alexandria, Virginia golf course but was sweltering by the end of his round. The heat sent temperatures soaring in more than twenty states to 105°F in Louisville, Kentucky; 101°F in Philadelphia; and 95°F in New York. (B)esides it reaching a record high of 105°F in Washington, a record of 104°F was set in Sioux Falls, S.D. At least thirty deaths were blamed on the heat—including nine in Maryland and ten in Chicago, mostly among the elderly.[239]

Colorado Wildfires 2012: Worst Wildfire Season In A Decade; Fires Close In On Tourist Destinations

COLORADO SPRINGS, Colorado—Flames forced thousands of Colorado residents from their homes over the weekend and disrupted vacation plans for countless visitors as smoke shrouded some of the

238 http://theextinctionprotocol.wordpress.com/2012/07/07/chaos-in-skies-over-britain-forecasters-describe-horrific-summer-as-the-worst-since-records-began/
239 http://theextinctionprotocol.wordpress.com/2012/07/07/sweltering-u-s-heat-wave-claims-30-lives/

state's top tourist destinations, including majestic Pike's Peak and tranquil Estes Park.

Colorado is having its worst wildfire season in a decade, with more than a half a dozen forest fires burning across the state's parched terrain. Some hotels and campgrounds are emptying ahead of the busy Fourth of July holiday.[240]

You can watch the DVD I put together in 2008 where I show you the extreme weather patterns of that time,[241] or you can watch the DVD that came out in January of 2012 when I spoke in Texas and directed my focus at the weather, severe drought and wildfires they were facing.[242] And as I write this Hurricane Sandy is flooding New York and New Jersey with million going without hydro or gasoline as temperatures drop, and at the same time Virginia is getting 2 feet of snow as a result of this monster size storm.

The dictionary definition of insanity is to keep doing the same thing over and over, expecting a different result. Many people, after a disaster, will return to the church they were at the week before, to pray to the same god who did not stop the tornado, wildfire, earthquake or whatever disaster it was they were dealing with at the time.

We are told in Proverbs if we are not keeping Torah even our prayers are an abomination to Yehovah.

> 9 He who turns away his ear from hearing the Torah, even his prayer is an abomination. (**Proverbs 28:9**)

Why wait then, until you have had your life destroyed before you repent and return to the one true God? Why wait until your property is destroyed or your loved ones are killed? Why gamble with the lives of those you love?

> 23 "Turn at my reproof. See, I pour out my spirit on you, I make my words known to you."[1] (**Proverbs 23:1** | Footnote: [1]See **Psalm 33:6**)

> 24 "Because I called and you refused, I have stretched out My hand and no one inclined, 25 and you spurned all My counsel, and would not yield to My reproof, 26 let Me also laugh at your calamity, mock when your

---

240 http://www.huffingtonpost.com/2012/06/25/colorado-wildfires-2012-v_n_1623695.html
241 *The Chronological Order of Prophecy In the Jubilees*:
http://www.sightedmoon.com/?page_id=251
242 *The Prophecies of Abraham*: http://www.sightedmoonnl.com/?page_id=771

dread comes, **27** when your dread comes like a storm, and your calamity comes like a whirlwind, when distress and anguish come upon you. **28** Let them then call on Me, but I answer not; let them seek Me, but not find me. **29** Because they hated knowledge and did not choose the fear of יהוה, **30** they did not accept My counsel, they despised all My reproof, **31** therefore let them eat the fruit of their own way, and be filled with their own counsels. **32** For the turning away of the simple slays them, and the complacency of fools destroys them. **33** But whoever listens to Me dwells safely, and is at ease from the dread of evil." (**Proverbs 1:24-33**)

In August of 2011, there were 600,000 less cattle in the state of Texas than on January 1ˢᵗ of that same year:

Texas Drought Shrinks State Cow Herd

December 17ᵗʰ, 2011

Since January of last year, the number of cows in Texas is expected to have decreased by about 600,000—a 12% drop from about five million cows at the beginning of the year. That's according to David Anderson, a livestock economist in College Station who monitors beef markets for the Texas AgriLife Extension Service.

The trend is likely the largest drop in the number of cows any state has ever seen, Anderson told *The Times*. Texas only had a larger percentage decline during the Great Depression.[243]

Texas Lake Turns Blood-Red & the Cause Is Disturbing

August 2ⁿᵈ, 2011

A lake and popular fishing spot in West Texas has turned blood-red this summer.

A drought has left the O.C. Fisher Reservoir in San Angelo State Park in West Texas almost entirely dry. The water that is left is stagnant, full of dead fish, and deep, opaque red in color.

According to officials from Texas Parks and Wildlife Inland Fisheries, the bloody color is the result of Chromatiaceae bacteria, which thrives

---

243 http://latimesblogs.latimes.com/nationnow/2011/12/texas-drought-shrinks-state-cow-herd.html

in oxygen-depleted water and often takes on an opaque red hue. Texas is experiencing a severe drought this summer, which in turn is causing water levels throughout the state to drop. What likely happened here is that the fish began to die as the lake dried up; the decomposing fish reduced the oxygen levels in the water leading to a rapid increase of this Chromatiaceae bacteria.[244]

This lake is in Texas. Does the Bible Belt of the USA get it? Do they know what is happening or is this just another "meanwhile, back at the ranch" occurrence? Every plague of Egypt is promised to happen to us if we will not guard The Commandments to keep the Sabbath, The Holy Days, and the Sabbatical Years—including the Jubilee Years. I admonish you, therefore, to take a much closer look at what is happening in your own backyard.

> **58** "If you do not guard to do all the Words of this Torah that are written in this book, to fear this esteemed and awesome Name, יהוה your Elohim, **59** then יהוה shall bring upon you *and your descendants* extraordinary plagues, great and lasting plagues, and grievous and lasting sicknesses. **60** And He shall bring back on you all the diseases of Mitsrayim (Egypt), of which you were afraid, and they shall cling to you, **61** also every sickness and every plague, which is not written in the book of this Torah, יהוה does bring upon you until you are destroyed. **62** And you shall be left with few men, although you had become as numerous as the stars of the heavens, because you did not obey the voice of יהוה your Elohim."
> **(Deuteronomy 28:58)**

What if we continue to not keep the Sabbatical Years? Then there are curses as laid out in Leviticus 26 which you can plan on receiving. This is what I am trying to show you and keep telling you. These curses are happening to you right here, right now—or are about to come upon you. Know and understand *why* they are happening—because you *have not kept* the Sabbatical Years. Most do not keep the Sabbath. Even fewer keep the Holy Days and hardly *anyone* at all keeps the Sabbatical Years. And yet, all this destruction comes and we cry out to the God of our churches saying, "Why me?" and "What have I done to deserve this?"

The answers to both of these questions are found in Proverbs:

> **24** "Because I called and you refused, I have stretched out my hand and no one inclined. **25** And you spurned all my counsel, and would not yield to my reproof. **26** Let me also laugh at your calamity, mock when your

244 http://thestir.cafemom.com/in_the_news/123981/texas_lake_turns_bloodred_the

dread comes. **27** When your dread comes like a storm, and your calamity comes like a whirlwind, when distress and anguish come upon you. **28** Let them then call on me, but I answer not. Let them seek me, but not find me. **29** Because they hated knowledge and did not choose the fear of יהוה. **30** They did not accept my counsel. They despised all my reproof." **(Proverbs 1:24-30)**

Although our country has made the "War On Terror" official as a direct response to terrorism, ironically we see an increase in terrorism on a global scale while The West keeps trying to defend itself from it. Even more ironically still, even though we see and hear of floods in one place, severe heat and drought in another, earthquakes, tsunamis, hurricanes, raging wildfires, torrential rains, severe tornadoes and cyclones, crop and cattle losses, unexplainable animal deaths of all different kinds in droves on a global scale and swarms of locusts, we still do not repent and return to the Torah. <u>We do not consider these things to be a clear and present warning from Yehovah, but instead chalk it up to "mother nature," thereby denying Yehovah and His mighty hand in any of it.</u>

Yet, in Isaiah it is written:

> **7** "I form the light, and create darkness: I make peace, and create evil: I YHVH do all these things." **(Isaiah 45:7 | KJV)**

(This is the true translation from the Hebrew word of "ra-ah" (resh ayin hey) which means "evil." All of the other later translations of the Bible from the Hebrew tried to find another word in English in order to get around this. Notice that it is in the PRESENT tense. That means that God is CONTINUALLY creating evil, even now![245]

In Isaiah 45, the word "evil" is used in … contrast to … peace and well-being.

I quote John Haley:

> Evil means natural, and ***not*** moral evil, or sin. Herderson says "affliction, adversity;" Calvin, "afflictions, wars, and other adverse occurrences."

God, in Hebrew thought, is considered the final authority over everything. If wars or famine happen, then God has allowed that to occur, and therefore controls evil.

---

245 http://www.comereason.org/phil_qstn/phi025.asp

The Amplified Bible says it even more clearly:

> 7 "I form the light and create darkness, I make peace (national well-being) and create (physical) evil (calamity); I am YHVH, Who does all these things." (**Isaiah 45:7**)

I have now covered the First Curse of Terror and the Second Curse of Drought (which includes severe weather) with you.

Also, for the record, we are now living during the third Sabbatical Cycle at the time of this writing in 2012. That being said, I will now go over the Third Curse with you.

This Third Curse is found in Leviticus:

> 21 "And if you walk contrary to Me, and refuse to obey Me, I shall bring on you seven times more plagues, according to your sins." (**Leviticus 26:21**)

> 22 "... and send wild beasts among you, which shall bereave you of your children. And I shall cut off your livestock, and make you few in number, and your highways shall be deserted." (**Leviticus 26:22**)

Once again we have the warning of the seven times (or seven years), which is again, one Sabbatical Cycle. This third Sabbatical Cycle begins in 2010 and extends into 2016.

The Third Curse then is: Pestilence, Famine and Earthquakes.

For the past six consecutive Jubilee Cycles, there has been Pestilence outbreak that began in the first year of the third Sabbatical Cycle and has extended into the first year of the fifth Sabbatical Cycle. I find this to be very alarming and something we would all do well to be mindful of.

When we look at the Spanish Flu, we can see that it came in the last two years of the third Sabbatical Cycle. This would match our time of 2015-2016.

The Influenza Pandemic of 1918 [246]

> The Influenza Pandemic of 1918-1919 killed more people than the Great War, known today as World War I (WWI), at somewhere between 20-40 million people. It has been cited as the most devastating Epidemic in recorded world history. More people died of Influenza in a *single year*

---

246 http://virus.stanford.edu/uda/

than in four years of the Black Death Bubonic Plague from 1347 C.E.–
1351 C.E. Known as the "Spanish Flu" or "La Grippe," the Influenza of
1918 C.E.–1919 C.E. was a global disaster.

As for recent outbreaks, the World Health Organization (W.H.O.) was
on the watch for something to happen soon, but they were not sure when or
where. When the Swine Flu broke out, they were quick to call it a Pandemic
and they are still watching it as it mutates into what is now called the Avian
(Bird) Flu and other names.

Outbreak of Swine-Origin Influenza; an (H1N1) Virus Infection—Mexico, March-April 2009[247]

In March and early April 2009, Mexico experienced outbreaks of
respiratory illness and increased reports of patients with influenza-like illness
(ILI) in several areas of the country. On April 12, the General Directorate
of Epidemiology (DGE) reported an outbreak of ILI in a small community
in the state of Veracruz to the Pan American Health Organization (PAHO)
in accordance with International Health Regulations. On April 17, a case
of atypical pneumonia in Oaxaca State prompted enhanced surveillance
throughout Mexico. On April 23, several cases of severe respiratory illness
laboratory confirmed as swine-origin influenza A (H1N1) virus (S-OIV)
infection were communicated to the PAHO. Sequence analysis revealed
that the patients were infected with the same S-OIV strain detected in two
children residing in California. This report describes the initial and ongoing
investigation of the S-OIV outbreak in Mexico.

W.H.O. Declares Global Swine Flu Pandemic

June 11th 2009

The World Health Organization on Thursday declared a Swine Flu
Pandemic, marking the first worldwide Flu Epidemic in forty-one
years.[248]

---

247 http://www.cdc.gov/mmwr/preview/mmwrhtml/mm58d0430a2.htm
248 http://www.pbs.org/newshour/updates/health/jan-june09/flupandemic_06-11.
html

W.H.O. Declares first 21ˢᵗ-Century Flu Pandemic

Thursday, June 11ᵗʰ, 2009 [249]

GENEVA (Reuters)—The World Health Organization declared an Influenza Pandemic on Thursday and advised governments to prepare for a long-term battle against an unstoppable new Flu Virus.

The United Nations agency raised its Pandemic Flu alert to phase six on a six-point scale, indicating the first Influenza Pandemic since 1968 is under way.

This Pandemic later turned out not to be as lethal as expected, but they did have legitimate cause to be concerned.

You can stay tuned into W.H.O. as they monitor the newest strains of the Flu around the world.[250]

When I was searching for Pestilence outbreaks in the Bible, I learned that most of them occurred at the *same time* as Famine. It was at this point I noticed what Yehshua said in Matthew:

> 4 And יהושע answering, said to them, "Take heed that no one leads you astray. 5 For many shall come in My Name, saying, 'I am the Messiah,' and they shall lead many astray. 6 And you shall begin to hear of fightings and reports of fightings. See that you are not troubled, for these have to take place, but the end is not yet. 7 For nation shall rise against nation, and reign against reign. And there shall be scarcities of food, and deadly diseases, and earthquakes in places. 8 And all these are the beginning of birth pains." (**Matthew 24:4-8**)

He lists Disease or Pestilence *along with* Famine and Earthquakes.

Rising Food Prices: It's No Small Potatoes

The Globe and Mail

Published Tuesday, April 19ᵗʰ 2011[251]

---

249 http://www.reuters.com/article/2009/06/11/us-flu-idUSTRE55A1U720090611
250 http://www.who.int/influenza/en/
251 http://www.theglobeandmail.com/report-on-business/economy/economy-lab/daily-mix/rising-food-prices-its-no-small-potatoes/article1990922/

The cost of food picked up to 3.3% in March, much higher than the 2.1% rate of food inflation a month earlier. The price of food bought from stores rose 3.7%—the biggest increase in a year and a half.

Factors driving food costs range from bad weather to rising energy prices.

Food Prices Are Expected To Keep Rising In 2012

A trip to the grocery store is going to cost more next year, according to a new report by the U.S. Department of Agriculture.

Federal officials expect grocery prices to rise 3-4 % overall in 2012. That change represents a slight tapering off from the 5% jump seen (in 2011). But it's still dramatically higher than 2009 and 2010, when food-based inflation rates were the lowest since the 1960's.

The jump in prices between 2010 and 2011 also turned up in the Tampa Tribune's own Market Basket Survey of the region's main grocery stores in September. An analysis of grocery prices from each year showed sharp jumps in eggs and dairy products, (as well as) week-to-week variations in meat prices.

That pattern is likely to continue, but at a slightly muted pace, federal officials said.[252]

Hyperinflation Warning: Why Food Prices Will Be Rising Even Faster in 2012.[253]

Speaking of hyperinflation, no other dissertation on this subject have I found to be more sobering, compelling and eye-opening than *The Porter-Stansberry Investment Advisory*.[254]

So what does this mean for Americans in 2012? At the very least, we will experience inflation like never before. At worst, we will experience hyperinflation, which means a double-digit rise in prices every month.

After the financial crisis of 2008-2009, respected economists like Marc Faber and Jim Rogers, along with trends forecaster Gerald Celente (who all have excellent track records of being right on with their predictions) explained that since the Federal Reserve had "fired all its bullets," the next time we hit

252 http://www2.tbo.com/news/business/2011/nov/28/food-prices-expected-to-keep-rising-in-2012-ar-327747/
253 http://ezinearticles.com/?Hyperinflation-Warning:-Why-Food-Prices-Will-Be-Rising-Even-Faster-in-2012&id=6723534
254 http://www.youtube.com/watch?v=tM-c8PxPZXQ

a bump in the road, there will be little, if anything, they can do. We are now living in that "next time …"

Rising food prices invariably stem from a complex set of dynamics, all of which are now coming together to create the "perfect storm" of hyperinflation. The global financial crisis, as I mentioned, is a huge contributing factor and gives every appearance of being the proverbial straw that is about to break the camel's back.

In addition, there have been very poor harvests from several major agricultural exporting countries, thus bringing the global food supply to an all-time low. This global food crisis, combined with increasing uncertainty in the Middle East (and how the price of gas is affected as a result), will contribute to food prices skyrocketing faster than ever.

Do you understand what is happening *right now* in 2012? The headlines in the news as of July 2012 warned of a failing corn crop and the potential for many other crops to be lost to a severe, nationwide drought.

The European economic crisis and the national debt of the U.S.A. will cause the banks to eventually fail.

If you look at the recessions over the past 100 years, you will notice how the majority of them occur during what I have been telling you are Sabbatical Years. The latest recession began with the collapse of Lehman's Bank in September 2008 causing a major panic throughout the inter-bank loan market.[255] And as of 2012, the world still has not recovered from this economic collapse.

The Sabbatical Year began in March-April 2009. One of the Commandments I have already shared with you that we are to do is found in Deuteronomy:

> **1** "At the end of every seven years you make a release of debts. **2** And this is the word of the release: Every creditor is to release what he has loaned to his neighbor, he does not require it of his neighbor or his brother, because it is called the release of יהוה." (**Deuteronomy 15:1-2**)

The reason I bring this up is because the next Sabbatical Year is 2016 and it too is a Year of Release. If the nations of the world have not forgiven the debts of those who owe them, then you can count on this shaky financial market to continue to be highly volatile and unstable up to this point and then another major downturn is expected.

---

255 http://en.wikipedia.org/wiki/Late-2000s_recession

This will result in the kind of hyperinflation that will cause the price of food to go through the roof and this, in turn, will cause many more people around the world to go with less and less food.

I have now addressed with you the Pestilence and Famine that will, for certain, factor into this third Sabbatical Cycle. But Yeshua also said there would be Earthquakes.

I have two charts from a U.S. Geological Survey but at present, they are no longer on the U.S.G.S. website. On these two charts it shows you that from the year 1900 until recently, the deadly and destructive earthquakes between 6.0 and 8.0 in magnitude had more or less flatlined until the year 2000 at a rate of about five per year. Between 2000 and 2008, however, it goes up to thirty-five times per year.

The other chart shows you from 1966 to 2010. It shows the number of 6.0 and greater earthquakes during this time period. It mirrors the one I have just spoken of. Up to the year 2000 it averages about five a year and then it goes up to 35 until 2008. But for 2009 and 2010 it goes to over forty-five per year.[256] Again those charts are not there today. And also the data for 2012 seems to show a decrease.

Earthquakes > M6.0

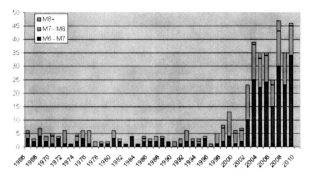

---

256 http://earthquake.usgs.gov/earthquakes/world/historical.php

The U.S. Geological Survey asks the following question:

Are Earthquakes Really On the Increase?[257]

I continue to be asked by many people throughout the world if Earthquakes are on the increase. Although it may seem that we have been experiencing more Earthquakes, Earthquakes of the magnitude 7.0 or greater have remained fairly constant throughout history.

A partial explanation may lie in the fact that in the last twenty years, we have definitely experienced a significant increase in the number of Earthquakes we have been able to locate each year. This is because of the tremendous increase in the number of seismograph stations in the world and the many improvements in global communications. In 1931, there were only about 350 stations operating in the world. Today, there are more than 8,000 stations and the data now comes in rapidly from these stations by electronic mail, internet and satellite. This increase in the number of stations and the more timely receipt of data has allowed seismological centers to pinpoint earthquakes more rapidly and positively identify many small earthquakes which went undetected in decades past. The N.E.I.C. (National Earthquake Information Center) now detects roughly 20,000 earthquakes each year or approximately fifty per day. Also, because of the improvements in communications and the increased interest in the environment and natural disasters, the public now hears more about earthquakes in the news, on channels like the Discovery Channel and the History Channel, not to mention the information at one's fingertips surfing the web.

According to seismology records dating back to 1900, one can expect, on the average, seventeen major earthquakes (7.0-7.9) and one cataclysmic earthquake (8.0 or above) in any given year.

You must decide for yourself, however, if they are on the rise or not.

But I have only covered the first three curses. We are currently in the third Sabbatical Cycle, which is accompanied by the respective curses of this third Sabbatical Cycle, alongside of the two curses that came before.

Just when you think it can't get any worse, you would do well to know

---

257 http://earthquake.usgs.gov/learn/topics/increase_in_earthquakes.php Copyright © 2005, The Geological Society of America, Inc. (GSA). All rights reserved. Copyright not claimed on content prepared wholly by U.S. government employees within scope of their employment.

there are two more curses we will all have to endure if we continue to refuse to obey Yehovah's Commandments.

> **23** "And if you are not instructed by Me by these, but walk contrary to Me, **24** then I also shall walk contrary to you, and I Myself shall smite you seven times for your sins. **25** And I shall bring against you a sword executing the vengeance of My covenant, and you shall gather together in your cities, and I shall send pestilence among you, and you shall be given into the hand of the enemy. **26** When I have cut off your supply of bread, ten women shall bake your bread in one oven, and they shall bring back to you your bread by weight, and you shall eat and not be satisfied."
> **(Leviticus 26:23-26)**

According to the Sabbatical Cycles as explained in my DVD[258] and illustrated to you in the charts in the back of *The Prophecies of Abraham*,[259] this Fourth Curse is to begin around 2017. With Pestilence and Famine being *a part of* the Third Curse, you can be assured in Yehovah's Word that all the underpinnings of the Third Curse will overlap into the Fourth Curse, but with the Fourth Curse being added to the previous three curses as a whole as well. This Fourth Curse then is the Sword of War. I will explain this Fourth Curse of War in my next book as I teach you the meaning of Daniel's 70 Weeks.

The U.S.A., the U.K. and her commonwealth countries will lose this upcoming war along with the State of Israel.

All the curses will then culminate in the Fifth and final Curse of Leviticus 26 that will follow on the heels of the other curses. You must read this and understand. It is speaking of you and those around you who will be forced into Captivity after losing the preceding war that was waged during the Fourth Curse.

> **27** "And if in spite of this, you do not obey Me, but walk contrary to Me, **28** then I shall walk contrary to you in wrath. And I Myself shall punish you seven times for your sins. **29** And you shall eat the flesh of your sons, and eat the flesh of your daughters. **30** And I shall destroy your high places, and cut down your sun-pillars, and put your carcasses on the carcasses of your idols. And My being shall loathe you. **31** And I shall turn your cities into ruins and lay your set-apart places waste, and not smell your sweet fragrances. **32** And I shall lay the land waste, and your enemies who dwell in it shall be astonished at it. **33** And I shall scatter

258 http://www.sightedmoon.com/?page_id=251
259 *The Prophecies of Abraham* by Joseph F. Dumond Published: February 2010 | ISBN: 9781449047528

you among the gentiles and draw out a sword after you. And your land shall be desert and your cities ruins, **34** and the land enjoy its Sabbaths as long as it lies waste and you are in your enemies' land. Then the land would rest and enjoy its Sabbaths. **35** As long as it lies waste it rests, for the time it did not rest on your Sabbaths when you dwelt in it. **36** And as for those of you who are left, I shall send faintness into their hearts in the lands of their enemies, and the sound of a shaken leaf shall cause them to flee. And they shall flee as though retreating from a sword, and they shall fall when no one pursues. **37** And they shall stumble over one another, as from before a sword, when no one pursues. And you shall be unable to stand before your enemies. **38** And you shall perish among the gentiles, and the land of your enemies shall eat you up, **39** and those of you who are left rot away in their crookedness in your enemies' lands, and also in their fathers' crookednesses rot away with them." (**Leviticus 26:27-39**)

This is the reason I began to speak out about this in 2005 and did the DVD in 2008 despite the fact I had never attempted anything like this ever before. This is also why I wrote *The Prophecies of Abraham* in 2009 and published it in 2010. Moreover, this is my primary motivation for why I am writing this book now and following up with another book shortly thereafter. Finally, this is why I remain faithful sharing prophecy as it unfolds each week around the world in my weekly newsletters.

It is because 90% of the U.S.A. and 90% of the U.K. and her Commonwealth are about to be destroyed from the coming War and subsequent Captivity that is about to strike. I will go into that in much more detail in my next book, as I have already mentioned.

The *Good News* being, you have the opportunity to repent *right now* and save yourself and your family from all of these terrors that are about to come upon you.

40 "But if they confess their crookedness and the crookedness of their fathers, with their trespass in which they trespassed against Me, and that they also have walked contrary to Me, **41** and that I also have walked contrary to them and have brought them into the land of their enemies—if their uncircumcised heart is then humbled, and they accept the punishment of their crookedness, **42** then I shall remember My covenant with Ya'aqob (Jacob), and also My covenant with Yitshaq (Isaac), and also remember My covenant with Abraham, and remember the land. **43** For the land was abandoned by them, and enjoying its Sabbaths while lying waste without them, and they were paying for their crookedness, because they rejected My right-rulings and because their being loathed My laws. **44** And yet for all this, when they are in the land of their enemies, I shall not reject them, nor shall I loathe them so as to destroy them and break My covenant with them. For I am יהוה their Elohim. **45** Then I shall remember for their sake the covenant of the ancestors whom I brought out of the land of Mitsrayim (Egypt) before the eyes of the nations to be their Elohim. I am יהוה." (**Leviticus 26:40-45**)

When Solomon had finished building the Temple and placed all the Holy things inside, he turned to the people and prayed this prayer:

26 "And now, O Elohim of Yisra'ĕl, please let Your word come true which You have spoken to Your servant Dawiḏ (David) my father. **27** For is it true: Elohim dwells on the earth? See, the heavens and the heavens of the heavens are unable to contain You, how much less this House which I have built! **28** Yet, shall You turn to the prayer of Your servant and his supplication, O יהוה my Elohim, and listen to the cry and the prayer which Your servant is praying before You today? **29** For Your eyes to be open toward this House night and day, toward the place of which You said, 'My Name is there,' to listen to the prayer which Your servant makes toward this place. **30** Then, shall You hear the supplication of Your servant and of Your people Yisra'ĕl when they pray toward this place, when You hear in Your dwelling place, in the heavens? And shall You hear, and forgive? **31** If anyone sins against his neighbor, and he has lifted up an oath on him, to cause him to swear, and comes and swears before Your altar in this House, **32** then hear in the heavens, and act and rightly rule Your servants, declaring the wrongdoer wrong, bringing his way on his head, and declaring the righteous right by giving him according to his righteousness. (**I Kings 8:26-32**)

33 "When Your people Yisra'ĕl are smitten before an enemy, because they have sinned against You, and they shall turn back to You and confess Your Name, and pray and make supplication to You in this House, **34** then hear in the heavens, and forgive the sin of Your people Yisra'ĕl, and bring them back to the land which You gave to their fathers. **35** When the heavens are shut up and there is no rain because they sin against You, when they pray toward this place and confess Your Name, and turn from their sin because You afflict them, **36** then hear in the heavens, and forgive the sin of Your servants, Your people Yisra'ĕl—for You teach them the good way in which they should walk—and shall give rain on Your land which You have given to Your people as an inheritance. **37** When there is scarcity of food in the land; when there is pestilence, blight, mildew, locusts, grasshoppers; when their enemy distresses them in the land of their cities; any plague, any sickness, **38** whatever prayer, whatever supplication made by anyone of all Your people Yisra'ĕl, each knowing the plague of his own heart, and shall spread out his hands toward this House, **39** then hear in the heavens, Your dwelling place, and forgive, and act, and render unto everyone according to all his ways, whose heart You know." (**I Kings 8:33-39**)

39 "Because You—You alone—know the hearts of all the sons of men, **40** so that they fear You all the days that they live in the land which You gave to our fathers. **41** Also, concerning a foreigner, who is not of Your people Yisra'ěl, but has come from a far land for Your Name's sake—**42** since they hear of Your great Name and Your strong hand and Your outstretched arm—and he shall come and pray toward this House, **43** hear in the heavens Your dwelling place, and do according to all for which the foreigner calls to You, so that all peoples of the earth know Your Name and fear You, as do Your people Yisra'ěl, and know that this House which I have built is called by Your Name. **44** When Your people go out to battle against their enemy, in the way that You send them, and they shall pray to יהוה toward the city which You have chosen and toward the House which I have built for Your Name, **45** then shall You hear in the heavens their prayer and their supplication, and maintain their cause?" (**I Kings 8:39-45**)

46 "When they sin against You—**for there is no one who does not sin**—and You become enraged with them and give them to the enemy, and they take them captive to the land of the enemy, far or near; **47** and they shall turn back unto their heart in the land where they have been taken captive, and shall turn, and make supplication to You in the land of those who took them captive, saying, 'We have sinned and acted crookedly, we have committed wrong,' **48** and they shall turn back to You with all their heart and with all their being in the land of their enemies who led them away captive, and shall pray to You toward their land which You gave to their fathers, the city which You have chosen and the House which I have built for Your Name, **49** then shall You hear in the heavens Your dwelling place their prayer and their supplication, and maintain their cause, **50** and forgive Your people who have sinned against You, and all their transgressions which they have transgressed against You? And give them compassion before those who took them captive, and they shall have compassion on them. **51** For they are Your people and Your inheritance, whom You brought out of Mitsrayim (Egypt), out of the iron furnace. **52** Let Your eyes be open to the supplication of Your servant and the supplication of Your people Yisra'ěl, to listen to them whenever they call to You. **53** For You have separated them unto Yourself for an inheritance, out of all the peoples of the earth, as You spoke by the hand of Your servant Mosheh (Moses), when You brought our fathers out of Mitsrayim (Egypt), O Masterיהוה ." (**I Kings 8:46-53**)

Brethren the time to repent is *now*. You need to ask Yehovah to forgive you, but you *also* need to begin walking in this new way of life with your whole heart and *in earnest*—which includes keeping the weekly seventh day Saturday Sabbath and the Holy Days of Leviticus 23 without adding to them or subtracting from them. Last, but not least, this also involves keeping the Sabbatical and Jubilee Years at the right time as they come upon you.

May Yehovah bless you and keep you from the coming terrors.

Appendix "A"

All the glory belongs to Yehovah. Now, more so than ever before, the following verse holds true:

> **19** For the intense longing of the creation eagerly waits for the revealing of the son of Elohim. (**Romans 8:19**)

I believe it to be His good and perfect will that we become intimately acquainted with the Sabbatical and Jubilee teachings at this time. It is all to His glory and any boasting I am about to do (or have done) is only because of what Yehovah reveals to all those who seek Him in earnest and look deeply into His Word of Truth. Keep in mind, I graduated from high school with an English GPA (grade point average) of only 51% and they gave that to me *only because* they did not want to see me back again. So, all the glory belongs to Yehovah and to no one else.

My first work (a DVD) came out in March of 2008. I had been speaking and writing about the Sabbatical and Jubilee years since August of 2005. I then began a series of newsletters in 2009 that would lead to the publishing of *The Prophecies of Abraham* in February, 2010. That being said, I would now like to take the time to share with you some new developments which have transpired since then that I have kept to myself until as of late.

Dear Joseph: March 20th, 2010

I have worked through your book as well as the DVD—two words: "mind-blowing!"

Apologies for taking some time, I did not want to rush through it. Please find attached the endorsement as requested. Hope this is what you were looking for.

p.s. Please feel free to improve the sentences if you need to.
p.p.s. See further below what this greeting entails.

With Shalom in Y'shua haMashiach I greet you, (see further below what this greeting entails)

Professor W.A. Liebenberg

Hebrew Roots Teaching Institute
Calvary University
South Africa

RE: Endorsement: *The Prophecies of Abraham*

Dear Joseph: March 19th, 2010

Herewith please find the endorsement as requested by you for the above mentioned book.

"If your future has always baffled you, this book is the key to unlock its mysteries. In my 15 years as an Eschatology and Hebraic Roots teacher, I've *never* run across a book that has made such an impact on me. I'm recommending this book to *every* student of mine who has been passionate with holy living and end-time events. If I knew then what I know now about YHWH's Jubilee Years, I'd rather become a Sabbatical/Jubilee researcher explaining YHWH's appointed judgments on an ignorant world not adhering to His instructions about His Appointed Times."

Thank you for your wisdom and sound teaching of this book. The video is well presented and to the point. It refutes any teaching attempting to prove that the Old Covenant and its principles are not in tact anymore.

Shalom,

Professor W.A. Liebenberg

Shalom Joseph:

Many thanks for your kind words.

I have spoken to the Professorate of Calvary University and they have accepted your book *Prophecies of Abraham* and your DVD *Chronological Order of Prophecies In the Jubilees* as part of the Curriculum for *both* Messianic Studies (Hebraic Roots) as well as for Midrashic Echatology (Jewish Eschatology). WELL DONE!!!

Again, well done my friend. Your material which you worked so hard on will now be ordered by every person globally enrolling from Diploma upwards. Your material is now University prescribed material. This does not happen every day!

Thanks a mill' Joseph, and once again, congratulations.

With Shalom in Y'shua haMashiach I greet you and yours, (see further below what this greeting entails).

Professor W.A. Liebenberg

Dear Joseph,   March 23rd, 2010

My friend, if YHWH can use a donkey and me, then surely He can use you as well. We are all simple people. Let me tell you something. Y'shua selected only the humble, simple man to become part of His team—tax collectors, fishermen, etc. Why will He not select you Joseph? He does not need the high and mighty professors and doctors who think they are clever enough to carry out His work. He needed you, and selected you out of 6.5 billion people in a single moment in time. He trusted you and birthed His ministry in you to execute it painstakingly.

You are a stunning presenter—I watched your DVD—and you are doing a tremendous work for YHWH. To be honest with you, your work is Doctorate Level research quality. You have proven something no man has proven before! Joseph, you must complete your Bachelor's Degree as soon as possible so that you can roll into go on to obtaining your Master's Degree!

Enjoy your visit in Jerusalem.

With Shalom in Y'shua haMashiach I greet you, (see further below what this greeting entails).

Professor W.A. Liebenberg

RE: Nomination of Joseph F. Dumond for a Nobel Humanitarian Prize

To the Nobel Committee:

RE: Nomination of Joseph F. Dumond for a Nobel Humanitarian Prize

Since 1901, the Nobel Prize has been awarded to men and women from all corners of the globe for outstanding achievements in physics, chemistry, physiology or medicine, literature, and for work in world peace. The Norwegian Nobel Committee defines humanitarian efforts as an essential part of promoting "fraternity among nations."

To my understanding, The Committee focused on a basic aspect of the word "humanitarian": helping to improve the lives of mankind and reduce suffering. Repeatedly, it has chosen human symbols, **or** people who, through their good deeds, can serve as examples for contemporary and future generations. According to The Committee, these "champions of brotherly love" or "self-sacrificing" men and women served the cause of peace by holding out a helping hand to victims of armed conflicts, etc. Men and women who wish to heal the wounds of war or to prevent a sure future catastrophic event, is in and of itself an important factor in the committee's deliberations.

The Committee strongly stressed that we *all* have a global responsibility and that the proud tradition of humanitarianism must also be put on the agenda of world politics. Therefore, I would like to nominate Mr. Joseph F. Dumond from Canada as a Laureate for the Humanitarian Prize, who in my mind, has put forth a tremendous effort to prevent a sure approaching catastrophic event.

Would you please be so kind to forward me the guidelines and procedure to nominate an individual? Thanking you kindly for your quick response.

Yours Sincerely,

Professor W.A. Liebenberg
Calvary University

The Swedish Academy
P.O. Box 2118
SE-103 13 Stockholm

Greetings to the Swedish Academy:

The Hebraic Roots Teaching Institute of South Africa has asked to have *The Prophecies of Abraham* added to your list of literature for nomination for the Nobel Prize In Literature.

The *Prophecies of Abraham* was published in March of 2010 and it has solved the question of when Sabbatical and Jubilee Years are and what it means for us today. Joseph F. Dumond the author of *The Prophecies of Abraham* has an international audience to whom he writes each week in which he explains the Sabbatical Years and how they repeatedly show us throughout history when diseases come at the same time during each Sabbatical and Jubilee Cycle. He also shows how major disasters come at the same repeated Sabbatical Cycles throughout history. You can read what other people have been saying about this most remarkable book at:

http://www.sightedmoonnl.com/?page_id=604

On your web page it is stated:

http://nobelprize.org/nobel_prizes/literature/articles/sture/index.html it is stated:

"What Strindberg is referring to is the fact that Alfred Nobel had stipulated in his will in 1895 that the Nobel Prize for literature should be awarded to the person who had produced 'the most outstanding work in an ideal direction.'"

With this in mind, Joseph F. Dumond has produced this year's most outstanding work—having proven beyond all doubt when the Sabbatical and Jubilee Years are. He also shows when the curses associated with these years are expected to come and what it means to us today. We strongly feel that this book must be seriously considered for this year's Nobel Prize.

Sincerely,

Professor W.A. Liebenberg
Calvary University

All of this I have kept under my hat and not said a word, as these things had to be done in secret. Today the awards were announced for the Nobel Prize In Literature:

Press Release
October 6th, 2011

The Nobel Prize In Literature 2011

Tomas Tranströmer

The Nobel Prize In Literature for 2011 is awarded to the Swedish Poet, Tomas Tranströmer.

Consequently, *The Prophecies of Abraham* did *not* win. But it *was* nominated, which is unbelievable in and of itself. I have shared this with you all so that this Feast year, you might tell others to read this book or watch the DVD and to give glory to Yehovah for the mighty things He is doing in all our lives in these Last Days.

Appendix "B"

There have been many things, which have taken place to date that I am currently at a loss to explain. I am now going to share with you these life-changing events in order to better show you how Yehovah has been very much at work *in* and a part *of* all of this.

I first began to question the validity of the Sabbath in 1982 and after proving it to be true, I began attending the Worldwide Church of God in Toronto, Canada. In 1994, I left this denomination as they began to return to the church teachings I had formerly stopped patterning my life after.

I then returned to working seven days a week for a time before I felt this huge hole in my innermost being. I began a day and night study to relay the foundation of all I had thought I believed in, not using any church literature. As I engaged in these studies, I began to write them down in article format.

In 1996, which I did not know at the time was the Jubilee Year, I learned of Noah's Ark and spoke at length to one Ron Wyatt on the phone just *one year prior to his death* in 1998. I was studying many things during this time and writing down everything I was learning along the way. I had an insatiable desire welling up from deep within me to prove everything from Noah's Ark to even the Messiah.

Then, in 2001, 9/11 took place and I thought the end was about to begin, so I returned to the United Church of God—one of over 800 offshoots of the Worldwide Church of God that came into existence after 1994. I was there for a season and during that time, they let me write for their church newspaper and their Good News magazine. I felt truly blessed by the magnanimous response from my readership and so many telling me how much they looked forward to reading my articles and contributions. The United Church of God was also grooming me to become a deacon during this time from 2001 until 2006 when I finally left.

In my researching and intensive study, I came under heavy conviction over the sins I was still engaging in and unable to stop doing. I felt spiritually sick and cut to the quick to where I felt I would never become a true, died in the wool, member of Yehovah's Kingdom if I kept it up.

In 2004, I read Daniel's confession in the following passage:

> **3** So I set my face toward יהוה the Elohim to seek by prayer and supplications, with fasting, and sackcloth, and ashes. **4** And I prayed to יהוה my Elohim, and made confession, and said, "O יהוה, great and awesome Ĕl, guarding the covenant and the kindness to those who love Him, and to those who guard His commands. **5** We have sinned and did crookedness, and did wrong and rebelled, to turn aside from Your commands and from Your right-rulings. **6** And we have not listened to Your servants the prophets, who spoke in Your Name to our sovereigns, our heads, and our fathers, and to all the people of the land. **7** O יהוה, to You is the righteousness, and to us the shame of face, as it is this day—to the men of Yehudah (Judah), to the inhabitants of Yerushalayim (Jerusalem) and all Yisra'ĕl, those near and those far off in all the lands to which You have driven them, because of their trespass which they have trespassed against You. **8** O Master, to us is the shame of face, to our sovereigns, to our heads, and to our fathers, because we have sinned against You. **9** To יהוה our Elohim are the compassions and forgivenesses, for we have rebelled against Him." **(Daniel 9:3-9)**

> **10** "And we have not obeyed the voice of יהוה our Elohim, to walk in His Torot (Torah plural), which He set before us through His servants the prophets. **11** And all Yisra'ĕl have transgressed Your Torah, and turned aside, so as not to obey Your voice. So the curse and the oath written in the Torah of Mosheh (Moses) the servant of Elohim have been poured out on us, for we have sinned against Him. **12** And He has confirmed His words, which He spoke against us and against our rulers who judged us, by bringing upon us great evil. For under all the heavens there has not been done like what was done to Yerushalayim (Jerusalem). **13** As it is written in the Torah of Mosheh (Moses), all this evil has come upon us, and we have not entreated the face of יהוה our Elohim, to turn back from our crookednesses, and to study Your truth. **14** Hence יהוה has watched over the evil and has brought it upon us. For יהוה our Elohim is righteous in all the works which He has done, but we have not obeyed His voice." **(Daniel 9:10-14)**

> **15** "And now, O יהוה our Elohim, who brought Your people out of the land of Mitsrayim (Egypt) with a strong hand, and made Yourself a Name, as it is this day—we have sinned, we have done wrong! **16** O יהוה, according to all Your righteousness, I pray, let Your displeasure and Your wrath be turned away from Your city Yerushalayim (Jerusalem),

Your set-apart mountain. For, because of our sins, and because of the crookednesses of our fathers, Yerushalayim (Jerusalem) and Your people have become a reproach to all those around us. **17** And now, our Elohim, hear the prayer of Your servant, and his supplications, and for the sake of יהוה cause Your face to shine on Your set-apart place, which is laid waste. **18** O my Elohim, incline Your ear and hear. Open Your eyes and see our wastes, and the city which is called by Your Name. For we do not present our supplications before You because of our righteous deeds, but because of Your great compassions. **19** O יהוה, hear! O יהוה, forgive! O יהוה, listen and act! Do not delay for Your own sake, my Elohim, for Your city and Your people are called by Your Name." (**Daniel 9:15-19**)

After reading this, I felt I had to repent and cry out to Yehovah in like manner. This passage began to prick my conscience the more I meditated upon it, to the point where, as I stated at the beginning of this book, I wrote out *all* my sins and made an appointment to meet with my pastor and confess my sins to him back in December of 2004. It took me the better part of two hours to read the entire account and he was willing to listen to it impartially and not judge me. Finally, someone knew my secret sins and was going to hold me accountable. A great weight had been lifted—or so it seemed.

It was shortly thereafter that I then learned about the debate between the Sighted Moon people, namely the Karaites and the Conjunction Moon adherents, namely the Hebrew Calendar devotees. I was quick to see the importance of learning all I possibly could about this, as it determined the beginning of the month and the count to each of the Holy Days of Leviticus 23. But, at that time, I was unable to prove which one was right.

After wrestling with it the entire winter and with Passover being only two months away, I prayed in earnest to Yehovah for an answer. He then led me to Isaiah 7 and Revelation 12. After that, He led me to the following passage in Matthew:

> **36** But concerning that day and the hour no one knows, not even the messengers of the heavens, but My Father only. (**Matthew 24:36**)

And it dawned on me that we could know when; we could not know the actual day and this is because this is speaking of the Feast of Trumpets, which depicts the day of the Messiah's triumphant return.[260] This was the day Yehshua was born on.[261]

---

260 *Conjunction or Sighted, Which?* http://www.sightedmoon.com/?page_id=22
261 *Return of Yehshua*, http://www.sightedmoon.com/?page_id=20

"Because you cannot know the day …" is a Hebrew idiom, which is indicative of the Feast of Trumpets. This then means the month begins *with* the Sighted Moon and *not* the Conjunction Moon currently being used in the Hebrew Calendar. I would later learn how this Hebrew Calendar came to be.

So I now had a test to pass in front of me. We are told in Exodus how Yehovah uses the Sabbath to test His people. So here you have a situation where the Passover season is just about to begin and my test was: which calendar was I going to keep? The unbiblical "Conjunction Moon" I had been following the past twenty-three years, or the biblically sanctioned Sighted Moon Method by which to begin the month?

I was still not 100% sure, so I decided to keep *both* Passovers on *both* days, and two Holy Days for the Days of Unleavened Bread and two more at the end of the Days of Unleavened Bread. Then the controversy really began because the Passovers would now be one month apart due to the barley being ripe early. This meant I had to keep the Holy Days of two calendar systems one month apart. So I set my mind to do *both* and to see for myself which one was right. This meant I was going to keep two Pentecosts, two Feast of Trumpets, two Day of Atonements and two Feasts of Tabernacles. And I did this.

As soon as I kept the first Passover according to the Sighted Moon Method with the barley being Aviv in Israel and before I had kept the second one, Yehovah revealed to me the Sabbatical Years.

I was wowed over this. I had been looking into this on and off for almost twenty years up until this point and now, "Voila!" there it was right in front of me as I read of the Sabbatical Years and Jubilee Cycles as explained by Qadesh La Yahweh Press.[262] And then I realized the curses that also lined up with this and began seeing it on the nightly news everywhere.

I tried to tell my pastor at the United Church of God, but he and the other elders did not want to hear me out on this or with regard to any of the other things I was learning.

I then wrote the article, *Time's Up! No More Excuses*,[263] in an effort to try and explain some of this, but I had not yet been asked the hard questions people ask in order to justify not keeping the Sabbatical Year.

As the Feast came in 2005, I decided to go with a group in New Hampshire who were keeping the Feast according to the barley and the Sighted Moon.

262 http://yahweh.org/yahweh2.html
263 http://www.sightedmoon.com/?page_id=53

I asked if I would be able to talk to someone about the Sabbatical Years and sent them my article entitled, *Time's Up! No More Excuses*. They wrote back and told me I *had* to teach this at the Feast that year, which was less than a month away.

I had never spoken at a Feast or Festival before and was scared to do so. They had me speak on the opening night. There were about fifty people presiding and I did a miserable job at presenting it. I went back to my tent and just cried.

That night I put a fleece out before Yehovah that if this was truly His message, He would make an opening in the speaking schedule as it currently was full with no wiggle room for anyone else. The very next morning as I entered the hall, the host was visibly upset. I went to talk to him and asked him what was wrong. He told me that one of his key speakers had just backed out and that this created three main teaching spots that were now vacant. I roared with laughter and then proceeded to explain to him what my prayer the night before had been all about. He wanted me to begin teaching that very same day, but I declined. I told him in three days' time I would be ready.

I then went and fasted for the entire time up to and including when I spoke. I also rewrote the entire message and prayed the entire three days.

At the onset of my presentation, there were over 100 people present and I remember like it was yesterday how not one person got up and moved the entire four hours while I presented this information to them. One fellow by the name of Steven Denke, who would later become a close friend, sat in the audience with an incredulous look upon his face the entire time. No one had heard anything like this before. They had kept the Sabbath and the Holy Days according to the Sighted Moon and the barley being Aviv, but never did they think they were still sinning because they had failed to keep the Sabbatical Years nor had they connected them to the curses happening then which are still happening now.

Yehovah had blessed my mouth, given them ears to hear and they "got" the message.

I then began to try and share this message and teaching with all the Church of God groups I could find, but was met with a great deal of resistance because I was not an elder, deacon or someone who had been raised up in the ministry.

For the second Feast I had determined in my heart to keep that year (2005), I was going to Israel for the first time on a tour with Don Esposito's group. We went to The North and to The South. I was very much in awe of

The Land and met so many people who actually *knew* their Bibles—at least they knew more than I did. While in Eliat, which is the southern tip of Israel, I was able to present this teaching for the second time to Don and about twelve others who joined us. Sadly, however, it was *not* well received.

On the last day of the tour, Don took us to the riverbed where David had, as a shepherd boy, picked up the stone he slew Goliath with. After reading the story, Don paused and then asked, "Who amongst you will stand in the gap? Which one of you are going to stand up and take on Goliath, despite the odds stacked against you and defend Yehovah's Torah and His way of life, come what may?"

I can remember saying to myself out loud that I would. I would stand up and do whatever needed to be done. Suffice it to say, I had *no* idea what I was in for. I was just responding to a question at the end of a Holy Land "tour of a lifetime."

On the last day of this tour, I went to where the Temple once stood in the Old City of David near the Gihon Spring. It was about 5:30am and the streets were empty. I went there to pray to Yehovah to thank Him for an awesome tour of His Land and for allowing me to finally see it for the very first time. I was, in fact, saying my goodbyes as I fully believed I would never be able to possibly afford to come back again.

The sun had not yet risen and the place where I was praying overlooked the Kidron Valley and was halfway down to the Gihon Spring. The hill in front of me was very steep and on that hill I suddenly saw two men stand up. I must have missed them before with my eyes closed praying. As I watched them, they began to walk up the hill in strides that seemed effortless. They then both jumped the railing just down the stairs from me and one began walking toward the Gihon Spring and the other came and stood at the edge of the platform I was praying on and fixed his gaze upon the Kidron Valley and never once looked at me.

I thought I was about to be mugged, so I clenched my fist just in case. I finished my prayer with one eye open, watching this guy closely the entire time. I said goodbye to Yehovah and left keeping an eye on this guy in case he followed me up the stairs. I went back to the group and finished the tour and then flew home.

By the end of that tour, Don had inspired and challenged me to engage in some deeper studies of the things he had spoken about on the tour. Once I had finished these studies, I could not believe what I had uncovered and had to come back to Israel in 2006 again for Sukkot.

I tried to speak to everyone I could about Israel and how awesome my first visit there was and also, about the things I was learning with regard to the Sighted Moon and the Sabbatical Years. By July of 2006, my pastor of the United Church of God asked me to come to a meeting and I thought this was going to be the perfect time to explain the Sabbatical Years without being interrupted.

But he had asked me to come to the meeting for no other reason than to determine if I wanted to keep attending. He then told me I had to stop talking about the Bible and the things I was studying. I was floored. I could not talk about these things at home with my unconverted wife, and now I was told I couldn't talk about them at church? What was I to do? Needless to say, my feet left that meeting and the rest of my body followed.

I contacted a certain individual and told him I had to get an Internet site up and running right away. The Internet was fairly new at this time so I did not know how to go about it. While we both were talking, he asked me what I wanted to call it. I said "The Berean Truth" site. Neither one of us could figure out how to spell "Berean" however. But, because we were also working on the moon logo, he proffered, "Why not call it "sightedmoon.com?" I took an instant liking to his suggestion and that was the beginning of my website. During the course of that very same week, I was asked not to come back by my pastor. I then posted all the articles I had researched on my new website and that is how it all started.

At the Feast of Tabernacles in 2006, I went back to Israel again and met many more brethren from around the world who were excited, studying, learning, and growing, just like me. I conducted my explorations at night and early in the morning. I was trying to prove the books I had read to be true or false as to the actual location of the Temple.

By the middle of the week, I had eliminated all the other potential sites and had taken a number of people on some small tours. There was only one place left to go at this point and this had to be the location of the crucifixion site for the Messiah. I attended a lesson led by Don and was just about to depart when a lady told me I had to hear her out. She had recently just had a dream about me and simply had to share it with me.

As a rule, I do not believe in dreams and am inclined to think those who tell others of their dreams are a bit loony. I was trying to ignore her and she grabbed my arm and pulled me closer to her and said, "Listen. I dreamed that Yehovah was drawing you closer to Himself." I asked her what it meant? She did not know, but she just had to tell me "That Yehovah was drawing me to Himself"

317

I said, "Thank you," and thought she was nuts. I then embarked upon my quest for the crucifixion site. Much to my surprise, I found it. But I could not be 100% sure, as there was no missing tomb and I could not find it anywhere. Yet, everything else lined up with what Josephus had said about the Temple.

Near the end of this tour, I brought some ladies over to the very same place and showed them what I had found and explained how. When they began to look around, one of them called me over to where she was standing and exclaimed, "Look at this!" And, lo and behold, it was an elaborate tomb with seven sepulchers inside. Moreover, it was just yards from the place I concluded to be the crucifixion site. I was beyond excited.

It was also on this trip that Don offered all of us an opportunity to mikveh (get re-baptized) in the Gihon Spring. The year before he did it in the Jordan, but it was green with sewage and I adamantly refused to get in the water. But the Gihon Spring was pure water that came roaring up from right out of the ground. I and a number of others were immersed that day and I remember the fellow who laid hands on me afterward while praying for my gifts to be enhanced. I did not think I had any gifts. Yet this was, in truth, what he had prayed.

Since that time, I have not been able to shut up about the Sabbatical and Jubilee Years. I have also been writing my weekly newsletters nonstop ever since Passover of 2007. I figured I only had enough material to write seven newsletters up to Pentecost that year. To date, as of 2012, there are now over 300 articles online—not all of them written by me.

I had now gone to Israel two times in my life and once again never conceived I would ever go back again. I had also just been kicked out of my church and, apart from the creation of my website, I was not exactly sure what to do next.

A friend then asked me to take him to Israel with me to show him all the things I had found and was talking about. He kept bugging me until I relented. In 2007, I again went to Jerusalem for Sukkot. That year, we booked our room right on the crucifixion site and my friend could not understand why we were staying there.

Each day I showed him all the things I had learned. Day by day we eliminated each of the traditional sites by exposing the facts found in the history books. By day three, he was ecstatic about all he was learning and wanted to mikveh in the Gihon Spring as I had. I also wanted to mikveh again in the Gihon Spring. While we were talking, a gentleman from France asked to join us and so the three of us raced down the path to the Gihon Spring to be the first ones in the spring to perform the mikveh.

In Leviticus it says that for each purification ceremony each thing that was required was done seven times and then the eighth time it was acceptable to Yehovah.

I told my friend from New Zealand this and we determined we would submerge ourselves seven times each and then once more for a total of eight times. When I was done, he followed suit and I then washed my new Tallit (Jewish prayer shawl) eight times over. We then prayed quietly. The man from France only watched and never mikveh'd. But he began to get excited and said, "What is happening?"

As we looked around, we were about twenty feet from the entrance into the waters of the Gihon Spring. We were in an underground tunnel that King Hezekiah had dug in 701 B.C. The air temperature was constant, but all around us a fog was forming and it was getting thicker and thicker as we looked on.

My friend Nevil asked me what was going on and I said I did not know. We could not even see our hands in front of us and each of us had become totally obscured by the fog yet we were all just a couple of feet apart.

While we were pondering the meaning or the cause of the fog that had just enveloped us, we began to hear footsteps from inside the tunnel coming toward us. This was very weird as we were the first ones in the tunnel. Again, each of asked the other what was going on and no one had the slightest clue. We started to walk in the direction of the footsteps which kept getting louder. Then suddenly, they stopped and the cloud lifted and we could all see each other again. Without uttering a single word, we all walked the rest of the way out of the tunnel and then back up to our rooms where we hung out our Tallits to dry on the Mount of Olives. It was noon before we would begin to talk about it, but we never were able to make sense of what had just happened.

The following year, I had decided to come *once again* to Israel in 2008. This time around, despite what little stock I take in dreams, it was I who had a dream. Three weeks before I came, I had a nightmare, no less. I dreamed I was in a German concentration camp as a P.O.W. (Prisoner of War). This was a war, still yet to come, set in the future. I and another fellow had asked the guards if we could go into this one building. We did and then when we came out my "master guard" was across the street from us diagonally speaking and began to yell at us and I did not understand him. But when he began to untie his whip, I understood and we both dropped to our knees and began to yell out, "We are guilty! We are guilty! WE *ARE* GUILTY!"

Each time he would crack the whip, it would snap right on the hairs of my nose, ears and cheeks. The whip never hit me, but the cracking of it was deafening. My guard cracked that whip twelve times and each time I screamed, "We are guilty!" The twelfth time, I yelled I was guilty and the whipping stopped. I awoke from the nightmare drenched with my own perspiration and my wife, whom I yelled at for not waking me, never heard a thing.

When I woke up, I knew the man in the dream doing the whipping was Yehshua and that is why He never *actually* struck me. But the part that was so upsetting to me was His face. It was the *very same* face of the man who had stood beside me in 2005 as I prayed above the Gihon Spring. He was right there and I did not recognize Him.

I returned to Israel in 2008 and gave a private tour of the things I had discovered and was also talking about.

At Passover in 2009, I had the privilege to meet the man who was going to be making the Korban (Corban) offering on the Temple mount on behalf of the Sanhedrin. I found him to be very interesting and wondered if this was going to start a "holy war" when he did it. It turned out that he was prohibited from making the Korban offering by the courts of Israel.

It was also in 2009 that I did a series of newsletters about the life of Abraham. People began to tell me I had to put all of the information contained within this newsletter series into one book so that it could be viewed all in one place instead of spread out over the course of so many newsletters. In response, I began to work on *The Prophecies of Abraham* at this time.

In 2009, many of us ended up staying at the Petra Hostel in the Old City. During our stay, we decided to organize our very own Feast site for those who were no longer allowed to fellowship with any of the other groups. We had walking tours and speakers each night and on one occasion there was a turnout of 175 people in all coming to the Petra to keep the Feast. We became the talk of the town that year and it was one of the best Feasts ever. This was also my first Sabbatical Year and I was determined to keep *all three* feasts in Israel that year and I did.

The Prophecies of Abraham was published in February 2010. And although I had never written anything except the News Letters, it has continued to be proven true in that it accurately mirrors the world events which have been taking place on the nightly news ever since.

Also in 2010, at Passover, a friend and I went to Israel for the purpose of making a freewill offering to Yehovah. We did not know how exactly to do this, so we finally decided upon the giving of a gift to a Jewish charity teaching about the Ten Tribes.

In 2010, we did as we had done in 2009 and hosted a Feast at the Petra. In addition, we conducted a couple of bus tours. Once again, we had a big turnout. We had a host of guest speakers each night and, like the year before; it proved itself to be another awesome Feast.

A lady came up to me during this Feast to remember. She was a good friend and went on to say, "I had a dream about you last night." Again I sighed, but she was a friend, so I listened. In her dream, all the leaders of the Hebraic Roots Movement were at a meeting in Jerusalem and they were all asking, "Where is Joe?" because I was not there. This lady then answered them in her dream saying, "He is in the outer courtyard, but can't find the door to get in. But he will be coming as soon as possible."

I asked her what it meant and she did not know. All she knew was that she felt compelled to share her dream with me. So I began to do some research. The outer courtyard was the courtyard of the Temple and this is where the lambs were sacrificed. The Door was and *is* Yehshua.

Now from the first dream of being drawn closer, when one makes an offering (or a freewill offering), that person is said to be drawing closer to Yehovah. So here I was in the outer courtyard making a freewill offering to Yehovah of myself—drawing closer to Him.

In 2011, there was a dispute, which caused us to separate from the Petra group. I then went with Avi Ben Mordechai[264] and co-hosted a tour in Israel for the Feast. It was another amazing time for me.

During this Feast, as I taught about the Sabbatical Years, I explained how this message was going to be taken from the Ten Lost Tribes and shared with the Asian world. This is what was impressed upon me from my study of Matthew 22. What was so amazing was that over half the audience that year *was* from Asia and we were witnessing prophetic history in the making, taking place right in front of us.

I was unable to announce it to anyone before the Feast in 2011, but *The Prophecies of Abraham* had been nominated that year for a Nobel Prize, of which you can read about in Appendix "A." My book did not win but it was nominated, which was a huge honor.

---

264 http://www.m7000.com/

This year—the year 2012—the breach between us and the Petra group was finally repaired, so we agreed to work together for the Feast this year.

As you can see, each and every year I have gone to Israel, something truly remarkable and inexplicable has taken place or, if nothing else, we have all been blessed beyond words while experiencing one incredible time after another with one another. I wanted to share these things with you so that 1). I do not forget and 2). To show you how Yehovah is at work in our lives. I am no different than you. All I did was say, "Here am I Yehovah, send me. I will stand in the gap." And somewhere in the midst of it all, my newsletter grew from being one in which no one read to one that has now caught the attention of over 11,000 readers who span the globe. The web site is about to pass 2 Million hits and all of this since 2005 when I was first shown these truths, and then in 2006 when the web site began and then from 2007 when I began to write on a weekly basis the News Letter for Sightedmoon.com.

Appendix "C"

During each one of these days of Counting the Omer to Pentecost, Jewish tradition has developed around reading the Psalms on certain days. I find this to be very beneficial. It is customary that following the "Counting of the Omer," one recites Psalm 67, for according to tradition, that Psalm has forty-nine words, which corresponds perfectly to the forty-nine days of the "Counting of the Omer."

And as you meditate on and do these readings, which includes the Counting of the Omer command, keep in mind what this symbolizes. It is the counting of the Sabbatical and Jubilee Years and where we are in that cycle. We are in the seventeenth year in 2012, which corresponds to the seventeenth day of the "Counting of the Omer."

Counting Of the Omer

WEEK ONE

Day One | The Law of Yehovah | Psalm 119:1-8
This first day will begin on the Sunday during the Days of Unleavened Bread.

Today is the first day of the first week of seven weeks. Today is the first day of the counting of fifty days from the day of the waving of the Omer on the morrow after the Sabbath.[265]

> **1** Elohim does favor us and bless us. Cause His face to shine upon us. Selah. (**Psalm 67:1**)

---

265 http://www.karaite-korner.org/omer.shtml

2 For Your way to be known on earth, Your deliverance among all nations. (**Psalm 67:2**)

3 Let the peoples praise You, O Elohim, let all the peoples praise You. (**Psalm 67:3**)

4 Let the nations be glad and sing for joy! For You judge the peoples uprightly, and lead the nations on earth. Selah. (**Psalm 67:4**)

5 Let the peoples praise You, O Elohim; let all the peoples praise You. (**Psalm 67:5**)

6 The earth shall give her increase; Elohim, our own Elohim, blesses us! (**Psalm 67:6**)

7 Elohim blesses us! And all the ends of the earth fear Him! (**Psalm 67:7**)

1 Blessed are the perfect in the way, who walk in the Torah of יהוה! (**Psalm 119:1**)

2 Blessed are those who observe His witnesses, who seek Him with all their heart! (**Psalm 119:2**)

3 Yea, they shall do no unrighteousness; they shall walk in His ways. (**Psalm 119:3**)

4 You have commanded us to guard Your orders diligently. (**Psalm 119:4**)

5 Oh, that my ways were established to guard Your laws! (**Psalm 119:5**)

6 Then I would not be ashamed, when I look into all Your commands. (**Psalm 119:6**)

7 I thank You with uprightness of heart, when I learn the right-rulings of Your righteousness. (**Psalm 119:7**)

8 I guard Your laws; oh, do not leave me entirely! (**Psalm 119:8**)

Day Two | Obedience To the Law of Yehovah | Psalm 119:9-16

Today is the second day of the first week of seven weeks. Today is the second day of the counting of fifty days from the day of the waving of the Omer on the morrow after the Sabbath.

1 Elohim does favor us and bless us. Cause His face to shine upon us. Selah. (**Psalm 67:1**)

2 For Your way to be known on earth, Your deliverance among all nations. (**Psalm 67:2**)

3 Let the peoples praise You, O Elohim, let all the peoples praise You. (**Psalm 67:3**)

4 Let the nations be glad and sing for joy! For You judge the peoples uprightly, and lead the nations on earth. Selah. (**Psalm 67:4**)

5 Let the peoples praise You, O Elohim; let all the peoples praise You. (**Psalm 67:5**)

6 The earth shall give her increase; Elohim, our own Elohim, blesses us! (**Psalm 67:6**)

7 Elohim blesses us! And all the ends of the earth fear Him! (**Psalm 67:7**)

9 How would a young man cleanse his path? To guard it according to Your Word? (**Psalm 119:9**)

10 I have sought You with all my heart; let me not stray from Your commands! (**Psalm 119:10**)

11 I have treasured up Your word in my heart, that I might not sin against You. (**Psalm 119:11**)

12 Blessed are You, O יהוה! Teach me Your laws. (**Psalm 119:12**)

13 With my lips I have recounted all the right-rulings of Your mouth. (**Psalm 119:13**)

14 I have rejoiced in the way of Your witnesses, as over all riches. (**Psalm 119:14**)

15 I meditate on Your orders, and regard Your ways. (**Psalm 119:15**)

16 I delight myself in Your laws; I do not forget Your Word. (**Psalm 119:16** | Footnote: ¹See also vv. **119:24, 119:35, 119:47, 119:70, 119:77, 119:92, 119:143, 119:174; Romans 7:22**)

Day Three | Happiness In the Law of Yehovah | Psalm 119:17-24

Today is the third day of the first week of seven weeks. Today is the third day of the counting of fifty days from the day of the waving of the Omer on the morrow after the Sabbath.

1 Elohim does favor us and bless us. Cause His face to shine upon us. Selah. (**Psalm 67:1**)

2 For Your way to be known on earth, Your deliverance among all nations. (**Psalm 67:2**)

3 Let the peoples praise You, O Elohim, let all the peoples praise You. (**Psalm 67:3**)

4 Let the nations be glad and sing for joy! For You judge the peoples uprightly, and lead the nations on earth. Selah. (**Psalm 67:4**)

5 Let the peoples praise You, O Elohim; let all the peoples praise You. (**Psalm 67:5**)

6 The earth shall give her increase; Elohim, our own Elohim, blesses us! (**Psalm 67:6**)

7 Elohim blesses us! And all the ends of the earth fear Him! (**Psalm 67:7**)

17 Do good to Your servant, let me live and I guard Your Word. (**Psalm 119:17**)

18 Open my eyes, that I might see wonders from Your Torah. (**Psalm 119:18**)

19 I am a sojourner in the earth. Do not hide Your commands from me. (**Psalm 119:19**)

20 My being is crushed with longing for Your right-rulings at all times. (**Psalm 119:20**)

21 You rebuked the proud, cursed ones, who are straying from Your commands. (**Psalm 119:21**)

22 Remove from me reproach and scorn, for I have observed Your witnesses. (**Psalm 119:22**)

23 Though princes sat, speaking against me, Your servant meditates on Your laws. (**Psalm 119:23**)

24 Your witnesses also are my delight, my counselors. (**Psalm 119:24**)

Day Four | Determination To Obey the Law of Yehovah | Psalm 119:25-32

Today is the fourth day of the first week of seven weeks. Today is the fourth day of the counting of fifty days from the day of the waving of the Omer on the morrow after the Sabbath.

1 Elohim does favor us and bless us. Cause His face to shine upon us. Selah. (**Psalm 67:1**)

2 For Your way to be known on earth, Your deliverance among all nations. (**Psalm 67:2**)

3 Let the peoples praise You, O Elohim, let all the peoples praise You. (**Psalm 67:3**)

4 Let the nations be glad and sing for joy! For You judge the peoples uprightly, and lead the nations on earth. Selah. (**Psalm 67:4**)

5 Let the peoples praise You, O Elohim; let all the peoples praise You. (**Psalm 67:5**)

6 The earth shall give her increase; Elohim, our own Elohim, blesses us! (**Psalm 67:6**)

7 Elohim blesses us! And all the ends of the earth fear Him! (**Psalm 67:7**)

25 My being has been clinging to the dust; revive me according to Your Word. (**Psalm 119:25**)

26 I have recounted my ways and You answered me; teach me Your laws. (**Psalm 119:26**)

27 Make me understand the way of Your orders; that I might meditate on Your wonders. (**Psalm 119:27**)

28 My being has wept from grief; strengthen me according to Your Word. (**Psalm 119:28**)

29 Remove from me the way of falsehood, and favor me with Your Torah. (**Psalm 119:29**)

30 I have chosen the way of truth; Your right-rulings I have held level. (**Psalm 119:30**)

31 I have clung to Your witnesses; O יהוה, do not put me to shame! (**Psalm 119:31**)

32 I run the way of Your commands, for You enlarge my heart. (**Psalm 119:32**)

Day Five | A Prayer For Understanding | Psalm 119:33-40

Today is the fifth day of the first week of seven weeks. Today is the fifth day of the counting of fifty days from the day of the waving of the Omer on the morrow after the Sabbath.

1 Elohim does favor us and bless us. Cause His face to shine upon us. Selah. (**Psalm 67:1**)

2 For Your way to be known on earth, Your deliverance among all nations. (**Psalm 67:2**)

3 Let the peoples praise You, O Elohim, let all the peoples praise You. (**Psalm 67:3**)

4 Let the nations be glad and sing for joy! For You judge the peoples uprightly, and lead the nations on earth. Selah. (**Psalm 67:4**)

5 Let the peoples praise You, O Elohim; let all the peoples praise You. (**Psalm 67:5**)

6 The earth shall give her increase; Elohim, our own Elohim, blesses us! (**Psalm 67:6**)

7 Elohim blesses us! And all the ends of the earth fear Him! (**Psalm 67:7**)

33 Teach me, O יהוה, the way of Your laws, and I observe it to the end. (**Psalm 119:33**)

34 Make me understand, that I might observe Your Torah, and guard it with all my heart. (**Psalm 119:34**)

35 Make me walk in the path of Your commands, for I have delighted in it. (**Psalm 119:35**)

36 Incline my heart to Your witnesses, and not to own gain. (**Psalm 119:36**)

37 Turn away my eyes from looking at falsehood, and revive me in Your way. (**Psalm 119:37**)

38 Establish Your Word to Your servant, which leads to the fear of You. (**Psalm 119:38**)

39 Turn away my reproach which I dread, for Your right-rulings are good. (**Psalm 119:39**)

40 See, I have longed for Your orders; revive me in Your righteousness. (**Psalm 119:40**)

Day Six | Trusting the Law of Yehovah | Psalm 119:41-48

Today is the sixth day of the first week of seven weeks. Today is the sixth day of the counting of fifty days from the day of the waving of the Omer on the morrow after the Sabbath.

> **1** Elohim does favor us and bless us. Cause His face to shine upon us. Selah. **(Psalm 67:1)**
> **2** For Your way to be known on earth, Your deliverance among all nations. **(Psalm 67:2)**
> **3** Let the peoples praise You, O Elohim, let all the peoples praise You. **(Psalm 67:3)**
> **4** Let the nations be glad and sing for joy! For You judge the peoples uprightly, and lead the nations on earth. Selah. **(Psalm 67:4)**
> **5** Let the peoples praise You, O Elohim; let all the peoples praise You. **(Psalm 67:5)**
> **6** The earth shall give her increase; Elohim, our own Elohim, blesses us! **(Psalm 67:6)**
> **7** Elohim blesses us! And all the ends of the earth fear Him! **(Psalm 67:7)**

> **41** And let Your kindnesses come to me, O יהוה; Your deliverance, according to Your Word. **(Psalm 119:41)**
> **42** So that I answer my reprover, for I have trusted in Your Word. **(Psalm 119:42)**
> **43** And do not take away from my mouth the word of truth entirely, for I have waited for Your right-rulings. **(Psalm 119:43)**
> **44** That I might guard Your Torah continually, forever and ever. **(Psalm 119:44)**
> **45** That I might walk in a broad place, for I have sought Your orders. **(Psalm 119:45)**
> **46** That I might speak of Your witnesses before sovereigns, and not be ashamed. **(Psalm 119:46)**
> **47** That I might delight myself in Your commands, which I have loved. **(Psalm 119:47)**
> **48** That I might lift up my hands to Your commands, which I have loved; while I meditate on Your laws. **(Psalm 119:48)**

Day Seven | Is the 1ˢᵗ Shabbat | Confidence In the Law of Yehovah | Psalm 119:49-56

Today is the seventh day of the first week of seven weeks. Today is the seventh day of the counting of fifty days from the day of the waving of the Omer on the morrow after the Sabbath. Today is Sabbath, the first Sabbath of seven Sabbaths. Today completes the first week of seven weeks.

1 Elohim does favor us and bless us. Cause His face to shine upon us. Selah. **(Psalm 67:1)**

2 For Your way to be known on earth, Your deliverance among all nations. **(Psalm 67:2)**

3 Let the peoples praise You, O Elohim, let all the peoples praise You. **(Psalm 67:3)**

4 Let the nations be glad and sing for joy! For You judge the peoples uprightly, and lead the nations on earth. Selah. **(Psalm 67:4)**

5 Let the peoples praise You, O Elohim; let all the peoples praise You. **(Psalm 67:5)**

6 The earth shall give her increase; Elohim, our own Elohim, blesses us! **(Psalm 67:6)**

7 Elohim blesses us! And all the ends of the earth fear Him! **(Psalm 67:7)**

49 Remember the word to Your servant, on which You have caused me to wait. **(Psalm 119:49)**

50 This is my comfort in my affliction, for Your word has given me life. **(Psalm 119:50)**

51 The proud have utterly scorned me, I did not turn aside from Your Torah. **(Psalm 119:51)**

52 I remembered Your right-rulings of old, O יהוה, and I comfort myself. **(Psalm 119:52)**

53 Rage has seized me because of the wrong who forsake Your Torah. **(Psalm 119:53)**

54 Your laws have been my songs in the place of my sojournings. **(Psalm 119:54)**

55 I have remembered Your Name in the night, O יהוה, and I guard Your Torah. **(Psalm 119:55)**

56 This has become mine, because I have observed Your orders. **(Psalm 119:56)**

WEEK TWO

Day Eight | Devotion To the Law of Yehovah | Psalm 119:57-64
Today is the first day of the second week of seven weeks. Today is the eighth day of the counting of fifty days from the day of the waving of the Omer on the morrow after the Sabbath.

1 Elohim does favor us and bless us. Cause His face to shine upon us. Selah. **(Psalm 67:1)**

2 For Your way to be known on earth, Your deliverance among all nations. **(Psalm 67:2)**

3 Let the peoples praise You, O Elohim, let all the peoples praise You. (**Psalm 67:3**)

4 Let the nations be glad and sing for joy! For You judge the peoples uprightly, and lead the nations on earth. Selah. (**Psalm 67:4**)

5 Let the peoples praise You, O Elohim; let all the peoples praise You. (**Psalm 67:5**)

6 The earth shall give her increase; Elohim, our own Elohim, blesses us! (**Psalm 67:6**)

7 Elohim blesses us! And all the ends of the earth fear Him! (**Psalm 67:7**)

57 You are my portion, O יהוה; I have promised to guard Your words. (**Psalm 119:57**)

58 I have sought Your face with all my heart. Show me favor according to Your Word. (**Psalm 119:58**)

59 I have thought upon my ways, and turned my feet to Your witnesses. (**Psalm 119:59**)

60 I have hurried, and did not delay to guard Your commands. (**Psalm 119:60**)

61 The cords of the wrong have surrounded me, Your Torah I have not forgotten. (**Psalm 119:61**)

62 At midnight I rise to give thanks to You, for Your righteous right-rulings. (**Psalm 119:62**)

63 I am a companion of all who fear You, and of those guarding Your orders. (**Psalm 119:63**)

64 O יהוה, Your kindness has filled the earth. Teach me Your laws. (**Psalm 119:64**)

Day Nine | The Value of the Law of Yehovah | Psalm 119:65-72

Today is the second day of the second week of seven weeks. Today is the ninth day of the counting of fifty days from the day of the waving of the Omer on the morrow after the Sabbath.

1 Elohim does favor us and bless us. Cause His face to shine upon us. Selah. (**Psalm 67:1**)

2 For Your way to be known on earth, Your deliverance among all nations. (**Psalm 67:2**)

3 Let the peoples praise You, O Elohim, let all the peoples praise You. (**Psalm 67:3**)

4 Let the nations be glad and sing for joy! For You judge the peoples uprightly, and lead the nations on earth. Selah. (**Psalm 67:4**)

5 Let the peoples praise You, O Elohim; let all the peoples praise You. (**Psalm 67:5**)

6 The earth shall give her increase; Elohim, our own Elohim, blesses us! (**Psalm 67:6**)

7 Elohim blesses us! And all the ends of the earth fear Him! (**Psalm 67:7**)

65 You have done good to Your servant, O יהוה, according to Your Word. (**Psalm 119:65**)

66 Teach me good **sense** and knowledge, for I have trusted in Your commands. (**Psalm 119:66**)

67 Before I was afflicted I myself was going astray, but now I have guarded Your Word. (**Psalm 119:67**)

68 You are good, and do good. Teach me Your laws. (**Psalm 119:68**)

69 The proud have forged a lie against me. With all *my* heart I observe Your orders. (**Psalm 119:69**)

70 Their heart has become like fat, without feeling. I have delighted in Your Torah. (**Psalm 119:70**)

71 It was good for me that I was afflicted, that I might learn Your laws. (**Psalm 119:71**)

72 The Torah of Your mouth is better to me than thousands of gold and silver pieces. (**Psalm 119:72**)

Day Ten | The Justice of the Law of Yehovah | Psalm 119:73-80

Today is the third day of the second week of seven weeks. Today is the tenth day of the counting of fifty days from the day of the waving of the Omer on the morrow after the Sabbath.

1 Elohim does favor us and bless us. Cause His face to shine upon us. Selah. (**Psalm 67:1**)

2 For Your way to be known on earth, Your deliverance among all nations. (**Psalm 67:2**)

3 Let the peoples praise You, O Elohim, let all the peoples praise You. (**Psalm 67:3**)

4 Let the nations be glad and sing for joy! For You judge the peoples uprightly, and lead the nations on earth. Selah. (**Psalm 67:4**)

5 Let the peoples praise You, O Elohim; let all the peoples praise You. (**Psalm 67:5**)

6 The earth shall give her increase; Elohim, our own Elohim, blesses us! (**Psalm 67:6**)

7 Elohim blesses us! And all the ends of the earth fear Him! (**Psalm 67:7**)

73 Your hands have made me and formed me; make me understand, that I might learn Your commands. (**Psalm 119:73**)

74 Those who fear You see me and rejoice, for I have waited for Your Word. **(Psalm 119:74)**

75 I know, O יהוה, that Your right-rulings are righteous, and in trustworthiness You have afflicted me. **(Psalm 119:75)**

76 Please let Your kindness be for my comfort, according to Your Word to Your servant. **(Psalm 119:76)**

77 Let Your compassions come to me, that I might live, for Your Torah is my delight. **(Psalm 119:77)**

78 Let the proud be put to shame, for with lies they perverted me; *but* I study Your orders. **(Psalm 119:78)**

79 Let those who fear You turn to me, and those who know Your witnesses. **(Psalm 119:79)**

80 Let my heart be perfect in Your laws, so that I am not put to shame. **(Psalm 119:80)**

Day Eleven | Prayer For Deliverance | Psalm 119:81-88

Today is the fourth day of the second week of seven weeks. Today is the eleventh day of the counting of fifty days from the day of the waving of the Omer on the morrow after the Sabbath.

1 Elohim does favor us and bless us. Cause His face to shine upon us. Selah. **(Psalm 67:1)**

2 For Your way to be known on earth, Your deliverance among all nations. **(Psalm 67:2)**

3 Let the peoples praise You, O Elohim, let all the peoples praise You. **(Psalm 67:3)**

4 Let the nations be glad and sing for joy! For You judge the peoples uprightly, and lead the nations on earth. Selah. **(Psalm 67:4)**

5 Let the peoples praise You, O Elohim; let all the peoples praise You. **(Psalm 67:5)**

6 The earth shall give her increase; Elohim, our own Elohim, blesses us! **(Psalm 67:6)**

7 Elohim blesses us! And all the ends of the earth fear Him! **(Psalm 67:7)**

81 For Your deliverance my being has pined away, for I have waited for Your Word. **(Psalm 119:81)**

82 My eyes have pined away for Your Word, saying, "When would it comfort me?" **(Psalm 119:82)**

83 For I have become like a wineskin in the smoke, Your laws I have not forgotten. **(Psalm 119:83)**

84 How many are the days of Your servant? When do You execute right-ruling on those who persecute me? **(Psalm 119:84)**

85 The proud have dug pits for me, which is not according to Your Torah. **(Psalm 119:85)**

86 All Your commands are trustworthy. They have persecuted me with lies. Help me! **(Psalm 119:86)**

87 They almost made an end of me on earth, but I, I did not forsake Your orders. **(Psalm 119:87)**

88 Revive me according to Your kindness, that I might guard the witness of Your mouth. **(Psalm 119:88)**

Day Twelve | In the Law of Yehovah | Psalm 119:89-96

Today is the fifth day of the second week of seven weeks. Today is the twelfth day of the counting of fifty days from the day of the waving of the Omer on the morrow after the Sabbath.

1 Elohim does favor us and bless us. Cause His face to shine upon us. Selah. **(Psalm 67:1)**

2 For Your way to be known on earth, Your deliverance among all nations. **(Psalm 67:2)**

3 Let the peoples praise You, O Elohim, let all the peoples praise You. **(Psalm 67:3)**

4 Let the nations be glad and sing for joy! For You judge the peoples uprightly, and lead the nations on earth. Selah. **(Psalm 67:4)**

5 Let the peoples praise You, O Elohim; let all the peoples praise You. **(Psalm 67:5)**

6 The earth shall give her increase; Elohim, our own Elohim, blesses us! **(Psalm 67:6)**

7 Elohim blesses us! And all the ends of the earth fear Him! **(Psalm 67:7)**

89 Forever, O יהוה, Your Word stands firm in the heavens. **(Psalm 119:89)**

90 Your trustworthiness is to all generations; You established the earth, and it stands. **(Psalm 119:90)**

91 According to Your right-rulings, they have stood to this day, for all are Your servants. **(Psalm 119:91)**

92 If Your Torah had not been my delight, I would have perished in my affliction. **(Psalm 119:92)**

93 Let me never forget Your orders, for by them You have given me life. **(Psalm 119:93)**

94 I am Yours, save me; for I have sought Your orders. **(Psalm 119:94)**

95 The wrong have waited for me to destroy me; I understand Your witnesses. **(Psalm 119:95)**

96 I have seen an end of all perfection; Your command is exceedingly broad. **(Psalm 119:96)**

Day Thirteen | Love For the Law of Yehovah | Psalm 119:97-104
Today is the sixth day of the second week of seven weeks. Today is the thirteenth day of the counting of fifty days from the day of the waving of the Omer on the morrow after the Sabbath.

> **1** Elohim does favor us and bless us. Cause His face to shine upon us. Selah. (**Psalm 67:1**)
> **2** For Your way to be known on earth, Your deliverance among all nations. (**Psalm 67:2**)
> **3** Let the peoples praise You, O Elohim, let all the peoples praise You. (**Psalm 67:3**)
> **4** Let the nations be glad and sing for joy! For You judge the peoples uprightly, and lead the nations on earth. Selah. (**Psalm 67:4**)
> **5** Let the peoples praise You, O Elohim; let all the peoples praise You. (**Psalm 67:5**)
> **6** The earth shall give her increase; Elohim, our own Elohim, blesses us! (**Psalm 67:6**)
> **7** Elohim blesses us! And all the ends of the earth fear Him! (**Psalm 67:7**)

> **97** O how I love Your Torah[1]! It is my study all day long. (**Psalm 119:97** | Footnote: [1]See also vv. **119:113, 119:119, 119:127, 119:163, 119:165, 119:167**)
> **98** Your commands make me wiser than my enemies; for it is ever before me. (**Psalm 119:98**)
> **99** I have more understanding than all my teachers, for Your witnesses are my study. (**Psalm 119:99**)
> **100** I understand more than the aged, for I have observed Your orders. (**Psalm 119:100**)
> **101** I have restrained my feet from every evil way, that I might guard Your Word. (**Psalm 119:101**)
> **102** I have not turned aside from Your right-rulings, for You Yourself have taught me. (**Psalm 119:102**)
> **103** How sweet to my taste has Your Word been, more than honey to my mouth! (**Psalm 119:103**)
> **104** From Your orders I get understanding; therefore I have hated every false way. (**Psalm 119:104**)

Day Fourteen | Light From the Law of Yehovah | Psalm 119:105-112
Today is the seventh day of the second week of seven weeks. Today is the fourteenth day of the counting of fifty days from the day of the waving of the Omer on the morrow after the Sabbath. Today is Sabbath, the second Sabbath of seven Sabbaths. Today completes the second week of seven weeks.

1 Elohim does favor us and bless us. Cause His face to shine upon us. Selah. **(Psalm 67:1)**

2 For Your way to be known on earth, Your deliverance among all nations. **(Psalm 67:2)**

3 Let the peoples praise You, O Elohim, let all the peoples praise You. **(Psalm 67:3)**

4 Let the nations be glad and sing for joy! For You judge the peoples uprightly, and lead the nations on earth. Selah. **(Psalm 67:4)**

5 Let the peoples praise You, O Elohim; let all the peoples praise You. **(Psalm 67:5)**

6 The earth shall give her increase; Elohim, our own Elohim, blesses us! **(Psalm 67:6)**

7 Elohim blesses us! And all the ends of the earth fear Him! **(Psalm 67:7)**

105 Your Word is a lamp to my feet and a light to my path. **(Psalm 119:105)**

106 I have sworn, and I confirm, to guard Your righteous right-rulings. **(Psalm 119:106)**

107 I have been afflicted very much; O יהוה, revive me according to Your Word. **(Psalm 119:107)**

108 Please accept the voluntary offerings of my mouth, O יהוה, and teach me Your right-rulings. **(Psalm 119:108)**

109 My life is in my hand continually, and Your Torah I have not forgotten. **(Psalm 119:109)**

110 The wrong have laid a snare for me, but I have not strayed from Your orders. **(Psalm 119:110)**

111 Your witnesses are my inheritance forever, for they are the joy of my heart. **(Psalm 119:111)**

112 I have inclined my heart to do Your laws forever, to the end. **(Psalm 119:112)**

WEEK THREE

Day Fifteen | Safety In the Law Of Yehovah | Psalm 119:113-120
Today is the first day of the third week of seven weeks. Today is the fifteenth day of the counting of fifty days from the day of the waving of the Omer on the morrow after the Sabbath.

1 Elohim does favor us and bless us. Cause His face to shine upon us. Selah. **(Psalm 67:1)**

2 For Your way to be known on earth, Your deliverance among all nations. **(Psalm 67:2)**

3 Let the peoples praise You, O Elohim, let all the peoples praise You. (**Psalm 67:3**)

4 Let the nations be glad and sing for joy! For You judge the peoples uprightly, and lead the nations on earth. Selah. (**Psalm 67:4**)

5 Let the peoples praise You, O Elohim; let all the peoples praise You. (**Psalm 67:5**)

6 The earth shall give her increase; Elohim, our own Elohim, blesses us! (**Psalm 67:6**)

7 Elohim blesses us! And all the ends of the earth fear Him! (**Psalm 67:7**)

113 I have hated doubting thoughts, but I have loved Your Torah. (**Psalm 119:113**)

114 You are my hiding place and my shield; I have waited for Your Word. (**Psalm 119:114**)

115 Turn away from me, you evil-doers, for I observe the commands of my Elohim! (**Psalm 119:115**)

116 Support me according to Your Word, that I might live; and put me not to shame because of my expectation. (**Psalm 119:116**)

117 Sustain me, that I might be saved, and always look to Your laws. (**Psalm 119:117**)

118 You have made light of all those who stray from Your laws, for falsehood is their deceit. (**Psalm 119:118**)

119 You have made to cease all the wrong of the earth, like dross; therefore I have loved Your witnesses. (**Psalm 119:119**)

120 My flesh has trembled for fear of You, and I am in awe of Your right-rulings. (**Psalm 119:120**)

Day Sixteen | Obedience To the Law of Yehovah | Psalm 119:121-128

Today is the second day of the third week of seven weeks. Today is the sixteenth day of the counting of fifty days from the day of the waving of the Omer on the morrow after the Sabbath.

1 Elohim does favor us and bless us. Cause His face to shine upon us. Selah. (**Psalm 67:1**)

2 For Your way to be known on earth, Your deliverance among all nations. (**Psalm 67:2**)

3 Let the peoples praise You, O Elohim, let all the peoples praise You. (**Psalm 67:3**)

4 Let the nations be glad and sing for joy! For You judge the peoples uprightly, and lead the nations on earth. Selah. (**Psalm 67:4**)

5 Let the peoples praise You, O Elohim; let all the peoples praise You. (**Psalm 67:5**)

6 The earth shall give her increase; Elohim, our own Elohim, blesses us! (**Psalm 67:6**)

7 Elohim blesses us! And all the ends of the earth fear Him! (**Psalm 67:7**)

121 I have done right-ruling and righteousness; leave me not to my oppressors. (**Psalm 119:121**)

122 Guarantee Your servant's well-being; let not the proud oppress me. (**Psalm 119:122**)

123 My eyes have pined away for Your deliverance, and for the Word of Your righteousness. (**Psalm 119:123**)

124 Do with Your servant according to Your kindness, and teach me Your laws. (**Psalm 119:124**)

125 I am Your servant—make me understand, that I might know Your witnesses. (**Psalm 119:125**)

126 It is time for יהוה to act! For they have broken Your Torah. (**Psalm 119:126**)

127 Therefore I have loved Your commands more than gold, even fine gold! (**Psalm 119:127**)

128 Therefore all Your orders I count as right; I have hated every false way. (**Psalm 119:128**)

Day Seventeen | Desire To Obey the Law of Yehovah | Psalm 119:129-136

Today is the third day of the third week of seven weeks. Today is the seventeenth day of the counting of fifty days from the day of the waving of the Omer on the morrow after the Sabbath.

1 Elohim does favor us and bless us. Cause His face to shine upon us. Selah. (**Psalm 67:1**)

2 For Your way to be known on earth, Your deliverance among all nations. (**Psalm 67:2**)

3 Let the peoples praise You, O Elohim, let all the peoples praise You. (**Psalm 67:3**)

4 Let the nations be glad and sing for joy! For You judge the peoples uprightly, and lead the nations on earth. Selah. (**Psalm 67:4**)

5 Let the peoples praise You, O Elohim; let all the peoples praise You. (**Psalm 67:5**)

6 The earth shall give her increase; Elohim, our own Elohim, blesses us! (**Psalm 67:6**)

7 Elohim blesses us! And all the ends of the earth fear Him! (**Psalm 67:7**)

129 Your witnesses are wonders; so my being observes them. (**Psalm 119:129**)

130 The opening up of Your words gives light, giving understanding to the simple. (**Psalm 119:130**)

131 I have opened my mouth and panted, for I have longed for Your commands. (**Psalm 119:131**)

132 Turn to me and show me favor, according to Your right-ruling, toward those who love Your Name. (**Psalm 119:132**)

133 Establish my footsteps by Your Word, and let no wickedness have rule over me. (**Psalm 119:133**)

134 Redeem me from the oppression of man, that I might guard Your orders. (**Psalm 119:134**)

135 Make Your face shine upon Your servant, and teach me Your laws. (**Psalm 119:135**)

136 Streams of water have run down from my eyes, because they did not guard Your Torah. (**Psalm 119:136**)

Day Eighteen | The Justice of the Law of Yehovah | Psalm 119:137-144

Today is the fourth day of the third week of seven weeks. Today is the eighteenth day of the counting of fifty days from the day of the waving of the Omer on the morrow after the Sabbath.

1 Elohim does favor us and bless us. Cause His face to shine upon us. Selah. (**Psalm 67:1**)

2 For Your way to be known on earth, Your deliverance among all nations. (**Psalm 67:2**)

3 Let the peoples praise You, O Elohim, let all the peoples praise You. (**Psalm 67:3**)

4 Let the nations be glad and sing for joy! For You judge the peoples uprightly, and lead the nations on earth. Selah. (**Psalm 67:4**)

5 Let the peoples praise You, O Elohim; let all the peoples praise You. (**Psalm 67:5**)

6 The earth shall give her increase; Elohim, our own Elohim, blesses us! (**Psalm 67:6**)

7 Elohim blesses us! And all the ends of the earth fear Him! (**Psalm 67:7**)

137 Righteous are You, O יהוה, and Your right-rulings are straight. (**Psalm 119:137**)

138 You have commanded Your witnesses in righteousness and truth, exceedingly. (**Psalm 119:138**)

139 My ardor has consumed me, for my adversaries have forgotten Your words. (**Psalm 119:139**)

140 Your Word is tried, exceedingly; and Your servant has loved it. **(Psalm 119:140)**

141 I am small and despised; I have not forgotten Your orders. **(Psalm 119:141)**

142 Your righteousness is righteousness forever, and Your Torah is truth. **(Psalm 119:142)**

143 Distress and anguish have found me; Your commands are my delight. **(Psalm 119:143)**

144 The righteousness of Your witnesses is forever. Make me understand, that I might live. **(Psalm 119:144)**

Day Nineteen | Prayer For Deliverance | Psalm 119:145-152

Today is the fifth day of the third week of seven weeks. Today is the nineteenth day of the counting of fifty days from the day of the waving of the Omer on the morrow after the Sabbath.

1 Elohim does favor us and bless us. Cause His face to shine upon us. Selah. **(Psalm 67:1)**

2 For Your way to be known on earth, Your deliverance among all nations. **(Psalm 67:2)**

3 Let the peoples praise You, O Elohim, let all the peoples praise You. **(Psalm 67:3)**

4 Let the nations be glad and sing for joy! For You judge the peoples uprightly, and lead the nations on earth. Selah. **(Psalm 67:4)**

5 Let the peoples praise You, O Elohim; let all the peoples praise You. **(Psalm 67:5)**

6 The earth shall give her increase; Elohim, our own Elohim, blesses us! **(Psalm 67:6)**

7 Elohim blesses us! And all the ends of the earth fear Him! **(Psalm 67:7)**

145 I have called with all my heart. Answer me, O יהוה! I observe Your laws. **(Psalm 119:145)**

146 I have called upon You. Save me, that I might guard Your witnesses. **(Psalm 119:146)**

147 I rise before dawn, and cry for help. I have waited for Your Word. **(Psalm 119:147)**

148 My eyes have gone before the night watches, to study Your Word. **(Psalm 119:148)**

149 Hear my voice according to Your kindness; O יהוה, revive me according to Your right-ruling. **(Psalm 119:149)**

150 Those who pursue mischief have drawn near; they have been far from Your Torah. **(Psalm 119:50)**

151 You are near, O יהוה, and all Your commands are truth. (**Psalm 119:51**)

152 Of old I have known Your witnesses, that You have founded them forever. (**Psalm 119:52**)

Day Twenty | Plea For Salvation | Psalm 119:153-160

Today is the sixth day of the third week of seven weeks. Today is the twentieth day of the counting of fifty days from the day of the waving of the Omer on the morrow after the Sabbath.

1 Elohim does favor us and bless us. Cause His face to shine upon us. Selah. (**Psalm 67:1**)

2 For Your way to be known on earth, Your deliverance among all nations. (**Psalm 67:2**)

3 Let the peoples praise You, O Elohim, let all the peoples praise You. (**Psalm 67:3**)

4 Let the nations be glad and sing for joy! For You judge the peoples uprightly, and lead the nations on earth. Selah. (**Psalm 67:4**)

5 Let the peoples praise You, O Elohim; let all the peoples praise You. (**Psalm 67:5**)

6 The earth shall give her increase; Elohim, our own Elohim, blesses us! (**Psalm 67:6**)

7 Elohim blesses us! And all the ends of the earth fear Him! (**Psalm 67:7**)

153 See my affliction and deliver me, for I have not forgotten Your Torah. (**Psalm 119:153**)

154 Plead my cause and redeem me. Revive me according to Your Word. (**Psalm 119:154**)

155 Deliverance is far from the wrong ones, for they have not sought Your laws. (**Psalm 119:155**)

156 Your compassions are many, O יהוה. Revive me according to Your right-rulings. (**Psalm 119:156**)

157 My persecutors and adversaries are many; I have not turned aside from Your witnesses. (**Psalm 119:157**)

158 I saw traitors and was grieved, because they did not guard Your Word. (**Psalm 119:158**)

159 See how I have loved Your orders, יהוה. Revive me according to Your kindness. (**Psalm 119:159**)

160 The sum of Your Word is truth, and all Your righteous right-rulings are forever. (**Psalm 119:160**)

Day Twenty-One | Dedication To the Law of Yehovah | Psalm 119:161-168

Today is the seventh day of the third week of seven weeks. Today is the twenty-first day of the counting of fifty days from the day of the waving of the Omer on the morrow after the Sabbath. Today is Sabbath, the third Sabbath of seven Sabbaths. Today completes the third week of seven weeks.

1 Elohim does favor us and bless us. Cause His face to shine upon us. Selah. (**Psalm 67:1**)

2 For Your way to be known on earth, Your deliverance among all nations. (**Psalm 67:2**)

3 Let the peoples praise You, O Elohim, let all the peoples praise You. (**Psalm 67:3**)

4 Let the nations be glad and sing for joy! For You judge the peoples uprightly, and lead the nations on earth. Selah. (**Psalm 67:4**)

5 Let the peoples praise You, O Elohim; let all the peoples praise You. (**Psalm 67:5**)

6 The earth shall give her increase; Elohim, our own Elohim, blesses us! (**Psalm 67:6**)

7 Elohim blesses us! And all the ends of the earth fear Him! (**Psalm 67:7**)

161 Rulers have persecuted me without a cause, but at Your Word my heart stood in awe. (**Psalm 119:161**)

162 I rejoice at Your Word as one who finds great treasure. (**Psalm 119:162**)

163 I have hated falsehood and loathe it, Your Torah I have loved. (**Psalm 119:163**)

164 I have praised You seven times a day, because of Your righteous right-rulings. (**Psalm 119:164**)

165 Great peace have those loving Your Torah, and for them there is no stumbling-block. (**Psalm 119:165**)

166 יהוה, I have waited for Your deliverance, and I have done Your commands. (**Psalm 119:166**)

167 My being has guarded Your witnesses, and I love them exceedingly. (**Psalm 119:167**)

168 I have guarded Your orders and Your witnesses, for all my ways are before You. (**Psalm 119:168**)

WEEK FOUR

Day Twenty-Two | A Prayer For Help | Psalm 119:169-176

Today is the first day of the fourth week of seven weeks. Today is the twenty-second day of the counting of fifty days from the day of the waving of the Omer on the morrow after the Sabbath.

> **1** Elohim does favor us and bless us. Cause His face to shine upon us. Selah. (**Psalm 67:1**)
> **2** For Your way to be known on earth, Your deliverance among all nations. (**Psalm 67:2**)
> **3** Let the peoples praise You, O Elohim, let all the peoples praise You. (**Psalm 67:3**)
> **4** Let the nations be glad and sing for joy! For You judge the peoples uprightly, and lead the nations on earth. Selah. (**Psalm 67:4**)
> **5** Let the peoples praise You, O Elohim; let all the peoples praise You. (**Psalm 67:5**)
> **6** The earth shall give her increase; Elohim, our own Elohim, blesses us! (**Psalm 67:6**)
> **7** Elohim blesses us! And all the ends of the earth fear Him! (**Psalm 67:7**)

> **169** My cry comes before You, O יהוה. Make me understand according to Your Word. (**Psalm 119:169**)
> **170** Let my prayer come before You. Deliver me according to Your Word. (**Psalm 119:170**)
> **171** My lips pour forth praise, for You teach me Your laws. (**Psalm 119:171**)
> **172** My tongue sings of Your Word, for all Your commands are righteousness. (**Psalm 119:172**)
> **173** Your hand is a help to me, for I have chosen Your orders. (**Psalm 119:173**)
> **174** I have longed for Your deliverance, O יהוה, and Your Torah is my delight. (**Psalm 119:174**)
> **175** My being lives, and it praises You; and Your right-rulings help me. (**Psalm 119:175**)
> **176** I have strayed like a lost sheep. Seek Your servant, for I have not forgotten Your commands. (**Psalm 119:176**)

Day Twenty-Three | True Happiness | Psalm 1:1-6

Today is the second day of the fourth week of seven weeks. Today is the twenty-third day of the counting of fifty days from the day of the waving of the Omer on the morrow after the Sabbath.

1 Elohim does favor us and bless us. Cause His face to shine upon us. Selah. (**Psalm 67:1**)

2 For Your way to be known on earth, Your deliverance among all nations. (**Psalm 67:2**)

3 Let the peoples praise You, O Elohim, let all the peoples praise You. (**Psalm 67:3**)

4 Let the nations be glad and sing for joy! For You judge the peoples uprightly, and lead the nations on earth. Selah. (**Psalm 67:4**)

5 Let the peoples praise You, O Elohim; let all the peoples praise You. (**Psalm 67:5**)

6 The earth shall give her increase; Elohim, our own Elohim, blesses us! (**Psalm 67:6**)

7 Elohim blesses us! And all the ends of the earth fear Him! (**Psalm 67:7**)

1 Blessed is the man who shall not walk in the counsel of the wrong, and shall not stand in the path of sinners, and shall not sit in the seat of scoffers. (**Psalm 1:1**)

2 But his delight is in the Torah of יהוה, and he meditates in His Torah day and night. (**Psalm 1:2**)

3 For he shall be as a tree planted by the rivers of water, that yields its fruit in its season, and whose leaf does not wither, and whatever he does prospers. (**Psalm 1:3**)

4 The wrong are not so, but are like the chaff which the wind blows away. (**Psalm 1:4**)

5 Therefore, the wrong shall not rise in the judgment, nor sinners in the congregation of the righteous. (**Psalm 1:5**)

6 For יהוה knows the way of the righteous, but the way of the wrong comes to naught. (**Psalm 1:6**)

Day Twenty-Four | Confidence In Yehovah | Psalm 11:1-7

Today is the third day of the fourth week of seven weeks. Today is the twenty-fourth day of the counting of fifty days from the day of the waving of the Omer on the morrow after the Sabbath.

1 Elohim does favor us and bless us. Cause His face to shine upon us. Selah. (**Psalm 67:1**)

2 For Your way to be known on earth, Your deliverance among all nations. (**Psalm 67:2**)

3 Let the peoples praise You, O Elohim, let all the peoples praise You. (**Psalm 67:3**)

4 Let the nations be glad and sing for joy! For You judge the peoples uprightly, and lead the nations on earth. Selah. (**Psalm 67:4**)

5 Let the peoples praise You, O Elohim; let all the peoples praise You. (**Psalm 67:5**)

6 The earth shall give her increase; Elohim, our own Elohim, blesses us! (**Psalm 67:6**)

7 Elohim blesses us! And all the ends of the earth fear Him! (**Psalm 67:7**)

1 In יהוה I have taken refuge. Why do you say to me, "Flee to your mountain like a bird?" (**Psalm 11:1**)

2 For look! The wrong bend a bow, they set their arrow on the string, to shoot in darkness at the upright in heart. (**Psalm 11:2**)

3 When the foundations are destroyed, what shall the righteous do? (**Psalm 11:3**)

4 יהוה is in His set-apart Hĕ₫al (Temple), the throne of יהוה is in the heavens. His eyes see, His eyelids examine the sons of men. (**Psalm 11:4**)

5 יהוה tries the righteous, but His being shall hate the wrong and the one who loves violence. (**Psalm 11:5**)

6 Upon the wrong He rains snares. Fire and sulphur and a scorching wind are the portion of their cup. (**Psalm 11:6**)

7 For יהוה is righteous, He has loved righteousness. The upright shall see His face. (**Psalm 11:7**)

Day Twenty-Five | What Yehovah Requires | Psalm 15:1-5

Today is the fourth day of the fourth week of seven weeks. Today is the twenty-fifth day of the counting of fifty days from the day of the waving of the Omer on the morrow after the Sabbath.

1 Elohim does favor us and bless us. Cause His face to shine upon us. Selah. (**Psalm 67:1**)

2 For Your way to be known on earth, Your deliverance among all nations. (**Psalm 67:2**)

3 Let the peoples praise You, O Elohim, let all the peoples praise You. (**Psalm 67:3**)

4 Let the nations be glad and sing for joy! For You judge the peoples uprightly, and lead the nations on earth. Selah. (**Psalm 67:4**)

5 Let the peoples praise You, O Elohim; let all the peoples praise You. (**Psalm 67:5**)

6 The earth shall give her increase; Elohim, our own Elohim, blesses us! (**Psalm 67:6**)

7 Elohim blesses us! And all the ends of the earth fear Him! (**Psalm 67:7**)

1 יהוה, who does sojourn in Your Tent? Who does dwell in Your set-apart mountain? (**Psalm 15:1**)

2 He who walks blamelessly, and does righteousness, and speaks the truth in his heart. (**Psalm 15:2**)

3 He has not slandered with his tongue, he has not done evil to his neighbor, nor lifted up a reproach against his friend. (**Psalm 15:3**)

4 In whose eyes a reprobate one is despised, but he esteems those who fear יהוה, he who swears to his own hurt and does not change. (**Psalm 15:4**)

5 He has not put out his silver at interest, and has not taken a bribe against the innocent. He who does these is never moved. (**Psalm 15:5**)

Day Twenty-Six | The Creation of Yehovah | Psalm 19:1-7

Today is the fifth day of the fourth week of seven weeks. Today is the twenty-sixth day of the counting of fifty days from the day of the waving of the Omer on the morrow after the Sabbath.

1 Elohim does favor us and bless us. Cause His face to shine upon us. Selah. (**Psalm 67:1**)

2 For Your way to be known on earth, Your deliverance among all nations. (**Psalm 67:2**)

3 Let the peoples praise You, O Elohim, let all the peoples praise You. (**Psalm 67:3**)

4 Let the nations be glad and sing for joy! For You judge the peoples uprightly, and lead the nations on earth. Selah. (**Psalm 67:4**)

5 Let the peoples praise You, O Elohim; let all the peoples praise You. (**Psalm 67:5**)

6 The earth shall give her increase; Elohim, our own Elohim, blesses us! (**Psalm 67:6**)

7 Elohim blesses us! And all the ends of the earth fear Him! (**Psalm 67:7**)

1 The heavens are proclaiming the esteem of Ěl; and the expanse is declaring the work of His hand. (**Psalm 19:1**)

2 Day to day pours forth speech, and night to night reveals knowledge. (**Psalm 19:2**)

3 There is no speech, and there are no words. Their voice is not heard. (**Psalm 19:3**)

4 Their line has gone out through all the earth, and their words to the end of the world. In them He set up a tent for the sun. (**Psalm 19:4**)

5 And it is like a bridegroom coming out of his room. It rejoices like a strong man to run the path. (**Psalm 19:5**)

6 Its rising is from one end of the heavens, and its circuit to the other end. And naught is hidden from its heat. (**Psalm 19:6**)

7 The Torah of יהוה is perfect, bringing back the being. The witness of יהוה is trustworthy, making wise the simple. (**Psalm 19:7**)

Day Twenty-Seven | A Prayer For Guidance | Psalm 25:4-10

Today is the sixth day of the fourth week of seven weeks. Today is the twenty-seventh day of the counting of fifty days from the day of the waving of the Omer on the morrow after the Sabbath.

> **1** Elohim does favor us and bless us. Cause His face to shine upon us. Selah. **(Psalm 67:1)**
> **2** For Your way to be known on earth, Your deliverance among all nations. **(Psalm 67:2)**
> **3** Let the peoples praise You, O Elohim, let all the peoples praise You. **(Psalm 67:3)**
> **4** Let the nations be glad and sing for joy! For You judge the peoples uprightly, and lead the nations on earth. Selah. **(Psalm 67:4)**
> **5** Let the peoples praise You, O Elohim; let all the peoples praise You. **(Psalm 67:5)**
> **6** The earth shall give her increase; Elohim, our own Elohim, blesses us! **(Psalm 67:6)**
> **7** Elohim blesses us! And all the ends of the earth fear Him! **(Psalm 67:7)**

> **4** Show me Your ways, O יהוה. Teach me Your paths. **(Psalm 25:4)**
> **5** Lead me in Your truth and teach me, for You are the Elohim of my deliverance. On You I wait all the day. **(Psalm 25:5)**
> **6** Remember, O יהוה, Your compassion and Your kindnesses, for they are from everlasting. **(Psalm 25:6)**
> **7** Do not remember the sins of my youth, and my transgressions. According to Your kindness remember me, for Your goodness' sake, O יהוה. **(Psalm 25:7)**
> **8** Good and straight is יהוה; therefore, He teaches sinners in the way. **(Psalm 25:8)**
> **9** He guides the meek ones in right-ruling, and He teaches the meek ones His way. **(Psalm 25:9)**
> **10** All the paths of יהוה are kindness and truth, to those who guard His covenant and His witnesses. **(Psalm 25:10)**

Day Twenty-Eight | Longing For Yehovah | Psalm 63:1-8

Today is the seventh day of the fourth week of seven weeks. Today is the twenty-eighth day of the counting of fifty days from the day of the waving of the Omer on the morrow after the Sabbath. Today is Sabbath, the fourth Sabbath of seven Sabbaths. Today completes the fourth week of seven weeks.

> **1** Elohim does favor us and bless us. Cause His face to shine upon us. Selah. **(Psalm 67:1)**

2 For Your way to be known on earth, Your deliverance among all nations. (**Psalm 67:2**)

3 Let the peoples praise You, O Elohim, let all the peoples praise You. (**Psalm 67:3**)

4 Let the nations be glad and sing for joy! For You judge the peoples uprightly, and lead the nations on earth. Selah. (**Psalm 67:4**)

5 Let the peoples praise You, O Elohim; let all the peoples praise You. (**Psalm 67:5**)

6 The earth shall give her increase; Elohim, our own Elohim, blesses us! (**Psalm 67:6**)

7 Elohim blesses us! And all the ends of the earth fear Him! (**Psalm 67:7**)

1 O Elohim, You are my Ěl; I earnestly seek You. My being has thirsted for You. My flesh has longed for You in a dry and thirsty land without water. (**Psalm 63:1**)

2 Therefore I have had a vision of You In the set-apart place, to see Your power and Your esteem. (**Psalm 63:2**)

3 Because Your kindness is better than life, my lips do praise You. (**Psalm 63:3**)

4 Therefore I bless You while I live. In Your Name I lift up my hands. (**Psalm 63:4**)

5 My being is satisfied as with marrow and fat, and my mouth praises You with singing lips. (**Psalm 63:5**)

6 When I remember You on my bed, I meditate on You in the night watches. (**Psalm 63:6**)

7 For You have been my help, and in the shadow of Your wings I sing. (**Psalm 63:7**)

8 My being has closely followed You. Your right hand did uphold me. (**Psalm 63:8**)

WEEK FIVE

Day Twenty-Nine | A Song of Thanksgiving | Psalm 67:1-7

Today is the first day of the fifth week of seven weeks. Today is the twenty-ninth day of the counting of fifty days from the day of the waving of the Omer on the morrow after the Sabbath.

1 Elohim does favor us and bless us. Cause His face to shine upon us. Selah. (**Psalm 67:1**)

2 For Your way to be known on earth, Your deliverance among all nations. (**Psalm 67:2**)

3 Let the peoples praise You, O Elohim, let all the peoples praise You. (**Psalm 67:3**)

4 Let the nations be glad and sing for joy! For You judge the peoples uprightly, and lead the nations on earth. Selah. (**Psalm 67:4**)

5 Let the peoples praise You, O Elohim; let all the peoples praise You. (**Psalm 67:5**)

6 The earth shall give her increase; Elohim, our own Elohim, blesses us! (**Psalm 67:6**)

7 Elohim blesses us! And all the ends of the earth fear Him! (**Psalm 67:7**)

Day Thirty | Yehovah & His People (Part I) | Psalm 78:1-16

Today is the second day of the fifth week of seven weeks. Today is the thirtieth day of the counting of fifty days from the day of the waving of the Omer on the morrow after the Sabbath.

1 Elohim does favor us and bless us. Cause His face to shine upon us. Selah. (**Psalm 67:1**)

2 For Your way to be known on earth, Your deliverance among all nations. (**Psalm 67:2**)

3 Let the peoples praise You, O Elohim, let all the peoples praise You. (**Psalm 67:3**)

4 Let the nations be glad and sing for joy! For You judge the peoples uprightly, and lead the nations on earth. Selah. (**Psalm 67:4**)

5 Let the peoples praise You, O Elohim; let all the peoples praise You. (**Psalm 67:5**)

6 The earth shall give her increase; Elohim, our own Elohim, blesses us! (**Psalm 67:6**)

7 Elohim blesses us! And all the ends of the earth fear Him! (**Psalm 67:7**)

1 My people, give ear to my Torah.[1] Incline your ears to the words of my mouth. (**Psalm 78:1** | Footnote: [1]In vv. 1-11 the words "teaching, words, witness, commands, covenant," are used interchangeably, almost synonymously. We find the same in **Psalm 119**.)

2 I open my mouth in a parable; I utter riddles of old. (**Psalm 78:2**)

3 Which we have heard and known, for our fathers have related *them* to us. (**Psalm 78:3**)

4 We do not hide *them* from their children, relating to the generation to come the praises of יהוה, and His strength and His wonders which He has done. (**Psalm 78:4**)

5 For He raised a witness in Ya'aqoḇ (Jacob), and set a Torah in Yisra'ěl, which He commanded our fathers, to teach them to their children. (**Psalm 78:5**)

6 That it might be known to a generation to come, to children who would be born, to rise up and relate *them* to their children. (**Psalm 78:6**)

7 And place their trust in Elohim, and not forget the works of Ěl, but watch over His commands. (**Psalm 78:7**)

8 And not be like their fathers, a stubborn and rebellious generation, a generation which did not prepare its heart, whose spirit was not steadfast to Ěl. (**Psalm 78:8**)

9 The children of Ephrayim (Ephraim), armed bowmen, turned back in the day of battle. (**Psalm 78:9**)

10 They did not guard the covenant of Elohim, and they refused to walk in His Torah. (**Psalm 78:10**)

11 And they forgot His deeds and His wonders which He had shown them. (**Psalm 78:11**)

12 He did wonders in the sight of their fathers, in the land of Mitsrayim (Egypt), in the field of Tso'an (Zoan). (**Psalm 78:12**)

13 He split the sea and caused them to pass through, and He made the waters stand up like a heap. (**Psalm 78:13**)

14 And led them with the cloud by day, and all the night with a light of fire. (**Psalm 78:14**)

15 He split the rocks in the wilderness, and made them drink, as from the great depths. (**Psalm 78:15**)

16 And brought forth streams from the rock, and caused waters to come down as rivers. (**Psalm 78:16**)

Day Thirty-One | Yehovah & His People (Part II) | Psalm 78:17-31

Today is the third day of the fifth week of seven weeks. Today is the thirty-first day of the counting of fifty days from the day of the waving of the Omer on the morrow after the Sabbath.

1 Elohim does favor us and bless us. Cause His face to shine upon us. Selah. (**Psalm 67:1**)

2 For Your way to be known on earth, Your deliverance among all nations. (**Psalm 67:2**)

3 Let the peoples praise You, O Elohim, let all the peoples praise You. (**Psalm 67:3**)

4 Let the nations be glad and sing for joy! For You judge the peoples uprightly, and lead the nations on earth. Selah. (**Psalm 67:4**)

5 Let the peoples praise You, O Elohim; let all the peoples praise You. (**Psalm 67:5**)

6 The earth shall give her increase; Elohim, our own Elohim, blesses us! (**Psalm 67:6**)

7 Elohim blesses us! And all the ends of the earth fear Him! (**Psalm 67:7**)

17 Yet they sinned still more against Him to rebel against the Most High in the desert. (**Psalm 78:17**)

18 And they tried Ěl in their heart by asking food according to their desire. **(Psalm 78:18)**

19 And they spoke against Elohim. They said, "Is Ěl able to set a table in the wilderness?" **(Psalm 78:19)**

20 "Look, He struck the rock, so that the waters gushed out, and the streams overflowed. Is He able to give bread also? Would He provide meat for His people?" **(Psalm 78:20)**

21 Therefore יהוה heard, and He was wroth. So a fire was kindled against Ya'aqoḇ (Jacob), and displeasure also came up against Yisra'ěl. **(Psalm 78:21)**

22 Because they did not believe in Elohim, neither did they trust in His deliverance. **(Psalm 78:22)**

23 Yet He had commanded the clouds above, and opened the doors of the heavens. **(Psalm 78:23)**

24 And He rained down manna on them to eat, and He gave them the grain of the heavens. **(Psalm 78:24)**

25 Men ate bread of the mighty; He sent them provisions to satisfaction. **(Psalm 78:25)**

26 He made an east wind blow in the heavens; and by His power He brought in the south wind. **(Psalm 78:26)**

27 And He rained meat on them like the dust, and winged birds like the sand of the seas. **(Psalm 78:27)**

28 And let them fall in the midst of His camp, all around His Dwelling Place. **(Psalm 78:28)**

29 So they ate and were completely satisfied, for He brought them what they desired. **(Psalm 78:29)**

30 They had not turned away from their desire, their food was still in their mouths. **(Psalm 78:30)**

31 When the wrath of Elohim came against them, and He slew among their fat ones, and He struck down the choice ones of Yisra'ěl. **(Psalm 78:31)**

Day Thirty-Two | Yehovah & His People (Part III) | Psalm 78:32-39

Today is the fourth day of the fifth week of seven weeks. Today is the thirty-second day of the counting of fifty days from the day of the waving of the Omer on the morrow after the Sabbath.

1 Elohim does favor us and bless us. Cause His face to shine upon us. Selah. **(Psalm 67:1)**

2 For Your way to be known on earth, Your deliverance among all nations. **(Psalm 67:2)**

3 Let the peoples praise You, O Elohim, let all the peoples praise You. **(Psalm 67:3)**

4 Let the nations be glad and sing for joy! For You judge the peoples uprightly, and lead the nations on earth. Selah. **(Psalm 67:4)**

5 Let the peoples praise You, O Elohim; let all the peoples praise You. **(Psalm 67:5)**

6 The earth shall give her increase; Elohim, our own Elohim, blesses us! **(Psalm 67:6)**

7 Elohim blesses us! And all the ends of the earth fear Him! **(Psalm 67:7)**

32 In spite of all this they still sinned, and did not believe in His wonders. **(Psalm 78:32)**

33 So He ended their days in a breath, and their years in trouble. **(Psalm 78:33)**

34 When He slew them, then they sought Him, and they returned and did earnestly seek Ěl. **(Psalm 78:34)**

35 And they remembered that Elohim was their rock, and the Most High Ěl their Redeemer. **(Psalm 78:35)**

36 But they flattered Him with their mouth, and they lied to Him with their tongue. **(Psalm 78:36)**

37 For their heart was not steadfast with Him, and they were not true to His covenant. **(Psalm 78:37)**

38 But He, the Compassionate One, pardoned crookedness, and did *not* destroy them. And many a time He turned His displeasure away, and did *not* stir up all His wrath. **(Psalm 78:38)**

39 For He remembered that they were but flesh, a passing breath that does not return. **(Psalm 78:39)**

Day Thirty-Three | Yehovah & His People (Part IV) | Psalm 78:40-55

Today is the fifth day of the fifth week of seven weeks. Today is the thirty-third day of the counting of fifty days from the day of the waving of the Omer on the morrow after the Sabbath.

1 Elohim does favor us and bless us. Cause His face to shine upon us. Selah. **(Psalm 67:1)**

2 For Your way to be known on earth, Your deliverance among all nations. **(Psalm 67:2)**

3 Let the peoples praise You, O Elohim, let all the peoples praise You. **(Psalm 67:3)**

4 Let the nations be glad and sing for joy! For You judge the peoples uprightly, and lead the nations on earth. Selah. **(Psalm 67:4)**

5 Let the peoples praise You, O Elohim; let all the peoples praise You. **(Psalm 67:5)**

6 The earth shall give her increase; Elohim, our own Elohim, blesses us! **(Psalm 67:6)**

7 Elohim blesses us! And all the ends of the earth fear Him! (**Psalm 67:7**)

40 How often they rebelled against Him in the wilderness, and grieved Him in the desert! (**Psalm 78:40**)
41 And again and again they tried Ěl, and provoked the Set-Apart One of Yisra'ěl. (**Psalm 78:41**)
42 They did not remember His hand, the day when He redeemed them from the adversary. (**Psalm 78:42**)
43 How He worked His signs in Mitsrayim (Egypt), and His wonders in the field of Tso'an (Zoan). (**Psalm 78:43**)
44 He turned their rivers into blood, and they could not drink their streams. (**Psalm 78:44**)
45 He sent among them swarms of flies which devoured them, and frogs which destroyed them. (**Psalm 78:45**)
46 And gave their crops to the caterpillar, and their labor to the locust. (**Psalm 78:46**)
47 He destroyed their vines with hail, and their sycamore trees with frost. (**Psalm 78:47**)
48 And gave their beasts over to the hail, and their livestock to bolts of fire. (**Psalm 78:48**)
49 He sent on them the burning of His displeasure, wrath, and rage, and distress, a deputation of messengers of evils. (**Psalm 78:49**)
50 He made a path for His displeasure. He did not spare their being from death, but gave their life over to the plague. (**Psalm 78:50**)
51 And He smote all the first-born in Mitsrayim (Egypt), the first-fruits of strength in the tents of Ḥam. (**Psalm 78:51**)
52 Then made His own people go forth like sheep, and led them in the wilderness like a flock. (**Psalm 78:52**)
53 And He led them on safely, and they did not fear, but the sea covered their enemies. (**Psalm 78:53**)
54 And He brought them to the border of His set-apart place, this mountain which His right hand had gained. (**Psalm 78:54**)
55 And drove out nations before them, and allotted them a measured inheritance, and made the tribes of Yisra'ěl dwell in their tents. (**Psalm 78:55**)

Day Thirty-Four | Yehovah & His People (Part V) | Psalm 78:56-72
Today is the sixth day of the fifth week of seven weeks. Today is the thirty-fourth day of the counting of fifty days from the day of the waving of the Omer on the morrow after the Sabbath.

1 Elohim does favor us and bless us. Cause His face to shine upon us. Selah. (**Psalm 67:1**)

2 For Your way to be known on earth, Your deliverance among all nations. (**Psalm 67:2**)

3 Let the peoples praise You, O Elohim, let all the peoples praise You. (**Psalm 67:3**)

4 Let the nations be glad and sing for joy! For You judge the peoples uprightly, and lead the nations on earth. Selah. (**Psalm 67:4**)

5 Let the peoples praise You, O Elohim; let all the peoples praise You. (**Psalm 67:5**)

6 The earth shall give her increase; Elohim, our own Elohim, blesses us! (**Psalm 67:6**)

7 Elohim blesses us! And all the ends of the earth fear Him! (**Psalm 67:7**)

56 Yet they tried and rebelled against the Most High Elohim, and did not guard His witnesses. (**Psalm 78:56**)

57 But they turned back and acted treacherously like their fathers. They twisted like a treacherous bow. (**Psalm 78:57**)

58 For they enraged Him with their high places, and moved Him to jealousy with their carved images. (**Psalm 78:58**)

59 When Elohim heard this, He was wroth, and greatly despised Yisra'ĕl, (**Psalm 58:59**)

60 And He left the Dwelling Place of Shiloh, the Tent which He had set up among men. (**Psalm 58:60**)

61 And He gave His strength¹ into captivity, and His comeliness¹ into the hand of the adversary. (**Psalm 78:61** | Footnote: ¹"Strength" & "comeliness" are used as symbolic names for His Ark. See also **Psalm 63:2, Psalm 132:8, & II Chronicles 6:41**)

62 And He gave His people over to the sword, and He was wroth with His inheritance. (**Psalm 78:62**)

63 His young men were consumed by fire, and His maidens were not praised. (**Psalm 78:63**)

64 His priests fell by the sword, and their widows could not weep. (**Psalm 78:64**)

65 Then יהוה awoke as one asleep, as a mighty man who shouts because of wine. (**Psalm 78:65**)

66 And He smote His adversaries backward. He put them to an everlasting reproach. (**Psalm 78:66**)

67 Then He rejected the tent of Yosĕph (Joseph), and did not choose the tribe of Ephrayim (Ephraim). (**Psalm 78:67**)

68 But chose the tribe of Yehud̲ah (Judah), Mount Tsiyon (Zion), which He loved. (**Psalm 78:68**)

69 And He built His set-apart place like the heights, like the earth He founded it forever. (**Psalm 78:69**)

70 And He chose Dawid̲ (David) His servant, and took him from the sheepfolds. (**Psalm 78:70**)

71 He brought him in from tending the ewes, to shepherd Ya'aqoḇ (Jacob) His people, and Yisra'ĕl His inheritance. (**Psalm 78:71**)

72 And He shepherded them according to the integrity of His heart, and led them by the skill of His hands. (**Psalm 78:72**)

Day Thirty-Five | Yehovah, the King | Psalm 93:1-5

Today is the seventh day of the fifth week of seven weeks. Today is the thirty-fifth day of the counting of fifty days from the day of the waving of the Omer on the morrow after the Sabbath. Today is Sabbath, the fifth Sabbath of seven Sabbaths. Today completes the fifth week of seven weeks.

> **1** Elohim does favor us and bless us. Cause His face to shine upon us. Selah. (**Psalm 67:1**)
>
> **2** For Your way to be known on earth, Your deliverance among all nations. (**Psalm 67:2**)
>
> **3** Let the peoples praise You, O Elohim, let all the peoples praise You. (**Psalm 67:3**)
>
> **4** Let the nations be glad and sing for joy! For You judge the peoples uprightly, and lead the nations on earth. Selah. (**Psalm 67:4**)
>
> **5** Let the peoples praise You, O Elohim; let all the peoples praise You. (**Psalm 67:5**)
>
> **6** The earth shall give her increase; Elohim, our own Elohim, blesses us! (**Psalm 67:6**)
>
> **7** Elohim blesses us! And all the ends of the earth fear Him! (**Psalm 67:7**)

> **1** יהוה shall reign, He shall put on excellency. יהוה shall put on strength. He shall gird Himself. Indeed, the world is established, immovable. (**Psalm 93:1**)
>
> **2** Your throne is established from of old. You are from everlasting. (**Psalm 93:2**)
>
> **3** Rivers shall lift up, O יהוה. Rivers shall lift up their voice. Rivers lift up their breakers. (**Psalm 93:3**)
>
> **4** יהוה on high is mightier than the noise of many waters, the mighty breakers of the sea. (**Psalm 93:4**)
>
> **5** Your witnesses have been very trustworthy. Set-apartness befits Your house, O יהוה, forever. (**Psalm 93:5**)

WEEK SIX

Day Thirty-Six | Yehovah, the Judge | Psalm 94:12-23

Today is the first day of the sixth week of seven weeks. Today is the thirty-sixth day of the counting of fifty days from the day of the waving of the Omer on the morrow after the Sabbath.

1 Elohim does favor us and bless us. Cause His face to shine upon us. Selah. (**Psalm 67:1**)

2 For Your way to be known on earth, Your deliverance among all nations. (**Psalm 67:2**)

3 Let the peoples praise You, O Elohim, let all the peoples praise You. (**Psalm 67:3**)

4 Let the nations be glad and sing for joy! For You judge the peoples uprightly, and lead the nations on earth. Selah. (**Psalm 67:4**)

5 Let the peoples praise You, O Elohim; let all the peoples praise You. (**Psalm 67:5**)

6 The earth shall give her increase; Elohim, our own Elohim, blesses us! (**Psalm 67:6**)

7 Elohim blesses us! And all the ends of the earth fear Him! (**Psalm 67:7**)

12 Blessed is the man You discipline, O Yah, and instruct out of Your Torah. (**Psalm 94:12**)

13 To give him rest from the days of evil, until the pit is dug for the wrong. (**Psalm 94:13**)

14 For יהוה does not leave His people, nor does He forsake His inheritance. (**Psalm 94:14**)

15 For right-ruling returns man to righteousness, and all the upright in heart follow it. (**Psalm 94:15**)

16 Who would rise up for me against evil-doers? Who would stand up for me against workers of wickedness? (**Psalm 94:16**)

17 If יהוה had not been my help, my being would soon have settled in silence. (**Psalm 94:17**)

18 When I said, "My foot has slipped," Your kindness, O יהוה, supported me. (**Psalm 94:18**)

19 When anxiety was great within me, Your comforts delighted my being. (**Psalm 94:19**)

20 Would a throne of destruction, which devises trouble by decree, be joined with You? (**Psalm 94:20**)

21 They band together against the life of the righteous, and declare innocent blood wrong. (**Psalm 94:21**)

22 But יהוה is my defense, and my Elohim the rock of my refuge. (**Psalm 94:22**)

23 And brings back on them their own wickedness, and cuts them off in their own wrongdoing; יהוה our Elohim does cut them off. (**Psalm 94:23**)

Day Thirty-Seven | A Song of Praise | Psalm 95:1-7

Today is the second day of the sixth week of seven weeks. Today is the thirty-seventh day of the counting of fifty days from the day of the waving of the Omer on the morrow after the Sabbath.

1 Elohim does favor us and bless us. Cause His face to shine upon us. Selah. **(Psalm 67:1)**

2 For Your way to be known on earth, Your deliverance among all nations. **(Psalm 67:2)**

3 Let the peoples praise You, O Elohim, let all the peoples praise You. **(Psalm 67:3)**

4 Let the nations be glad and sing for joy! For You judge the peoples uprightly, and lead the nations on earth. Selah. **(Psalm 67:4)**

5 Let the peoples praise You, O Elohim; let all the peoples praise You. **(Psalm 67:5)**

6 The earth shall give her increase; Elohim, our own Elohim, blesses us! **(Psalm 67:6)**

7 Elohim blesses us! And all the ends of the earth fear Him! **(Psalm 67:7)**

1 Come, let us sing to יהוה! Let us raise a shout to the Rock of our deliverance. **(Psalm 95:1)**

2 Let us come before His face with thanksgiving. Let us raise a shout to Him in song. **(Psalm 95:2)**

3 For יהוה is a great Ěl, and a great Sovereign above all mighty ones. **(Psalm 95:3)**

4 In whose hand are the depths of the earth. The mountain peaks are His also. **(Psalm 95:4)**

5 His is the sea, for He made it; and His hands formed the dry land. **(Psalm 95:5)**

6 Come, let us bow down and bend low. Let us kneel before יהוה our Maker. **(Psalm 95:6)**

7 For He is our Elohim, and we are the people of His pasture, and the sheep of His hand. **(Psalm 95:7)**

Day Thirty-Eight | Yehovah, the Supreme King | Psalm 96:1-13 (14)
Today is the third day of the sixth week of seven weeks. Today is the thirty-eighth day of the counting of fifty days from the day of the waving of the Omer on the morrow after the Sabbath.

1 Elohim does favor us and bless us. Cause His face to shine upon us. Selah. **(Psalm 67:1)**

2 For Your way to be known on earth, Your deliverance among all nations. **(Psalm 67:2)**

3 Let the peoples praise You, O Elohim, let all the peoples praise You. **(Psalm 67:3)**

4 Let the nations be glad and sing for joy! For You judge the peoples uprightly, and lead the nations on earth. Selah. **(Psalm 67:4)**

5 Let the peoples praise You, O Elohim; let all the peoples praise You. (**Psalm 67:5**)

6 The earth shall give her increase; Elohim, our own Elohim, blesses us! (**Psalm 67:6**)

7 Elohim blesses us! And all the ends of the earth fear Him! (**Psalm 67:7**)

1 Sing to יהוה a new song. Sing to יהוה, all the earth! (**Psalm 96:1**)

2 Sing to יהוה, bless His Name. Proclaim His deliverance from day to day. (**Psalm 96:2**)

3 Declare His esteem among the nations; His wonders among all peoples. (**Psalm 96:3**)

4 For great is יהוה and greatly to be praised. He is to be feared above all mighty ones. (**Psalm 96:4**)

5 For all the mighty ones of the peoples are matters of naught, but יהוה made the heavens. (**Psalm 96:5**)

6 Excellency and splendor are before Him. Strength and comeliness are in His set-apart place. (**Psalm 96:6**)

7 Ascribe to יהוה, O clans of the peoples. Ascribe to יהוה esteem and strength. (**Psalm 96:7**)

8 Ascribe to יהוה the esteem of His Name. Bring an offering, and come into His courts. (**Psalm 96:8**)

9 Bow yourselves to יהוה, in the splendor of set-apartness! Tremble before Him, all the earth. (**Psalm 96:9**)

10 Say among nations, "יהוה shall reign. The world also is established, immovable. He judges the peoples in straightness." (**Psalm 96:10**)

11 Let the heavens rejoice, and let the earth be glad. Let the sea roar, and all that fills it. (**Psalm 96:11**)

12 Let the field exult, and all that is in it. Let all the trees of the forest then shout for joy. (**Psalm 96:12**)

13 At the presence of יהוה. For He shall come, for He shall come to judge the earth. He judges the world in righteousness[1], and the peoples with His truth. (**Psalm 96:13** | Footnote: [1]See also **98:9**; **Acts 17:31**; **Revelation 19:11**)

Day Thirty-Nine | Yehovah, the Ruler of the World | Psalm 98:1-9

Today is the fourth day of the sixth week of seven weeks. Today is the thirty-ninth day of the counting of fifty days from the day of the waving of the Omer on the morrow after the Sabbath.

1 Elohim does favor us and bless us. Cause His face to shine upon us. Selah. (**Psalm 67:1**)

2 For Your way to be known on earth, Your deliverance among all nations. (**Psalm 67:2**)

3 Let the peoples praise You, O Elohim, let all the peoples praise You. (**Psalm 67:3**)

4 Let the nations be glad and sing for joy! For You judge the peoples uprightly, and lead the nations on earth. Selah. (**Psalm 67:4**)

5 Let the peoples praise You, O Elohim; let all the peoples praise You. (**Psalm 67:5**)

6 The earth shall give her increase; Elohim, our own Elohim, blesses us! (**Psalm 67:6**)

7 Elohim blesses us! And all the ends of the earth fear Him! (**Psalm 67:7**)

1 Sing to יהוה a new song!, for He has done wonders. His right hand and His set-apart arm have brought Him deliverance. (**Psalm 98:1**)

2 יהוה has made known His deliverance. His righteousness He has openly shown before the eyes of the nations. (**Psalm 98:2**)

3 He has remembered His kindness and His trustworthiness to the house of Yisra'ĕl. All the ends of the earth have seen the deliverance of our Elohim. (**Psalm 98:3**)

4 Raise a shout to יהוה, all the earth. Break forth in song, rejoice, and sing praises. (**Psalm 98:4**)

5 Sing to יהוה with the lyre, with the lyre and the voice of a song. (**Psalm 98:5**)

6 With trumpets and the sound of a horn, raise a shout before יהוה, the Sovereign. (**Psalm 98:6**)

7 Let the sea roar, and all that fills it, the world and those who dwell in it. (**Psalm 98:7**)

8 Let the rivers clap their hands, let the mountains sing together for joy before יהוה. (**Psalm 98:8**)

9 For He shall come to judge the earth. He judges the world in righteousness, and the people in straightness. (**Psalm 98:9**)

Day Forty | Yehovah, the Supreme King | Psalm 99:1-9

Today is the fifth day of the sixth week of seven weeks. Today is the fortieth day of the counting of fifty days from the day of the waving of the Omer on the morrow after the Sabbath.

1 Elohim does favor us and bless us. Cause His face to shine upon us. Selah. (**Psalm 67:1**)

2 For Your way to be known on earth, Your deliverance among all nations. (**Psalm 67:2**)

3 Let the peoples praise You, O Elohim, let all the peoples praise You. (**Psalm 67:3**)

4 Let the nations be glad and sing for joy! For You judge the peoples uprightly, and lead the nations on earth. Selah. **(Psalm 67:4)**

5 Let the peoples praise You, O Elohim; let all the peoples praise You. **(Psalm 67:5)**

6 The earth shall give her increase; Elohim, our own Elohim, blesses us! **(Psalm 67:6)**

7 Elohim blesses us! And all the ends of the earth fear Him! **(Psalm 67:7)**

1 יהוה shall reign; peoples tremble! He is enthroned on the kerubim (cherubim); the earth shakes! **(Psalm 99:1)**

2 יהוה is great in Tsiyon (Zion), and He is high above all the peoples. **(Psalm 99:2)**

3 They praise Your Name, great and awesome, it is set-apart. **(Psalm 99:3)**

4 And the strength of the Sovereign shall love right-ruling. You Yourself shall establish straightness; You shall execute right-ruling and righteousness in Ya'aqob (Jacob). **(Psalm 99:4)**

5 Exalt יהוה our Elohim, and bow yourselves at His footstool. He is set-apart. **(Psalm 99:5)**

6 Mosheh (Moses) and Aharon (Aaron) were among His priests, and Shemu'ĕl (Samuel) was among those calling upon His Name. They called upon יהוה, and He answered them. **(Psalm 99:6)**

7 He spoke to them in the column of cloud. They guarded His witnesses and the Law He gave them. **(Psalm 99:7)**

8 You answered them, O יהוה our Elohim. You were a forgiving Ěl to them, though You took vengeance on their deeds. **(Psalm 99:8)**

9 Exalt יהוה our Elohim, and bow down toward His set-apart mountain; for יהוה our Elohim is set-apart. **(Psalm 99:9)**

Day Forty-One | The Love of Yehovah | Psalm 103:1-22

Today is the sixth day of the sixth week of seven weeks. Today is the forty-first day of the counting of fifty days from the day of the waving of the Omer on the morrow after the Sabbath.

1 Elohim does favor us and bless us. Cause His face to shine upon us. Selah. **(Psalm 67:1)**

2 For Your way to be known on earth, Your deliverance among all nations. **(Psalm 67:2)**

3 Let the peoples praise You, O Elohim, let all the peoples praise You. **(Psalm 67:3)**

4 Let the nations be glad and sing for joy! For You judge the peoples uprightly, and lead the nations on earth. Selah. **(Psalm 67:4)**

5 Let the peoples praise You, O Elohim; let all the peoples praise You. (**Psalm 67:5**)

6 The earth shall give her increase; Elohim, our own Elohim, blesses us! (**Psalm 67:6**)

7 Elohim blesses us! And all the ends of the earth fear Him! (**Psalm 67:7**)

1 Bless יהוה, O my being, and all that is within me. Bless His set-apart Name! (**Psalm 103:1**)

2 Bless יהוה, O my being, and do not forget all His dealings. (**Psalm 103:2**)

3 Who forgives all your crookednesses, Who heals all your diseases. (**Psalm 103:3**)

4 Who redeems your life from destruction, Who crowns you with kindness and compassion. (**Psalm 103:4**)

5 Who satisfies your desire with the good. Your youth is renewed like the eagle's. (**Psalm 103:5**)

6 יהוה is doing righteousness and right-ruling for all the oppressed. (**Psalm 103:6**)

7 He made known His ways to Mosheh (Moses), His acts to the children of Yisra'ěl. (**Psalm 103:7**)

8 יהוה is compassionate and showing favor, patient, and great in kindness. (**Psalm 103:8**)

9 He does not always strive, nor maintain it forever. (**Psalm 103:9**)

10 He has not done to us according to our sins, nor rewarded us according to our crookednesses. (**Psalm 103:10**)

11 For as the heavens are high above the earth, so great is His kindness toward those who fear Him. (**Psalm 103:11**)

12 As far as east is from west, so far has He removed our transgressions from us. (**Psalm 103:12**)

13 As a father has compassion for his children, so יהוה has compassion for those who fear Him. (**Psalm 103:13**)

14 For He knows how we are made; He remembers that we are dust. (**Psalm 103:14**)

15 As a flower of the field, so he flourishes. (**Psalm 103:15**)

16 For the wind blows over it, and it is no more, and its place no longer remembers it. (**Psalm 103:16**)

17 But the kindness of יהוה is from everlasting to everlasting upon those who fear Him, and His righteousness to children's children. (**Psalm 103:17**)

18 To those who guard His covenant, and to those who remember His orders to do them. (**Psalm 103:18**)

19 יהוה has established His throne in the heavens, and His reign shall rule over all. (**Psalm 103:19**)

20 Bless יהוה, you His messengers, mighty in power, who do His Word, listening to the voice of His Word. **(Psalm 103:20)**

21 Bless יהוה, all you His hosts, You His servants, who do His pleasure. **(Psalm 103:21)**

22 Bless יהוה, all His works, in all places of His rule. Bless יהוה, O my being! **(Psalm 103:22)**

Day Forty-Two | Yehovah & His People (Part VI) | Psalm 105:1-11

Today is the seventh day of the sixth week of seven weeks. Today is the forty-second day of the counting of fifty days from the day of the waving of the Omer on the morrow after the Sabbath. Today is Sabbath, the sixth Sabbath of seven Sabbaths. Today completes the sixth week of seven weeks.

1 Elohim does favor us and bless us. Cause His face to shine upon us. Selah. **(Psalm 67:1)**

2 For Your way to be known on earth, Your deliverance among all nations. **(Psalm 67:2)**

3 Let the peoples praise You, O Elohim, let all the peoples praise You. **(Psalm 67:3)**

4 Let the nations be glad and sing for joy! For You judge the peoples uprightly, and lead the nations on earth. Selah. **(Psalm 67:4)**

5 Let the peoples praise You, O Elohim; let all the peoples praise You. **(Psalm 67:5)**

6 The earth shall give her increase; Elohim, our own Elohim, blesses us! **(Psalm 67:6)**

7 Elohim blesses us! And all the ends of the earth fear Him! **(Psalm 67:7)**

1 Give thanks to יהוה! Call upon His Name. Make known His deeds among the peoples. **(Psalm 105:1)**

2 Sing to Him, sing praise to Him. Speak of all His wonders. **(Psalm 105:2)**

3 Make your boast in His set-apart Name. Let the hearts rejoice of those seeking יהוה. **(Psalm 105:3)**

4 Seek יהוה and His strength. Seek His face always. **(Psalm 105:4)**

5 Remember His wonders which He has done, His miracles, and the right-rulings of His mouth. **(Psalm 105:5)**

6 O seed of Avraham (Abraham) His servant, children of Ya'aqob (Jacob), His chosen ones! **(Psalm 105:6)**

7 He is יהוה our Elohim; His right-rulings are in all the earth. **(Psalm 105:7)**

8 He has remembered His covenant forever, the Word He commanded, for a thousand generations. **(Psalm 105:8)**

9 The covenant He made with Avraham (Aḇraham), and His oath to Yitsḥaq (Isaac). **(Psalm 105:9)**

10 And established it to Ya'aqoḇ (Jacob) for a Law, to Yisra'ĕl—an everlasting covenant. **(Psalm 105:10)**

11 Saying, "To you I give the land of Kena'an (Canaan), the portion of your inheritance." **(Psalm 105:11)**

WEEK SEVEN

Day Forty-Three | Yehovah's Graciousness | Psalm 106:1-5

Today is the first day of the seventh week of seven weeks. Today is the forty-third day of the counting of fifty days from the day of the waving of the Omer on the morrow after the Sabbath.

1 Elohim does favor us and bless us. Cause His face to shine upon us. Selah. **(Psalm 67:1)**

2 For Your way to be known on earth, Your deliverance among all nations. **(Psalm 67:2)**

3 Let the peoples praise You, O Elohim, let all the peoples praise You. **(Psalm 67:3)**

4 Let the nations be glad and sing for joy! For You judge the peoples uprightly, and lead the nations on earth. Selah. **(Psalm 67:4)**

5 Let the peoples praise You, O Elohim; let all the peoples praise You. **(Psalm 67:5)**

6 The earth shall give her increase; Elohim, our own Elohim, blesses us! **(Psalm 67:6)**

7 Elohim blesses us! And all the ends of the earth fear Him! **(Psalm 67:7)**

1 Praise Yah! Oh, give thanks to יהוה, for He is good! For His kindness is everlasting. **(Psalm 106:1)**

2 Who does relate the mighty acts of יהוה? Or declare all His praise? **(Psalm 106:2)**

3 Blessed are those who guard right-ruling, who do righteousness at all times! **(Psalm 106:3)**

4 Remember me, O יהוה, in the acceptance of Your people. Visit me with Your deliverance. **(Psalm 106:4)**

5 To see the good of Your chosen ones, to rejoice in the gladness of Your nation, to make my boast with Your inheritance. **(Psalm 106:5)**

Day Forty-Four | In Praise of Yehovah| Psalm 111:1-10

Today is the second day of the seventh week of seven weeks. Today is the forty-fourth day of the counting of fifty days from the day of the waving of the Omer on the morrow after the Sabbath.

1 Elohim does favor us and bless us. Cause His face to shine upon us. Selah. (**Psalm 67:1**)
2 For Your way to be known on earth, Your deliverance among all nations. (**Psalm 67:2**)
3 Let the peoples praise You, O Elohim, let all the peoples praise You. (**Psalm 67:3**)
4 Let the nations be glad and sing for joy! For You judge the peoples uprightly, and lead the nations on earth. Selah. (**Psalm 67:4**)
5 Let the peoples praise You, O Elohim; let all the peoples praise You. (**Psalm 67:5**)
6 The earth shall give her increase; Elohim, our own Elohim, blesses us! (**Psalm 67:6**)
7 Elohim blesses us! And all the ends of the earth fear Him! (**Psalm 67:7**)

1 Praise Yah! I thank יהוה with all my heart, in the company of the straight, and of the congregation. (**Psalm 111:1**)
2 Great are the works of יהוה, searched for by all who delight in them. (**Psalm 111:2**)
3 Splendor and greatness are His work, and His righteousness stands forever. (**Psalm 111:3**)
4 He has made His wonders to be remembered. יהוה shows favor and is compassionate. (**Psalm 111:4**)
5 He has given food to those who fear Him. He remembers His covenant forever. (**Psalm 111:5**)
6 He has shown His people the power of His works, to give to them the inheritance of the Gentiles. (**Psalm 111:6**)
7 The works of His hands are truth and right-ruling, all His orders are trustworthy. (**Psalm 111:7**)
8 They are upheld forever and ever, performed in truth and straightness. (**Psalm 111:8**)
9 He sent redemption to His people. He has commanded His covenant forever. Set-apart and awesome is His Name. (**Psalm 111:9**)
10 The fear of יהוה is the beginning of wisdom. All those doing them have a good understanding. His praise is standing forever. (**Psalm 111:10**)

Day Forty-Five | The Happiness of a Good Person | Psalm 112:1-10

Today is the third day of the seventh week of seven weeks. Today is the forty-fifth day of the counting of fifty days from the day of the waving of the Omer on the morrow after the Sabbath.

1 Elohim does favor us and bless us. Cause His face to shine upon us. Selah. (**Psalm 67:1**)
2 For Your way to be known on earth, Your deliverance among all nations. (**Psalm 67:2**)
3 Let the peoples praise You, O Elohim, let all the peoples praise You. (**Psalm 67:3**)
4 Let the nations be glad and sing for joy! For You judge the peoples uprightly, and lead the nations on earth. Selah. (**Psalm 67:4**)
5 Let the peoples praise You, O Elohim; let all the peoples praise You. (**Psalm 67:5**)
6 The earth shall give her increase; Elohim, our own Elohim, blesses us! (**Psalm 67:6**)
7 Elohim blesses us! And all the ends of the earth fear Him! (**Psalm 67:7**)

1 Praise Yah! Blessed is the man, who fears יהוה, who has greatly delighted in His commands. (**Psalm 112:1**)
2 Mighty in the earth shall be his seed, the generation of the straight ones shall be blessed. (**Psalm 112:2**)
3 Wealth and riches are in his house, and his righteousness is standing forever. (**Psalm 112:3**)
4 Light has risen in the darkness to the straight ones, *those* showing favor, the compassionate, and the righteous. (**Psalm 112:4**)
5 Good is a man showing favor and lending, he sustains his matters in right-ruling. (**Psalm 112:5**)
6 For he is never shaken; the righteous is remembered forever. (**Psalm 112:6**)
7 He is not afraid of an evil report. His heart is steadfast, trusting in יהוה. (**Psalm 112:7**)
8 His heart is upheld, he is not afraid, while he looks on his adversaries. (**Psalm 112:8**)
9 He scattered abroad, he gave to the poor. His righteousness is standing forever. His horn is exalted with esteem. (**Psalm 112:9**)
10 The wrong one sees it and shall be vexed. He gnashes his teeth and shall melt. The desire of the wrong ones does perish. (**Psalm 112:10**)

Day Forty-Six | The Reward of Obedience | Psalm 128:1-6

Today is the fourth day of the seventh week of seven weeks. Today is the forty-sixth day of the counting of fifty days from the day of the waving of the Omer on the morrow after the Sabbath.

1 Elohim does favor us and bless us. Cause His face to shine upon us. Selah. (**Psalm 67:1**)

2 For Your way to be known on earth, Your deliverance among all nations. (**Psalm 67:2**)

3 Let the peoples praise You, O Elohim, let all the peoples praise You. (**Psalm 67:3**)

4 Let the nations be glad and sing for joy! For You judge the peoples uprightly, and lead the nations on earth. Selah. (**Psalm 67:4**)

5 Let the peoples praise You, O Elohim; let all the peoples praise You. (**Psalm 67:5**)

6 The earth shall give her increase; Elohim, our own Elohim, blesses us! (**Psalm 67:6**)

7 Elohim blesses us! And all the ends of the earth fear Him! (**Psalm 67:7**)

1 Blessed are all who fear יהוה, who walk in His ways. (**Psalm 128:1**)

2 You shall eat the labor of your hands. Be blessed, and let it be well with you. (**Psalm 128:2**)

3 Let your wife be as a fruit-bearing vine within your house, your sons like olive plants all around your table. (**Psalm 128:3**)

4 Look, so shall the man be blessed who fears יהוה. (**Psalm 128:4**)

5 יהוה shall bless you out of Tsiyon (Zion), and let you see the good of Yerushalayim (Jerusalem), all the days of your life. (**Psalm 128:5**)

6 And let you see your children's children! Peace be upon Yisra'ěl! (**Psalm 128:6**)

Day Forty-Seven | A Prayer For Help | Psalm 130:1-8
Today is the fifth day of the seventh week of seven weeks. Today is the forty-seventh day of the counting of fifty days from the day of the waving of the Omer on the morrow after the Sabbath.

1 Elohim does favor us and bless us. Cause His face to shine upon us. Selah. (**Psalm 67:1**)

2 For Your way to be known on earth, Your deliverance among all nations. (**Psalm 67:2**)

3 Let the peoples praise You, O Elohim, let all the peoples praise You. (**Psalm 67:3**)

4 Let the nations be glad and sing for joy! For You judge the peoples uprightly, and lead the nations on earth. Selah. (**Psalm 67:4**)

5 Let the peoples praise You, O Elohim; let all the peoples praise You. (**Psalm 67:5**)

6 The earth shall give her increase; Elohim, our own Elohim, blesses us! (**Psalm 67:6**)

7 Elohim blesses us! And all the ends of the earth fear Him! (**Psalm 67:7**)

1 Out of the depths I have cried to You, O יהוה. (**Psalm 130:1**)

2 O יהוה, hear my voice! Let Your ears be attentive to the voice of my prayers. (**Psalm 130:2**)

3 O Yah, if You should watch crookednesses, O יהוה, who would stand? (**Psalm 130:3**)

4 But with You there is forgiveness, that You might be feared. (**Psalm 130:4**)

5 I looked to יהוה, my being has looked, and for His Word I have waited. (**Psalm 130:5**)

6 My being *looks* to יהוה more than those watching for morning, watching for morning. (**Psalm 130:6**)

7 O Yisra'ĕl, wait for יהוה; for with יהוה there is kindness. And with Him is much redemption. (**Psalm 130:7**)

8 For He shall redeem Yisra'ĕl from all his crookednesses. (**Psalm 130:8**)

Day Forty-Eight | A Call For the Universe To Praise Yehovah | Psalm 148:1-14

Today is the sixth day of the seventh week of seven weeks. Today is the forty-eighth day of the counting of fifty days from the day of the waving of the Omer on the morrow after the Sabbath.

1 Elohim does favor us and bless us. Cause His face to shine upon us. Selah. (**Psalm 67:1**)

2 For Your way to be known on earth, Your deliverance among all nations. (**Psalm 67:2**)

3 Let the peoples praise You, O Elohim, let all the peoples praise You. (**Psalm 67:3**)

4 Let the nations be glad and sing for joy! For You judge the peoples uprightly, and lead the nations on earth. Selah. (**Psalm 67:4**)

5 Let the peoples praise You, O Elohim; let all the peoples praise You. (**Psalm 67:5**)

6 The earth shall give her increase; Elohim, our own Elohim, blesses us! (**Psalm 67:6**)

7 Elohim blesses us! And all the ends of the earth fear Him! (**Psalm 67:7**)

1 Praise Yah! Praise יהוה from the heavens. Praise Him in the heights! (**Psalm 148:1**)

2 Praise Him, all His messengers. Praise Him, all His hosts! (**Psalm 148:2**)

3 Praise Him, sun and moon. Praise Him, all you stars of light! (**Psalm 148:3**)

4 Praise Him, heavens of heavens, and you waters above the heavens! (**Psalm 148:4**)

5 Let them praise the Name of יהוה, for He commanded and they were created. (**Psalm 148:5**)

6 And He established them forever and ever. He gave a law and they pass not beyond. (**Psalm 148:6**)

7 Praise יהוה from the earth, you great sea creatures and all the depths. (**Psalm 148:7**)

8 Fire and hail, snow and clouds, stormy wind that does His Word. (**Psalm 148:8**)

9 The mountains and all hills, fruit trees and all cedars. (**Psalm 148:9**)

10 Wild beasts and all cattle, creeping creatures and flying birds. (**Psalm 148:10**)

11 Sovereigns of the earth and all peoples, rulers and all judges of the earth. (**Psalm 148:11**)

12 Both young men and maidens, old men and children. (**Psalm 148:12**)

13 Let them praise the Name of יהוה, for His Name alone is exalted, His splendor is above the earth and heavens. (**Psalm 148:13**)

14 He also lifts up the horn of His people, the praise of all His kind ones; of the children of Yisra'ěl, a people near to Him. Praise Yah! (**Psalm 148:14**)

Day Forty-Nine | A Prayer of Thanksgiving | Psalm 138:1-8

Today is the seventh day of the seventh week of seven weeks. Today is the forty-ninth day of the counting of fifty days from the day of the waving of the Omer on the morrow after the Sabbath. Today is the seventh Sabbath of seven Sabbaths. Today completes the seventh week of seven weeks.

1 Elohim does favor us and bless us. Cause His face to shine upon us. Selah. (**Psalm 67:1**)

2 For Your way to be known on earth, Your deliverance among all nations. (**Psalm 67:2**)

3 Let the peoples praise You, O Elohim, let all the peoples praise You. (**Psalm 67:3**)

4 Let the nations be glad and sing for joy! For You judge the peoples uprightly, and lead the nations on earth. Selah. (**Psalm 67:4**)

5 Let the peoples praise You, O Elohim; let all the peoples praise You. (**Psalm 67:5**)

6 The earth shall give her increase; Elohim, our own Elohim, blesses us! (**Psalm 67:6**)

7 Elohim blesses us! And all the ends of the earth fear Him! (**Psalm 67:7**)

1 I give You thanks with all my heart. Before the mighty ones I sing praises to You. (**Psalm 138:1**)
2 I bow myself toward Your set-apart Hĕḵal (Temple), and give thanks to Your Name for Your kindness and for Your truth; for You have made great Your Word, Your Name, above all. (**Psalm 138:2**)
3 On the day I called, You did answer me. You made me bold with strength in my being. (**Psalm 138:3**)
4 Let all the sovereigns of the earth give thanks to You, O יהוה, when they shall hear the words of Your mouth. (**Psalm 138:4**)
5 And let them sing of the ways of יהוה, for great is the esteem of יהוה. (**Psalm 138:5**)
6 Though יהוה is exalted, He looks on the humble; but the proud He perceives from a distance. (**Psalm 138:6**)
7 Though I walk in the midst of distress, You revive me. You stretch out Your hand against the wrath of my enemies, and Your right hand saves me. (**Psalm 138:7**)
8 יהוה does perfect for me. O יהוה, Your kindness is everlasting. Do not forsake the works of Your hands. (**Psalm 138:8**)

SHAVUOT | FEAST OF PENTECOST

This Feast of the fiftieth day has been a many-sided one and as a consequence, has been called by many names.[266] The names are as follows:

- Chag Ha-Shavuot or Ḥag Shabu'ot (Feast of Weeks)
- Azeret shel Pesah (Closing Season Of the Passover)
- Yom ha-Bikkurim (Day of the First-Fruits)
- Feast of Shabua or Ḥagga di-Shebu'aya
- Ḥag ha-Ḳaẓir (Feast of Harvest)
- Azeret (Closing Festival)

Day Fifty | Praise Yehovah! | Psalm 150:1-6

Today is the fiftieth *and final day* of the counting from the day of the waving of the Omer on the morrow after the Sabbath. Today is the morrow of the seventh Sabbath, the Feast of Weeks, the Feast of Harvest, or the Day of First-Fruits.

1 Elohim does favor us and bless us. Cause His face to shine upon us. Selah. (**Psalm 67:1**)

---

266 http://www.jewishencyclopedia.com/articles/12012-pentecost

2 For Your way to be known on earth, Your deliverance among all nations. **(Psalm 67:2)**

3 Let the peoples praise You, O Elohim, let all the peoples praise You. **(Psalm 67:3)**

4 Let the nations be glad and sing for joy! For You judge the peoples uprightly, and lead the nations on earth. Selah. **(Psalm 67:4)**

5 Let the peoples praise You, O Elohim; let all the peoples praise You. **(Psalm 67:5)**

6 The earth shall give her increase; Elohim, our own Elohim, blesses us! **(Psalm 67:6)**

7 Elohim blesses us! And all the ends of the earth fear Him! **(Psalm 67:7)**

1 Praise Yah! Praise Ěl in His set-apart place. Praise Him in His mighty expanse! **(Psalm 150:1)**

2 Praise Him for His mighty acts. Praise Him according to His excellent greatness! **(Psalm 150:2)**

3 Praise Him with the blowing of the ram's horn. Praise Him with the harp and lyre! **(Psalm 150:3)**

4 Praise Him with tambourine and dance. Praise Him with stringed instruments and flutes! **(Psalm 150:4)**

5 Praise Him with sounding cymbals. Praise Him with resounding cymbals! **(Psalm 150:5)**

6 Let all that have breath praise Yah. Praise Yah! **(Psalm 150:6)**

CPSIA information can be obtained at www.ICGtesting.com
Printed in the USA
BVOW05s1902120815

413118BV00001B/2/P